152.4 FX: Gali gali (scrape scratch)

153.4 FX: Ba (whump)

155.2 FX: Suu (zzzz)
155.4 FX: Su (swish)

CHAPTER TWENTY-FOUR: A BATTLE OF ANGUISH

158.2 FX: Byu (vwoosh)

160.1 FX: Nyaa (meoow)
160.6 FX: Pata (plunk)
160.6 FX: Doki doki doki (ba-dump ba-dump ba-dump)

161.4 FX: Yoro (wobble)
161.4 FX: Haa haa (huff huff)
161.5 FX: Giku (shock)

164.1 FX: Gishi (glink)
164.2 FX: Bishi (whip)
164.3 FX: Kui (shove)

165.2 FX: Fu (hmph)
165.2 FX: Byu (vwip)
165.3 FX: Bishi (whip whip)

166.3 FX: Chi (tsk)

167.4 FX: Doki doki doki doki (ba-dump ba-dump ba-dump ba-dump)
167.4 FX: Ittadakimaaasu (Thanks for the food.)
167.4 FX: Tamaage (Fried Tamahome – abbreviated)

168.1 FX: Yoro yoro (stumble)
168.4 FX: Ka (krah)
168.5 FX: Gooo (gwooooh)

169.1 FX: Ka (klang)
169.1 FX: Hihiiin (neigh)
169.2 FX: Zolo zolo (plod plod)
169.4 FX: Ba (pounce)

170.1 FX: Hihiiin (neigh)

171.1 FX: Do (bam)
171.4 FX: Yura (shuffle)

172.1 FX: Dan (bam)
172.3 FX: Ka (krah)

173.1 FX: Ga (grip)
173.2 FX: Gili gili gili (cruuush)
173.3 FX: Zu (zsh)
173.5 FX: Da (dash)

174.1 FX: Su (swff)
174.4 FX: Dosheeee (whaaaaa?)

179.4 FX: Heta (slump)

180.1 FX: Gaba (gwahh)
180.3 FX: Shulululu (shwwrrrrl)

181.1 FX: Shulululu (shwwrrrrl)

182.4 FX: Shaaaa (shraaaaah)

183.3 FX: Shulu (fwoosh)
183.5 FX: Su (shff)

184.2 FX: don (boom)

185.3 FX: Fu (fwoosh)

186.3 FX: Kui (tug)
186.4 FX: Su (shwa)
186.4 FX: Pou (glow)
187.1 FX: Boya (bwhh)

188.1 FX: Su (shff)

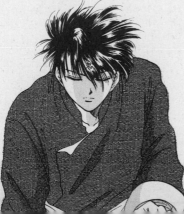

123.1 FX: Suto (shtf)
123.1 FX: Busu busu (sizzle)

CHAPTER TWENTY-THREE:
IN THE DARKNESS

130.1 FX: Ga (grrr)
130.4 FX: Kyu (tie)

131.4 FX: Doki doki (ba-dump ba-dump)
131.5 FX: Su (step)

133.3 FX: Dokun dokun dokun dokun (ba-dump
       ba-dump ba-dump ba-dump)

134.4 FX: Batan (bam)

135.1 FX: So (pat)
135.3 FX: Gashi (grab)
135.3 FX: Tatata (scurry)

136.1 FX: Poto (plop)

138.1 FX: Ba (wrench)
138.2 FX: Da (dash)

139.3 FX: Nyaa nyaa (meow)

140.6 FX: Pui (hmph)

141.3 FX: Pun Pun (grr grrr)

142.3 FX: Kalan (klank)

143.4 FX: Gyu (squeeze)

145.3 FX: Chaki (klick)
145.4 FX: Batan (bam)

146.2-.4 FX: Dokun dokun dokun dokun (ba-dump
       ba-dump ba-dump ba-dump)

147.1 FX: Butsu butsu (mumble mumble)
147.4 FX: Giku (urk)

149.3 FX: Dodododo
       (thump thump thump thump)

CHAPTER TWENTY-TWO:
CITY OF RESURRECTION

102.5 FX: Su (stand)

104.1 FX: Doki (ba-dump)
104.3 FX: Nu (nwoink)

105.3 FX: Chichichi (chirp chirp chirp)

106.3 FX: Gaba (gwah)
106.4 FX: Dokin (ba-dump)

107.1 FX: Pa (push)
107.5 FX: Fu (huh)

108.4 FX: Su (swoosh)

109.1 FX: Gyaa gyaa (caw caw)
109.4 FX: Galagalagala (gatunk gatunk gatunk)

112.3 FX: Yoro yoro (wobble wobble)

113.1 FX: Ban (bam)
113.4 FX: Suu (fshhh)

116.3 FX: Gyaa gyaa (screech caw caw)

117.1 FX: Gyaa gyaa (screech caw caw)

118.5 FX: Biku biku (twitch twitch)
118.5 FX: Zuzu (zggghh)

119.2 FX: Zulu (slither)
119.3 FX: Zu (slither)

120.1 FX: Zulu (drag)
120.2 FX: Gu (grip)
120.3 FX: Su (shff)
120.5 FX: Bota zulu (thud drag)

121.1 FX: Doka (donk)
121.2 FX: Ba (bwish)
121.3 FX: Zulu (drag)
121.3 FX: Zuzu (drag)

122.3 FX: Za (zash)
122.4 FX: Ton (tump)

fushigi yûgi™

The Mysterious Play
VOL. 4: BANDIT

Story & Art By
YÛ WATASE

FUSHIGI YÛGI
THE MYSTERIOUS PLAY
VOL. 4: BANDIT
SHÔJO EDITION

This volume contains the FUSHIGI YÛGI installments from Animerica Extra Vol. 3, No. 5 through No. 10, in their entirety.

STORY AND ART BY YÛ WATASE

English Adaptation/Yuji Oniki
Translation Assist/Kaori Kawakubo Inoue
Touch-up Art & Lettering/Andy Ristaino & Walden Wong
Design/Hidemi Sahara
Shôjo Edition Editor/Yuki Takagaki

Managing Editor/Annette Roman
Director of Production/Noboru Watanabe
Editorial Director/Alvin Lu
Sr. Director of Licensing & Acquisitions/Rika Inouye
Vice President of Marketing/Liza Coppola
Vice President of Sales/Joe Morici
Executive Vice President/Hyoe Narita
Publisher/Seiji Horibuchi

Printed in Canada

Published by VIZ, LLC
P.O. Box 77010
San Francisco, CA 94107

Shôjo Edition
10 9 8 7 6 5 4 3 2 1
First printing, September 2004
1st English edition published February 2001

www.viz.com   store.viz.com

CONTENTS

Chapter Nineteen
Wo Ai Ni.. 5

Chapter Twenty
Wolf of the Fortress.................................... 35

Chapter Twenty-one
Illusion's Embrace....................................... 65

Chapter Twenty-two
City of Resurrection.................................... 97

Chapter Twenty-three
In the Darkness... 127

Chapter Twenty-four
A Battle of Anguish..................................... 156

Glossary... 191

STORY THUS FAR

Junior high school girl Miaka and her best friend Yui are physically drawn into the world of a strange book—THE UNIVERSE OF THE FOUR GODS. Miaka is offered the role of the lead character, the Priestess of the god Suzaku, and is charged with gathering the seven Celestial Warriors of Suzaku who will help her complete a quest to save the nation of Hong-Nan, and in the process grant her any wish she wants. She has already found four warriors: dashing-but-greedy Tamahome, the noble emperor Hotohori, cross-dressing and impossibly strong Nuriko, and the mysterious monk Chichiri.

Yui's fate was much crueler than Miaka's. Upon entering the book, Yui suffered rape and manipulation, and she attempted suicide. Now, Yui has become the Priestess of the god Seiryu, the enemy of Suzaku and Miaka.

Before Miaka can set out to find the three remaining Celestial Warriors, Seiryu's country of Qu-Dong begins invading the weaker Hong-Nan. Qu-Dong declares that outright war will be averted by one thing only—if Hong-Nan surrenders Miaka's love, Tamahome!

THE UNIVERSE OF THE FOUR GODS is based on ancient Chinese legend, but Japanese pronunciation of Chinese names differs slightly from their Chinese equivalents. Here is a short glossary of the Japanese pronunciation of the Chinese names in this graphic novel:

CHINESE	JAPANESE	PERSON OR PLACE	MEANING
Hong-Nan	Konan	Southern Kingdom	Crimson South
Qu-Dong	Kutô	Eastern Kingdom	Gathered East
Tai Yi-Jun	Tai Itsukun	An Oracle	Preeminent Person
Shou-Shuang	Jusô	A Province	Lasting Frost
Ligé-San	Reikakuzan	A Mountain	Strength Tower
Knei-Gong	Kôji	A Bandit	Young Victor
Rui-Nei	Eiken	A Bandit	Imperial Likeness
Huan-Lang	Genrô	A Bandit Leader	Phantom Wolf
Changhung	Chôkô	A Northern Town	Expansive Place
Shao-Huan	Shôka	A Mystical Person	Small Flower
Miao Nioh-An	Myo Ju-An	A Hermit	Miracle Peaceful Life

No da: An emphatic. A verbal exclamation point placed at the end of a sentence or phrase.

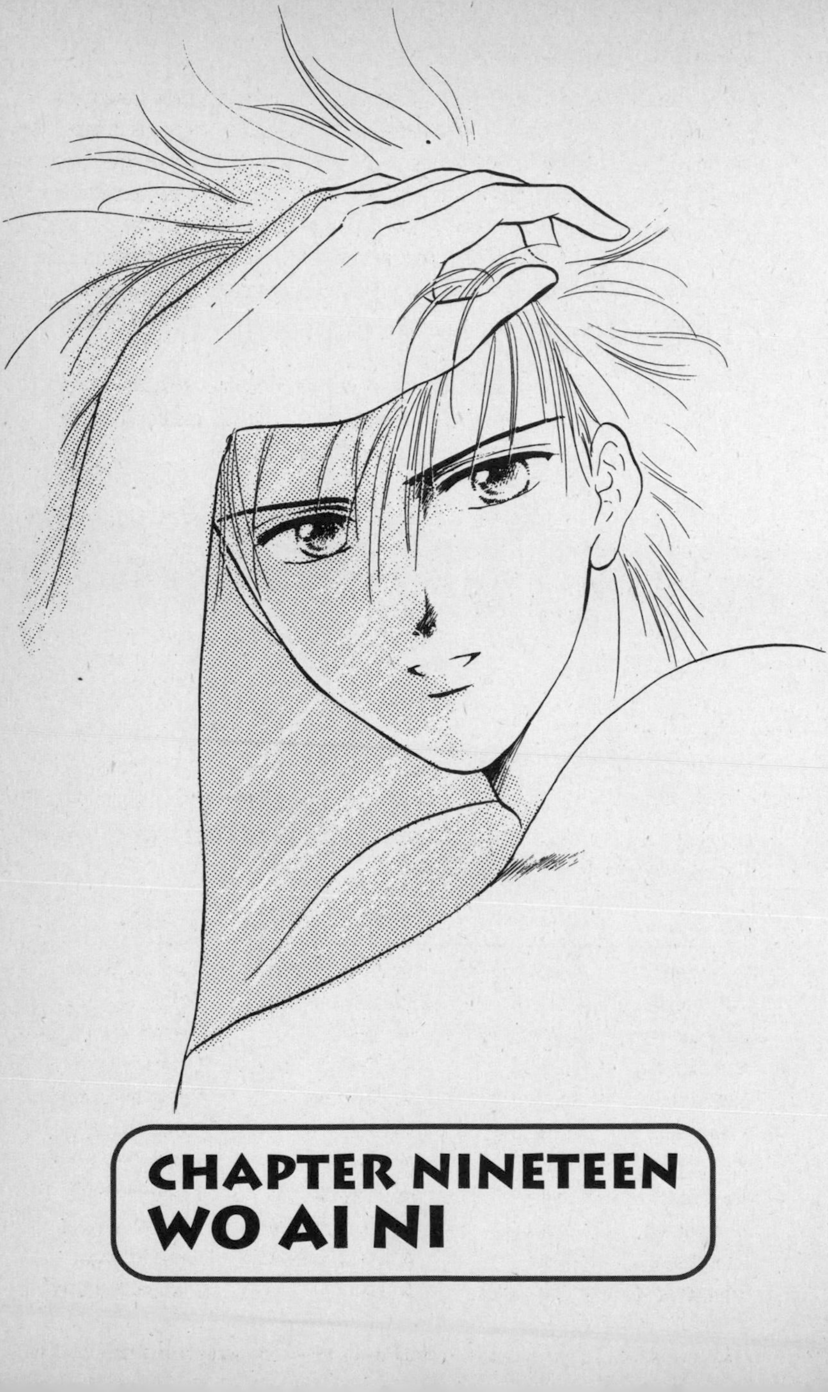

CHAPTER NINETEEN
WO AI NI

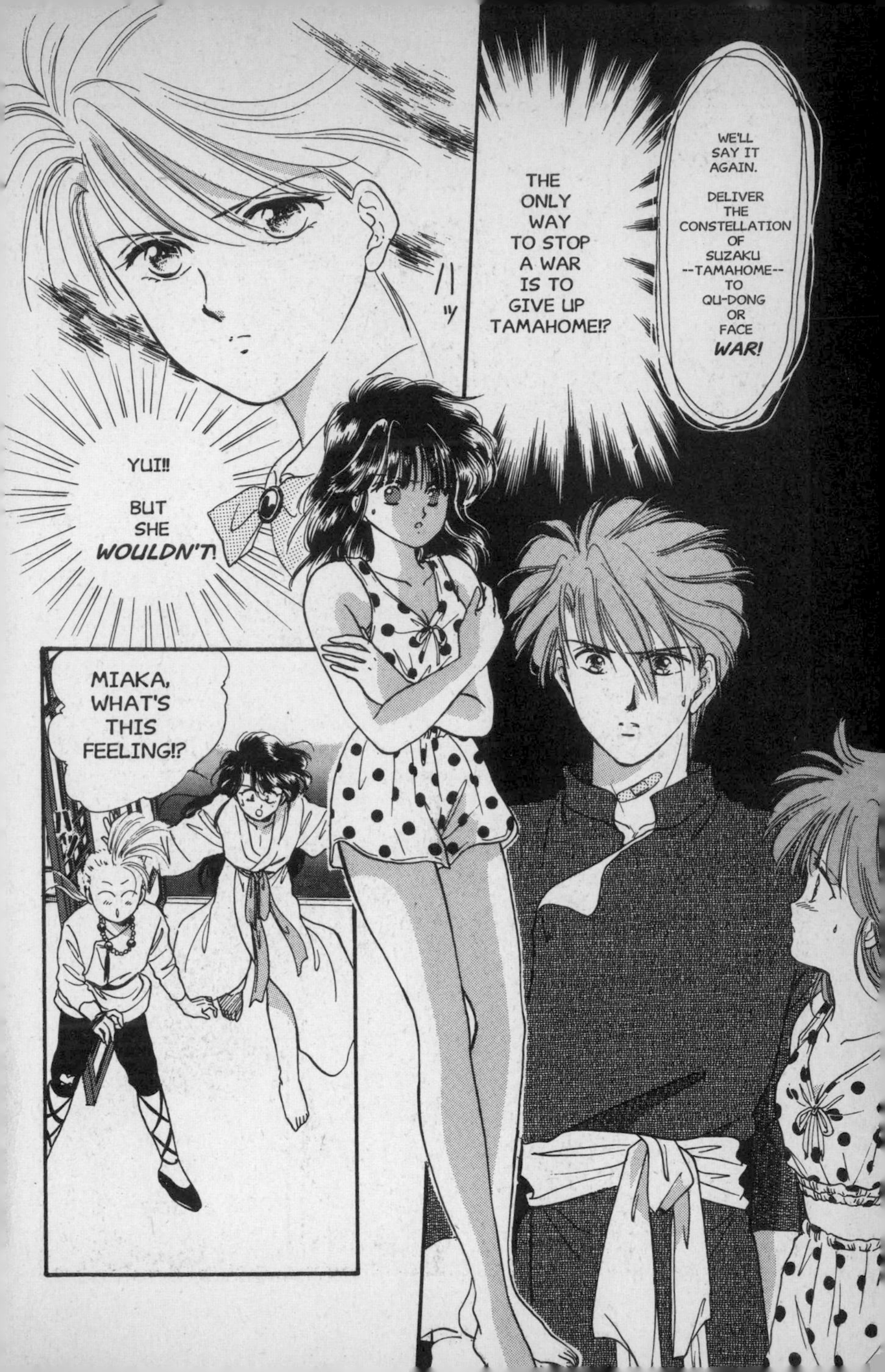
WE'LL SAY IT AGAIN. DELIVER THE CONSTELLATION OF SUZAKU --TAMAHOME-- TO QU-DONG OR FACE *WAR!*
THE ONLY WAY TO STOP A WAR IS TO GIVE UP TAMAHOME!?
YUI!!
BUT SHE *WOULDN'T!*
MIAKA, WHAT'S THIS FEELING!?

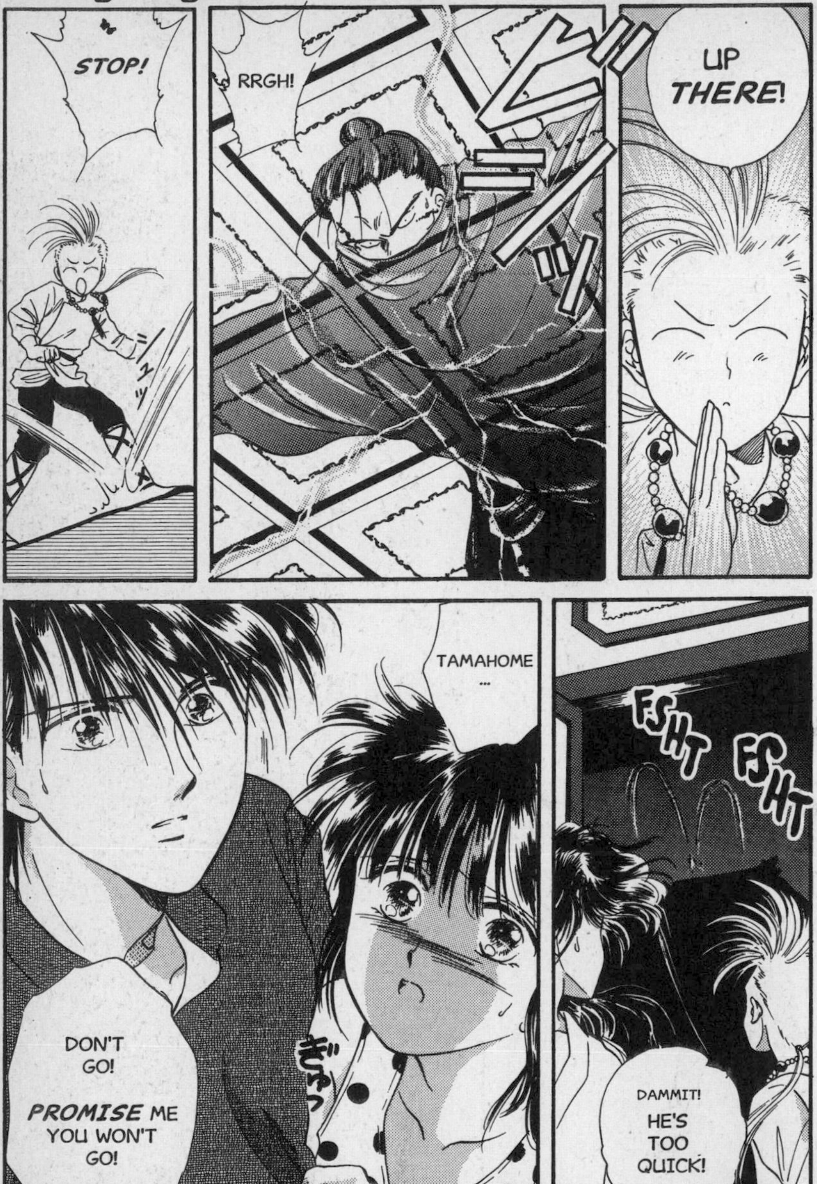
UP THERE!
RRGH!
STOP!
FSHT FSHT
DAMMIT! HE'S TOO QUICK!
TAMAHOME ...
DON'T GO! PROMISE ME YOU WON'T GO!

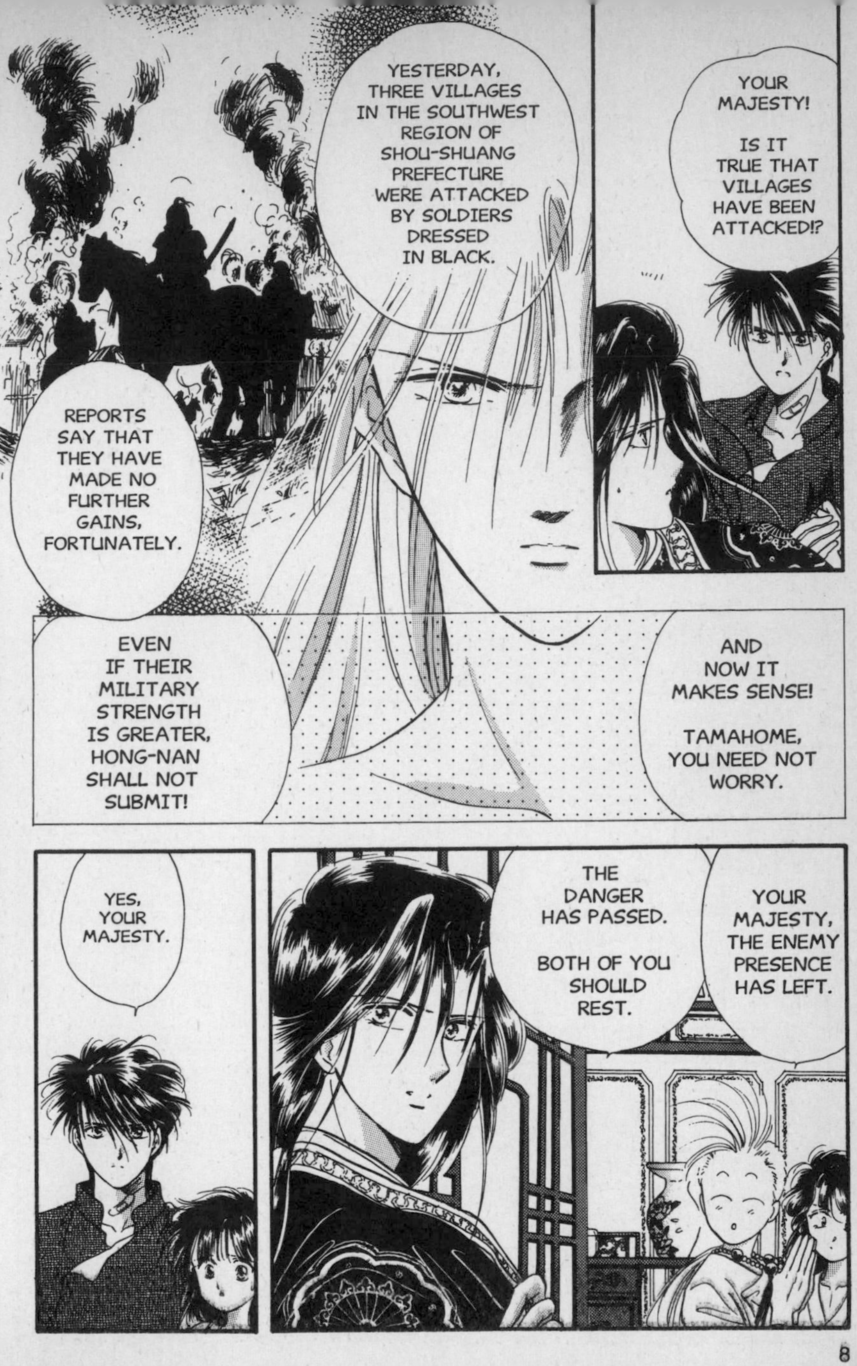
YOUR MAJESTY! IS IT TRUE THAT VILLAGES HAVE BEEN ATTACKED!?
YESTERDAY, THREE VILLAGES IN THE SOUTHWEST REGION OF SHOU-SHUANG PREFECTURE WERE ATTACKED BY SOLDIERS DRESSED IN BLACK.
REPORTS SAY THAT THEY HAVE MADE NO FURTHER GAINS, FORTUNATELY.
AND NOW IT MAKES SENSE! TAMAHOME, YOU NEED NOT WORRY.
EVEN IF THEIR MILITARY STRENGTH IS GREATER, HONG-NAN SHALL NOT SUBMIT!
YOUR MAJESTY, THE ENEMY PRESENCE HAS LEFT.
THE DANGER HAS PASSED. BOTH OF YOU SHOULD REST.
YES, YOUR MAJESTY.

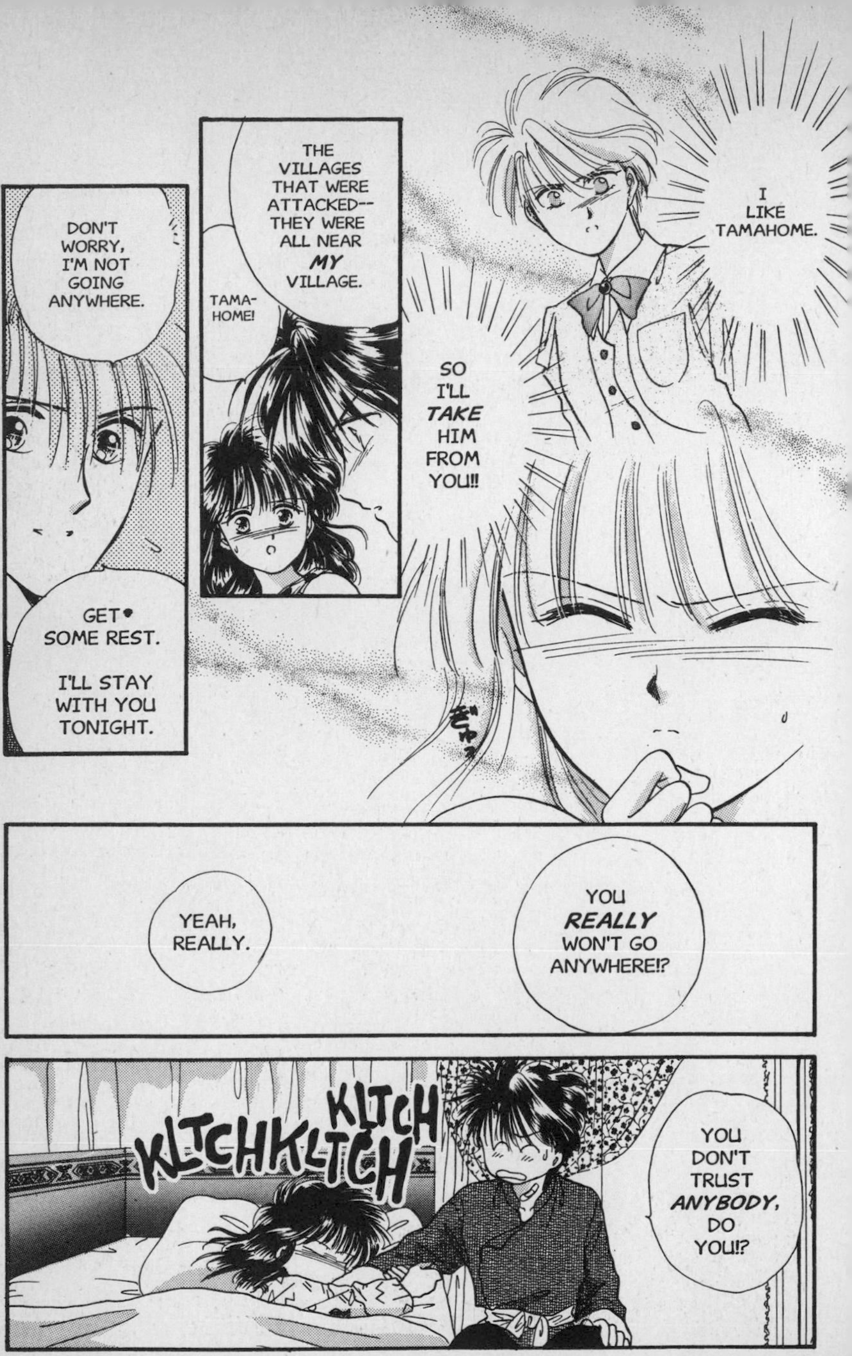
I LIKE TAMAHOME.
SO I'LL *TAKE* HIM FROM YOU!!
THE VILLAGES THAT WERE ATTACKED-- THEY WERE ALL NEAR *MY* VILLAGE.
TAMA-HOME!
DON'T WORRY, I'M NOT GOING ANYWHERE.
GET SOME REST.
I'LL STAY WITH YOU TONIGHT.
YOU *REALLY* WON'T GO ANYWHERE!?
YEAH, REALLY.
YOU DON'T TRUST *ANYBODY*, DO YOU!?
KLTCH
KLTCHKLTCH

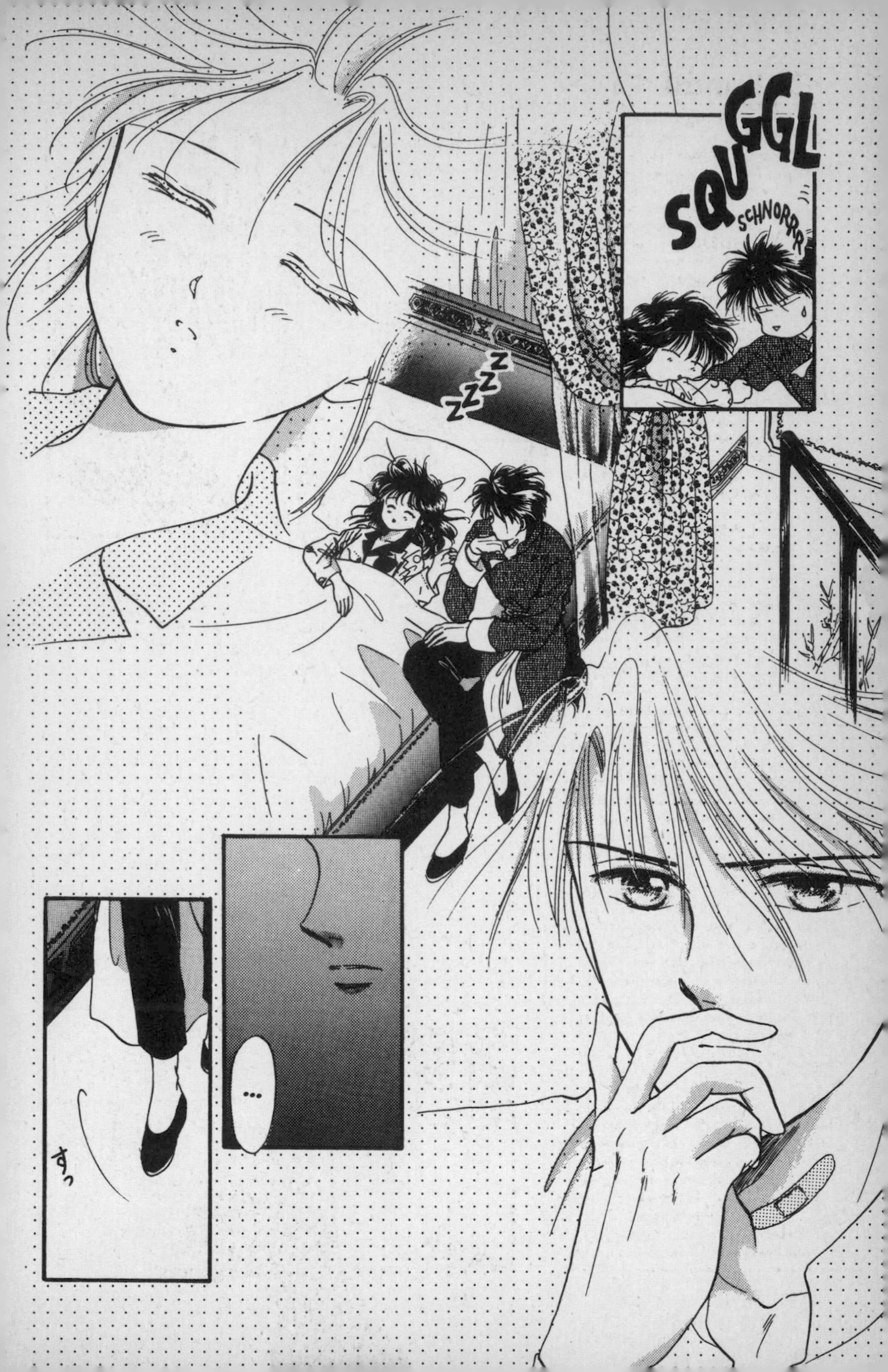
SQUGGL
SCHNORRRR
ZZZZ
...
すっ

Bandit

Tan-ta-dahhh! (the curtain rises) (applause) Thank you, thank you, thank you. Thank you for your warm reception as you read this. Thank you. Soooo-- (adjusts the microphone) Winter's really hit us hard, hasn't it? My hands are so cold, it's making a mess of my handwriting. What's that? "What else is new?" Usually my hand measures 5 on the Richter scale! That's a good one! (a roar of laughter and applause) Enough with the standup routine! It's so cold, my hands are like ice. I don't have much time either, so I'll have to write this in my usual Speed Racer quickness. It reminds me of when I began writing this column in volume 1, I had all these opinions crowding themselves into the column... Ahh, I'm driving myself nuts! I can't write properly at this speed with these numb fingers. But don't worry, when I fill out important documents, I write very prim and proper. Everyday I take my medicine for my muscle pains (fortified with vitamins),and then I set down to work. If I don't, my arm is just... I take antacids, vitamins, health drinks, and herbal medicine. So even though I don't get much sleep, I'm still feeling energetic. I'm grateful! I've heard of experienced manga artists who're carted off by an ambulance after they've finished their pages. They're hospitalized with the IV needle inserted in one arm, menthol patches on the other, and a pen taped to their fingers as they draw more manga. Who knows, I might be next. It brings tears to your eyes. Sometimes, while working, I start to worry about it. Mmmm...this hot Calpis tastes great! I've done quite a few columns now and when I reread them I'm really shocked!! My mental state at the time I was writing is so obvious!! I have to start remembering what I've written in every chapter!! One thing I'm certain of--everyone must think I'm weird!! Bonkers!! She's a total weirdo!! Read the next chapter to find out how that's a complete misconception.

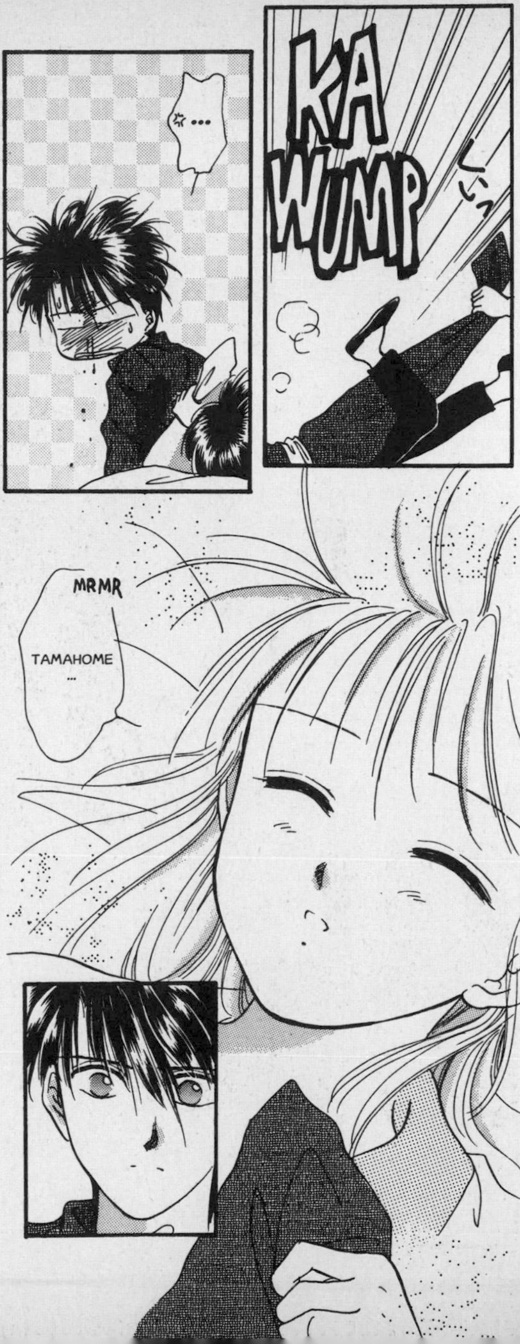
KA WUMP
...
MRMR
TAMAHOME ...

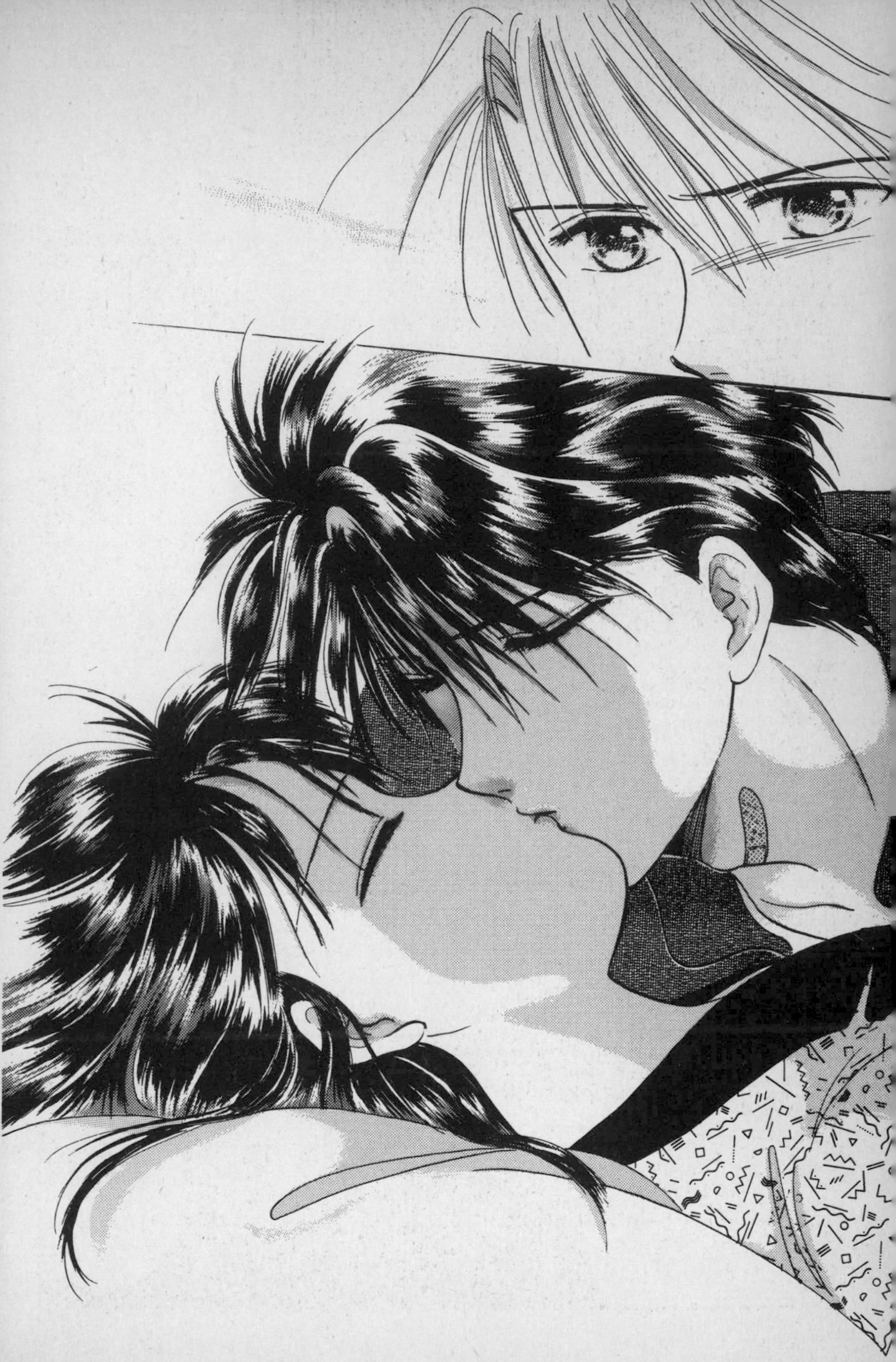

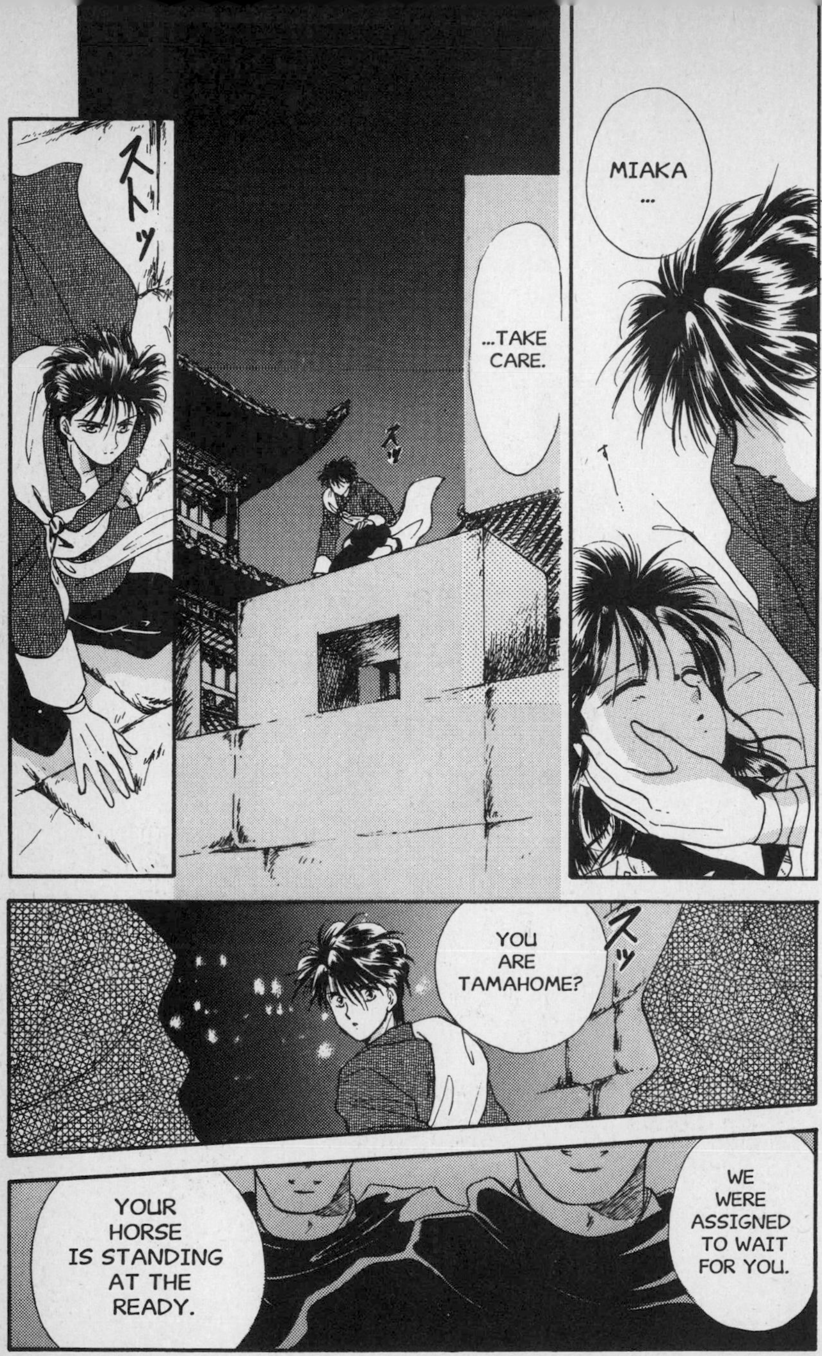
MIAKA ...
...TAKE CARE.
ストッ
YOU ARE TAMAHOME?
スッ
WE WERE ASSIGNED TO WAIT FOR YOU.
YOUR HORSE IS STANDING AT THE READY.

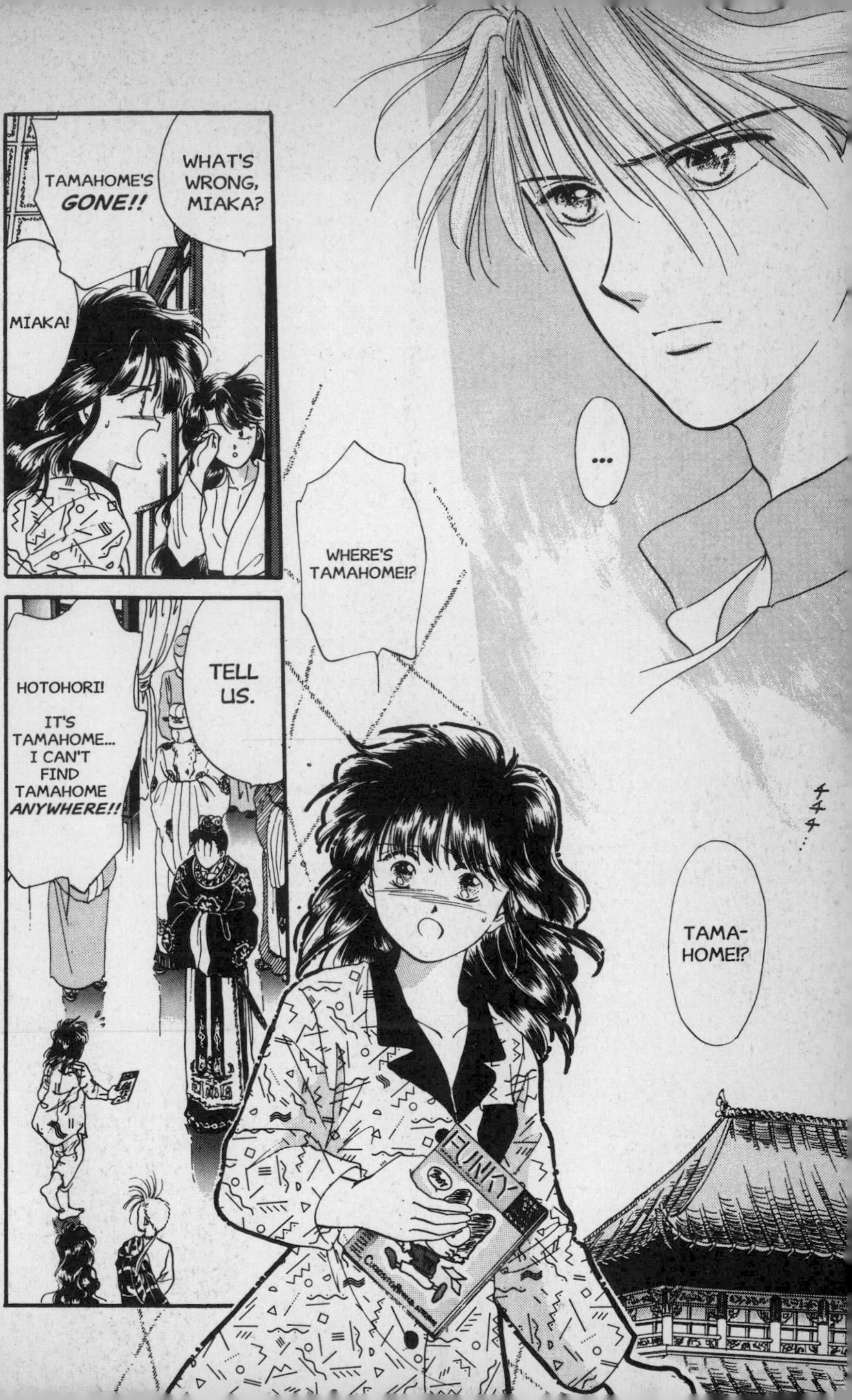
...
WHERE'S TAMAHOME!?
TAMA-HOME!?
WHAT'S WRONG, MIAKA?
TAMAHOME'S *GONE!!*
MIAKA!
TELL US.
HOTOHORI! IT'S TAMAHOME... I CAN'T FIND TAMAHOME *ANYWHERE!!*

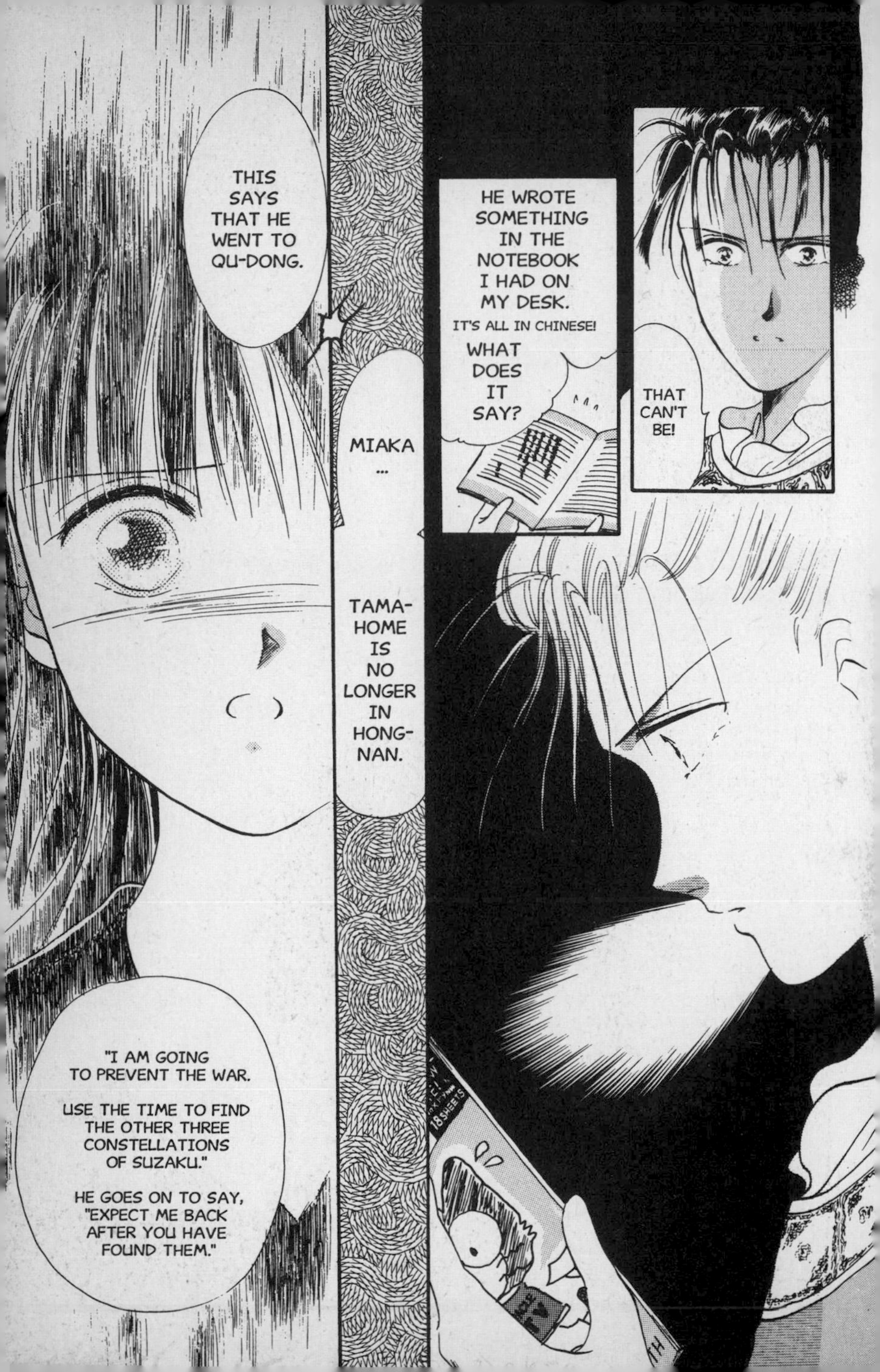
THAT CAN'T BE!
HE WROTE SOMETHING IN THE NOTEBOOK I HAD ON MY DESK.
IT'S ALL IN CHINESE!
WHAT DOES IT SAY?
MIAKA ...
TAMA-HOME IS NO LONGER IN HONG-NAN.
THIS SAYS THAT HE WENT TO QU-DONG.
"I AM GOING TO PREVENT THE WAR. USE THE TIME TO FIND THE OTHER THREE CONSTELLATIONS OF SUZAKU." HE GOES ON TO SAY, "EXPECT ME BACK AFTER YOU HAVE FOUND THEM."

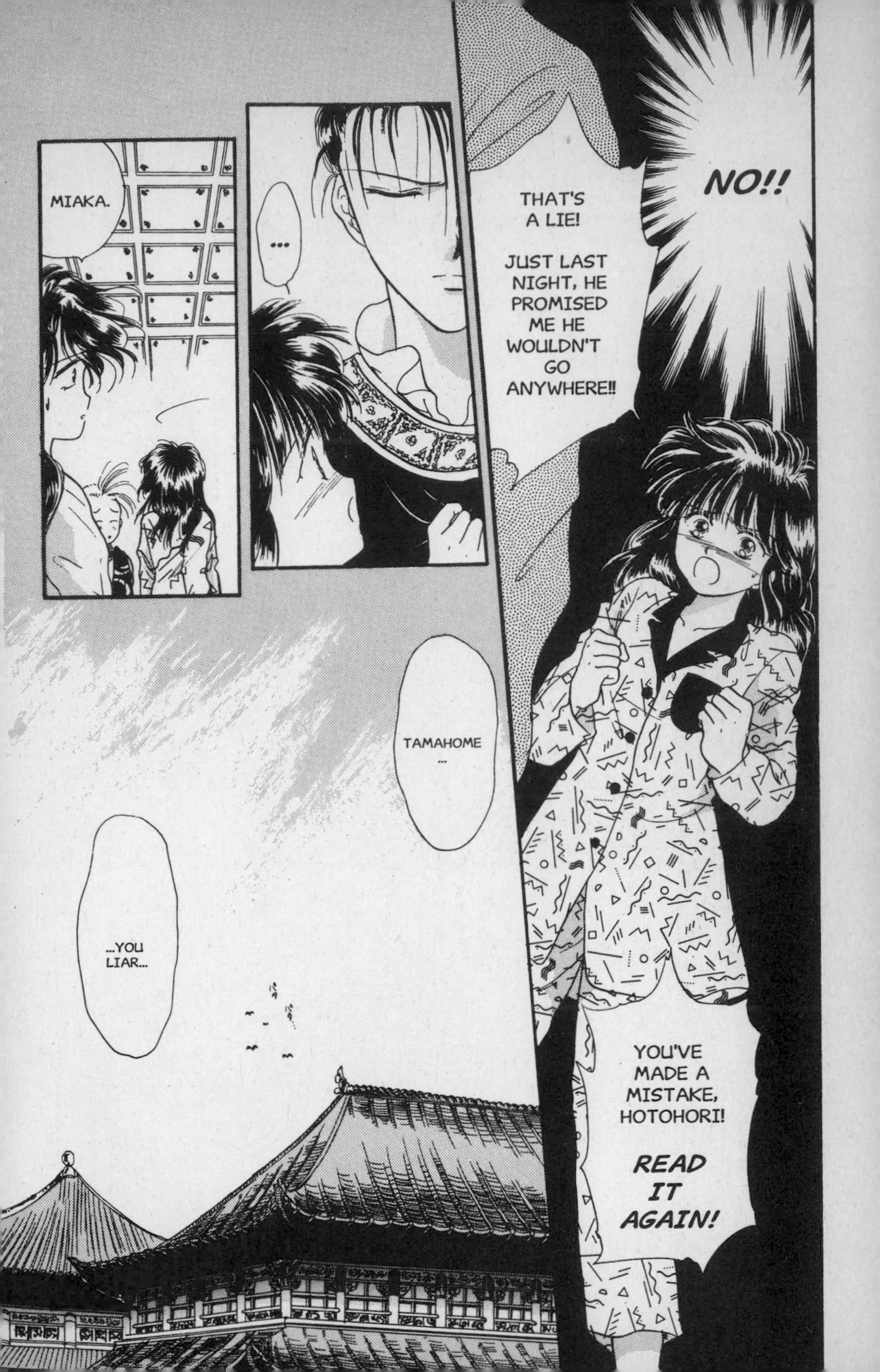
NO!!
THAT'S A LIE!
JUST LAST NIGHT, HE PROMISED ME HE WOULDN'T GO ANYWHERE!!
YOU'VE MADE A MISTAKE, HOTOHORI!
READ IT AGAIN!
...
MIAKA.
TAMAHOME ...
...YOU LIAR...

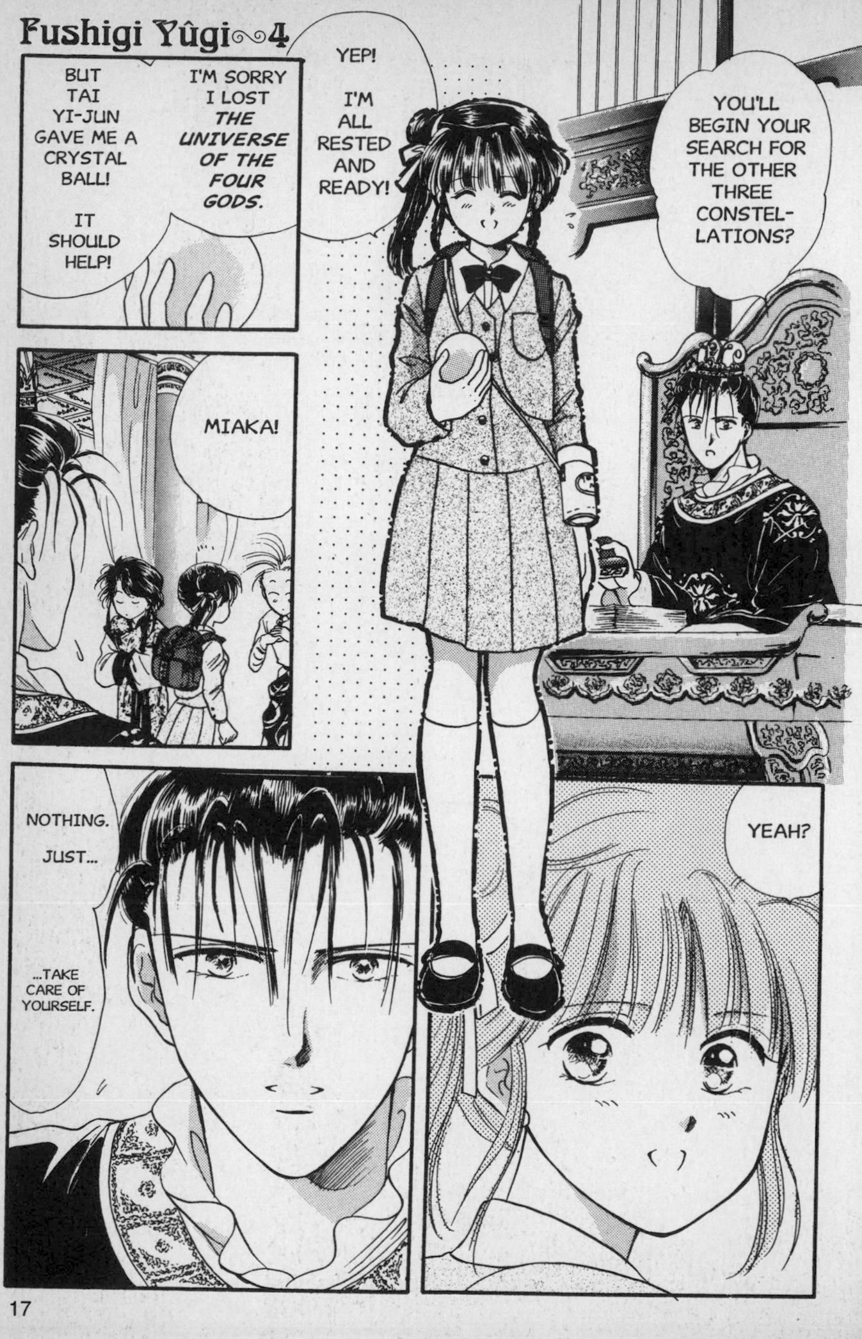
YOU'LL BEGIN YOUR SEARCH FOR THE OTHER THREE CONSTEL-LATIONS?
YEP! I'M ALL RESTED AND READY!
I'M SORRY I LOST *THE UNIVERSE OF THE FOUR GODS.*
BUT TAI YI-JUN GAVE ME A CRYSTAL BALL! IT SHOULD HELP!
MIAKA!
YEAH?
NOTHING. JUST...
...TAKE CARE OF YOURSELF.

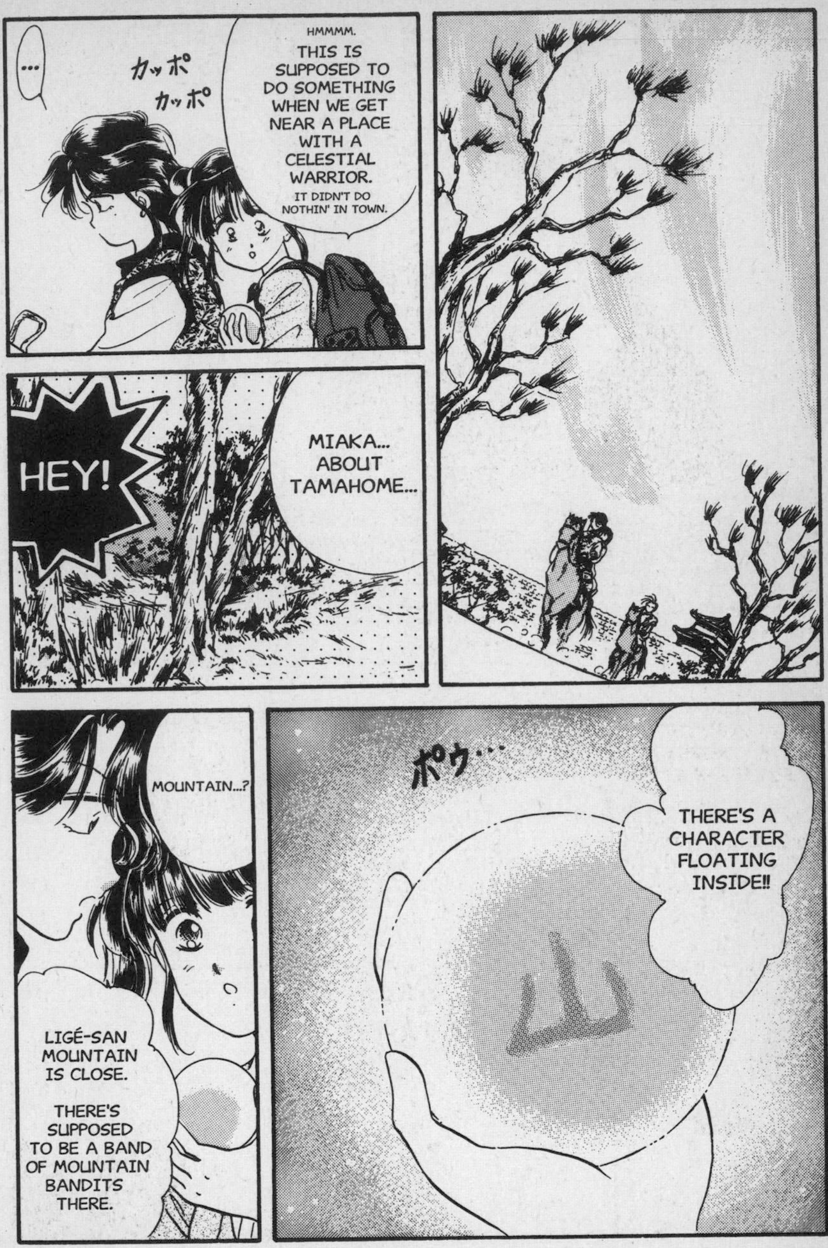
HMMMM.
THIS IS SUPPOSED TO DO SOMETHING WHEN WE GET NEAR A PLACE WITH A CELESTIAL WARRIOR.
IT DIDN'T DO NOTHIN' IN TOWN.
カッポ
カッポ
...
MIAKA... ABOUT TAMAHOME...
HEY!
THERE'S A CHARACTER FLOATING INSIDE!!
ポウ…
山
MOUNTAIN...?
LIGÉ-SAN MOUNTAIN IS CLOSE.
THERE'S SUPPOSED TO BE A BAND OF MOUNTAIN BANDITS THERE.

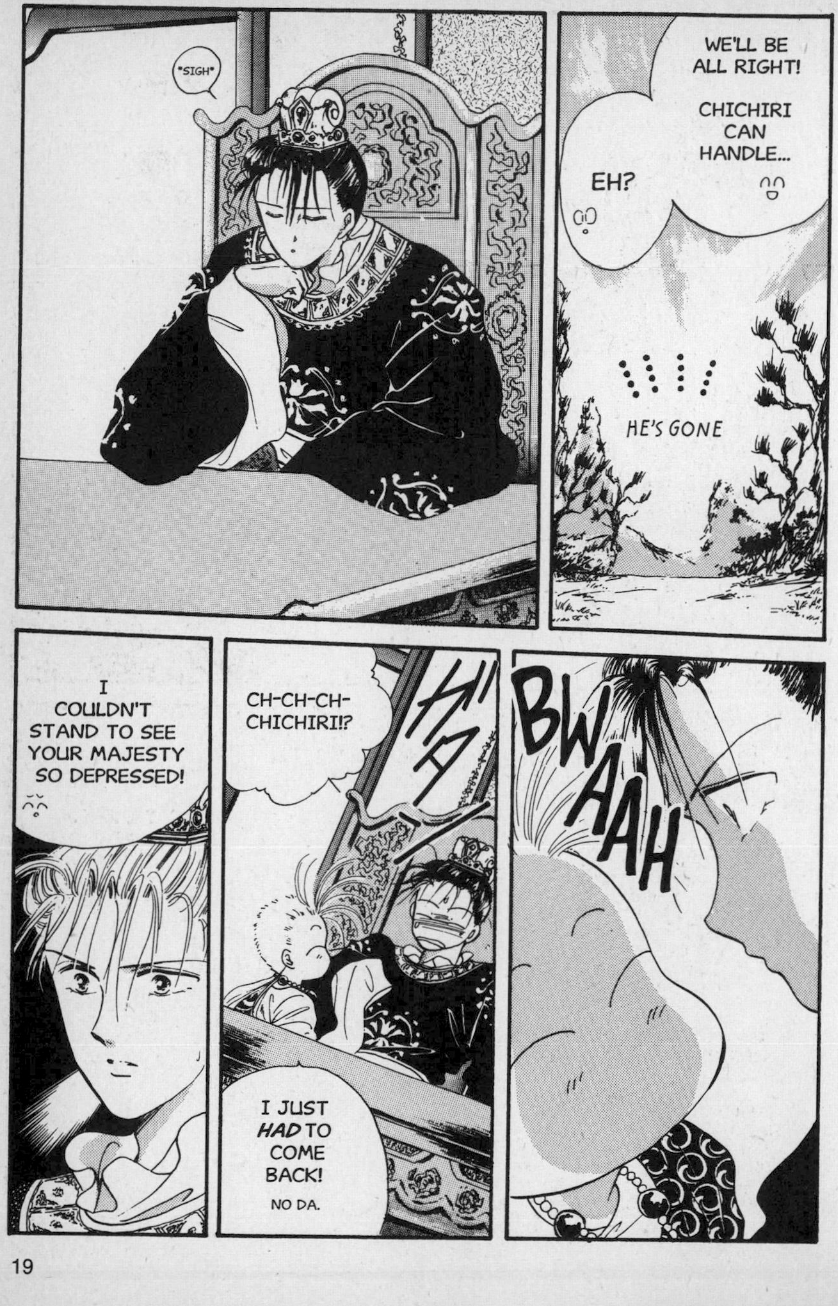
WE'LL BE ALL RIGHT!
CHICHIRI CAN HANDLE...
EH?
HE'S GONE
SIGH
BWAAAH
CH-CH-CH-CHICHIRI!?
I JUST *HAD* TO COME BACK!
NO DA.
I COULDN'T STAND TO SEE YOUR MAJESTY SO DEPRESSED!

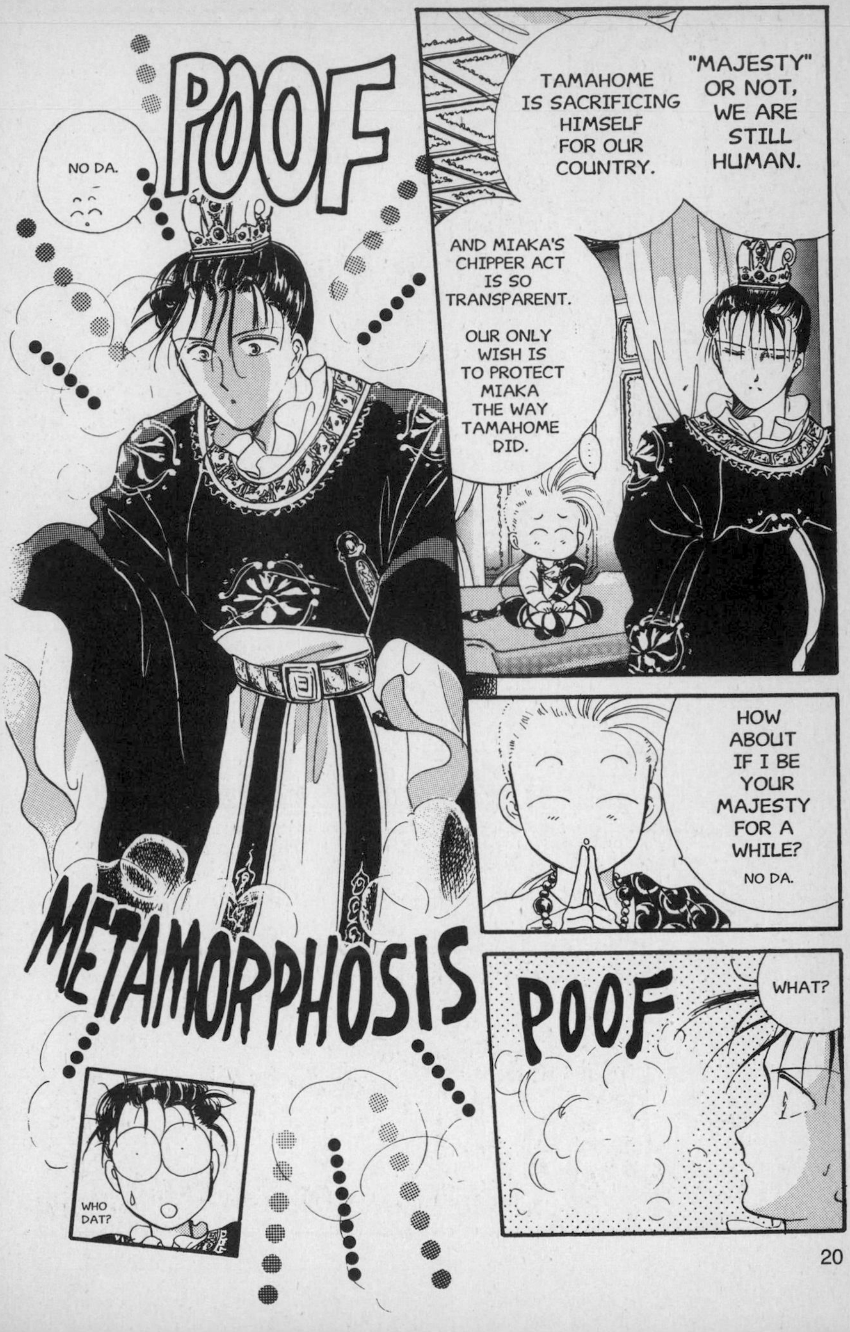
"MAJESTY" OR NOT, WE ARE STILL HUMAN.
TAMAHOME IS SACRIFICING HIMSELF FOR OUR COUNTRY.
AND MIAKA'S CHIPPER ACT IS SO TRANSPARENT.
OUR ONLY WISH IS TO PROTECT MIAKA THE WAY TAMAHOME DID.
...
HOW ABOUT IF I BE YOUR MAJESTY FOR A WHILE?
NO DA.
WHAT?
POOF
POOF
NO DA.
METAMORPHOSIS
WHO DAT?

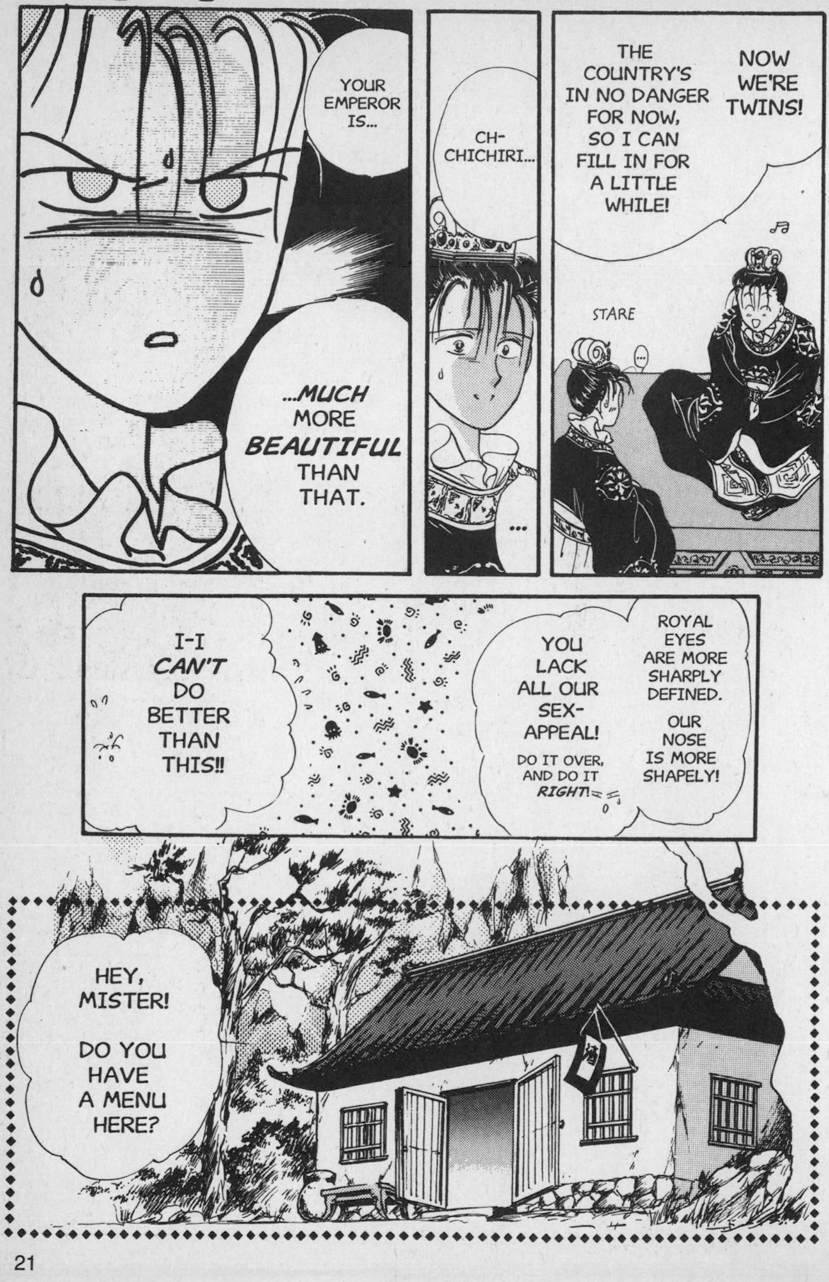
NOW WE'RE TWINS!
THE COUNTRY'S IN NO DANGER FOR NOW, SO I CAN FILL IN FOR A LITTLE WHILE!
STARE
...
CH-CHICHIRI...
...
YOUR EMPEROR IS...
...MUCH MORE BEAUTIFUL THAN THAT.
ROYAL EYES ARE MORE SHARPLY DEFINED.
OUR NOSE IS MORE SHAPELY!
YOU LACK ALL OUR SEX-APPEAL!
DO IT OVER, AND DO IT RIGHT!
I-I CAN'T DO BETTER THAN THIS!!
HEY, MISTER!
DO YOU HAVE A MENU HERE?

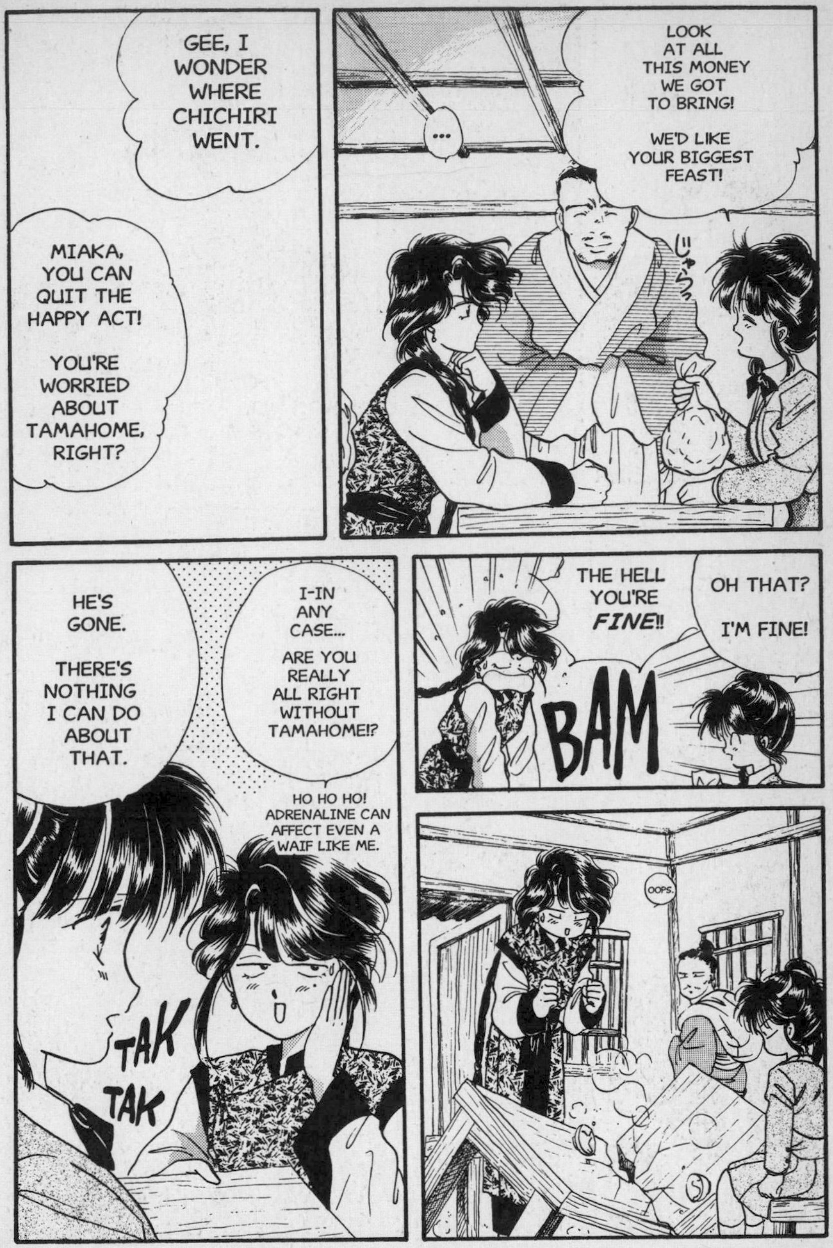
LOOK AT ALL THIS MONEY WE GOT TO BRING!
WE'D LIKE YOUR BIGGEST FEAST!
...
じゃらっ
GEE, I WONDER WHERE CHICHIRI WENT.
MIAKA, YOU CAN QUIT THE HAPPY ACT!
YOU'RE WORRIED ABOUT TAMAHOME, RIGHT?
OH THAT?
I'M FINE!
THE HELL YOU'RE *FINE*!!
BAM
OOPS.
I-IN ANY CASE...
ARE YOU REALLY ALL RIGHT WITHOUT TAMAHOME!?
HE'S GONE.
THERE'S NOTHING I CAN DO ABOUT THAT.
HO HO HO! ADRENALINE CAN AFFECT EVEN A WAIF LIKE ME.
TAK
TAK

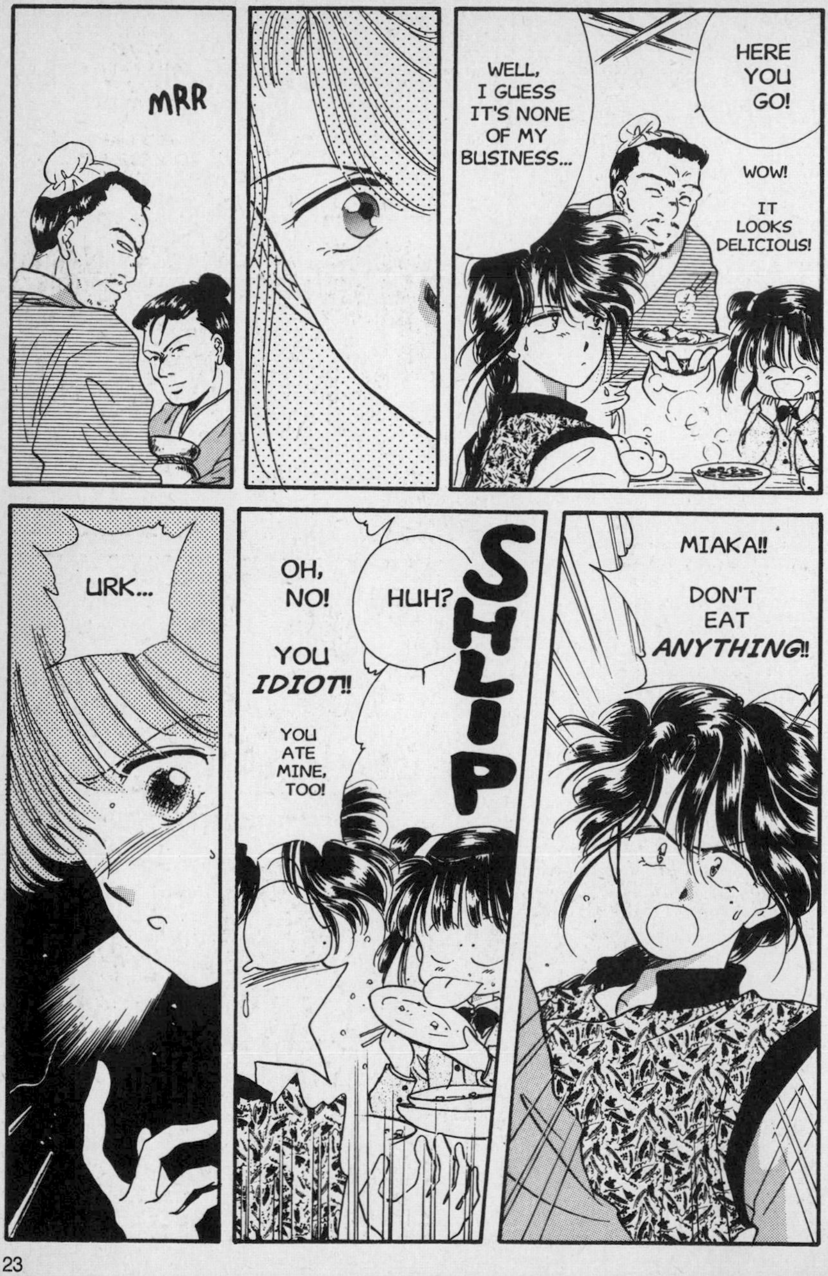
HERE YOU GO!
WELL, I GUESS IT'S NONE OF MY BUSINESS...
WOW! IT LOOKS DELICIOUS!
MRR
MIAKA!! DON'T EAT *ANYTHING*!!
SHLIP
HUH?
OH, NO! YOU *IDIOT*!!
YOU ATE MINE, TOO!
URK...

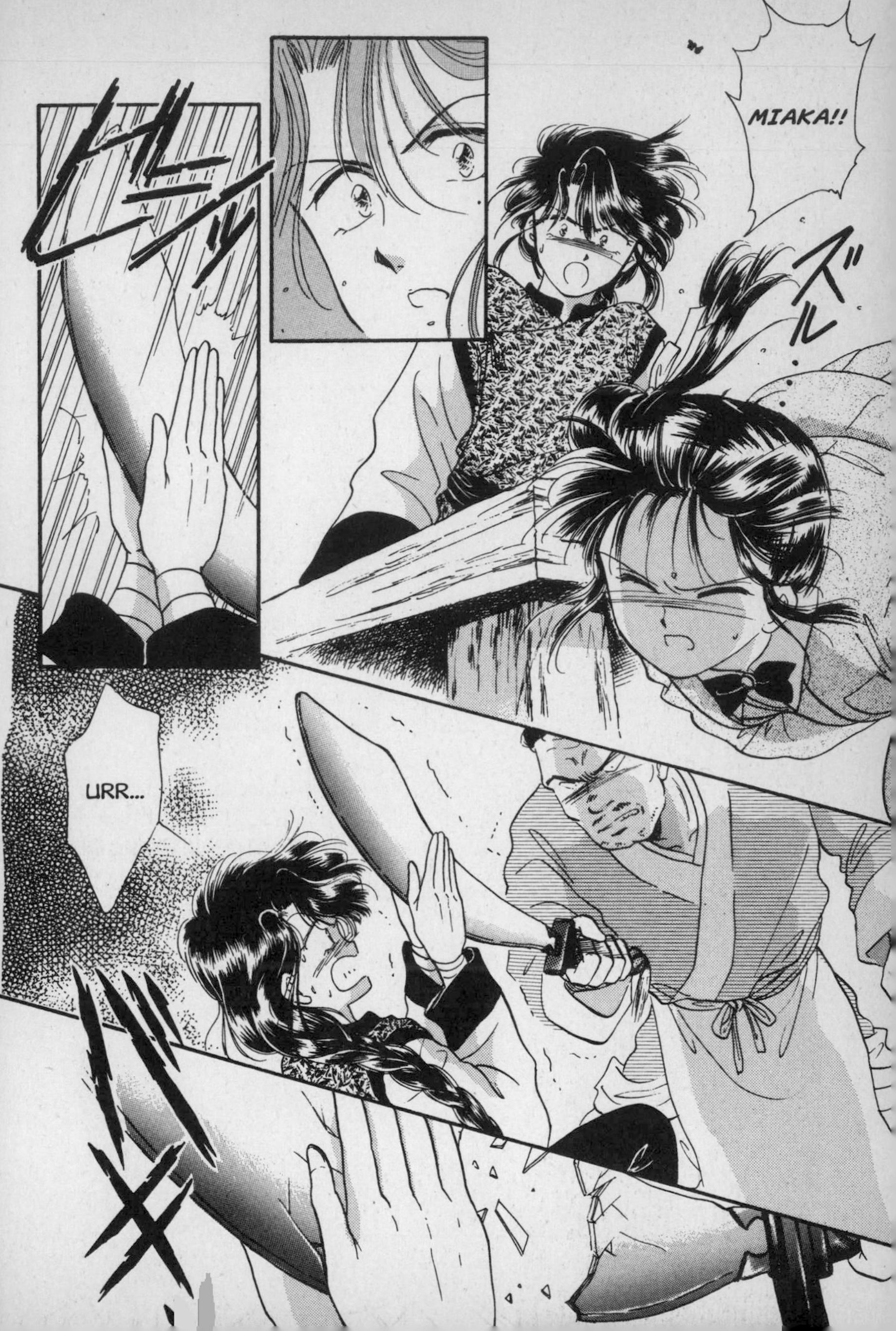
MIAKA!!
ズル
URR...

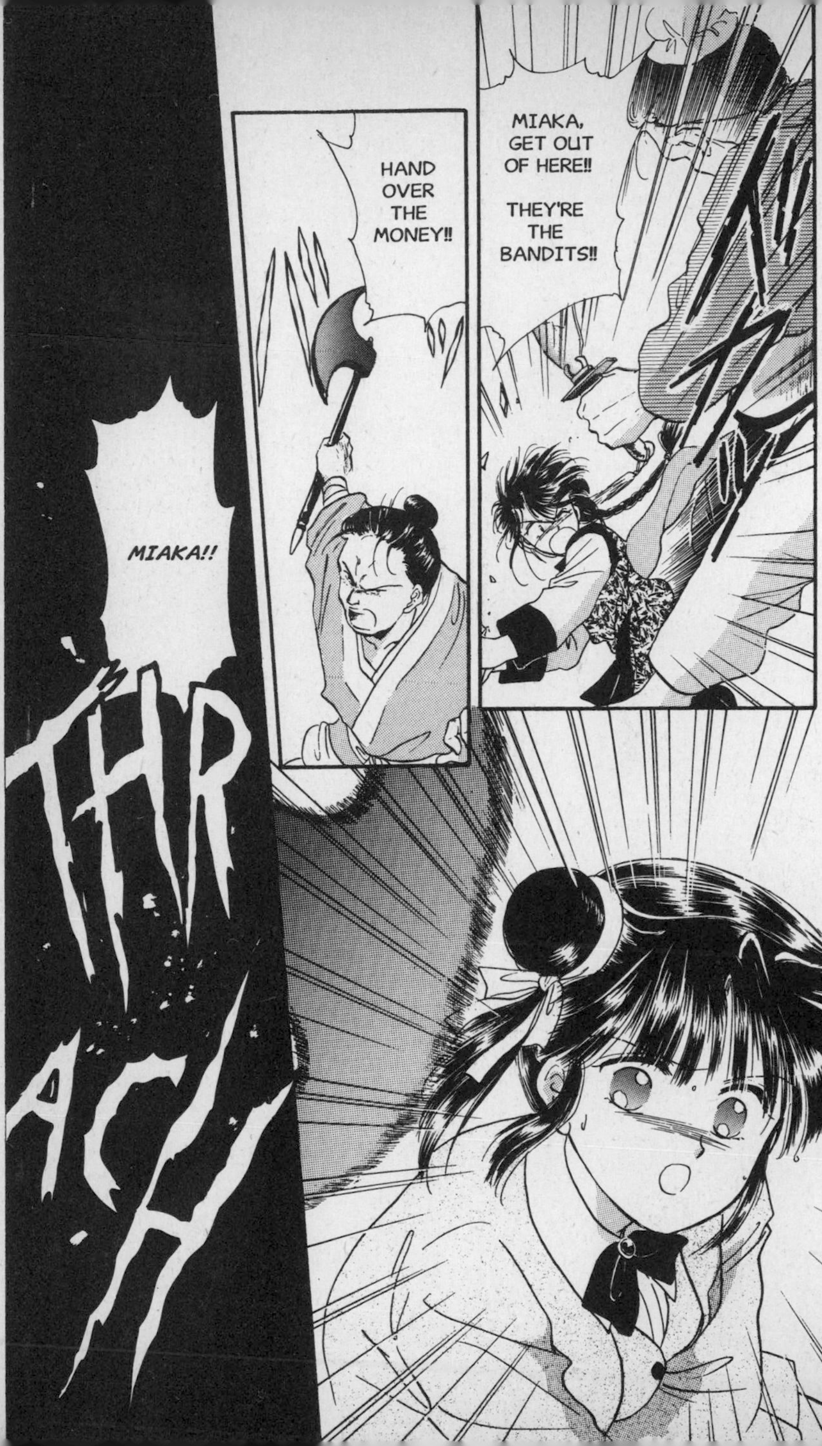
MIAKA, GET OUT OF HERE!!
THEY'RE THE BANDITS!!
HAND OVER THE MONEY!!
MIAKA!!
THRACH

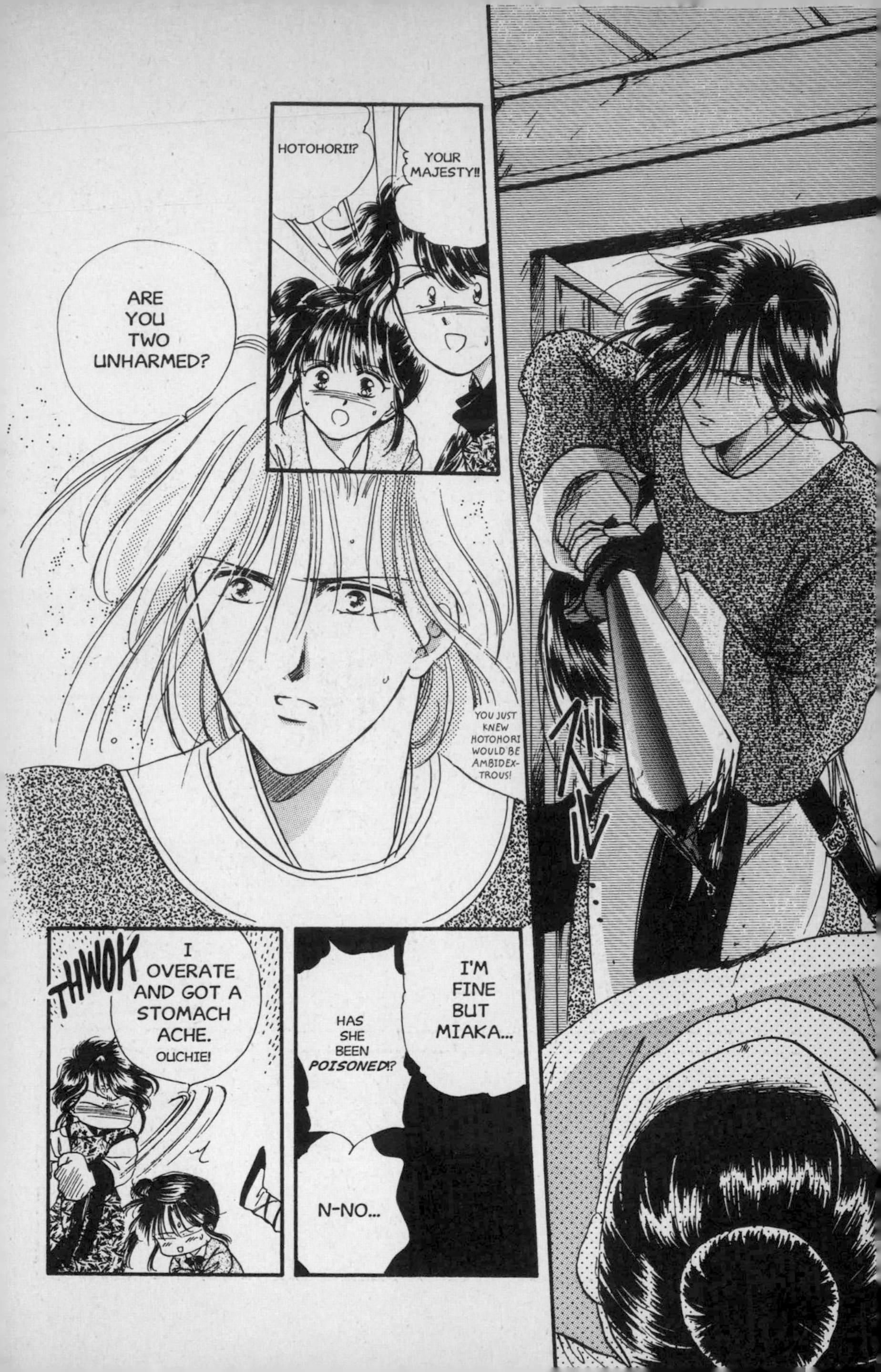
YOUR MAJESTY!!
HOTOHORI!?
ARE YOU TWO UNHARMED?
YOU JUST KNEW HOTOHORI WOULD BE AMBIDEXTROUS!
I'M FINE BUT MIAKA...
HAS SHE BEEN POISONED!?
N-NO...
THWOK
I OVERATE AND GOT A STOMACH ACHE.
OUCHIE!

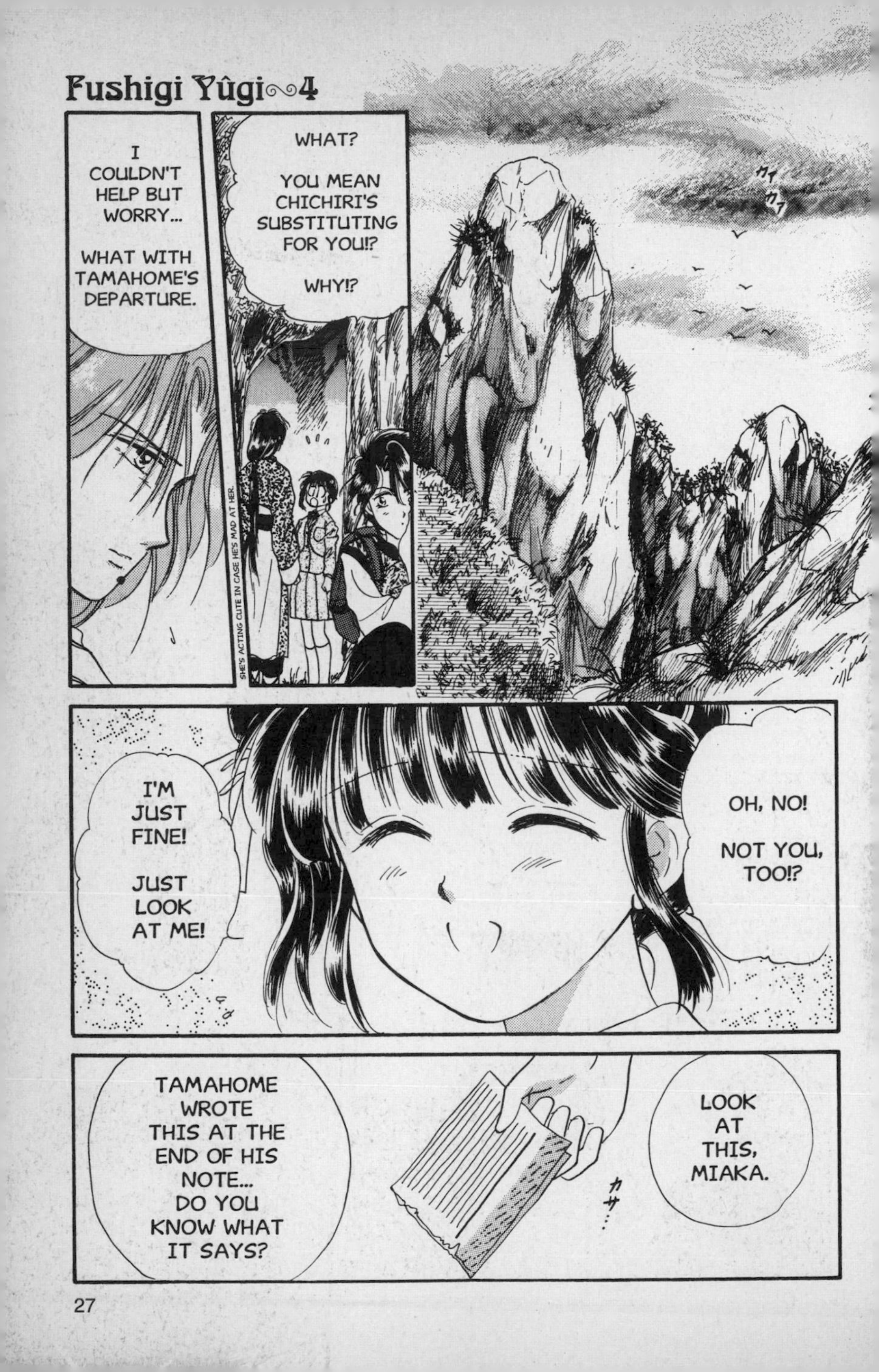
カァ カァ
WHAT? YOU MEAN CHICHIRI'S SUBSTITUTING FOR YOU!? WHY!?
SHE'S ACTING CUTE IN CASE HE'S MAD AT HER.
I COULDN'T HELP BUT WORRY... WHAT WITH TAMAHOME'S DEPARTURE.
OH, NO! NOT YOU, TOO!?
I'M JUST FINE! JUST LOOK AT ME!
LOOK AT THIS, MIAKA.
カサ…
TAMAHOME WROTE THIS AT THE END OF HIS NOTE... DO YOU KNOW WHAT IT SAYS?

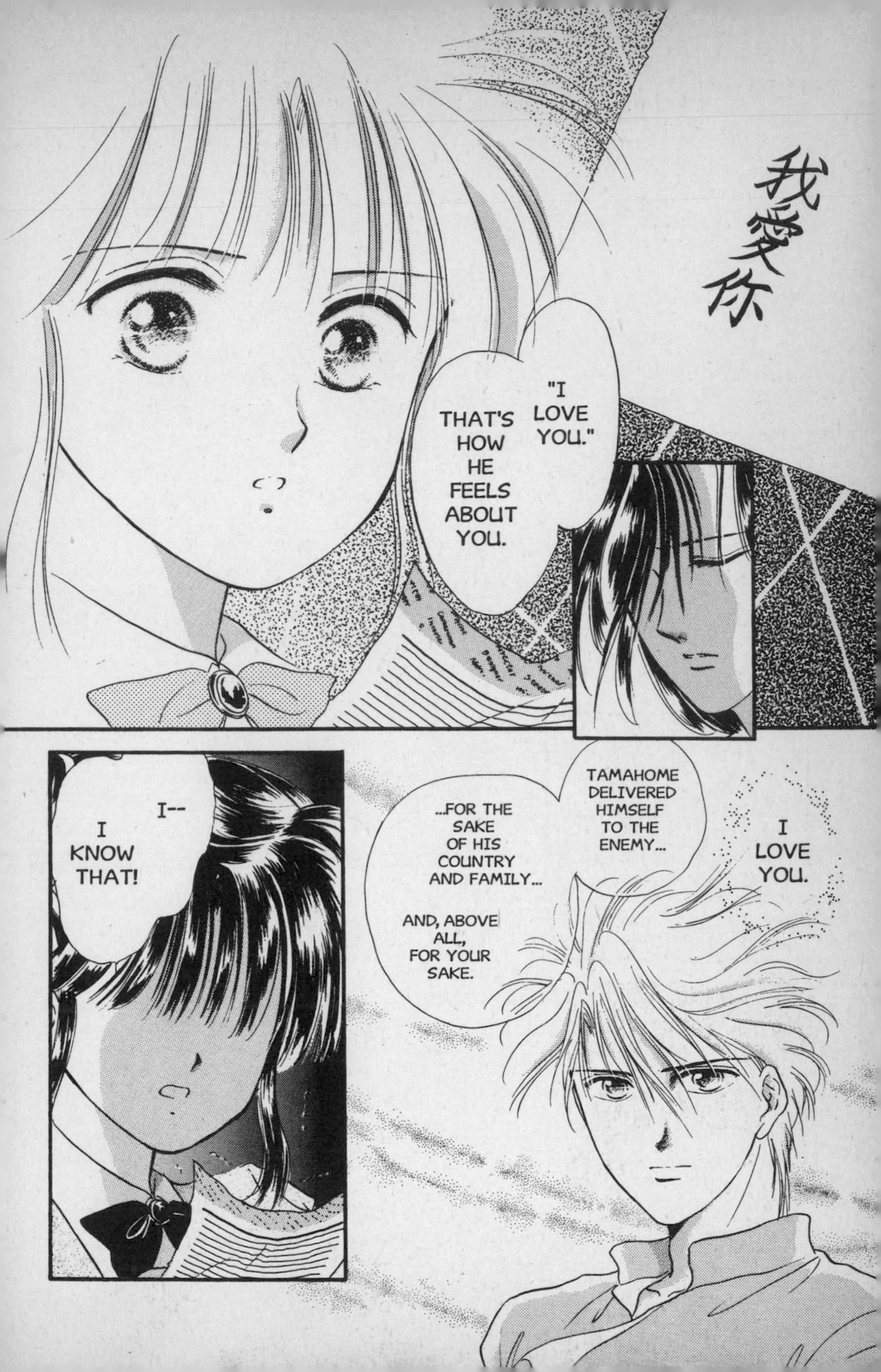
我愛你
"I LOVE YOU."
THAT'S HOW HE FEELS ABOUT YOU.
I LOVE YOU.
TAMAHOME DELIVERED HIMSELF TO THE ENEMY...
...FOR THE SAKE OF HIS COUNTRY AND FAMILY...
AND, ABOVE ALL, FOR YOUR SAKE.
I--
I KNOW THAT!

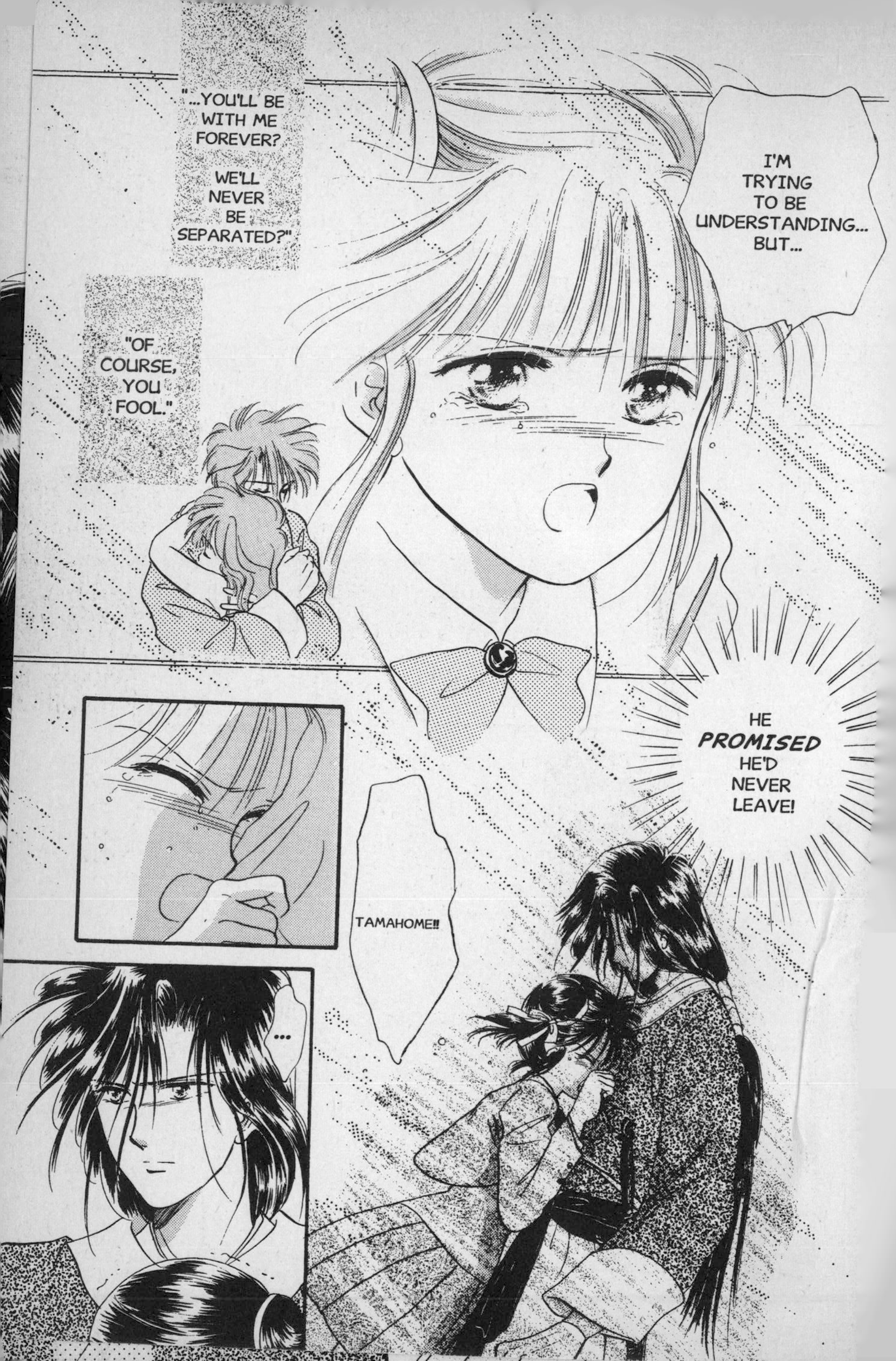
I'M TRYING TO BE UNDERSTANDING... BUT...
"...YOU'LL BE WITH ME FOREVER? WE'LL NEVER BE SEPARATED?"
"OF COURSE, YOU FOOL."
HE *PROMISED* HE'D NEVER LEAVE!
TAMAHOME!!
...

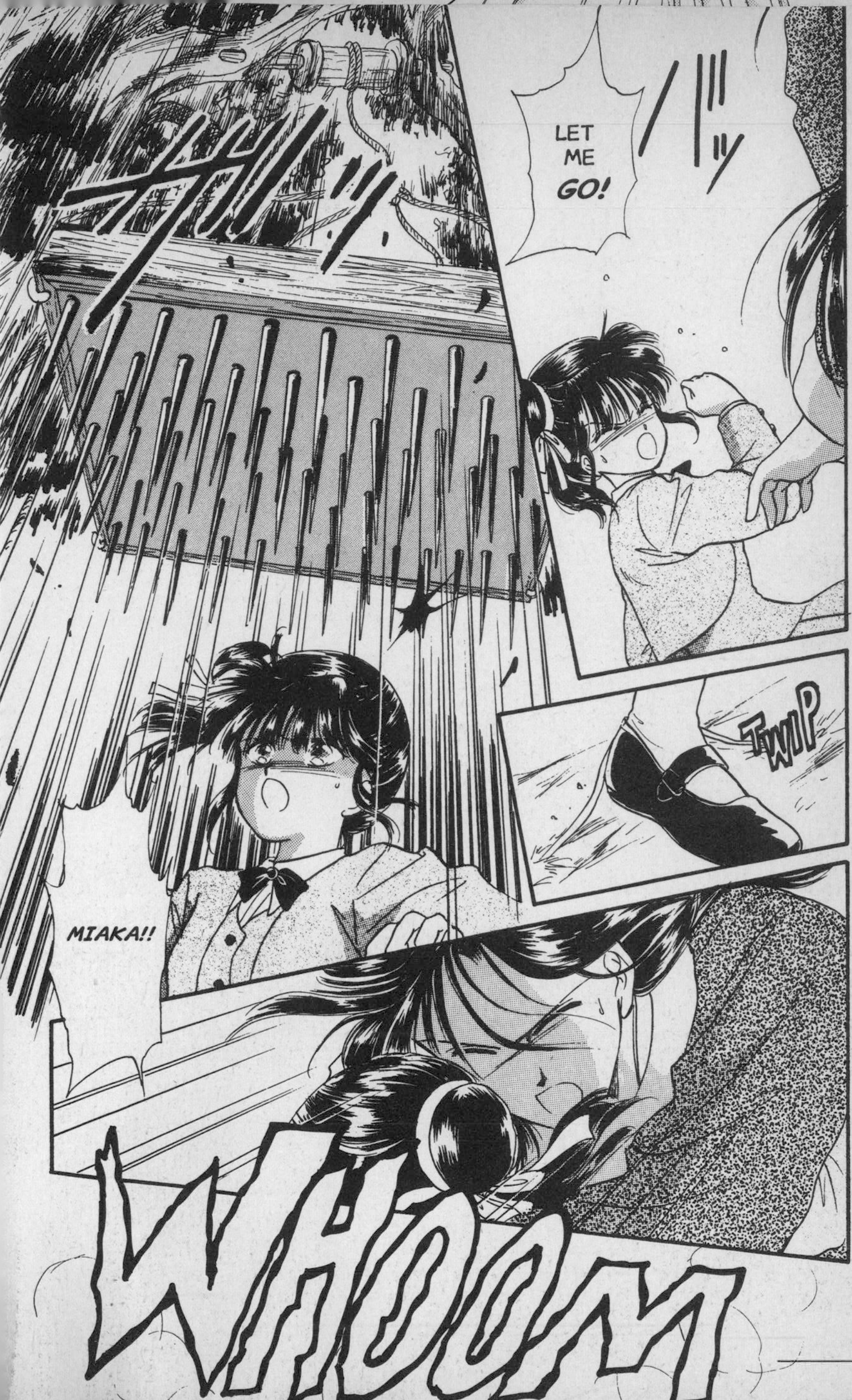
LET ME GO!
TWIP
MIAKA!!
WHOOM

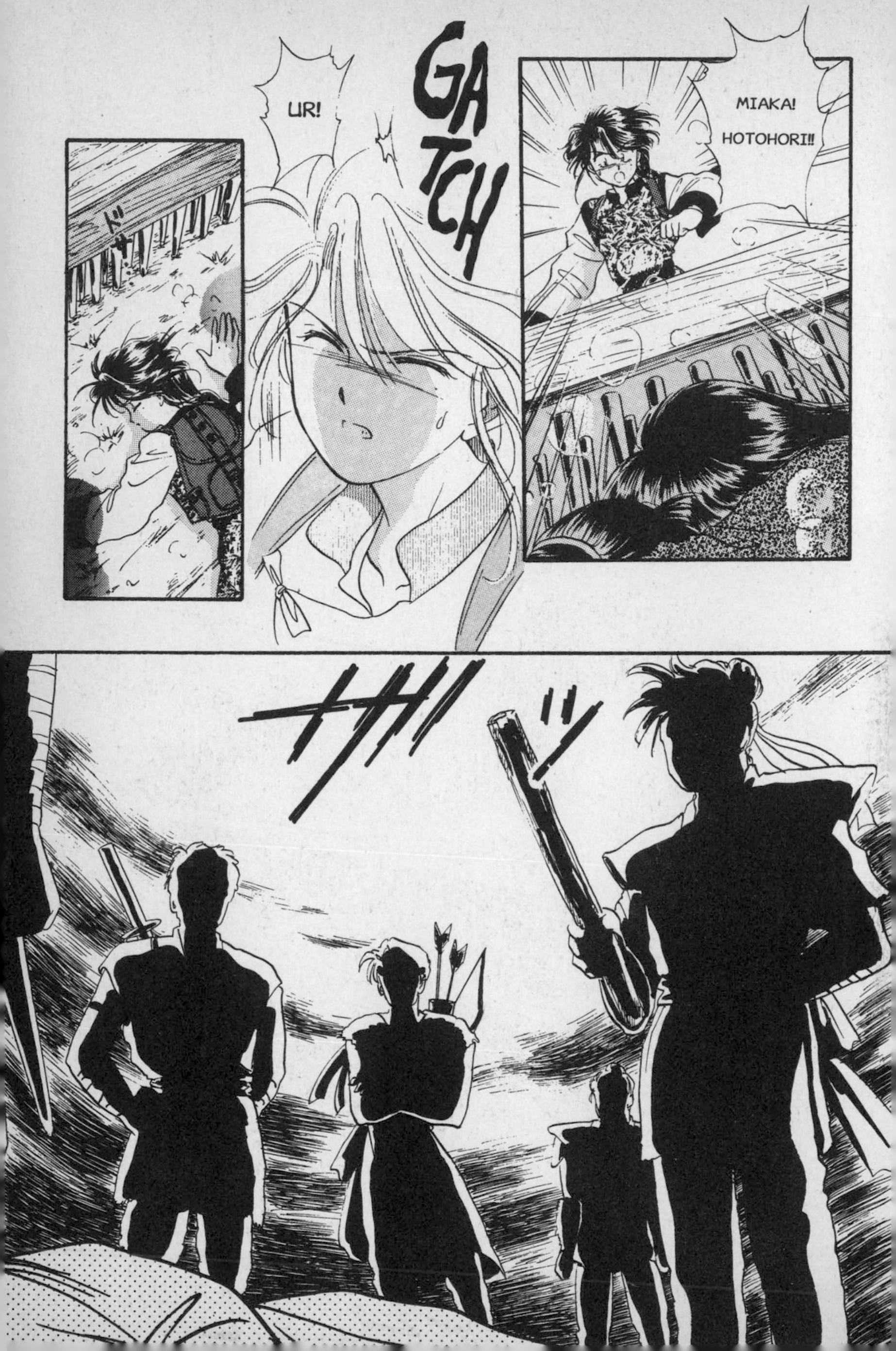
MIAKA!
HOTOHORI!!
GATCH
UR!

Fushigi Akugi has been canceled for this chapter!
(I don't have the originals to copy from)   I spaced out.
I can use any interesting ideas. Send any suggestions you may have my way.
I'll give you credit!
But will this series go on if the story gets any more serious?   We may get canceled here...
You'll have to be reading it in the (Japanese) anthology magazine to get your idea
to me in time for it to be included.

To readers of the English version: Sorry!
As much as we would love some of your
suggestions to be made into comics, it's too late!

TAMAHOME
(10 years old)

CHAPTER TWENTY
WOLF OF THE FORTRESS

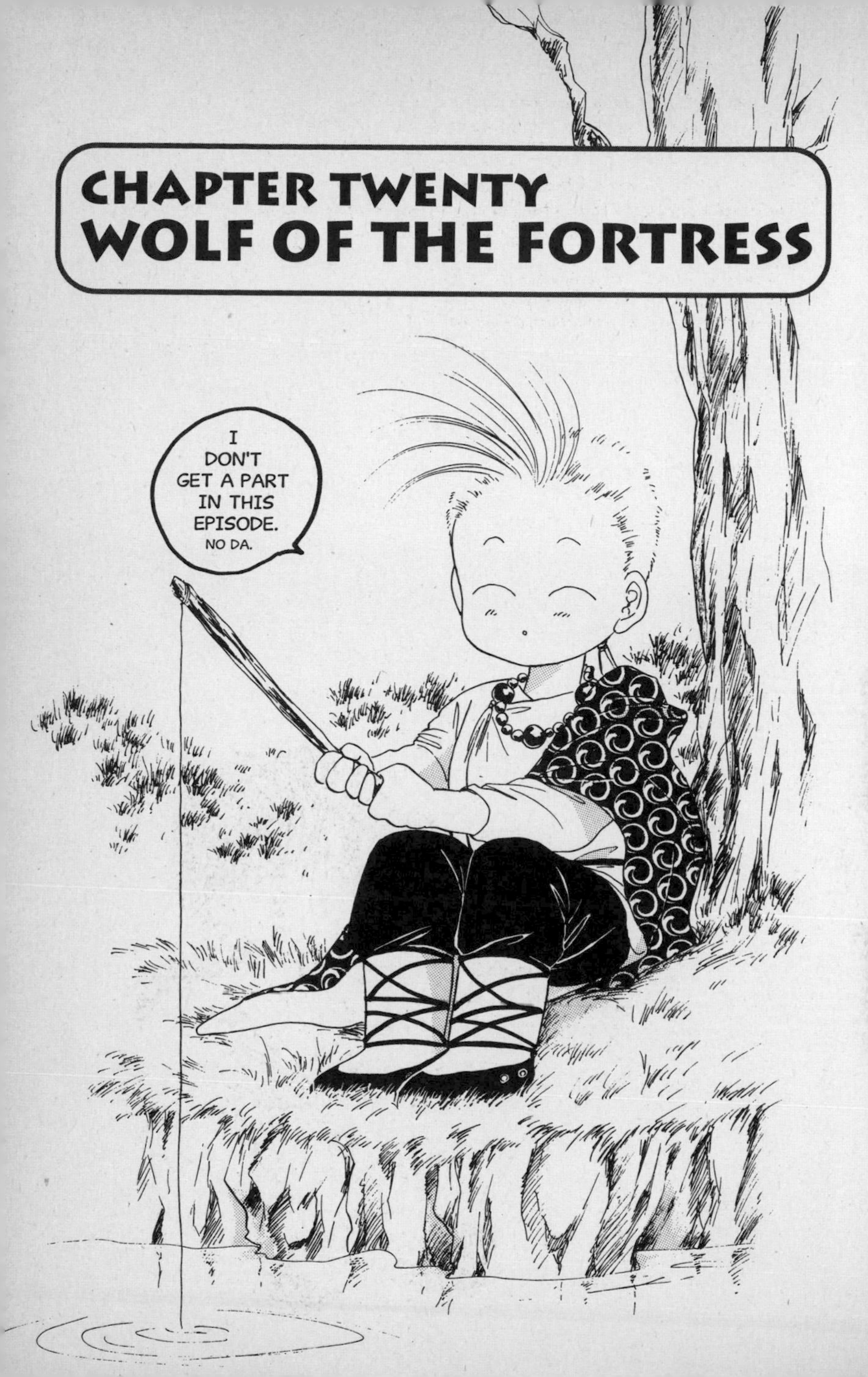
I DON'T GET A PART IN THIS EPISODE. NO DA.

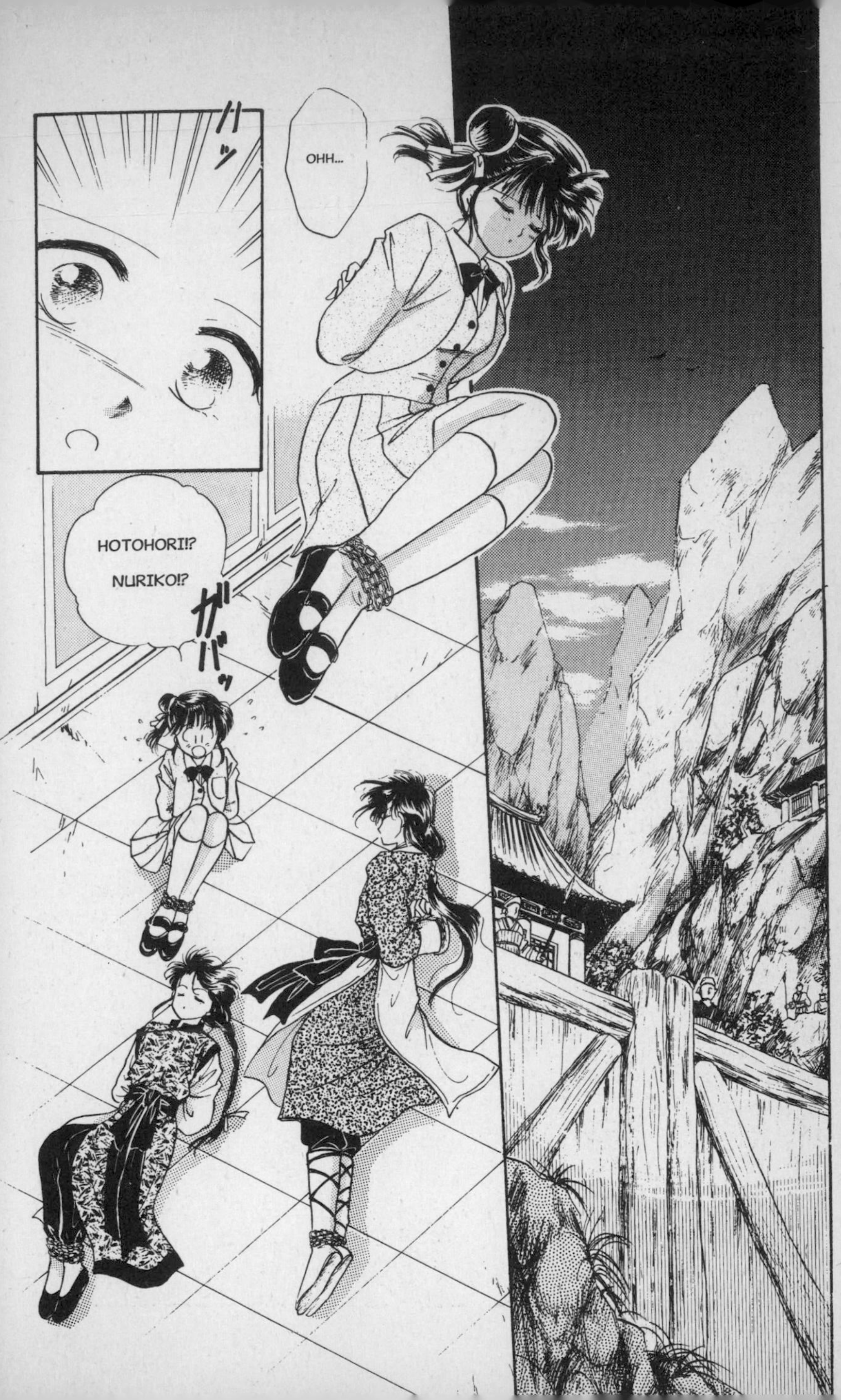
OHH...
ハッ
HOTOHORI!?
NURIKO!?
ガバッ

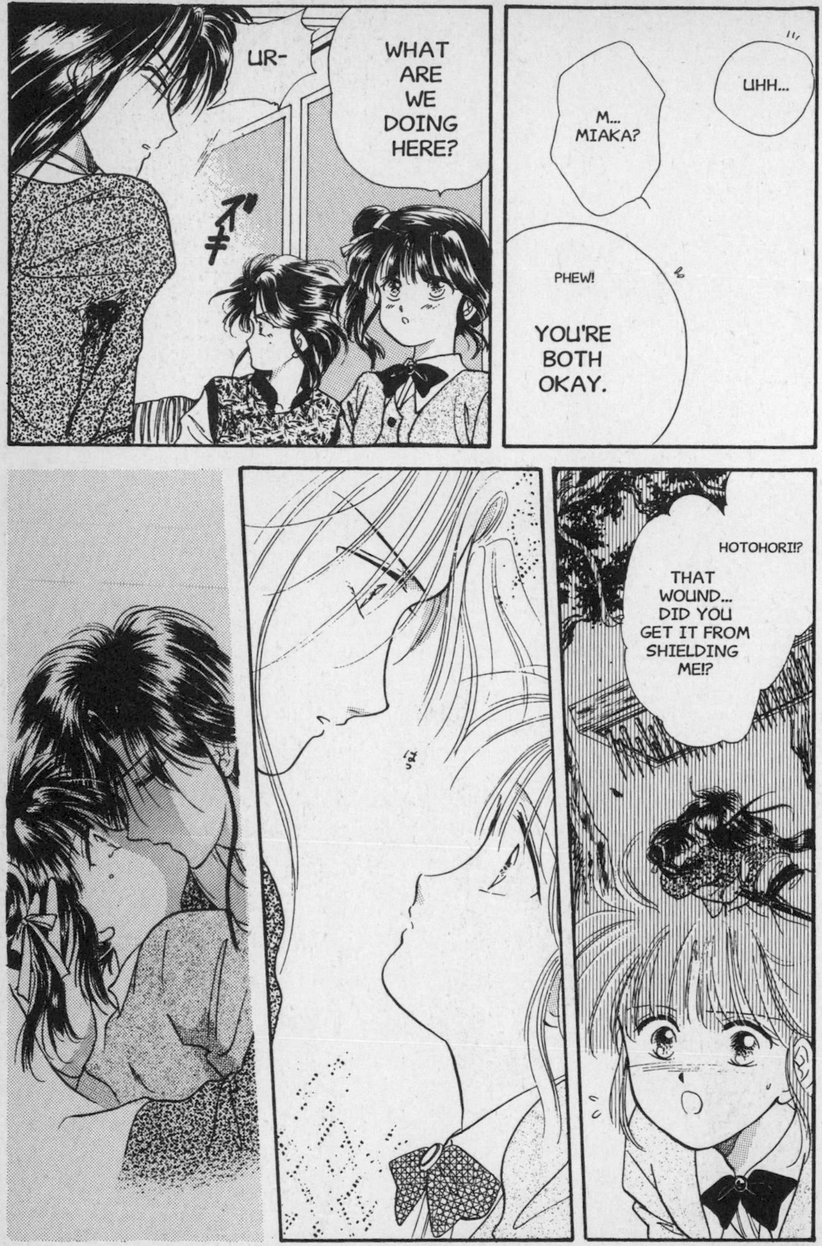
UHH...
M... MIAKA?
PHEW!
YOU'RE BOTH OKAY.
WHAT ARE WE DOING HERE?
UR-
HOTOHORI!?
THAT WOUND... DID YOU GET IT FROM SHIELDING ME!?

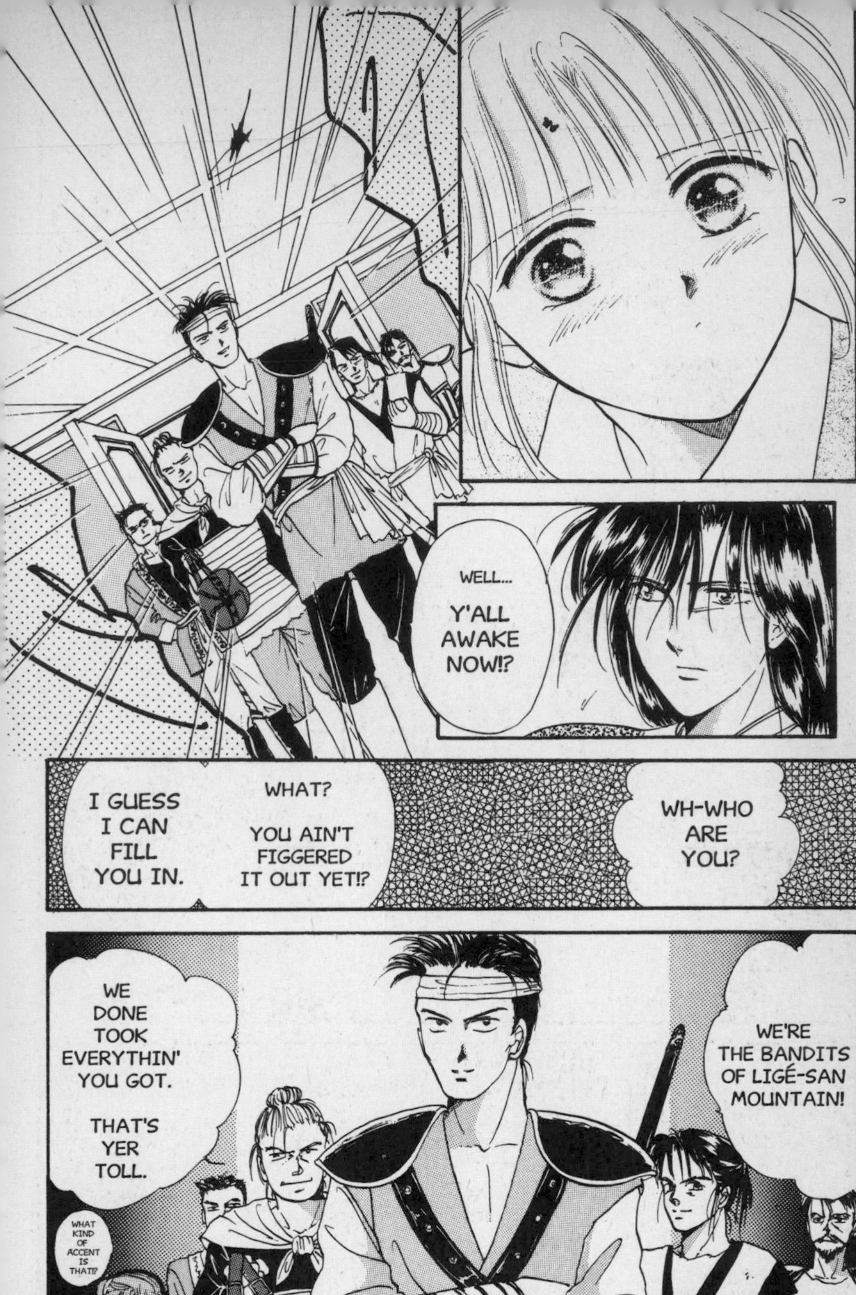
WELL... Y'ALL AWAKE NOW!?
WH-WHO ARE YOU?
WHAT? YOU AIN'T FIGGERED IT OUT YET!?
I GUESS I CAN FILL YOU IN.
WE'RE THE BANDITS OF LIGÉ-SAN MOUNTAIN!
WE DONE TOOK EVERYTHIN' YOU GOT. THAT'S YER TOLL.
WHAT KIND OF ACCENT IS THAT!?

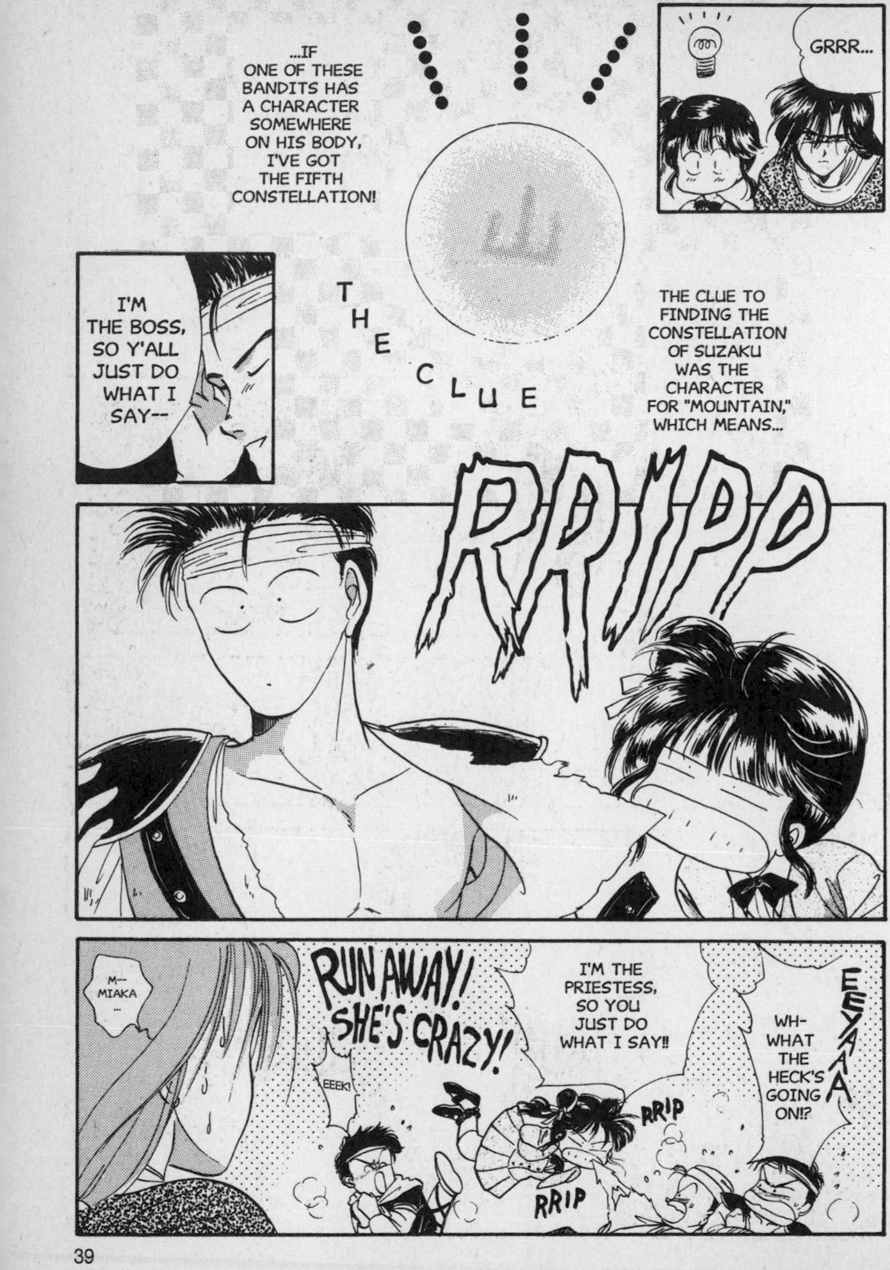
GRRR...
...IF ONE OF THESE BANDITS HAS A CHARACTER SOMEWHERE ON HIS BODY, I'VE GOT THE FIFTH CONSTELLATION!
THE CLUE TO FINDING THE CONSTELLATION OF SUZAKU WAS THE CHARACTER FOR "MOUNTAIN," WHICH MEANS...
THE CLUE
I'M THE BOSS, SO Y'ALL JUST DO WHAT I SAY--
RRIPP
EEYAAA
WH-WHAT THE HECK'S GOING ON!?
I'M THE PRIESTESS, SO YOU JUST DO WHAT I SAY!!
RRIP
RRIP
RUN AWAY! SHE'S CRAZY!
EEEK!
M--MIAKA...

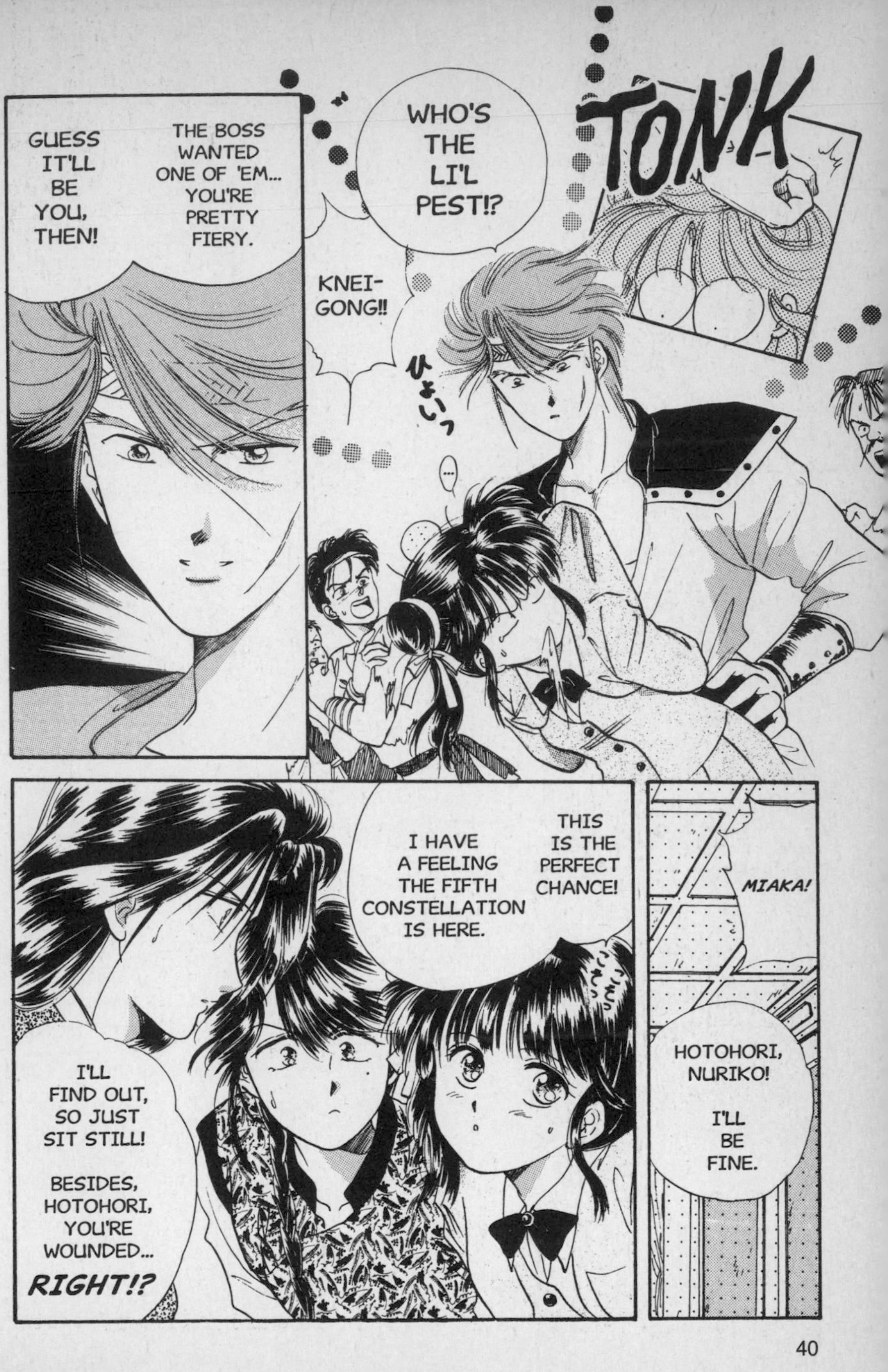
TONK
WHO'S THE LI'L PEST!?
KNEI-GONG!!
ひょいっ
...
THE BOSS WANTED ONE OF 'EM... YOU'RE PRETTY FIERY.
GUESS IT'LL BE YOU, THEN!
MIAKA!
HOTOHORI, NURIKO!
I'LL BE FINE.
THIS IS THE PERFECT CHANCE!
I HAVE A FEELING THE FIFTH CONSTELLATION IS HERE.
I'LL FIND OUT, SO JUST SIT STILL!
BESIDES, HOTOHORI, YOU'RE WOUNDED... **RIGHT!?**

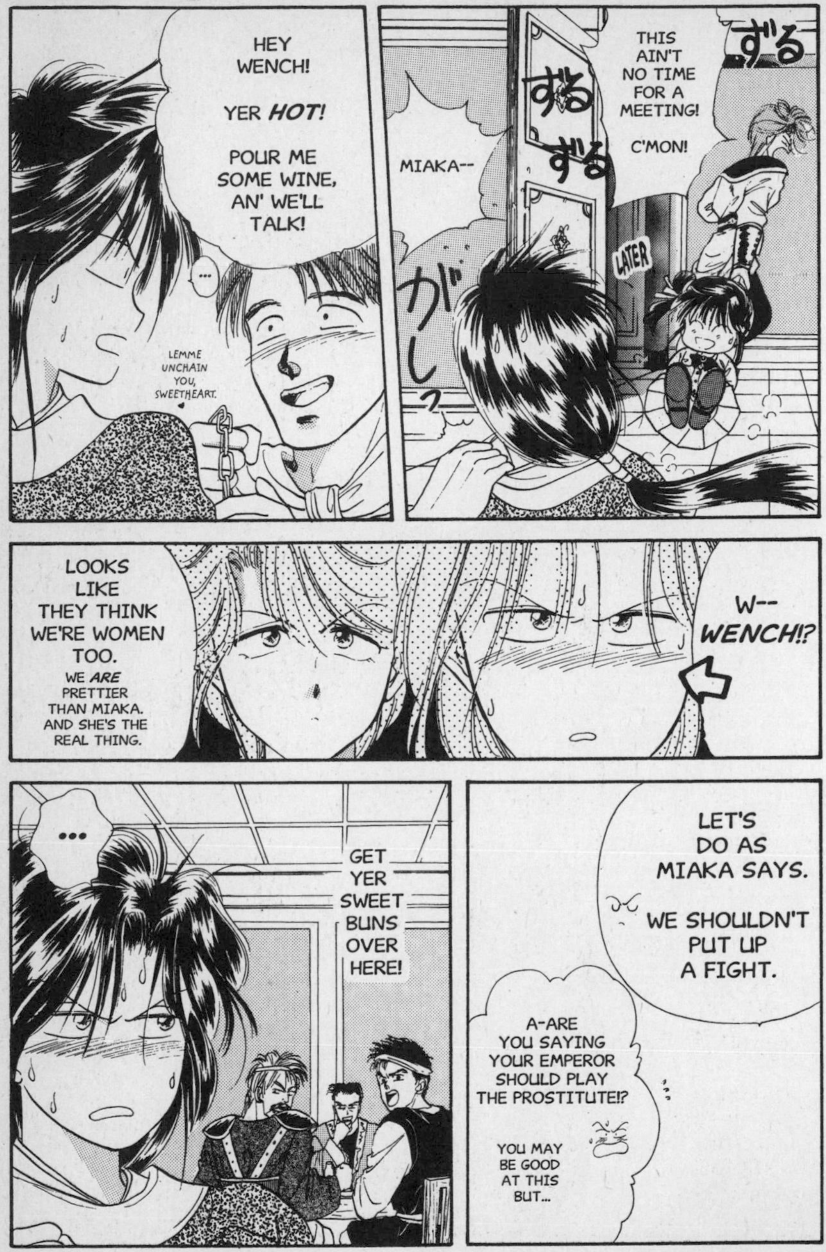
ずる
THIS AIN'T NO TIME FOR A MEETING!
C'MON!
ずる
ずる
MIAKA--
LATER
がしっ
HEY WENCH!
YER *HOT*!
POUR ME SOME WINE, AN' WE'LL TALK!
...
LEMME UNCHAIN YOU, SWEETHEART.
W-- *WENCH!?*
LOOKS LIKE THEY THINK WE'RE WOMEN TOO.
WE *ARE* PRETTIER THAN MIAKA. AND SHE'S THE REAL THING.
LET'S DO AS MIAKA SAYS.
WE SHOULDN'T PUT UP A FIGHT.
A-ARE YOU SAYING YOUR EMPEROR SHOULD PLAY THE PROSTITUTE!?
YOU MAY BE GOOD AT THIS BUT...
...
GET YER SWEET BUNS OVER HERE!

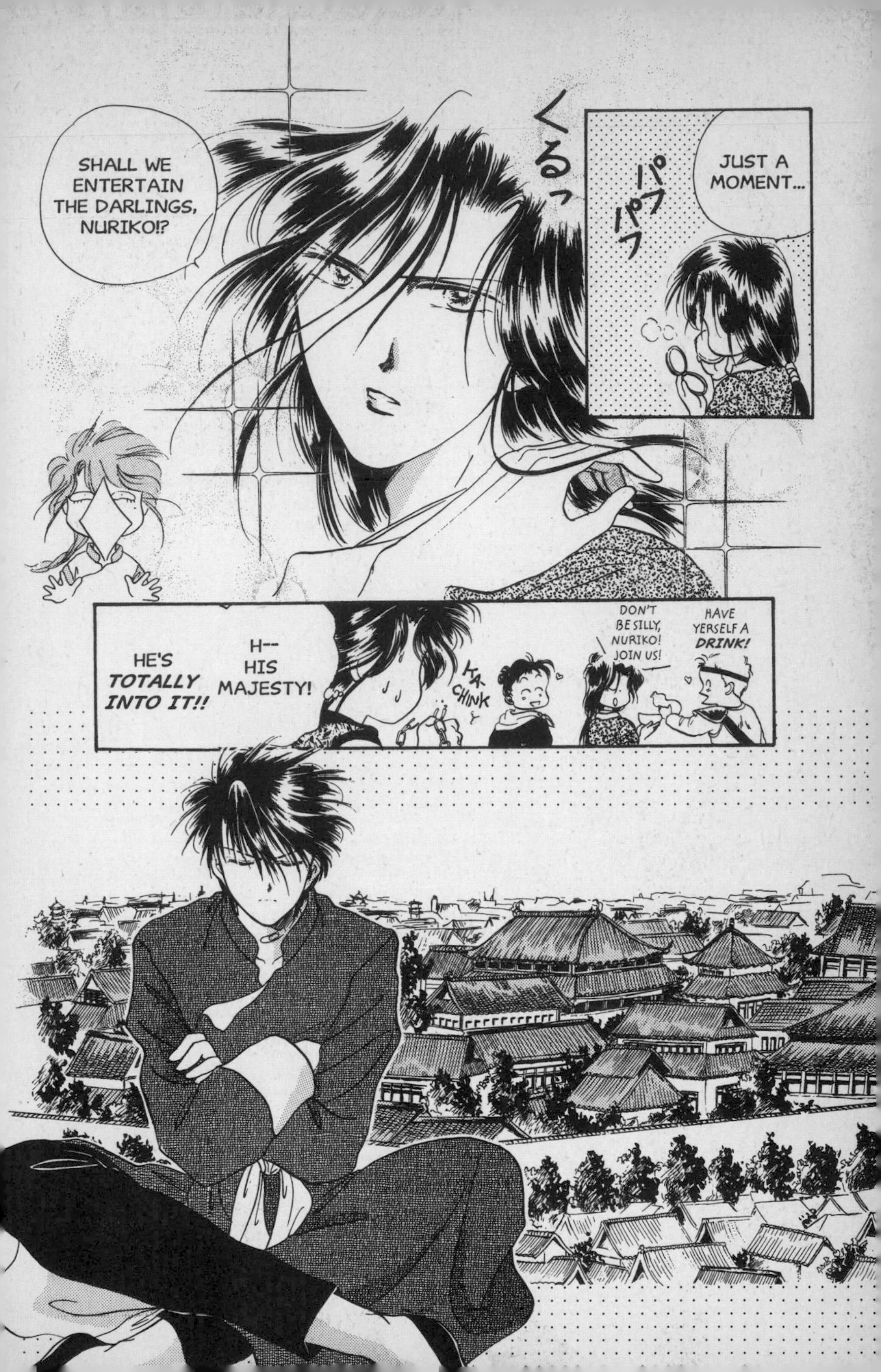
JUST A MOMENT...
パフパフ
くるっ
SHALL WE ENTERTAIN THE DARLINGS, NURIKO!?
HAVE YOURSELF A DRINK!
DON'T BE SILLY, NURIKO! JOIN US!
KA-CHINK
H-- HIS MAJESTY!
HE'S TOTALLY INTO IT!!

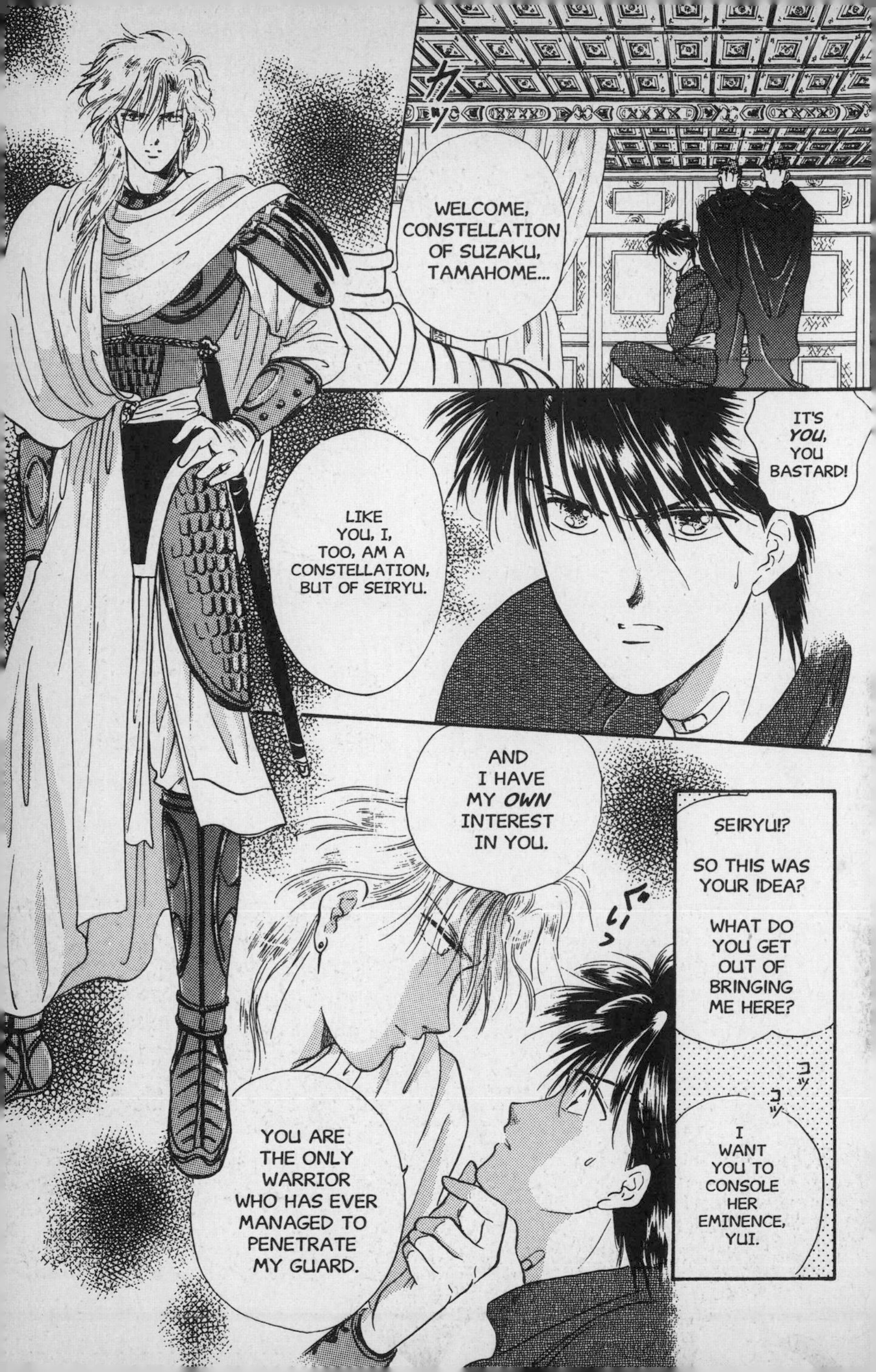
WELCOME, CONSTELLATION OF SUZAKU, TAMAHOME...
IT'S *YOU*, YOU BASTARD!
LIKE YOU, I, TOO, AM A CONSTELLATION, BUT OF SEIRYU.
SEIRYU!?
SO THIS WAS YOUR IDEA?
WHAT DO YOU GET OUT OF BRINGING ME HERE?
I WANT YOU TO CONSOLE HER EMINENCE, YUI.
AND I HAVE MY *OWN* INTEREST IN YOU.
YOU ARE THE ONLY WARRIOR WHO HAS EVER MANAGED TO PENETRATE MY GUARD.

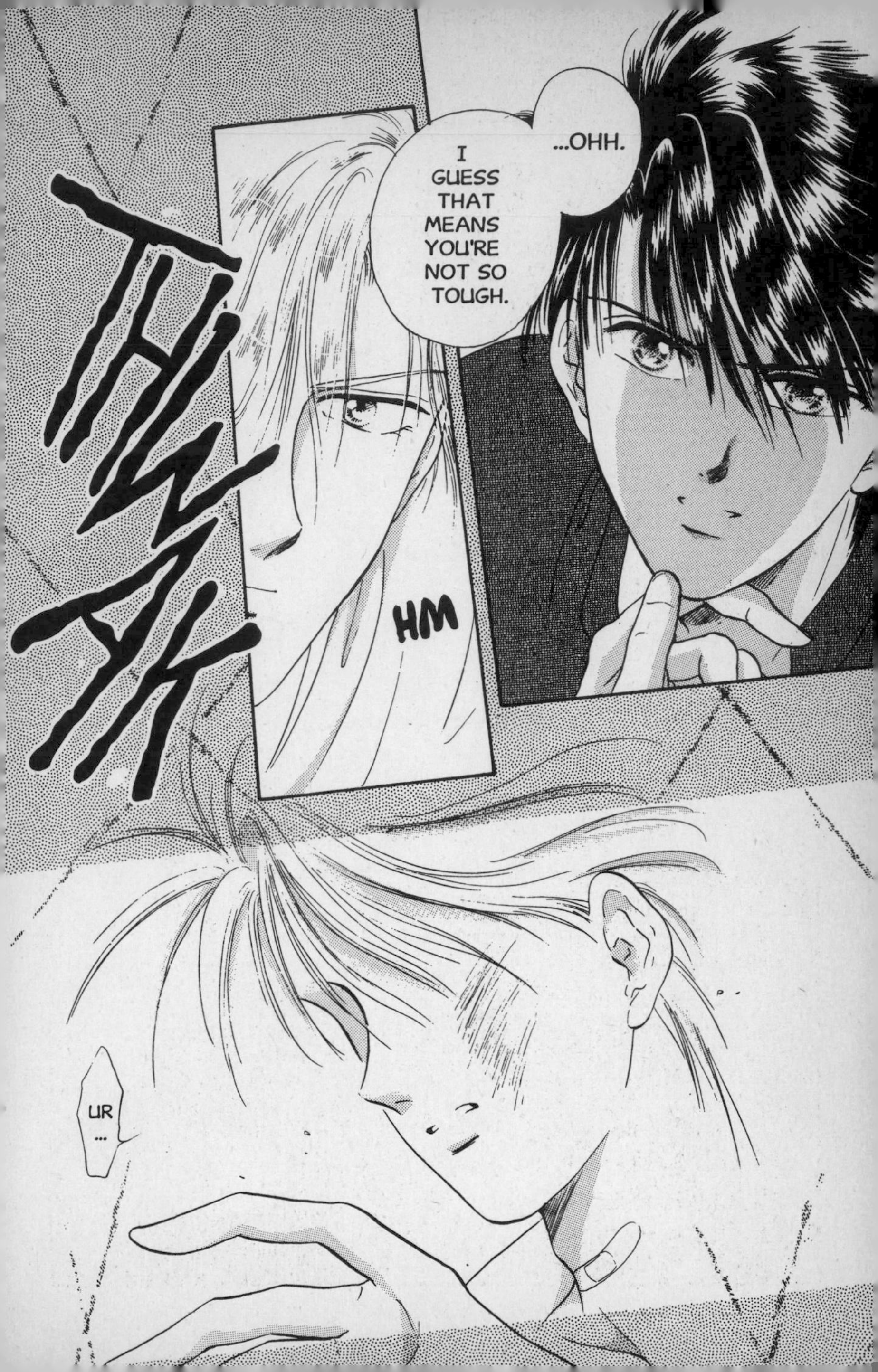
...OHH.
I GUESS THAT MEANS YOU'RE NOT SO TOUGH.
THWAK
HM
UR ...

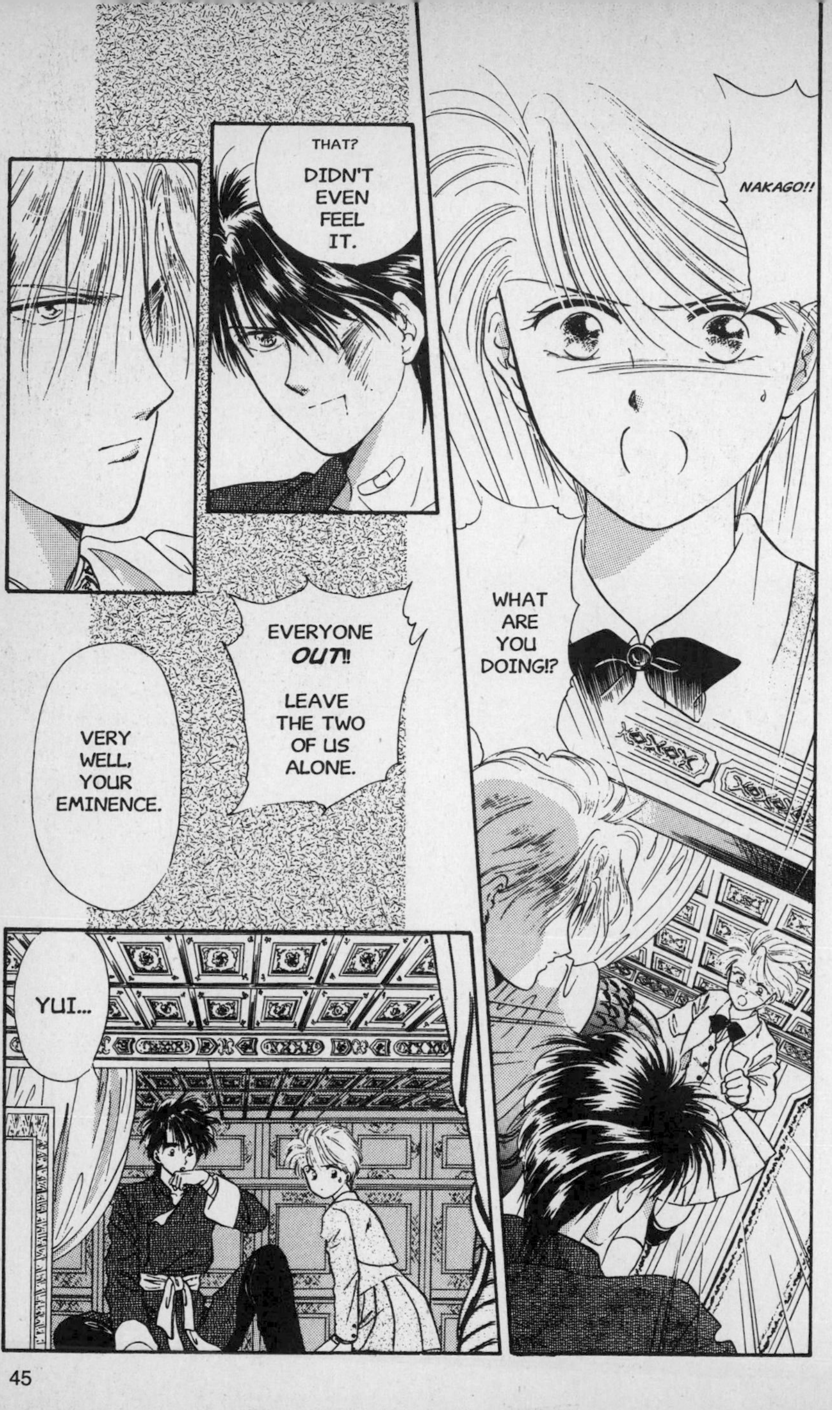
NAKAGO!!
WHAT ARE YOU DOING!?
THAT? DIDN'T EVEN FEEL IT.
EVERYONE OUT!! LEAVE THE TWO OF US ALONE.
VERY WELL, YOUR EMINENCE.
YUI...

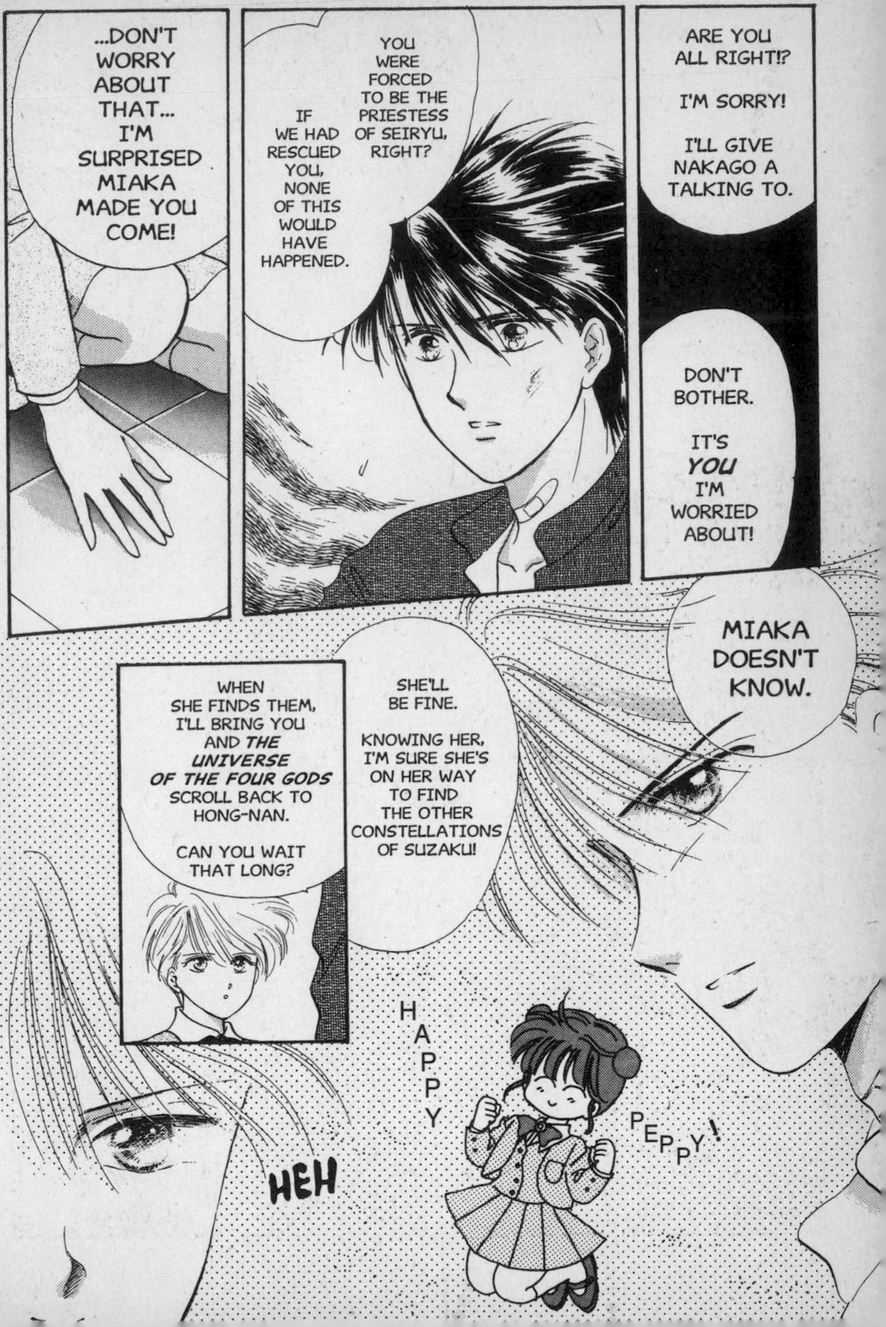
ARE YOU ALL RIGHT!? I'M SORRY! I'LL GIVE NAKAGO A TALKING TO.
DON'T BOTHER. IT'S *YOU* I'M WORRIED ABOUT!
YOU WERE FORCED TO BE THE PRIESTESS OF SEIRYU, RIGHT?
IF WE HAD RESCUED YOU, NONE OF THIS WOULD HAVE HAPPENED.
...DON'T WORRY ABOUT THAT... I'M SURPRISED MIAKA MADE YOU COME!
MIAKA DOESN'T KNOW.
SHE'LL BE FINE. KNOWING HER, I'M SURE SHE'S ON HER WAY TO FIND THE OTHER CONSTELLATIONS OF SUZAKU!
WHEN SHE FINDS THEM, I'LL BRING YOU AND *THE UNIVERSE OF THE FOUR GODS* SCROLL BACK TO HONG-NAN. CAN YOU WAIT THAT LONG?
PEPPY!
HAPPY
HEH

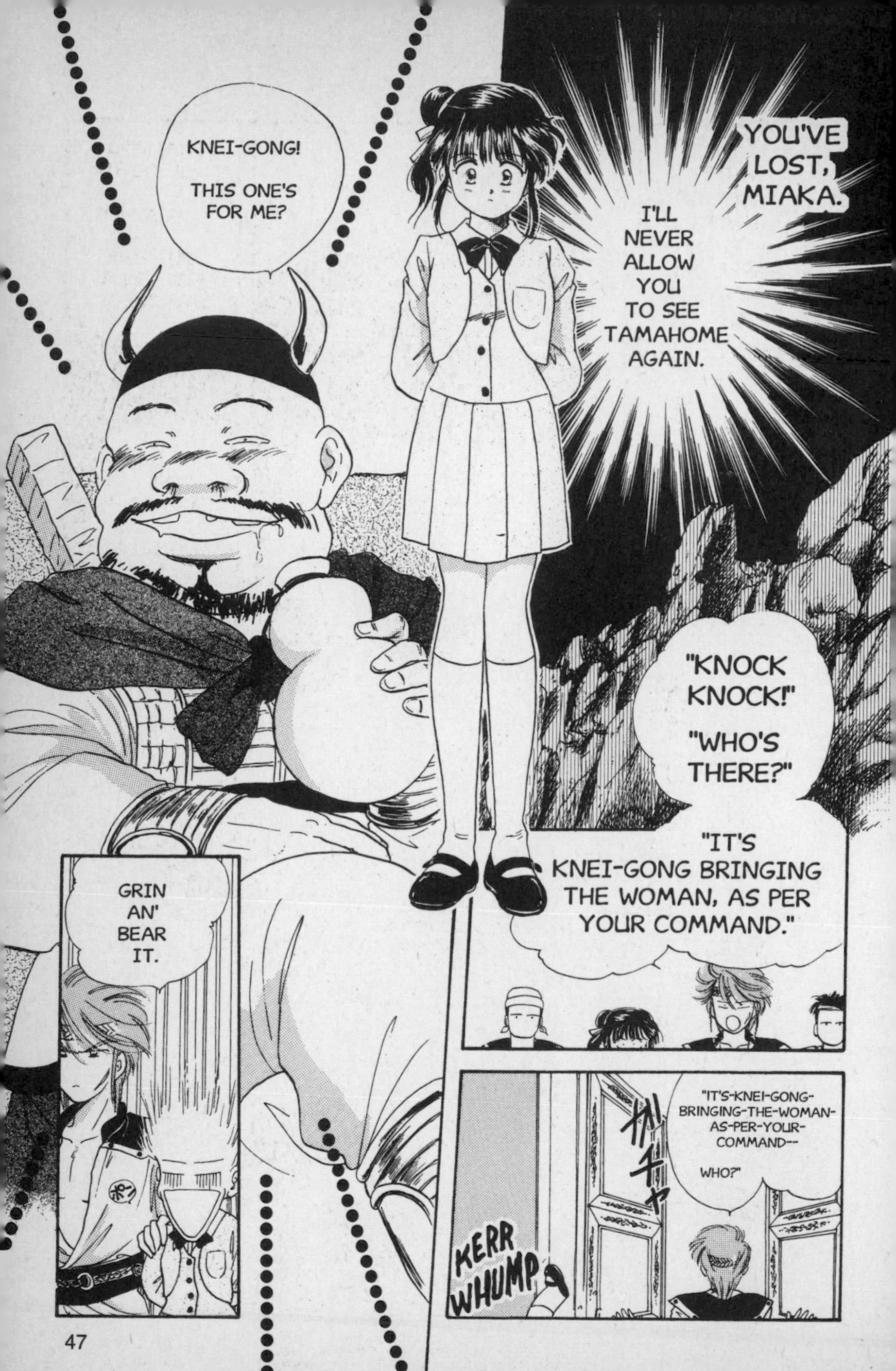
YOU'VE LOST, MIAKA.
I'LL NEVER ALLOW YOU TO SEE TAMAHOME AGAIN.
KNEI-GONG! THIS ONE'S FOR ME?
"KNOCK KNOCK!"
"WHO'S THERE?"
"IT'S KNEI-GONG BRINGING THE WOMAN, AS PER YOUR COMMAND."
"IT'S-KNEI-GONG-BRINGING-THE-WOMAN-AS-PER-YOUR-COMMAND--
WHO?"
ガチャ
KERR WHUMP
GRIN AN' BEAR IT.

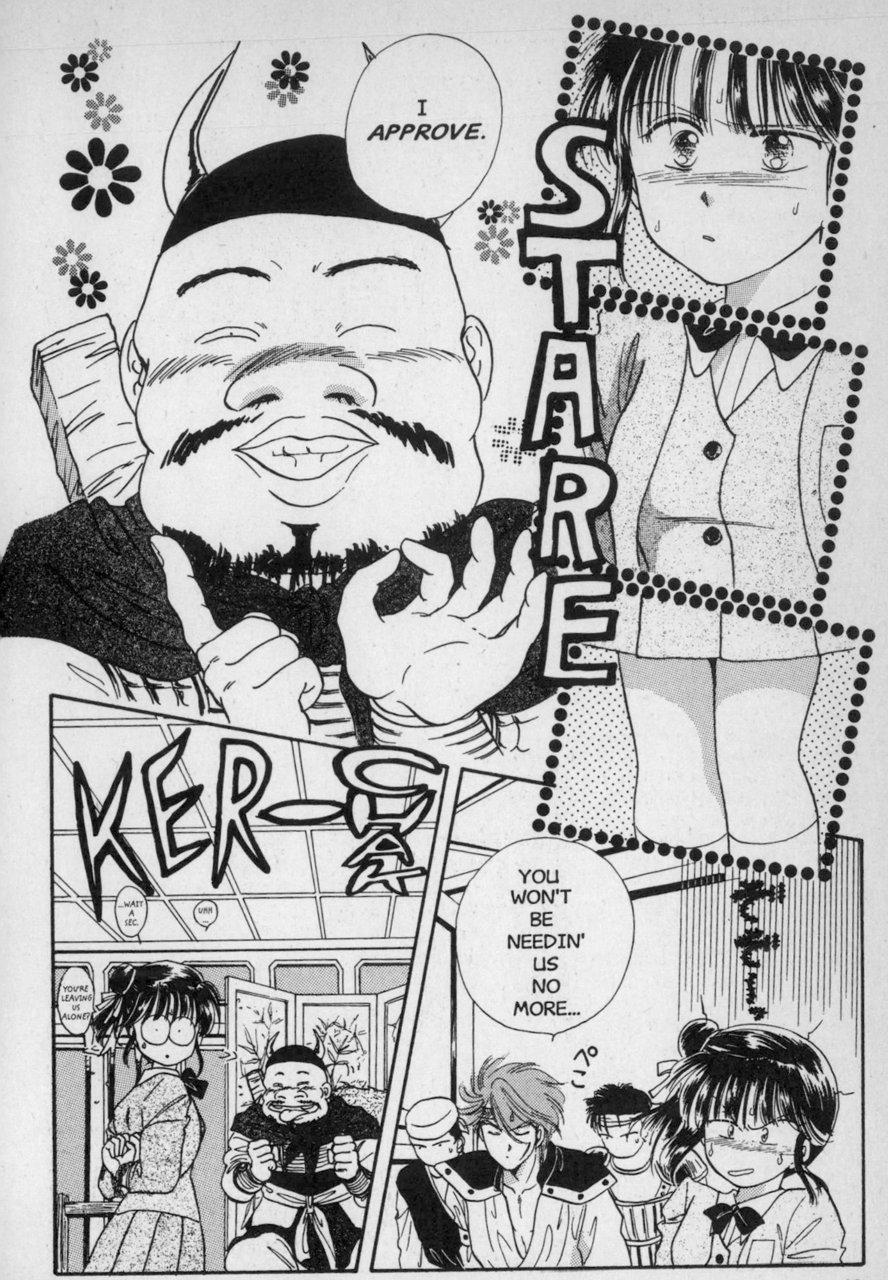
STARE
I APPROVE.
YOU WON'T BE NEEDIN' US NO MORE...
ぺこ
KER-
UHH ...
...WAIT A SEC.
YOU'RE LEAVING US ALONE?

Bandit

Hey, I can hear the music for "The Heroic Legend of Arslan" playing in the background. A reader sent me music that she thought would match Fushigi Yûgi. I wish I had the whole album! I read Tanaka's novels, but when I saw the anime version recently on video, I was brought up short. It ended too quickly! Narcasse's design was gorgeous, but he was different from how I'd imagined him. But the original novel series was really great (I've only read parts), so I'd been expecting a lot of story development. I've always liked heroic fantasy. But the recent fantasy craze is a little.... I do love it, tho. They usually do something that contradicts the setting—fantasy is hard! A different fan sent me five tapes! I was so happy! And a big thank you to everyone who spent six months producing a drama version of Suna no Tiara ("Tiara of Sand," a Watase short story from the collection of the same name--Ed.). For everyone else who's sent in material, I've kept it all, so thanks! Speaking of videos, when we have anime playing at work, M, who used to be an animator, will pipe in at the end of every movie when the credits scroll, "Huh, there's O, and there's P!" They're all her friends. Strange to hear. What do you think about Cyber Formula? I hear it's popular among you readers. (Thanks for the CD, by the way.) One of our staff apparently helped out on it. I think she was a key animator! Times are tough all over. In any case, she knows a lot about voice acting and Western art so I'm learning everything from her. She's an amazing illustrator. S has been here for about a year, and she can be a little odd. She's gonna be mad at me! She really wants to become a manga artist, and I'm no expert on the application of screen tones, so I am just amazed when I see her work. Volume 4 will be the last time I work with U, another screen-tone magician, who will be starting her own comic! All your hard work has finally paid off, and you've become a pro! I loved your proportions.... I wonder how you're doing. What a loss for us.

Huh? How'd this one end up being a column about my staff?

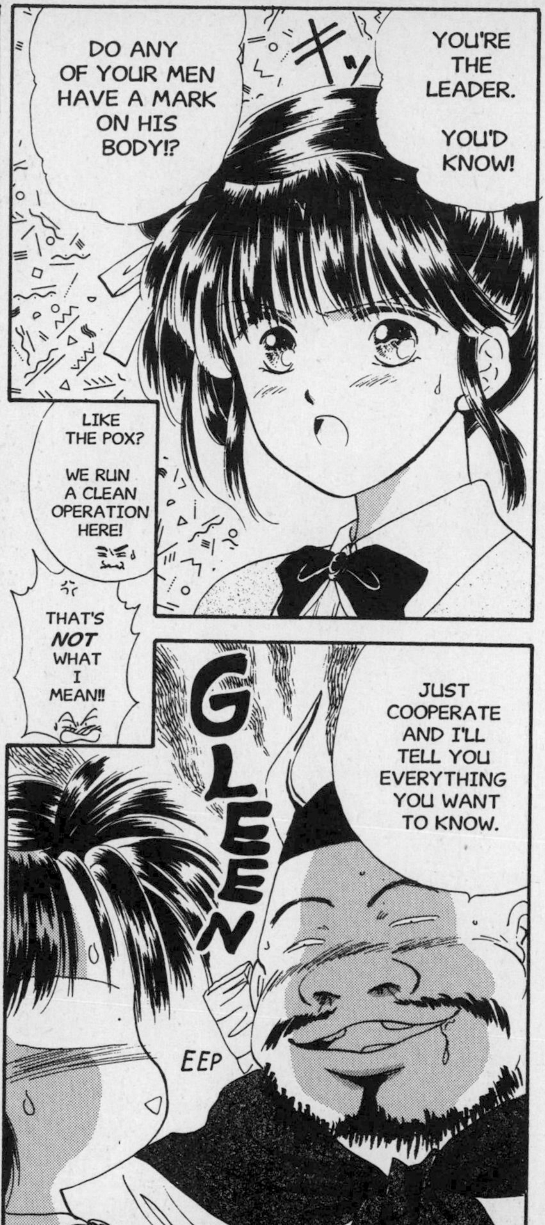
YOU'RE THE LEADER. YOU'D KNOW!
DO ANY OF YOUR MEN HAVE A MARK ON HIS BODY!?
LIKE THE POX? WE RUN A CLEAN OPERATION HERE!
THAT'S NOT WHAT I MEAN!!
JUST COOPERATE AND I'LL TELL YOU EVERYTHING YOU WANT TO KNOW.
GLEEN
EEP

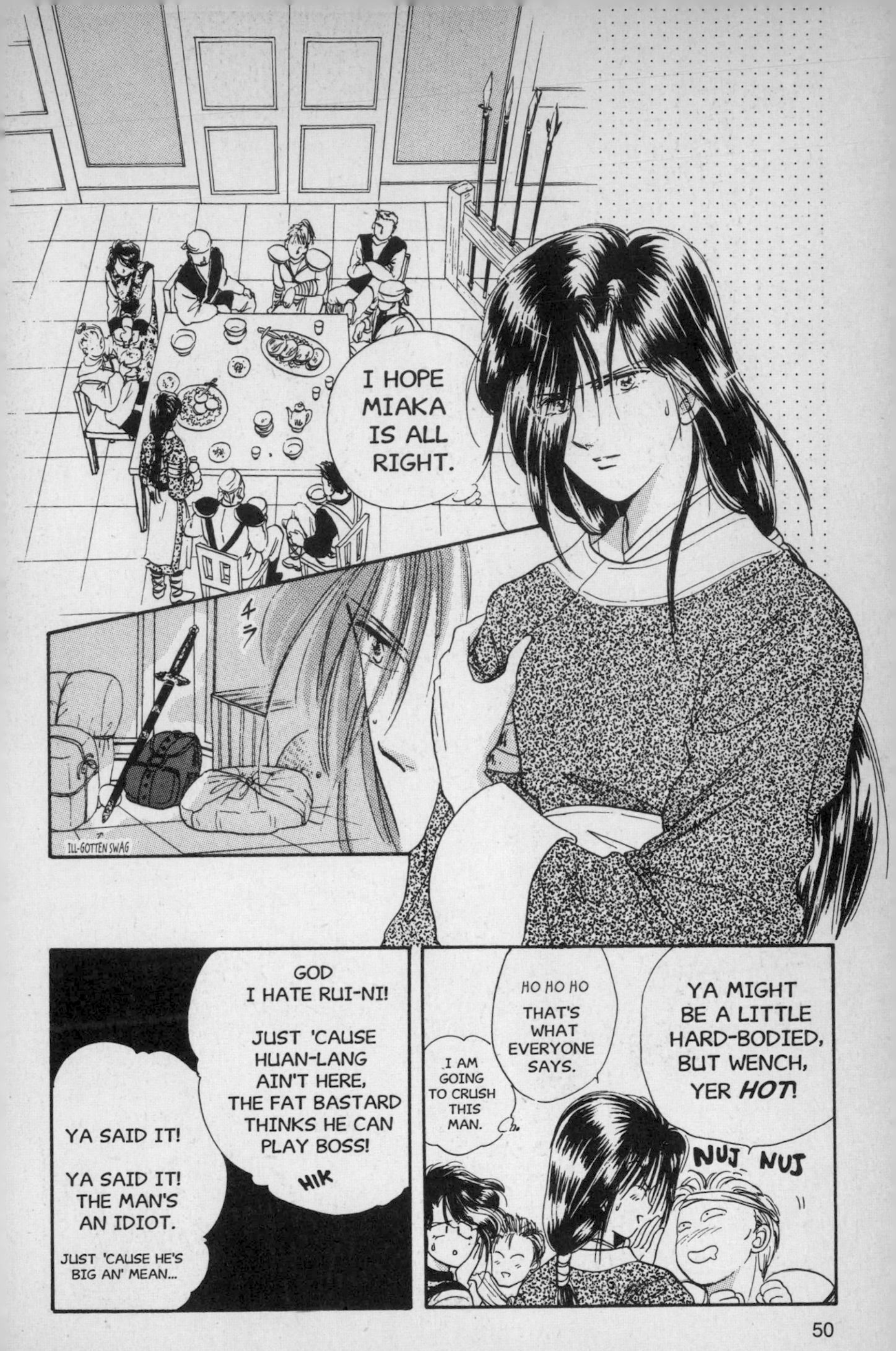
I HOPE MIAKA IS ALL RIGHT.
イラ
ILL-GOTTEN SWAG
YA MIGHT BE A LITTLE HARD-BODIED, BUT WENCH, YER *HOT*!
NUJ NUJ
HO HO HO
THAT'S WHAT EVERYONE SAYS.
I AM GOING TO CRUSH THIS MAN.
GOD I HATE RUI-NI!
JUST 'CAUSE HUAN-LANG AIN'T HERE, THE FAT BASTARD THINKS HE CAN PLAY BOSS!
HIK
YA SAID IT!
YA SAID IT! THE MAN'S AN IDIOT.
JUST 'CAUSE HE'S BIG AN' MEAN...

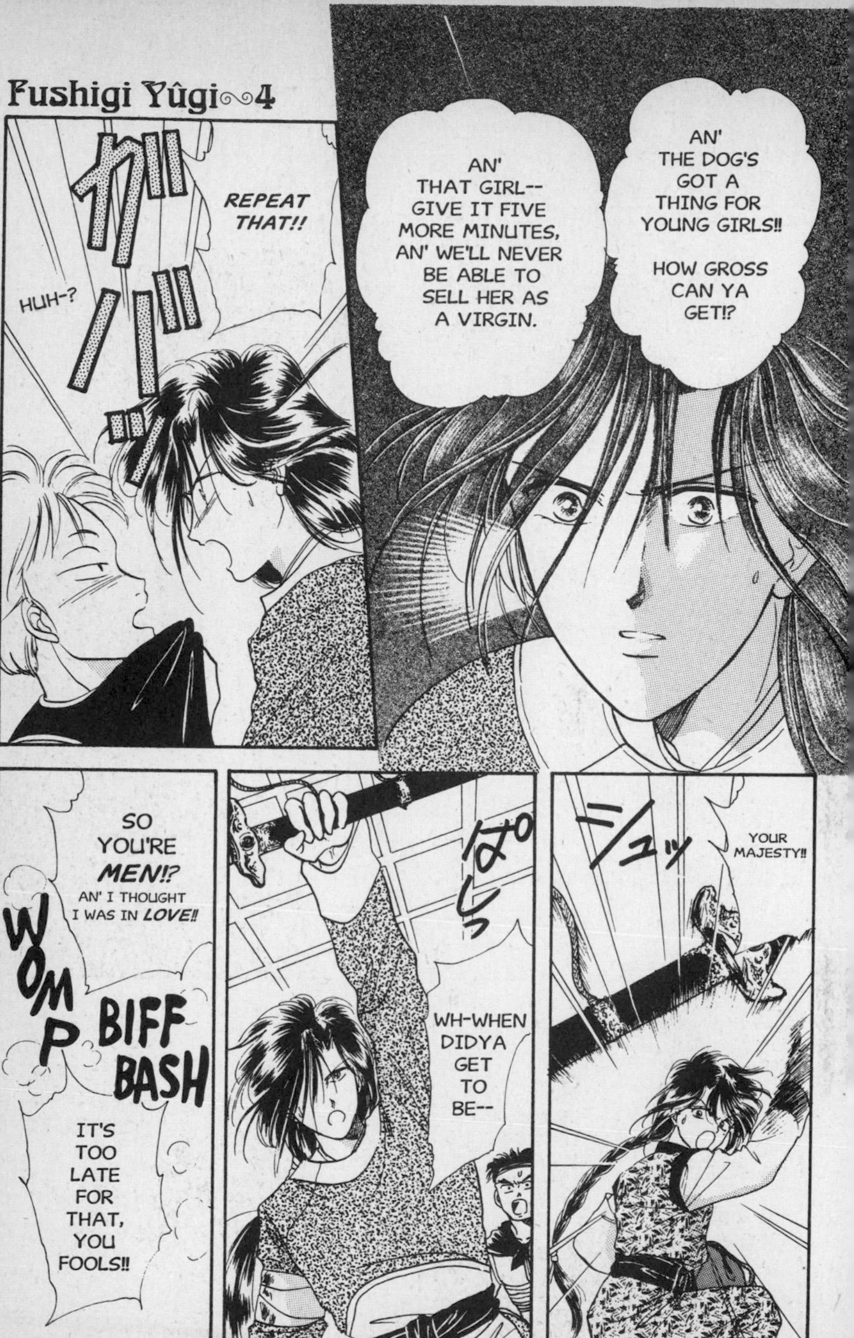
AN' THE DOG'S GOT A THING FOR YOUNG GIRLS!! HOW GROSS CAN YA GET!?
AN' THAT GIRL-- GIVE IT FIVE MORE MINUTES, AN' WE'LL NEVER BE ABLE TO SELL HER AS A VIRGIN.
REPEAT THAT!!
HUH-?
シュッ
YOUR MAJESTY!!
ぱしっ
WH-WHEN DIDYA GET TO BE--
SO YOU'RE MEN!? AN' I THOUGHT I WAS IN LOVE!!
WOMP
BIFF
BASH
IT'S TOO LATE FOR THAT, YOU FOOLS!!

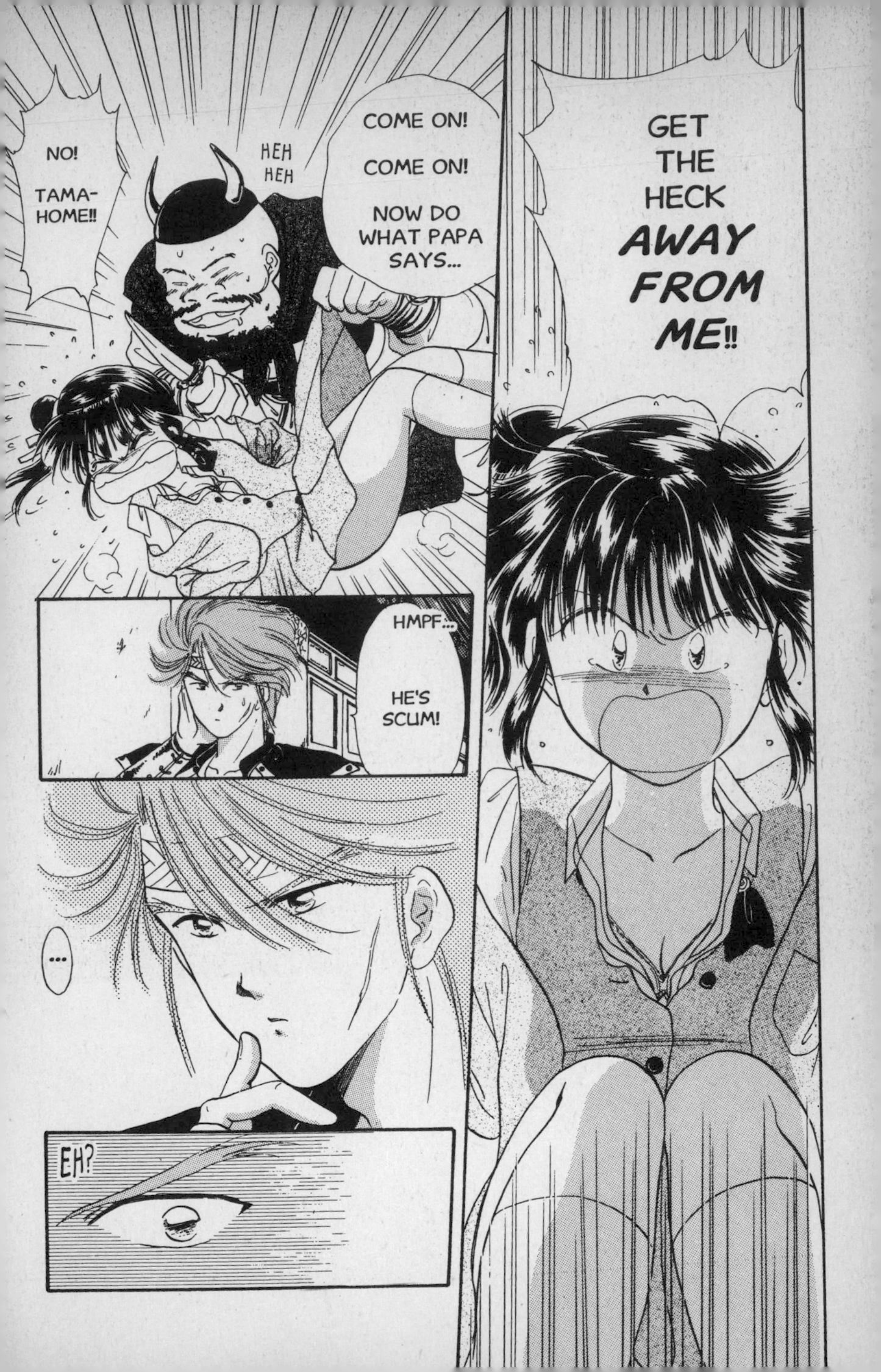
GET THE HECK AWAY FROM ME!!
COME ON! COME ON! NOW DO WHAT PAPA SAYS...
HEH HEH
NO! TAMA-HOME!!
HMPF... HE'S SCUM!
...
EH?

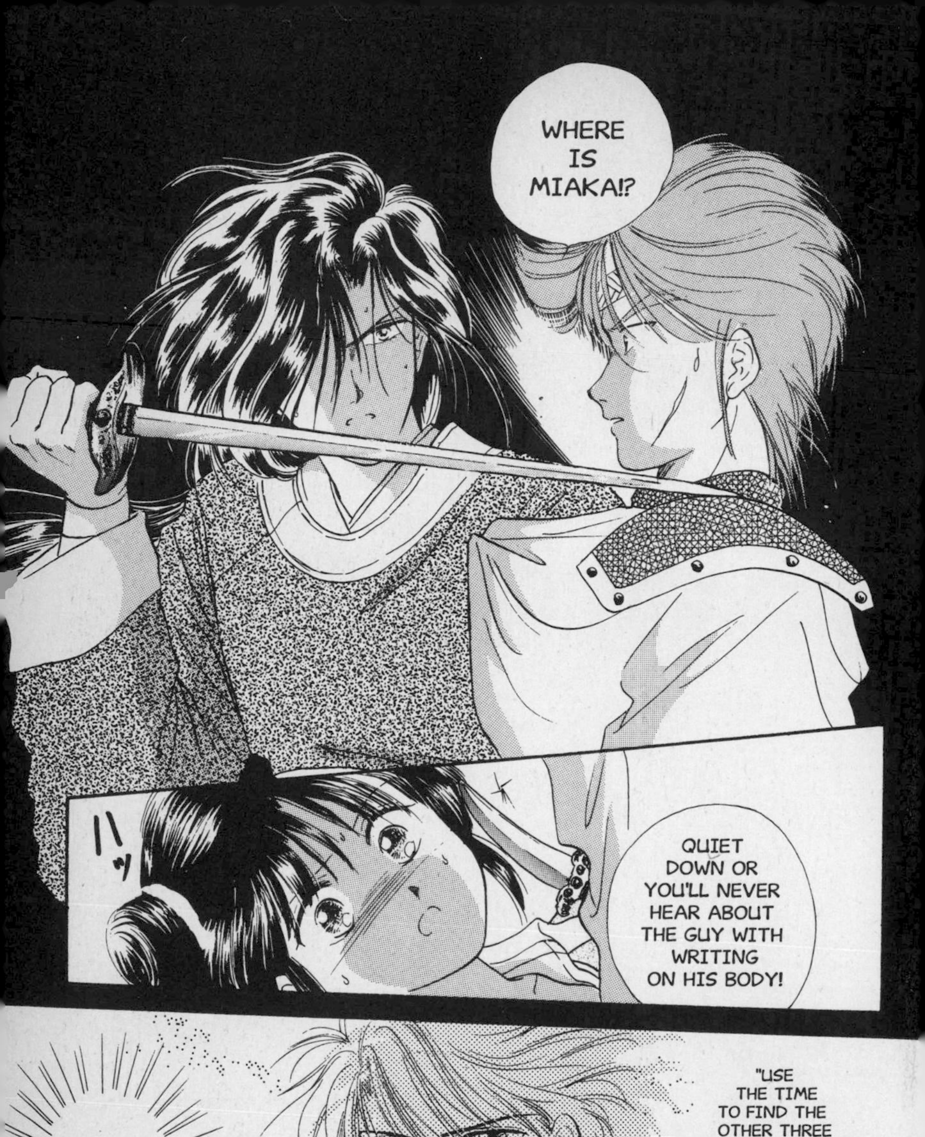
WHERE IS MIAKA!?
QUIET DOWN OR YOU'LL NEVER HEAR ABOUT THE GUY WITH WRITING ON HIS BODY!
ハッ
"USE THE TIME TO FIND THE OTHER THREE CONSTELLATIONS OF SUZAKU.
EXPECT ME BACK AFTER YOU HAVE FOUND THEM."
TAMAHOME...

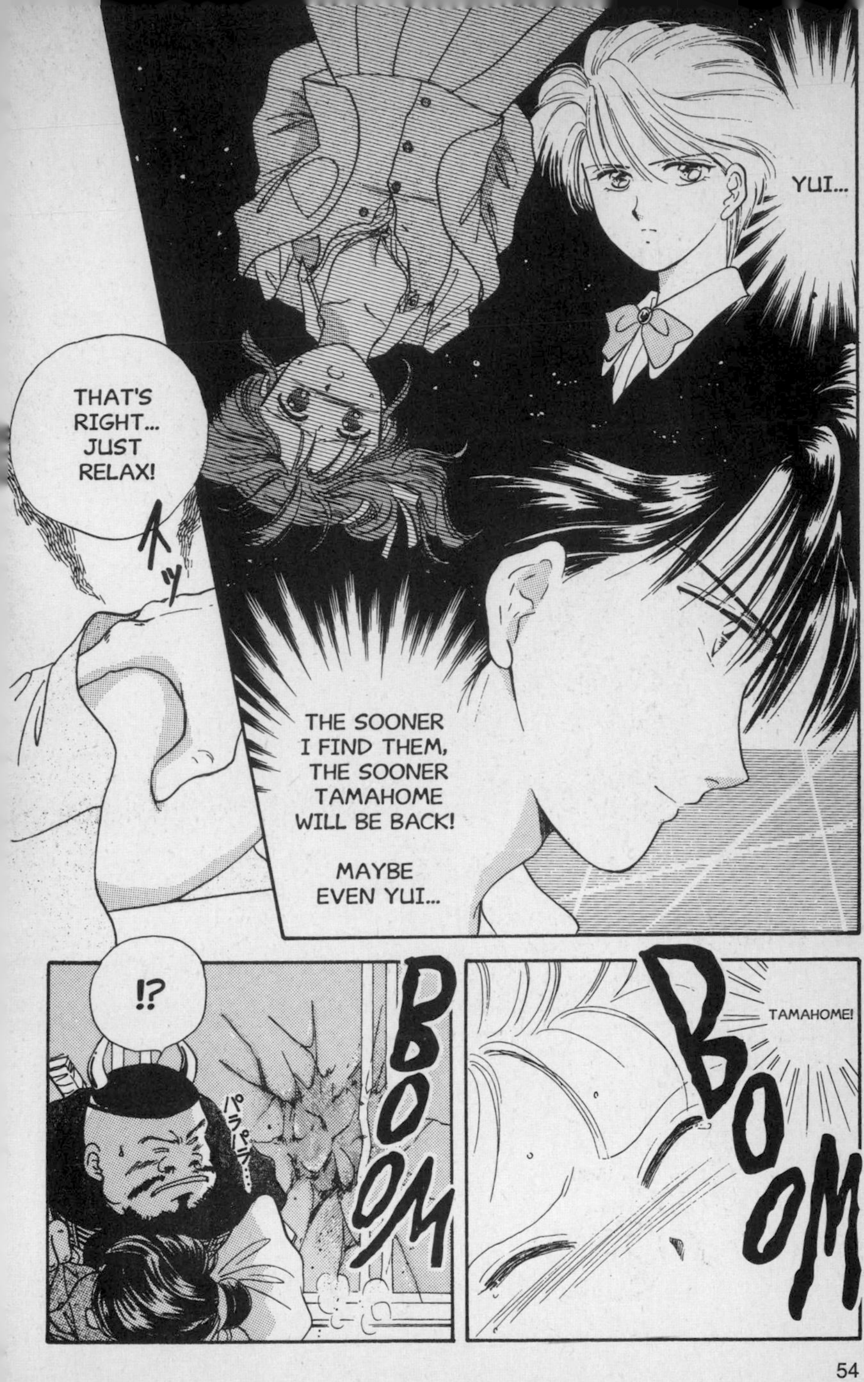
YUI...
THE SOONER I FIND THEM, THE SOONER TAMAHOME WILL BE BACK!
MAYBE EVEN YUI...
THAT'S RIGHT... JUST RELAX!
BOOM
TAMAHOME!
!?
パラパラ...
BOOM

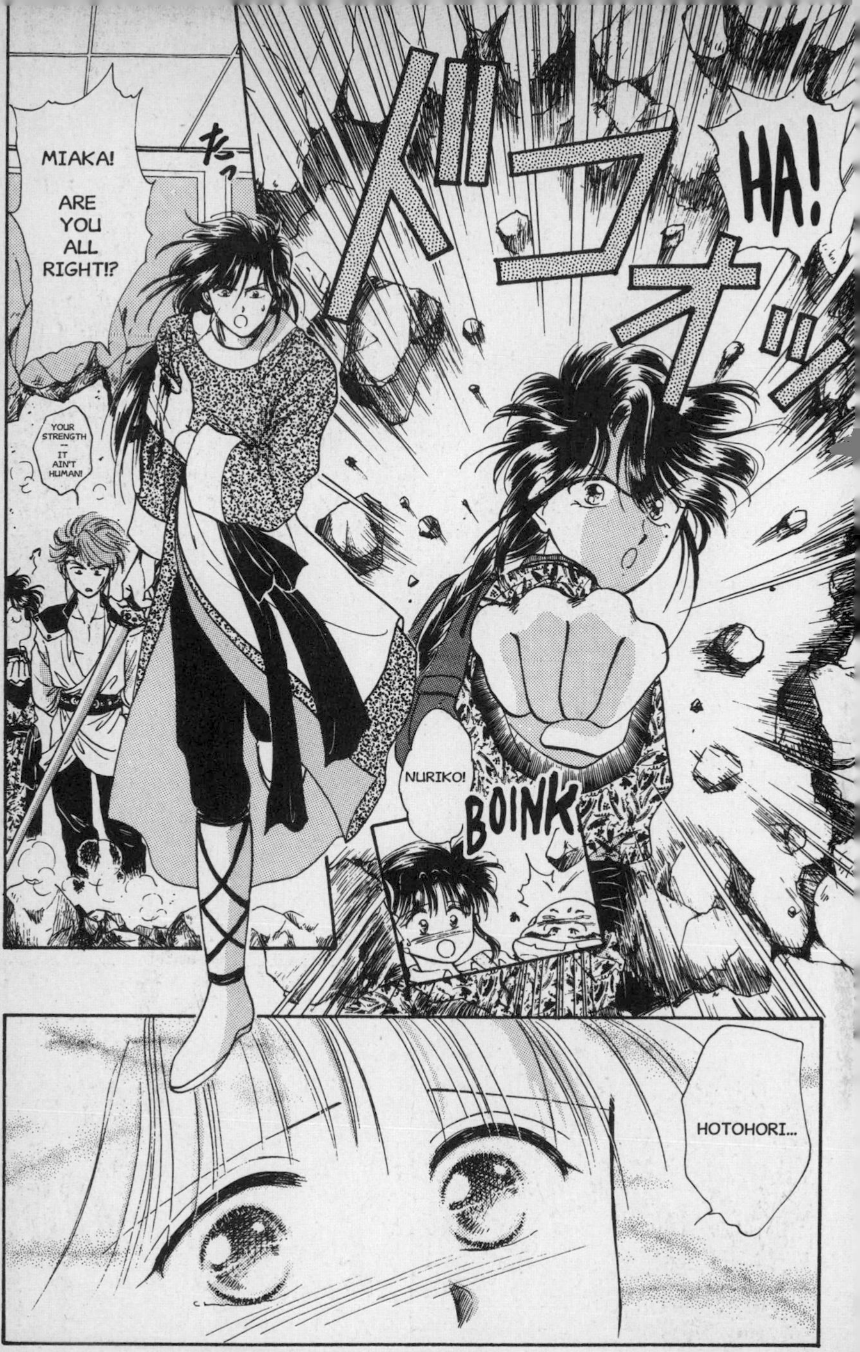

ズゴォッ
HA!
MIAKA!
ARE YOU ALL RIGHT!?
YOUR STRENGTH — IT AIN'T HUMAN!
NURIKO!
BOINK
HOTOHORI...

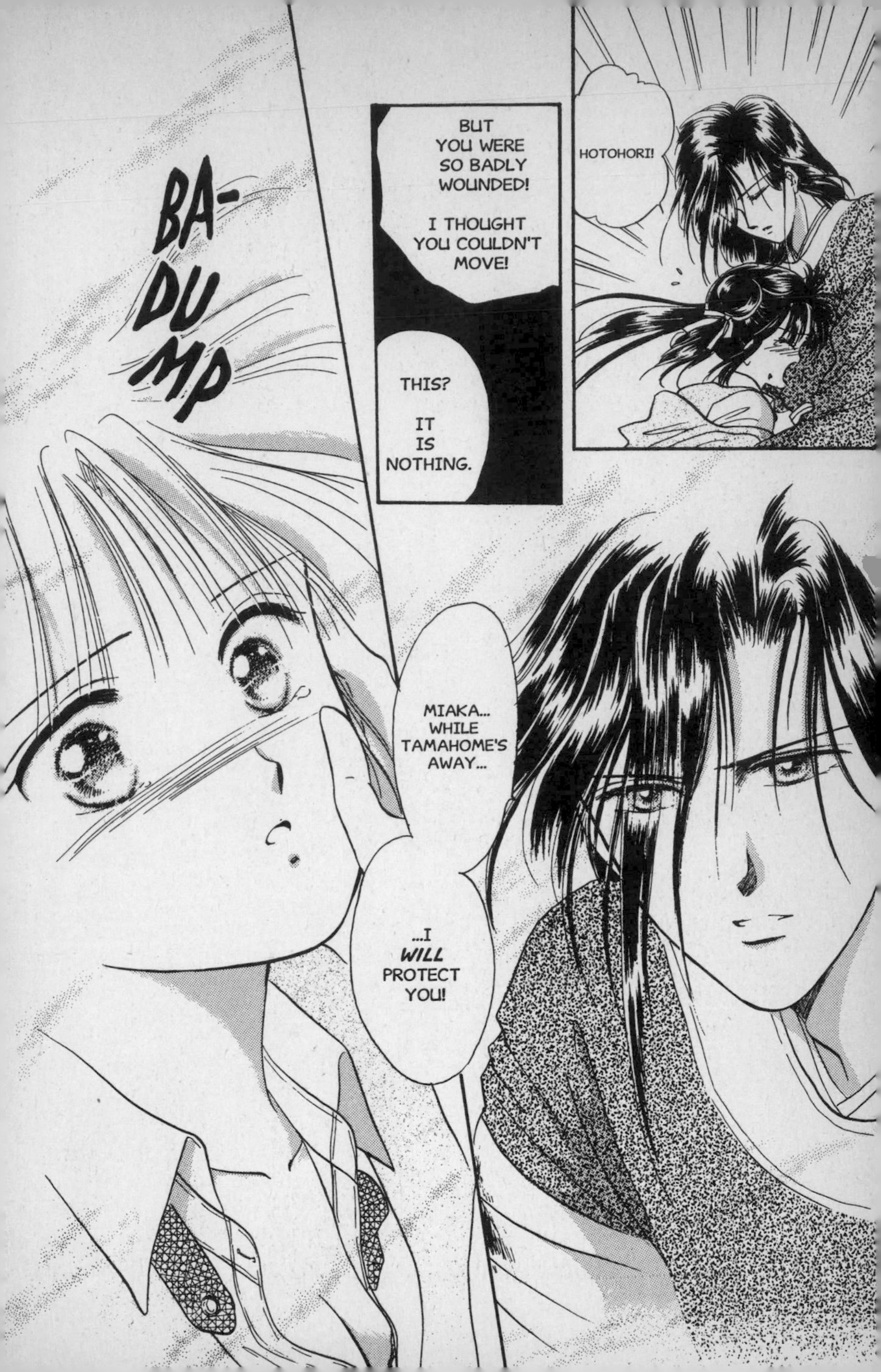
HOTOHORI!
BUT YOU WERE SO BADLY WOUNDED!
I THOUGHT YOU COULDN'T MOVE!
THIS? IT IS NOTHING.
MIAKA... WHILE TAMAHOME'S AWAY...
...I *WILL* PROTECT YOU!
BA-DUMP

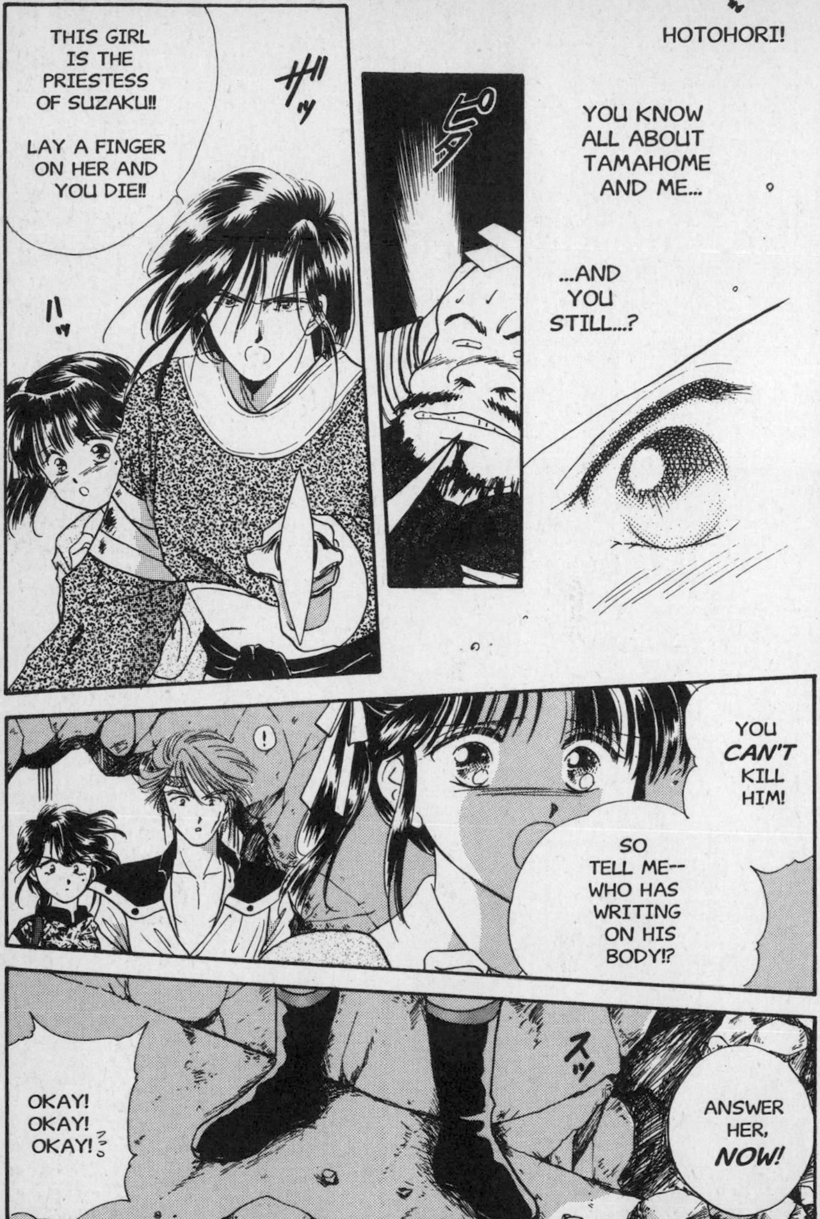
HOTOHORI!
YOU KNOW ALL ABOUT TAMAHOME AND ME...
...AND YOU STILL...?
ピタ
ザッ
THIS GIRL IS THE PRIESTESS OF SUZAKU!!
LAY A FINGER ON HER AND YOU DIE!!
ハッ
YOU *CAN'T* KILL HIM!
SO TELL ME-- WHO HAS WRITING ON HIS BODY!?
!
ANSWER HER, *NOW!*
スッ
OKAY! OKAY! OKAY!

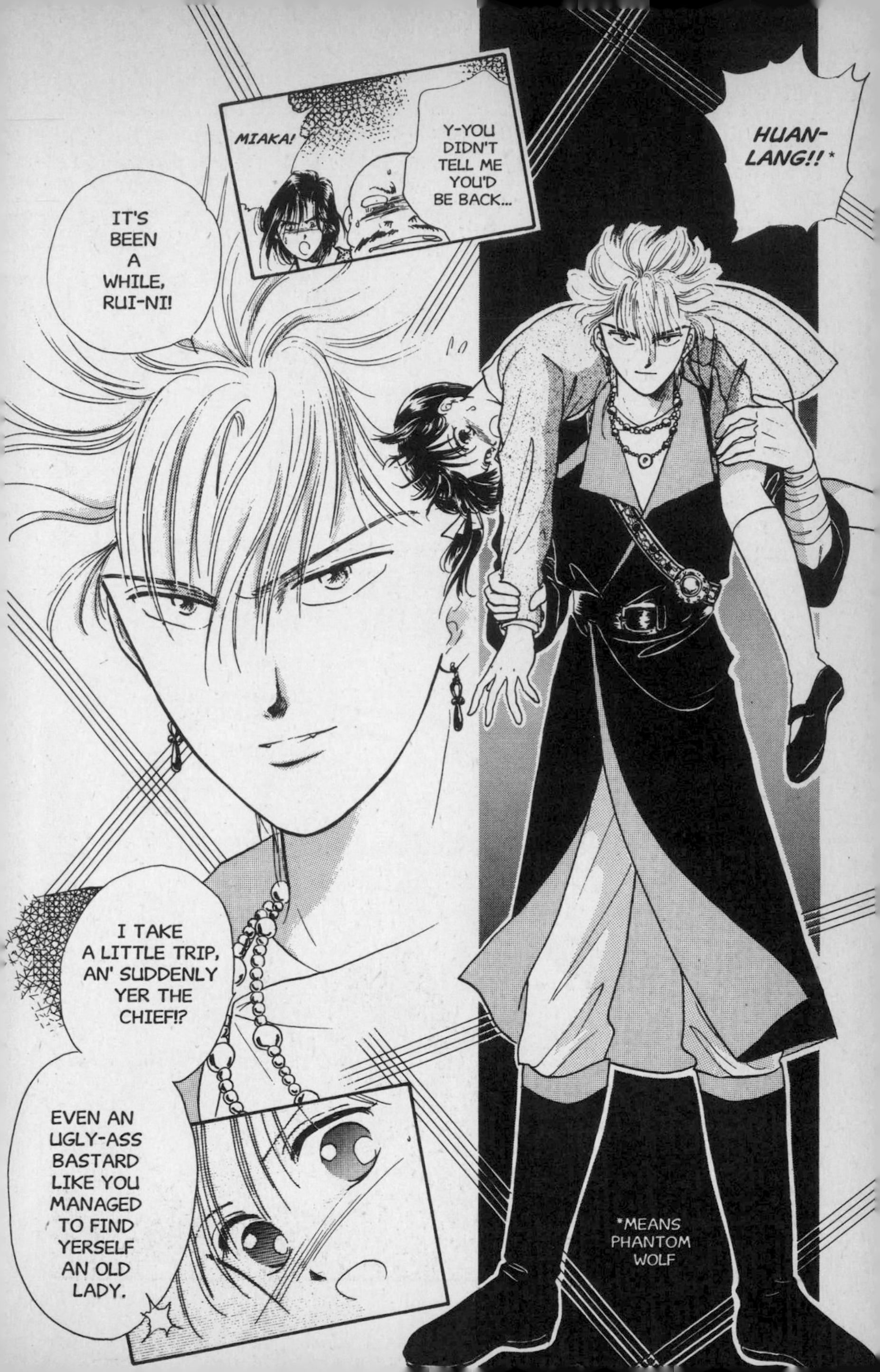
HUAN-LANG!!*
Y-YOU DIDN'T TELL ME YOU'D BE BACK...
MIAKA!
IT'S BEEN A WHILE, RUI-NI!
*MEANS PHANTOM WOLF
I TAKE A LITTLE TRIP, AN' SUDDENLY YER THE CHIEF!?
EVEN AN UGLY-ASS BASTARD LIKE YOU MANAGED TO FIND YERSELF AN OLD LADY.

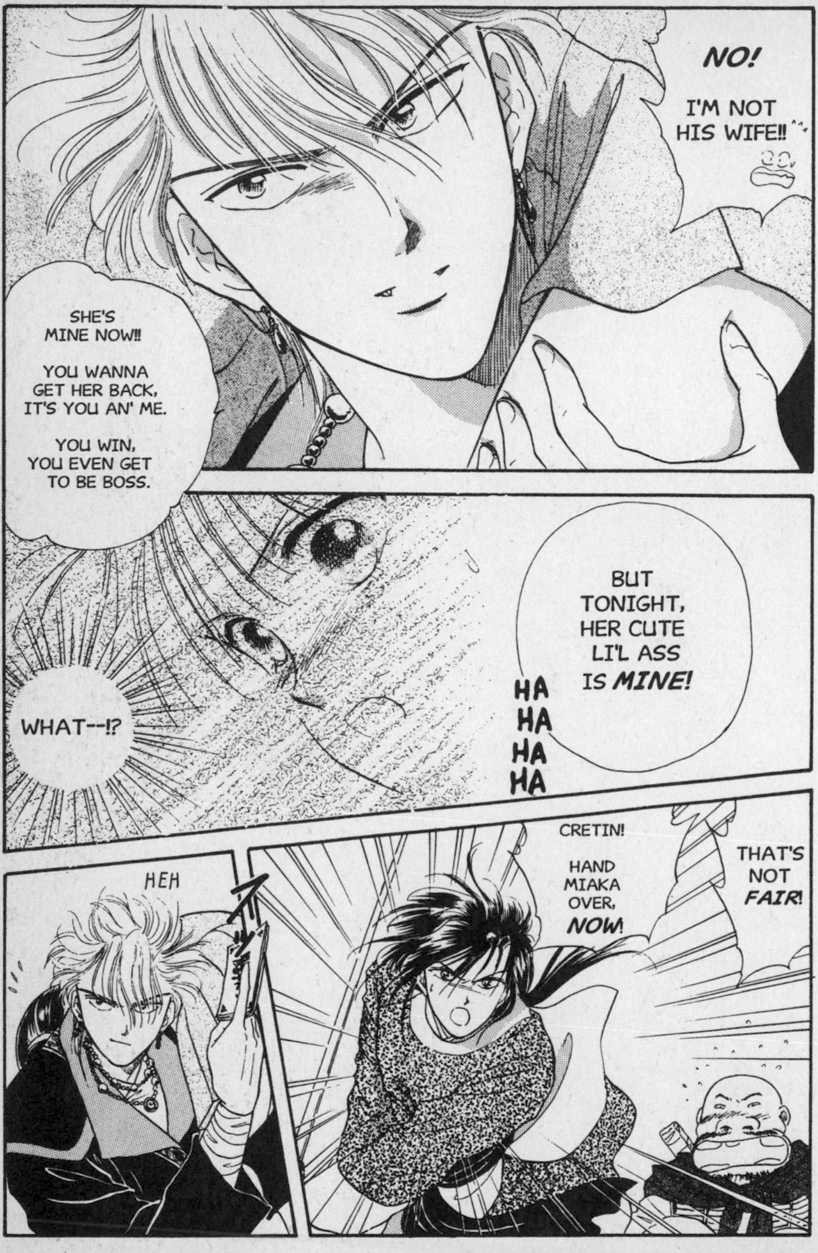
NO!
I'M NOT HIS WIFE!!
SHE'S MINE NOW!!
YOU WANNA GET HER BACK, IT'S YOU AN' ME.
YOU WIN, YOU EVEN GET TO BE BOSS.
BUT TONIGHT, HER CUTE LI'L ASS IS MINE!
HA HA HA HA
WHAT--!?
THAT'S NOT FAIR!
CRETIN!
HAND MIAKA OVER, NOW!
HEH

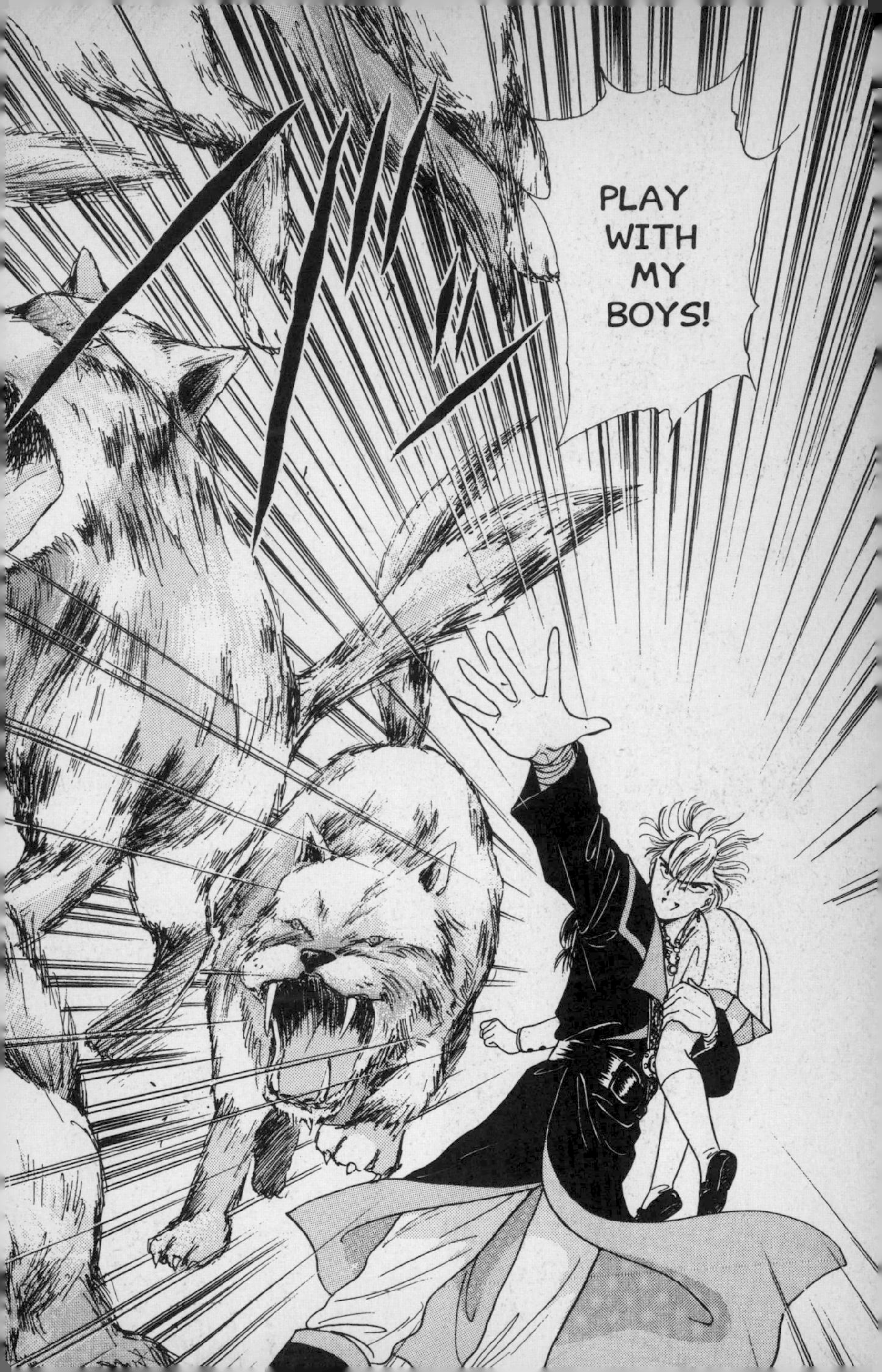
PLAY WITH MY BOYS!

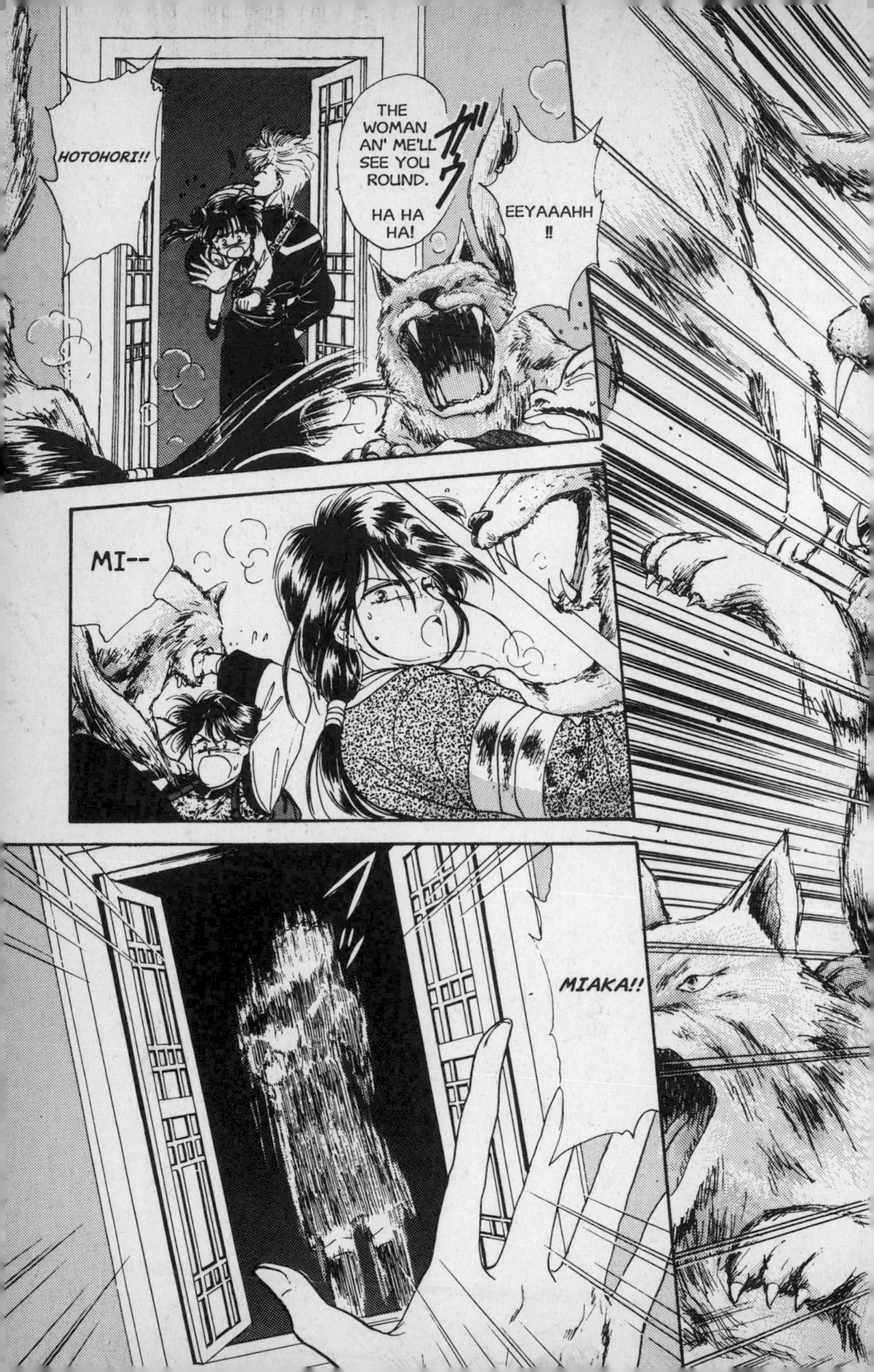
EEYAAAHH!!
ガウ
THE WOMAN AN' ME'LL SEE YOU ROUND.
HA HA HA!
HOTOHORI!!
MI--
MIAKA!!

XING SHU CAI PI DI
星 宿（彩 賁 帝）

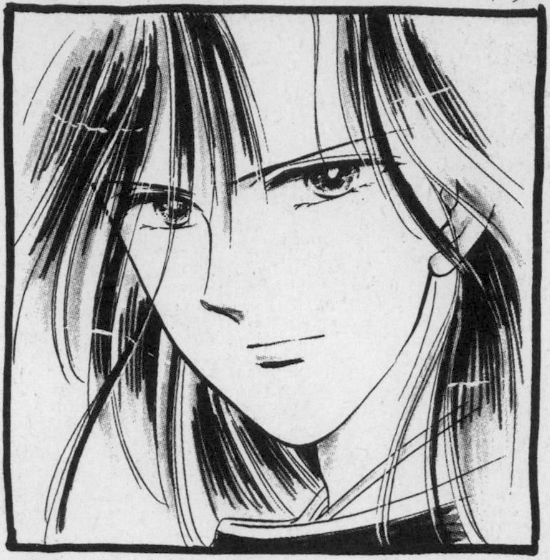

HOTOHORI

DIGRESSION: I hear there used to be a lake which used the kanji ⇨ 星宿海 in its name.

HYDRA

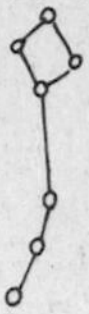

- Fourth Emperor of Hong-Nan. His palace is in the capital city of Rong-Yang where he reigns.
- Birthdate sometime between February and May. They don't make a big deal of it.
- He has two older brothers and one younger. Two younger sisters (something like that). (There was probably quite a battle for succession.)
- 18 years old but he looks older.
- Height 6 foot or thereabouts. Blood type A? I don't know!!
- His specialty is fencing. But since he has had the world's finest teachers since he was small, he can probably do anything.
- Personality: He seems like the type that hides his feelings, but he's actually a warm and gentle man. As the ruler of his kingdom, he was raised surrounded by adults, so it's no wonder he looks old for his age. He looks cold and harsh when he's sitting on the throne because of his isolated and lonely upbringing.
  I figure he never had any love from his parents, the previous emperor and empress, so he's very attracted to Miaka's warmth. When he's around her, he turns into a normal young man. The worst part (or best part) about him is that he's a total narcissist. Due to his sheltered background he doesn't know much about the world.

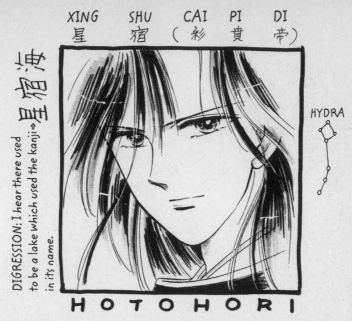

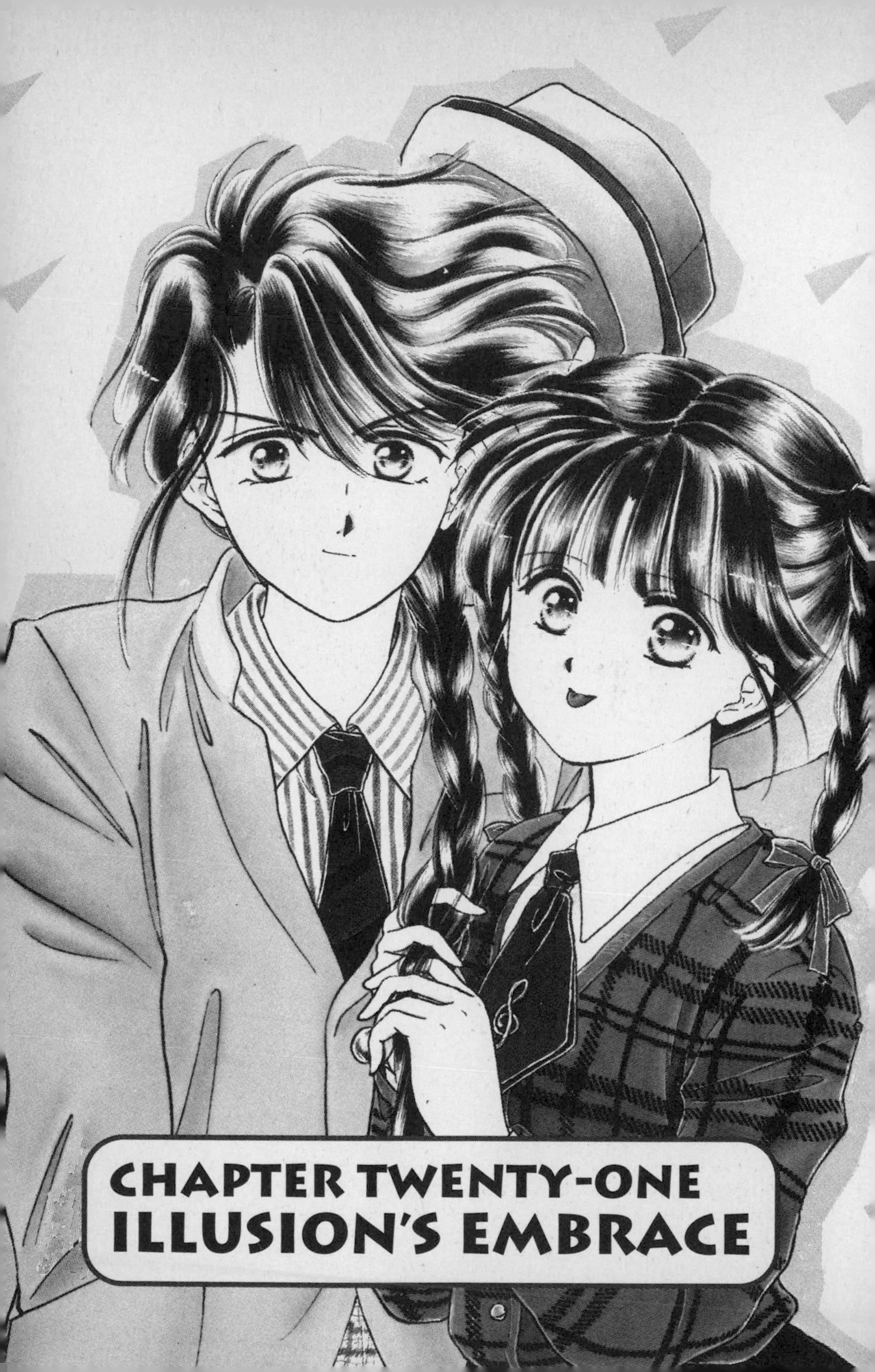
CHAPTER TWENTY-ONE
ILLUSION'S EMBRACE

NURIKO

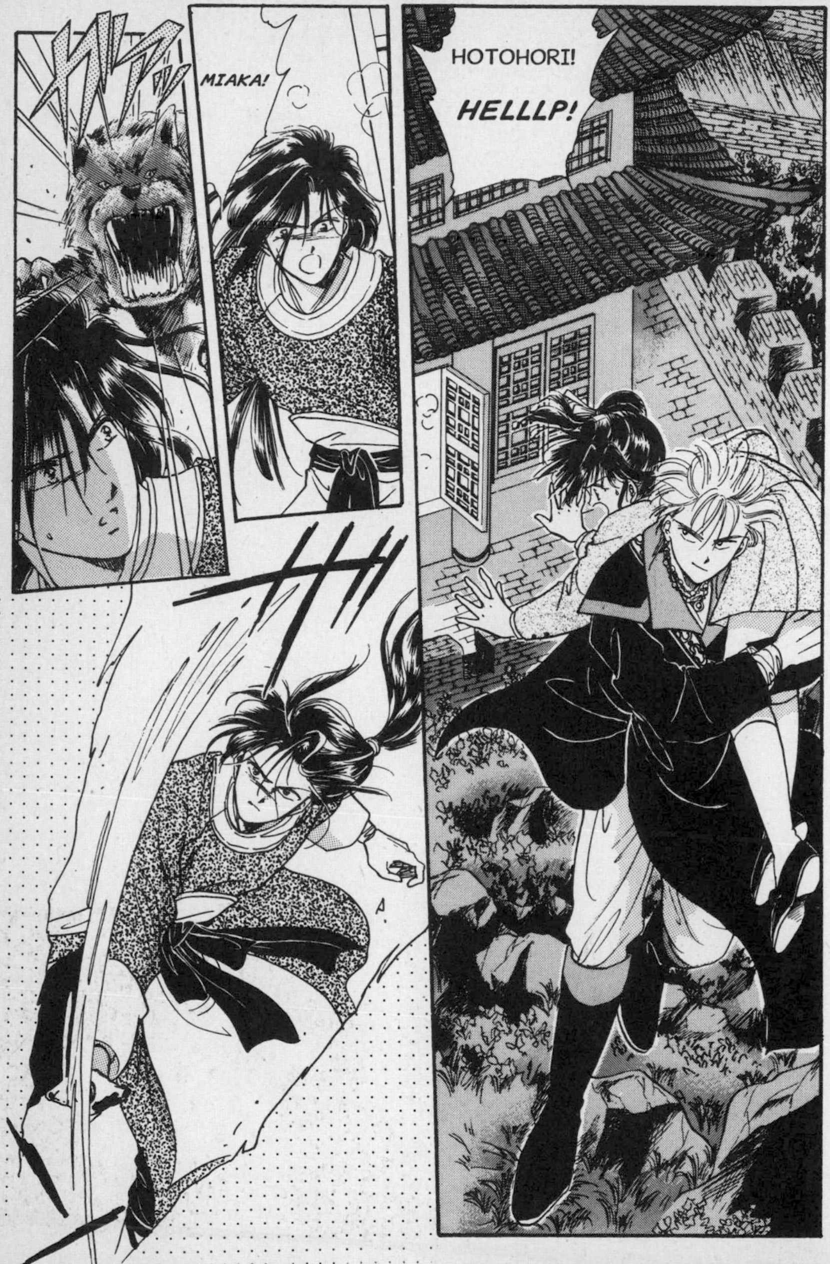
HOTOHORI!
HELLLP!
MIAKA!

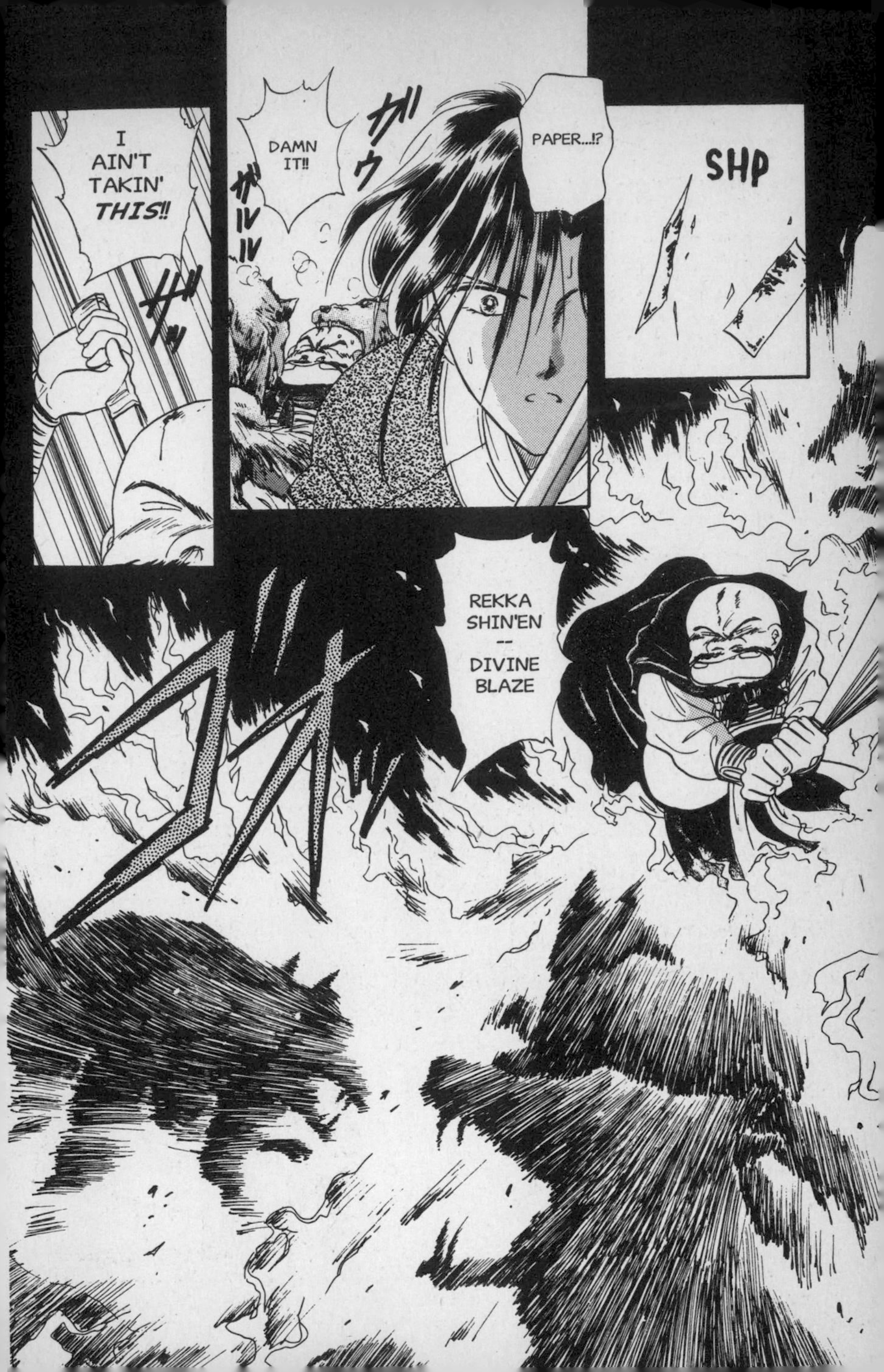
SHP
PAPER...!?
DAMN IT!!
I AIN'T TAKIN' *THIS!!*
REKKA SHIN'EN -- DIVINE BLAZE

Now I'm listening to the music for Street Fighter II. I just love the songs that sound Chinese. The commercial for the game has been playing since summer. It's sooo pretty! I love it!! That line, "I'll wander the Earth until I find someone stronger than I am," is so great. That reminds me! A buddy of mine works at Capcom. Are you reading this? You're responsible for the computer backgrounds, right? I wonder if you're involved in the Street Fighter series. I wanna play computer games, I wish I had free time. Come to think of it, I can't think of any ♪ of my friends who work normal office jobs (i.e. Office Ladies or OL). One of them, a friend from middle school, is in a puppet troupe (I get tapes from her that you can't find anywhere). Another one's in a "human" theater troupe (or something like that). One who works at a bookstore told a customer who was buying one of my books, "I'm pals with Yû Watase." I don't know what she was thinking! (Sometimes she'll send me faxes with no warning.) Then there's one who's a newlywed housewife, and another who's a nurse. I guess Ms. A works at an office. Then there's one friend in a musical troupe (hurry and get a leading role. As a high school senior I drew Scarlett O'Hara for you, right?) What does that have to do with anything? The rest are manga artists. Birds of a feather, huh? Oh, yeah! There was one who became a banker. In any case they're all good people, which would have to mean that I'm good, too. (Hold on a sec...) But with the distance between Tokyo and Osaka being 1/3 the entire length of Japan, I hardly ever see them. There's something comforting about friends who call you by your real name. I mean I've gotten used to being called "Ms. Watase." Which reminds me, someone who wrote to me had the same first and last name as me. I was amazed. (The characters were different, though.) That was more surprising than the time I received a letter from a boy with the same name as Manato Sudô in "Prepubescence" (I'm a little suspicious of this). How weird can this world be? Oh yes, a fan who's a housewife sent me a postcard saying that she named her son Manato. Isn't there a Tamahome out there somewhere?

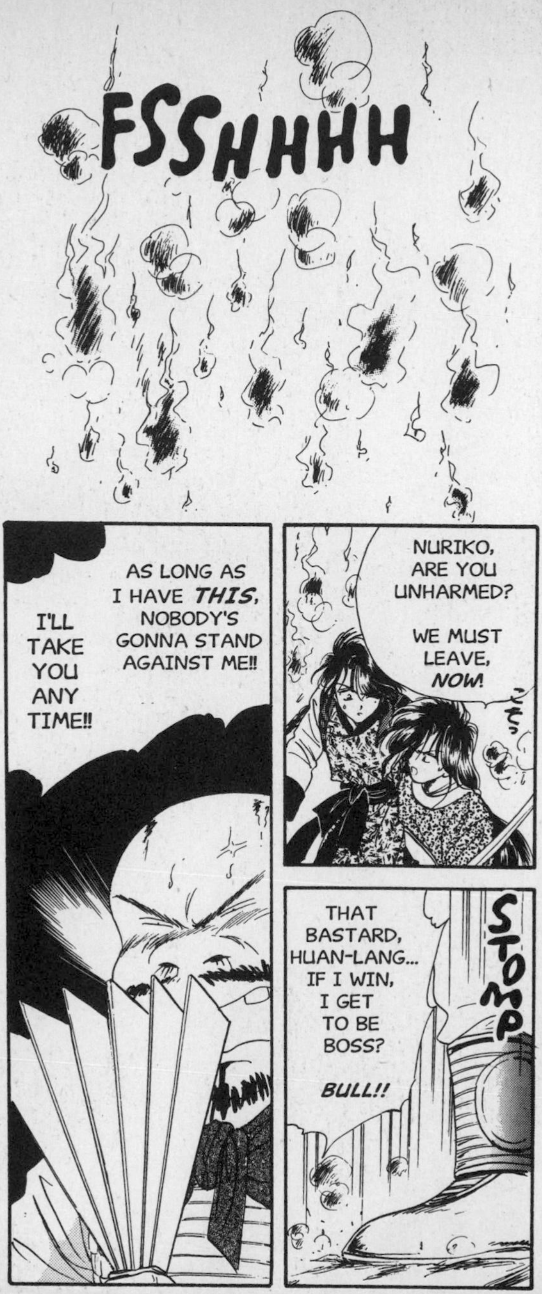
FSSHHHH
NURIKO, ARE YOU UNHARMED?
WE MUST LEAVE, *NOW*!
STOMP
THAT BASTARD, HUAN-LANG... IF I WIN, I GET TO BE BOSS?
BULL!!
AS LONG AS I HAVE *THIS*, NOBODY'S GONNA STAND AGAINST ME!!
I'LL TAKE YOU ANY TIME!!

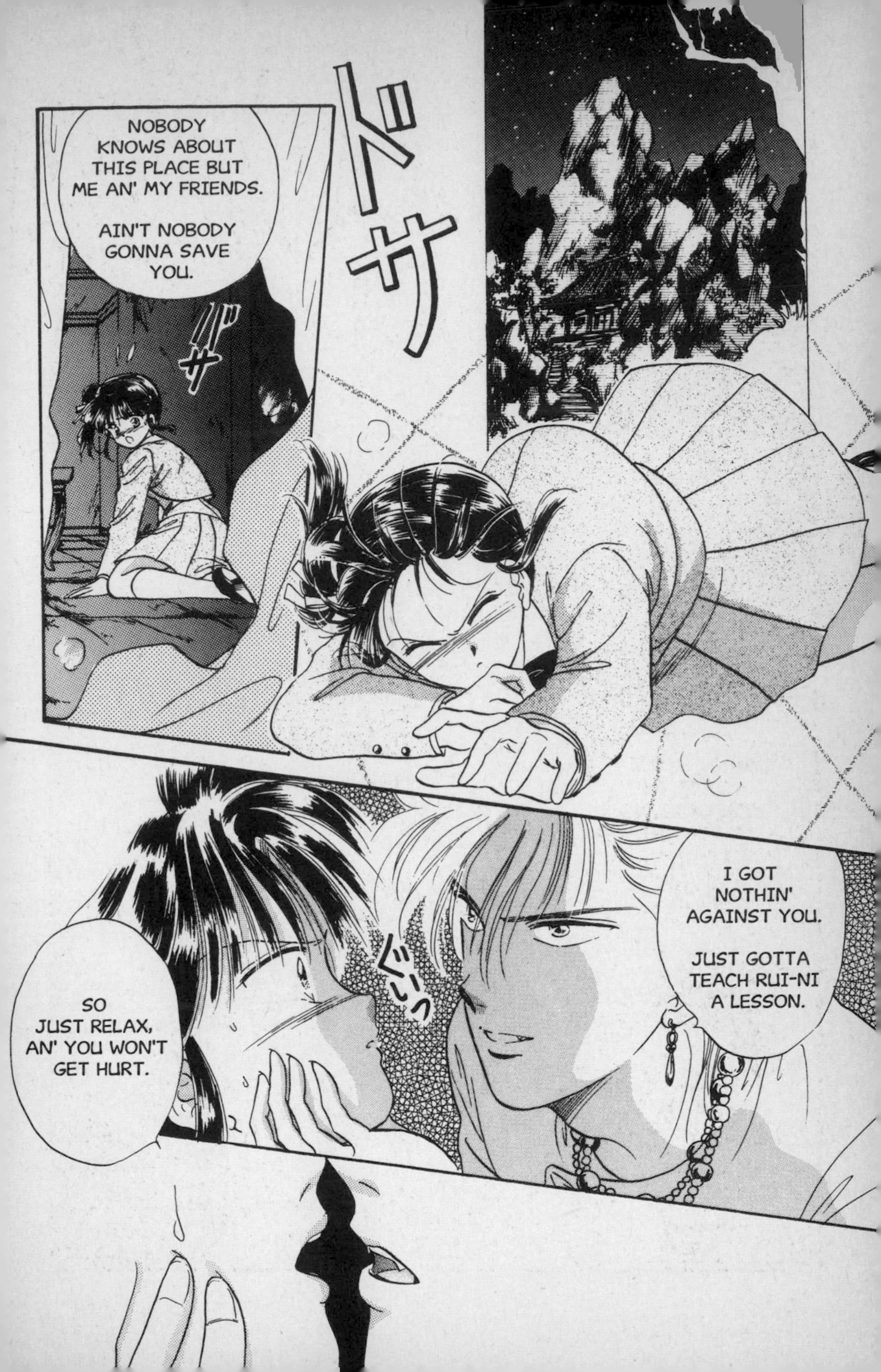
ドサ
NOBODY KNOWS ABOUT THIS PLACE BUT ME AN' MY FRIENDS.
AIN'T NOBODY GONNA SAVE YOU.
バサ
I GOT NOTHIN' AGAINST YOU.
JUST GOTTA TEACH RUI-NI A LESSON.
ぐいっ
SO JUST RELAX, AN' YOU WON'T GET HURT.

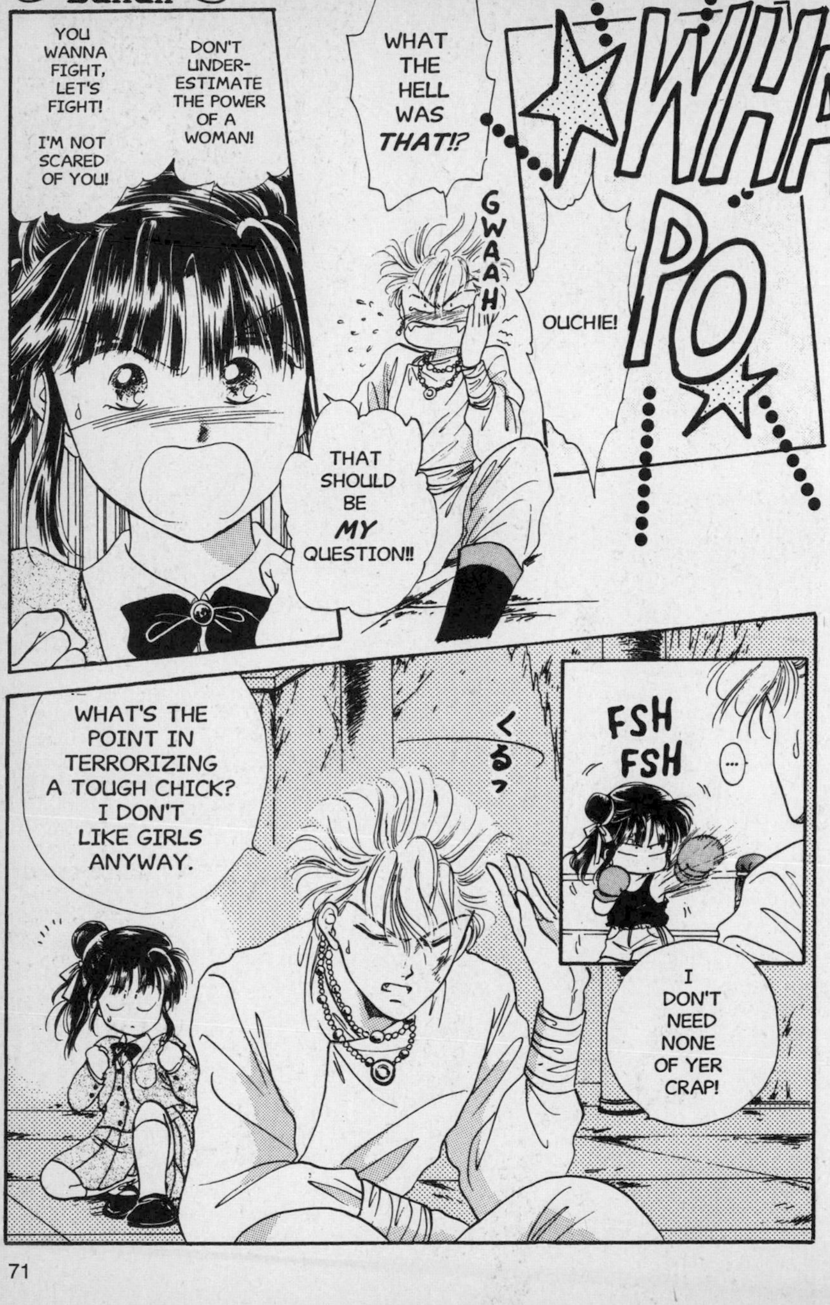
WHAPO
OUCHIE!
WHAT THE HELL WAS *THAT!?*
GWAAH
DON'T UNDER-ESTIMATE THE POWER OF A WOMAN!
YOU WANNA FIGHT, LET'S FIGHT!
I'M NOT SCARED OF YOU!
THAT SHOULD BE *MY* QUESTION!!
FSH FSH
...
I DON'T NEED NONE OF YER CRAP!
くるっ
WHAT'S THE POINT IN TERRORIZING A TOUGH CHICK? I DON'T LIKE GIRLS ANYWAY.

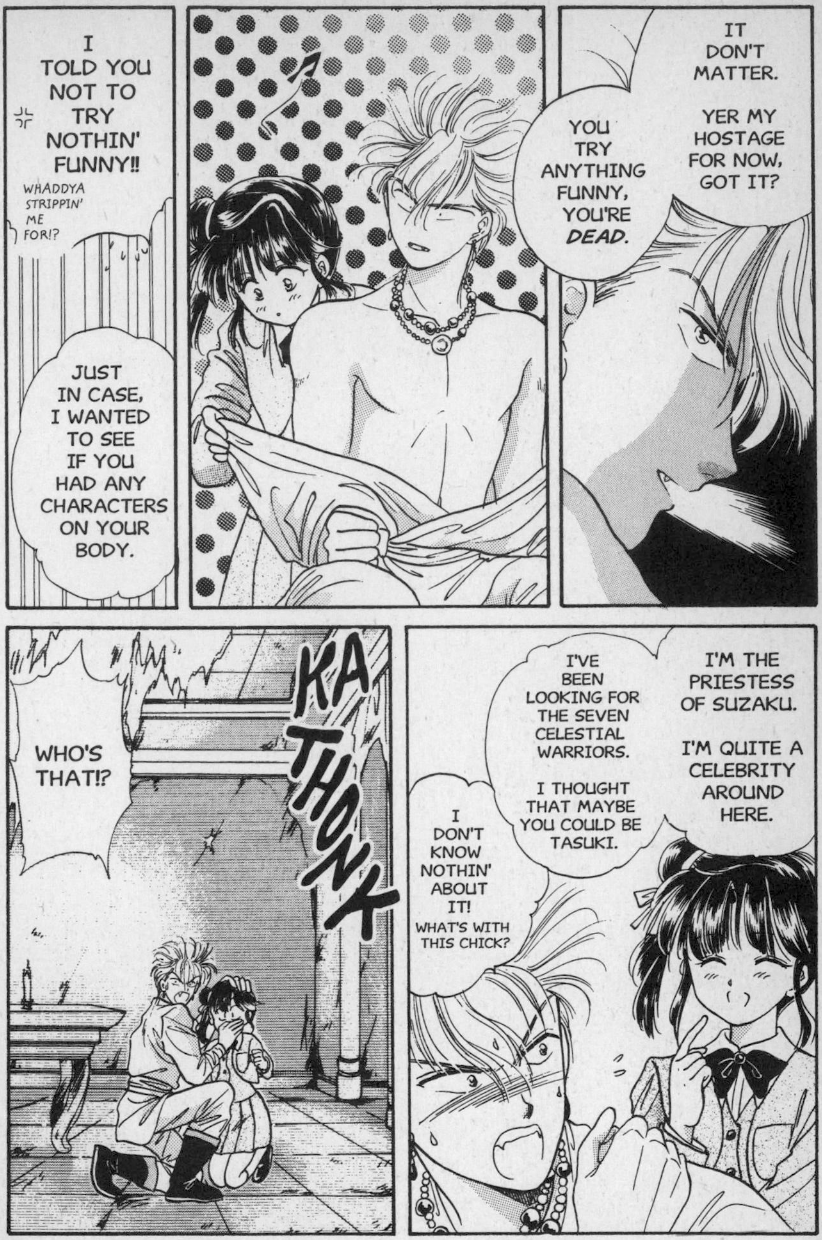
IT DON'T MATTER. YER MY HOSTAGE FOR NOW, GOT IT?
YOU TRY ANYTHING FUNNY, YOU'RE *DEAD.*
I TOLD YOU NOT TO TRY NOTHIN' FUNNY!!
WHADDYA STRIPPIN' ME FOR!?
JUST IN CASE, I WANTED TO SEE IF YOU HAD ANY CHARACTERS ON YOUR BODY.
I'M THE PRIESTESS OF SUZAKU. I'M QUITE A CELEBRITY AROUND HERE.
I'VE BEEN LOOKING FOR THE SEVEN CELESTIAL WARRIORS. I THOUGHT THAT MAYBE YOU COULD BE TASUKI.
I DON'T KNOW NOTHIN' ABOUT IT!
WHAT'S WITH THIS CHICK?
KA THONK
WHO'S THAT!?

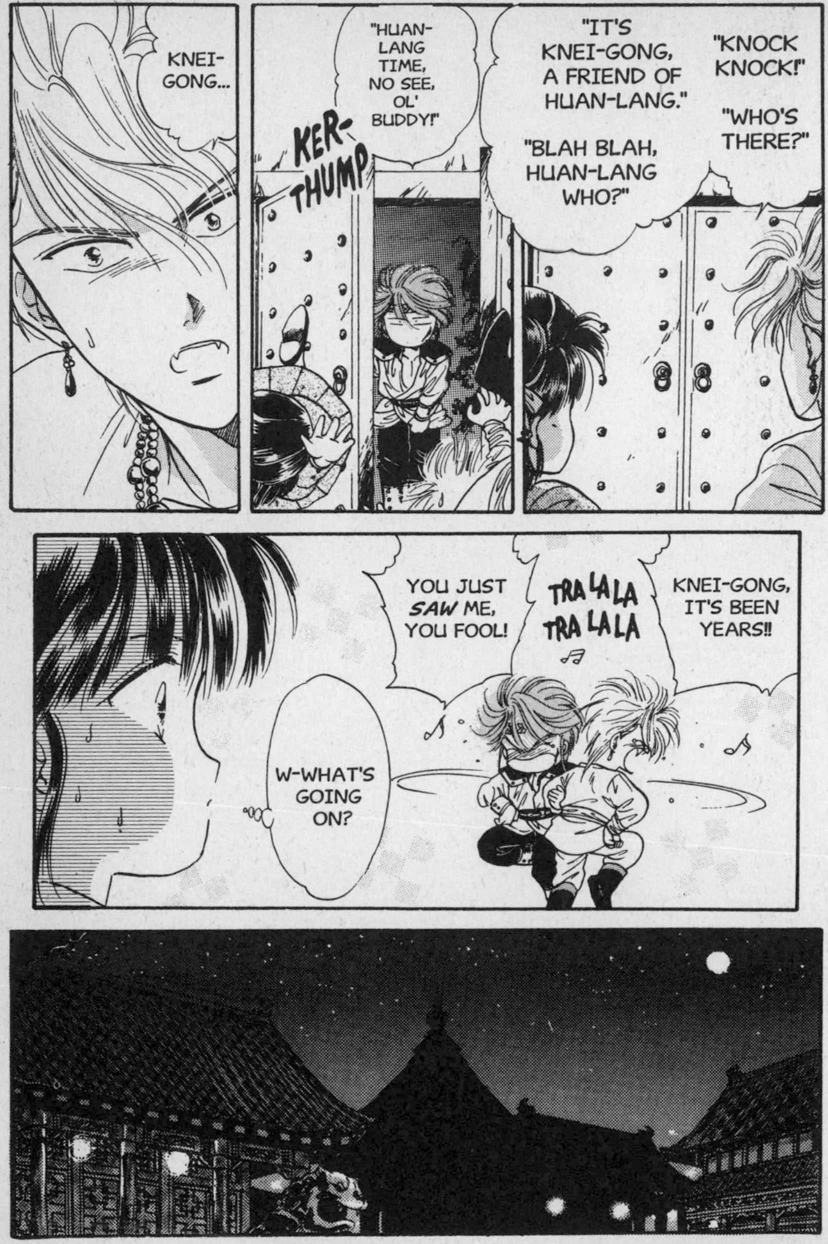
"KNOCK KNOCK!"
"WHO'S THERE?"
"IT'S KNEI-GONG, A FRIEND OF HUAN-LANG."
"BLAH BLAH, HUAN-LANG WHO?"
"HUAN-LANG TIME, NO SEE, OL' BUDDY!"
KER-THUMP
KNEI-GONG...
KNEI-GONG, IT'S BEEN YEARS!!
TRA LA LA TRA LA LA
YOU JUST *SAW* ME, YOU FOOL!
W-WHAT'S GOING ON?

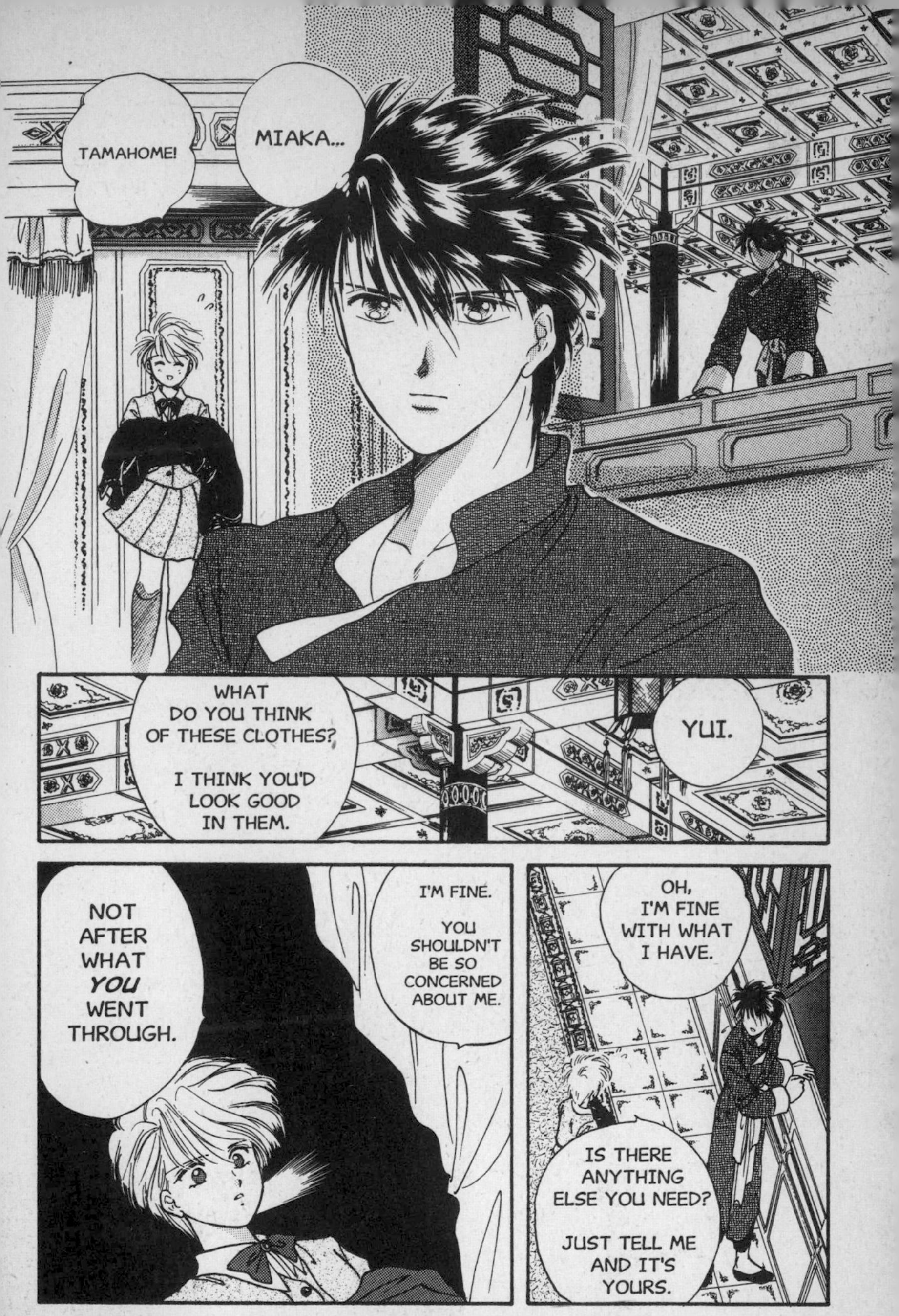
MIAKA...
TAMAHOME!
YUI.
WHAT DO YOU THINK OF THESE CLOTHES? I THINK YOU'D LOOK GOOD IN THEM.
OH, I'M FINE WITH WHAT I HAVE.
IS THERE ANYTHING ELSE YOU NEED? JUST TELL ME AND IT'S YOURS.
I'M FINE. YOU SHOULDN'T BE SO CONCERNED ABOUT ME.
NOT AFTER WHAT *YOU* WENT THROUGH.

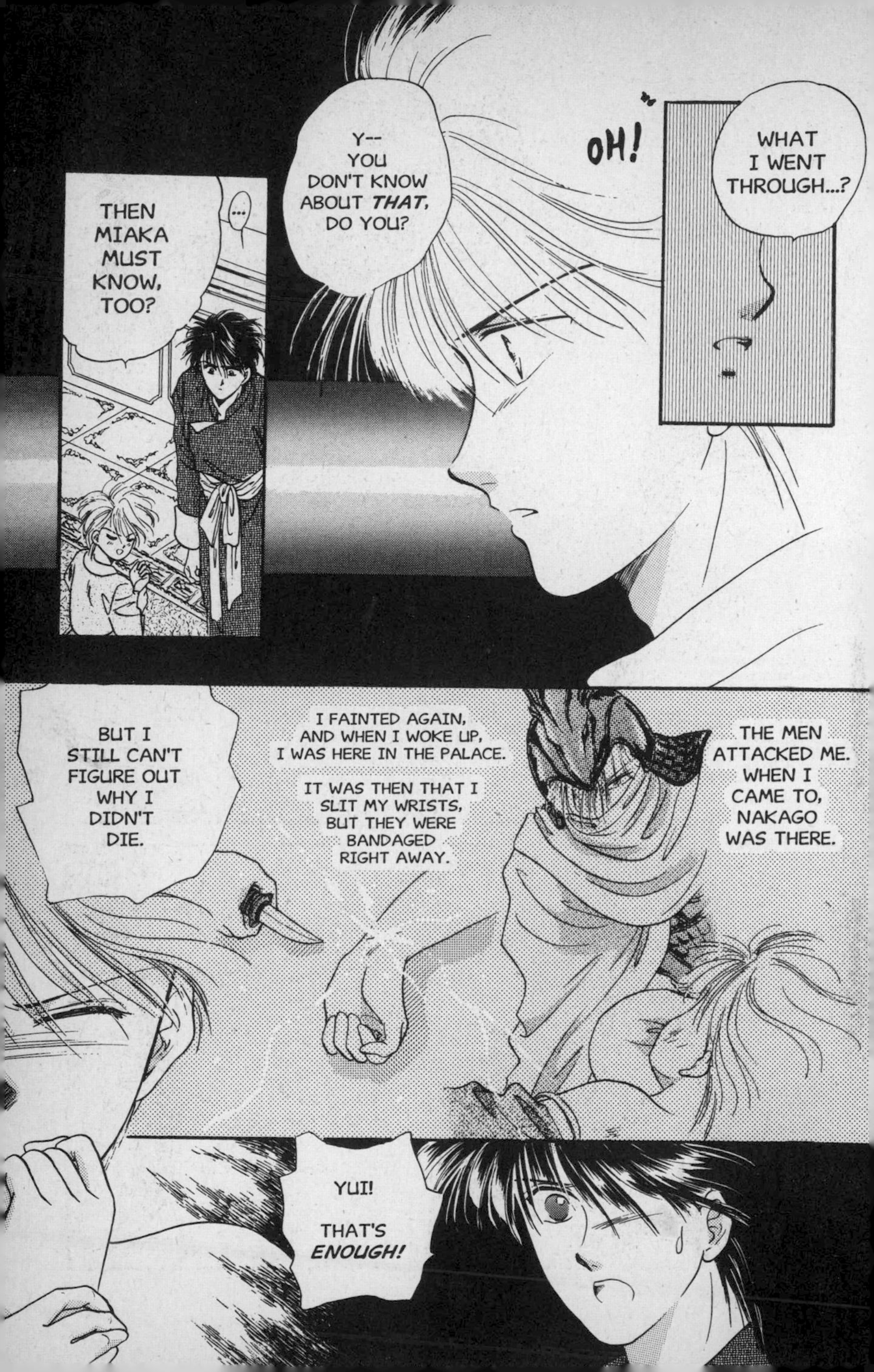
WHAT I WENT THROUGH...?
OH!
Y-- YOU DON'T KNOW ABOUT *THAT*, DO YOU?
...
THEN MIAKA MUST KNOW, TOO?
THE MEN ATTACKED ME. WHEN I CAME TO, NAKAGO WAS THERE.
I FAINTED AGAIN, AND WHEN I WOKE UP, I WAS HERE IN THE PALACE.
IT WAS THEN THAT I SLIT MY WRISTS, BUT THEY WERE BANDAGED RIGHT AWAY.
BUT I STILL CAN'T FIGURE OUT WHY I DIDN'T DIE.
YUI!
THAT'S *ENOUGH!*

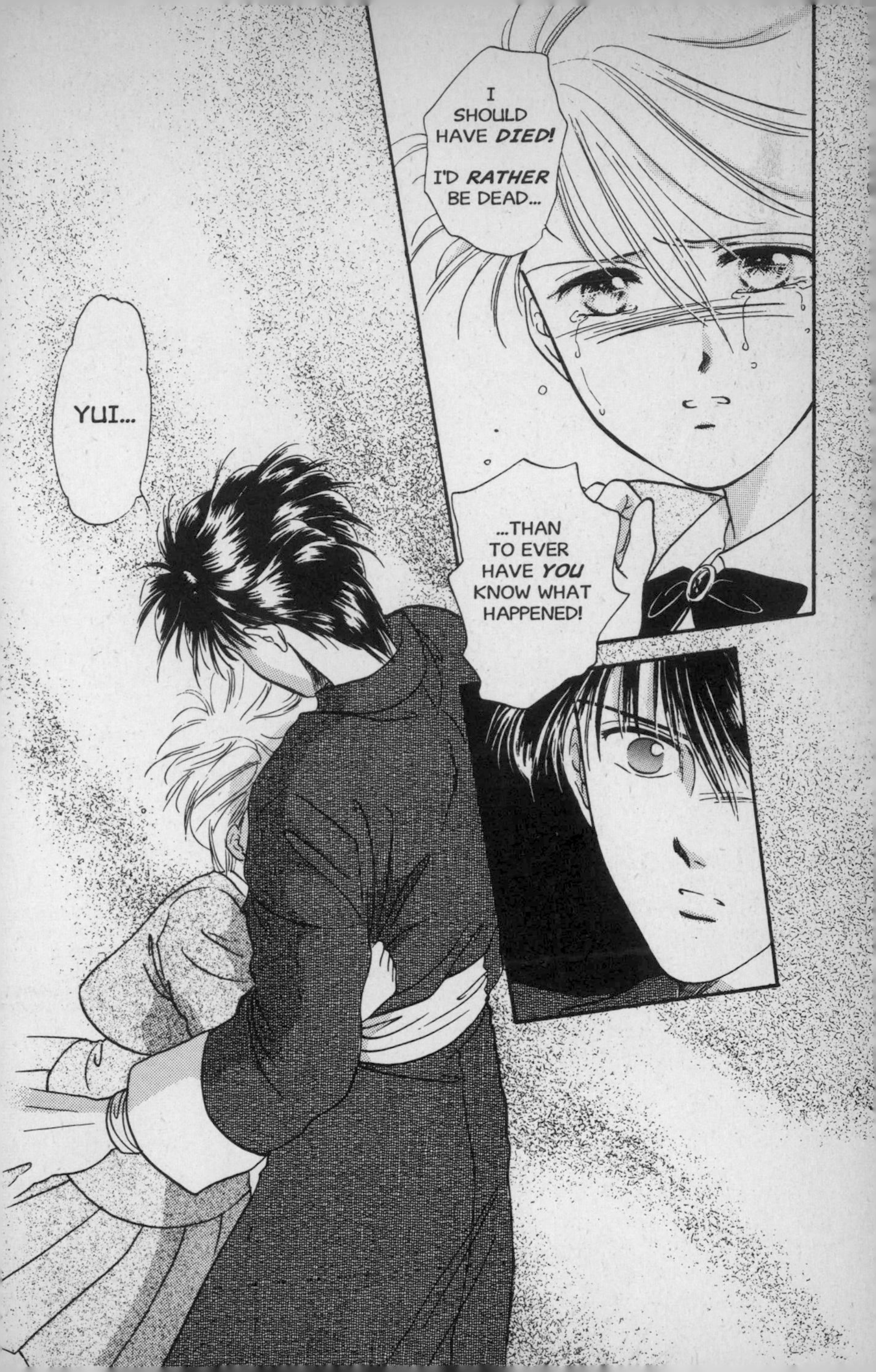

I SHOULD HAVE *DIED!*
I'D *RATHER* BE DEAD...
...THAN TO EVER HAVE *YOU* KNOW WHAT HAPPENED!
YUI...

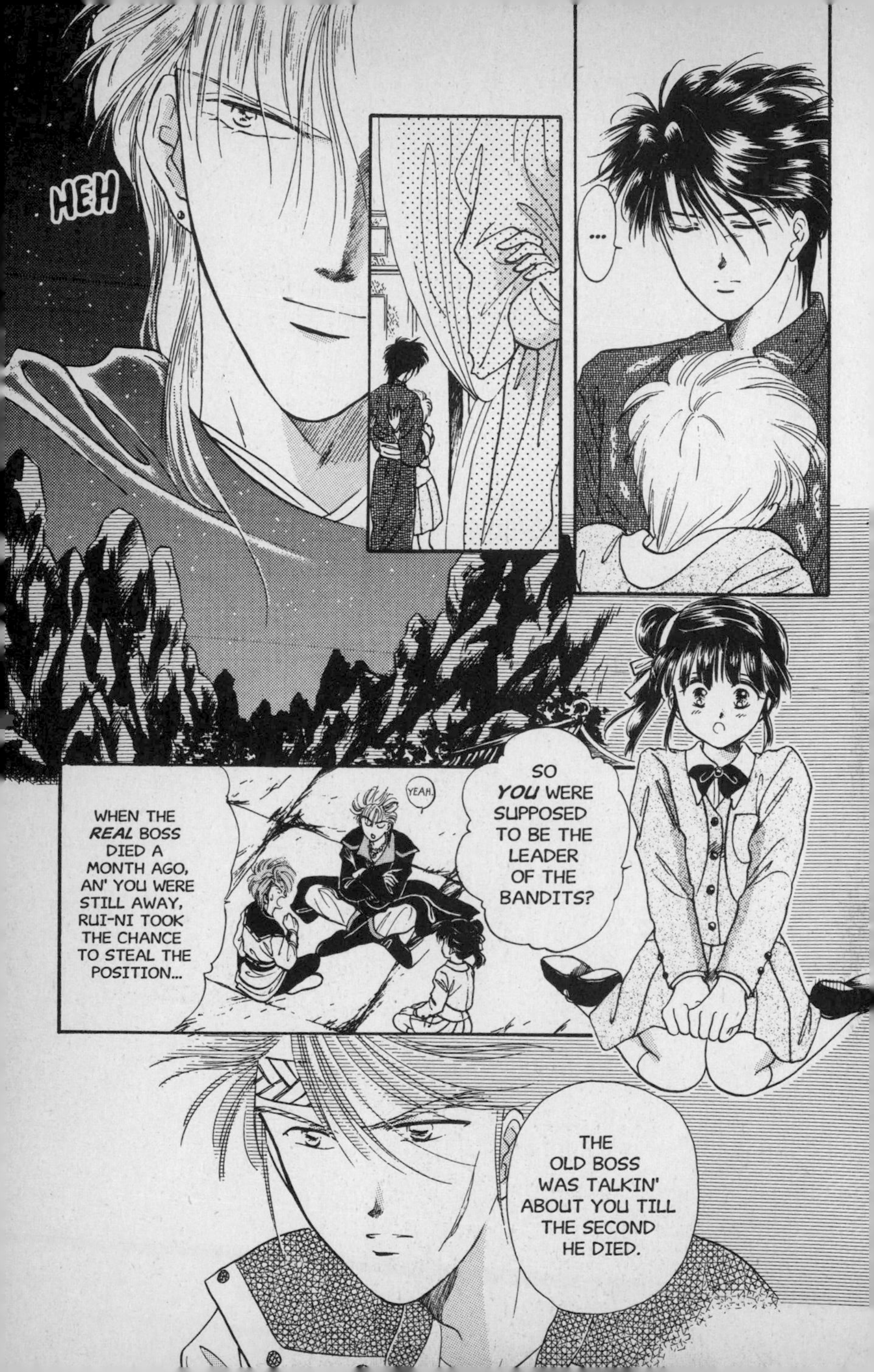
...
HEH
SO *YOU* WERE SUPPOSED TO BE THE LEADER OF THE BANDITS?
YEAH.
WHEN THE *REAL* BOSS DIED A MONTH AGO, AN' YOU WERE STILL AWAY, RUI-NI TOOK THE CHANCE TO STEAL THE POSITION...
THE OLD BOSS WAS TALKIN' ABOUT YOU TILL THE SECOND HE DIED.

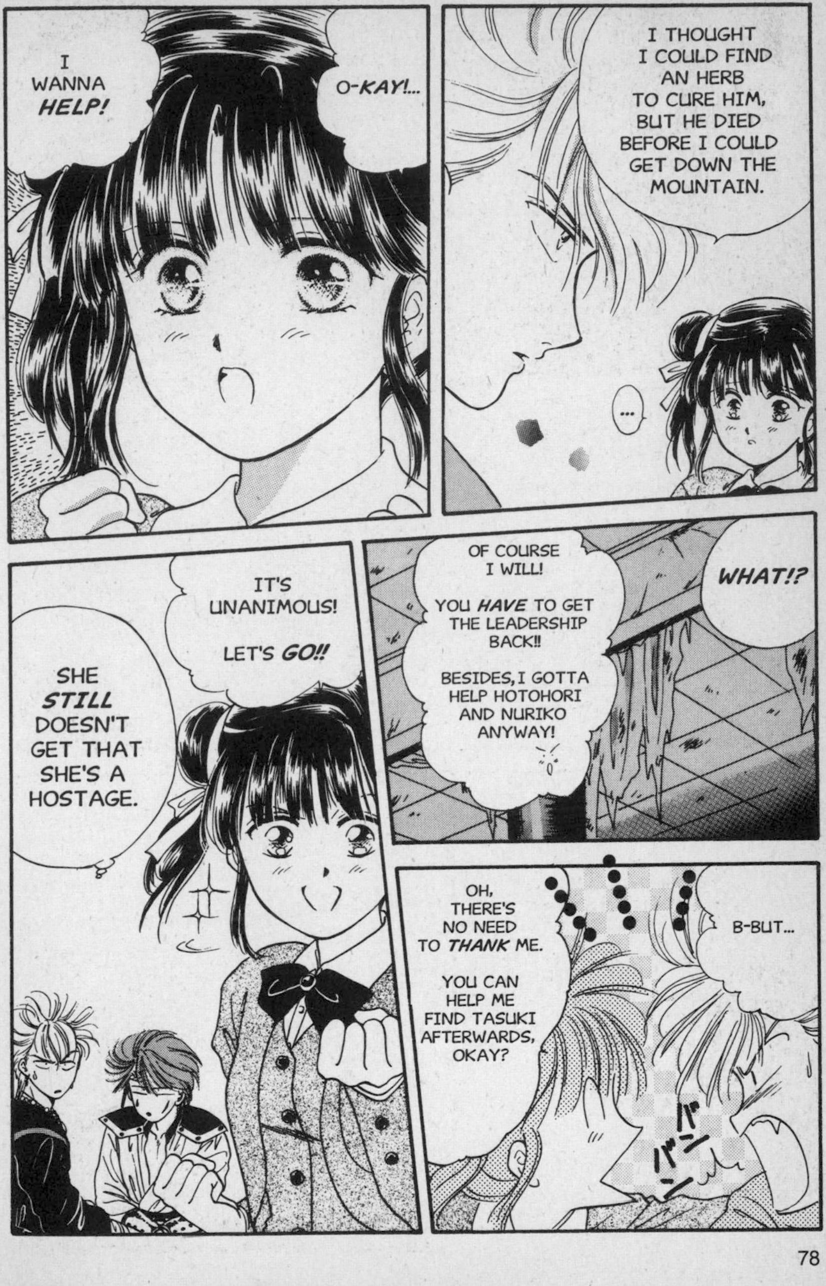
I THOUGHT I COULD FIND AN HERB TO CURE HIM, BUT HE DIED BEFORE I COULD GET DOWN THE MOUNTAIN.
...
O-*KAY!*...
I WANNA ***HELP!***
WHAT!?
OF COURSE I WILL!
YOU ***HAVE*** TO GET THE LEADERSHIP BACK!!
BESIDES, I GOTTA HELP HOTOHORI AND NURIKO ANYWAY!
B-BUT...
OH, THERE'S NO NEED TO ***THANK*** ME.
YOU CAN HELP ME FIND TASUKI AFTERWARDS, OKAY?
IT'S UNANIMOUS!
LET'S ***GO!!***
SHE ***STILL*** DOESN'T GET THAT SHE'S A HOSTAGE.

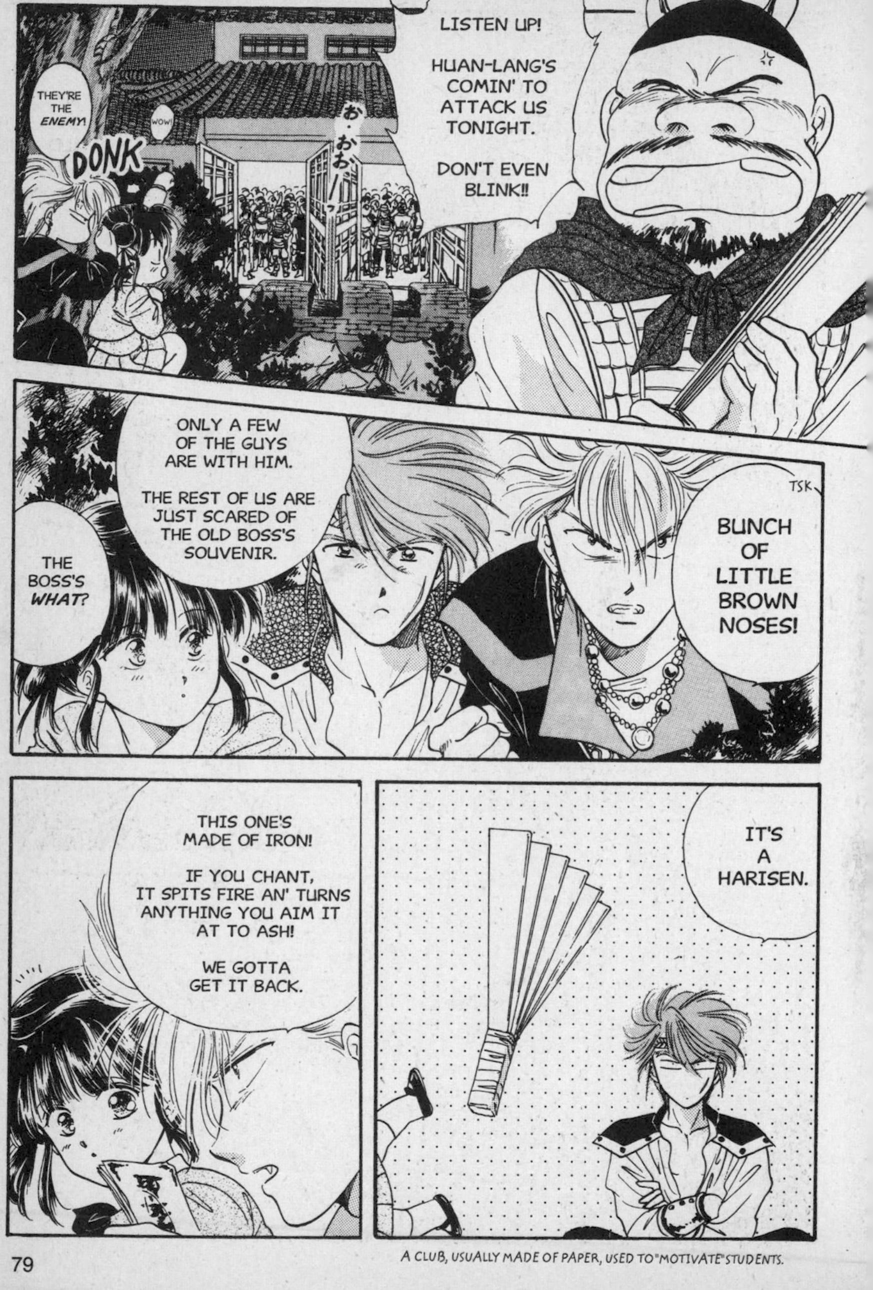
LISTEN UP!
HUAN-LANG'S COMIN' TO ATTACK US TONIGHT.
DON'T EVEN BLINK!!
お・おお!!っ
WOW!
THEY'RE THE *ENEMY*!
DONK
TSK
BUNCH OF LITTLE BROWN NOSES!
ONLY A FEW OF THE GUYS ARE WITH HIM.
THE REST OF US ARE JUST SCARED OF THE OLD BOSS'S SOUVENIR.
THE BOSS'S *WHAT*?
IT'S A HARISEN.
THIS ONE'S MADE OF IRON!
IF YOU CHANT, IT SPITS FIRE AN' TURNS ANYTHING YOU AIM IT AT TO ASH!
WE GOTTA GET IT BACK.

A CLUB, USUALLY MADE OF PAPER, USED TO "MOTIVATE" STUDENTS.

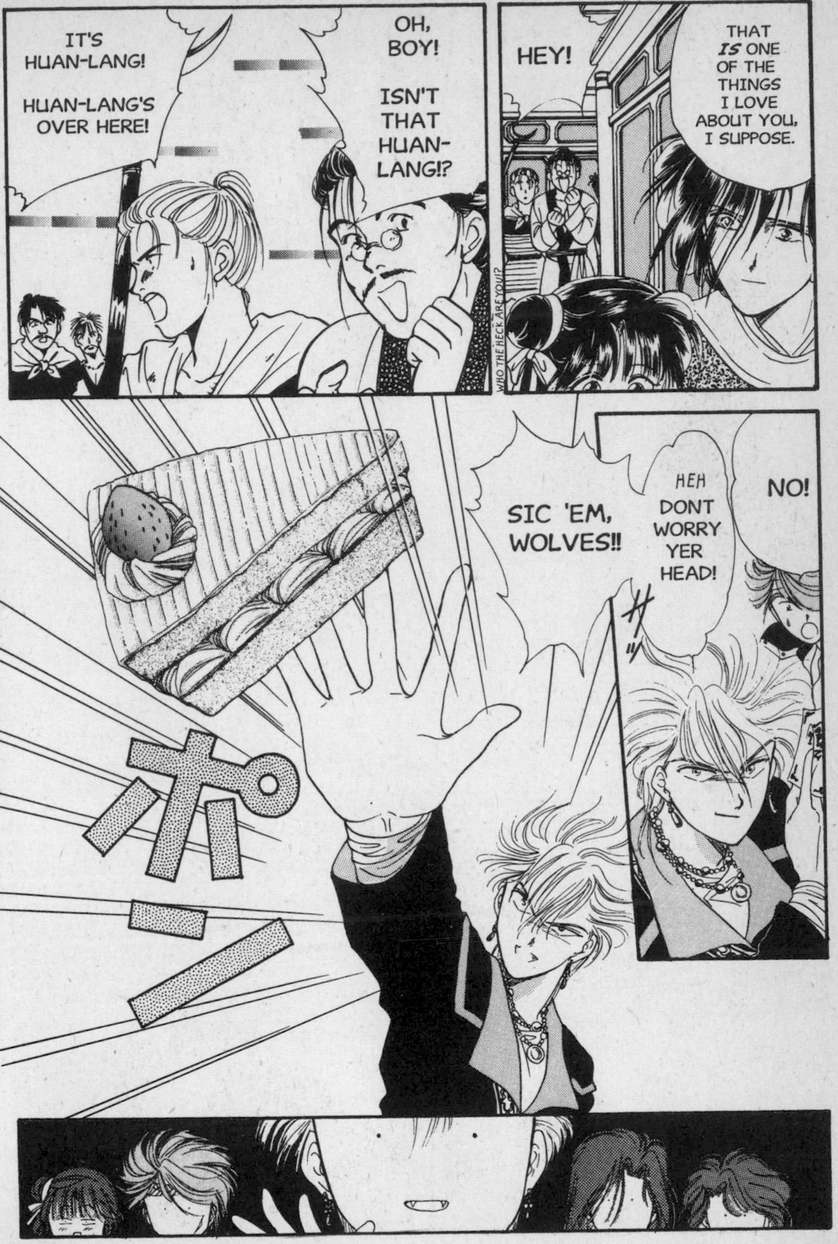
THAT *IS* ONE OF THE THINGS I LOVE ABOUT YOU, I SUPPOSE.
HEY!
WHO THE HECK ARE YOU!?
OH, BOY!
ISN'T THAT HUAN-LANG!?
IT'S HUAN-LANG!
HUAN-LANG'S OVER HERE!
NO!
HEH
DONT WORRY YER HEAD!
SIC 'EM, WOLVES!!
ポー

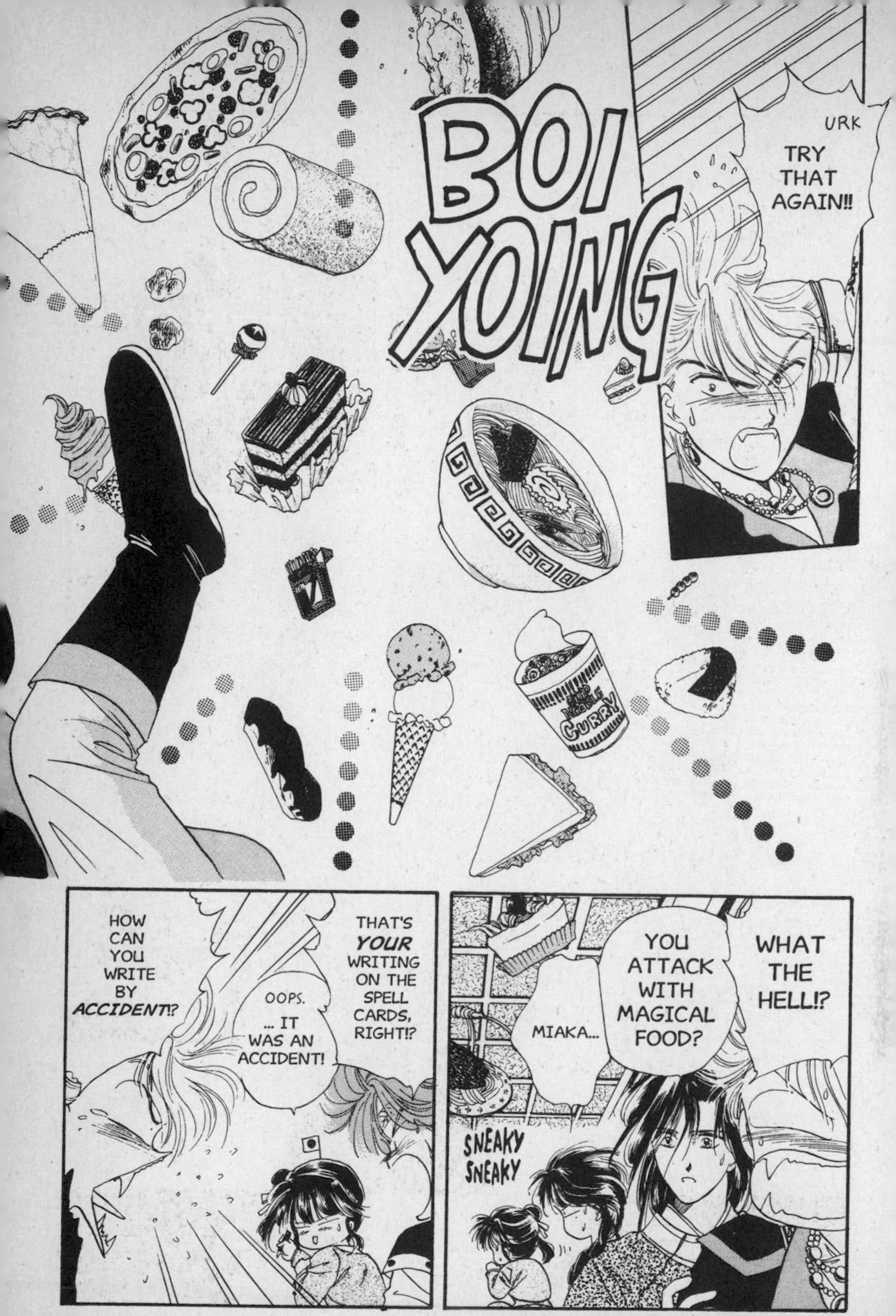
URK
TRY THAT AGAIN!!
BOI YOING
WHAT THE HELL!?
YOU ATTACK WITH MAGICAL FOOD?
MIAKA...
SNEAKY SNEAKY
THAT'S *YOUR* WRITING ON THE SPELL CARDS, RIGHT!?
OOPS. ... IT WAS AN ACCIDENT!
HOW CAN YOU WRITE BY *ACCIDENT*!?

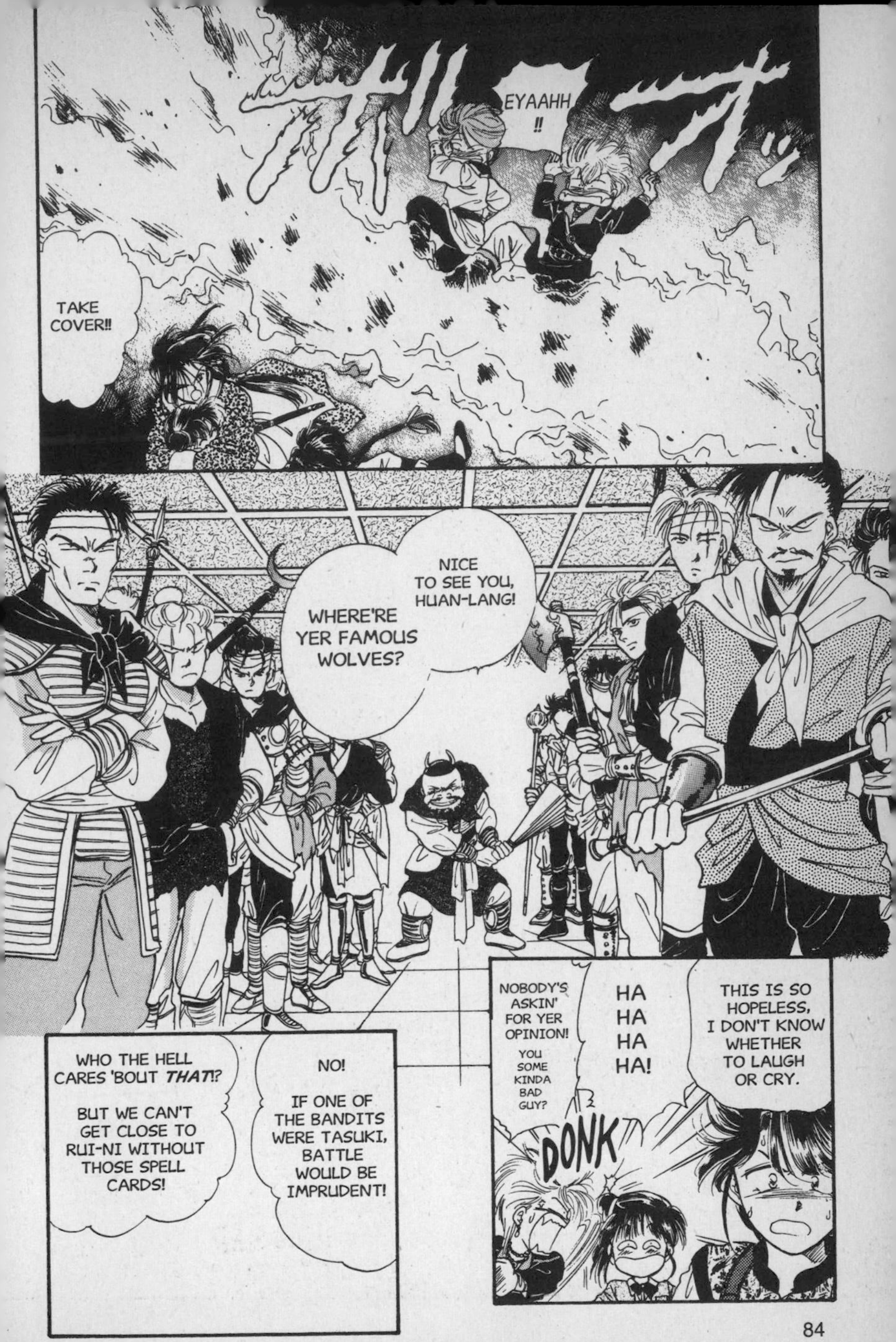
EYAAHH!!
TAKE COVER!!
NICE TO SEE YOU, HUAN-LANG!
WHERE'RE YER FAMOUS WOLVES?
THIS IS SO HOPELESS, I DON'T KNOW WHETHER TO LAUGH OR CRY.
HA HA HA HA!
NOBODY'S ASKIN' FOR YER OPINION!
YOU SOME KINDA BAD GUY?
DONK
NO!
IF ONE OF THE BANDITS WERE TASUKI, BATTLE WOULD BE IMPRUDENT!
WHO THE HELL CARES 'BOUT *THAT*!?
BUT WE CAN'T GET CLOSE TO RUI-NI WITHOUT THOSE SPELL CARDS!

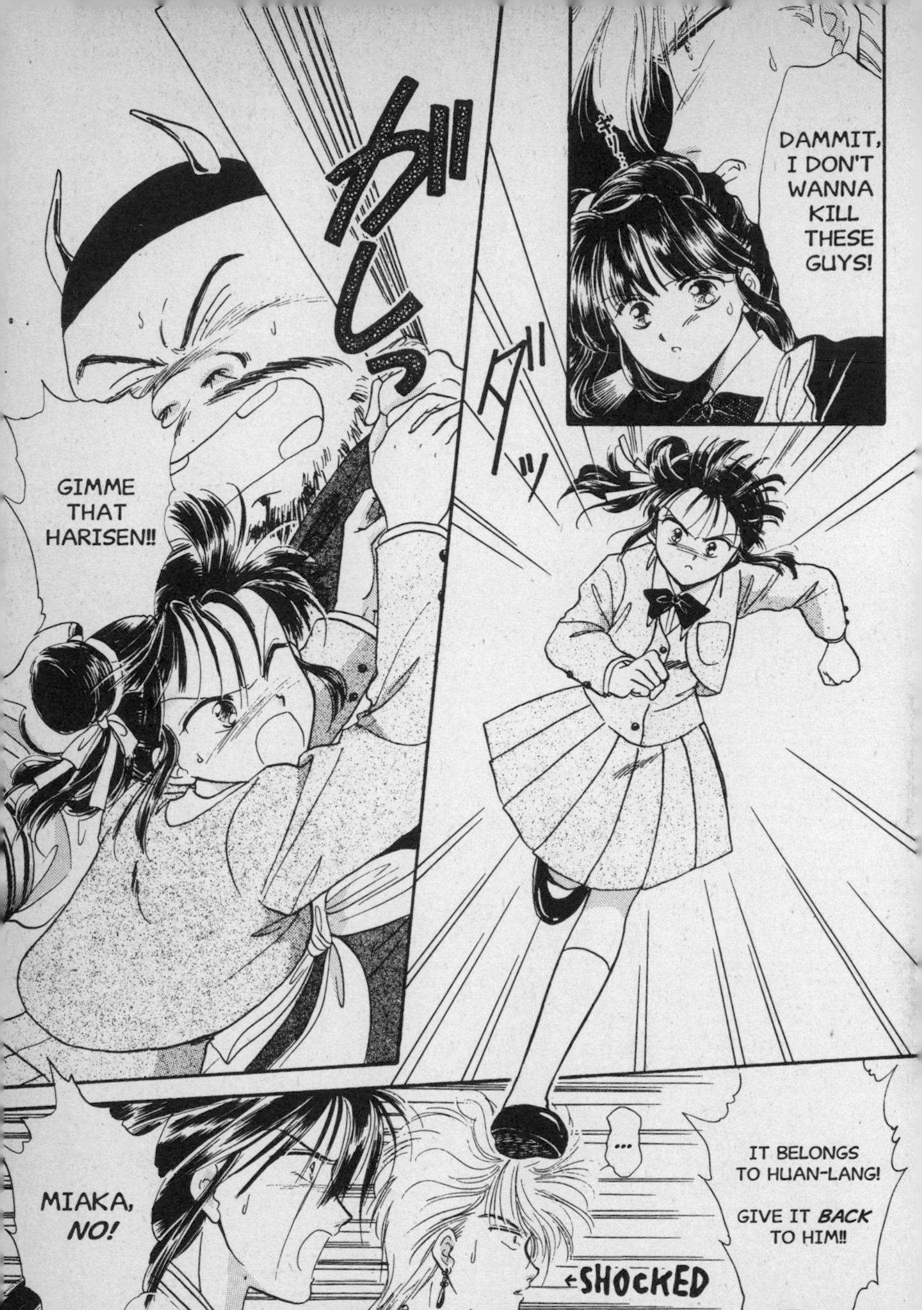
DAMMIT, I DON'T WANNA KILL THESE GUYS!
ダッ
がしっ
GIMME THAT HARISEN!!
IT BELONGS TO HUAN-LANG!
GIVE IT *BACK* TO HIM!!
...
←SHOCKED
MIAKA, *NO!*

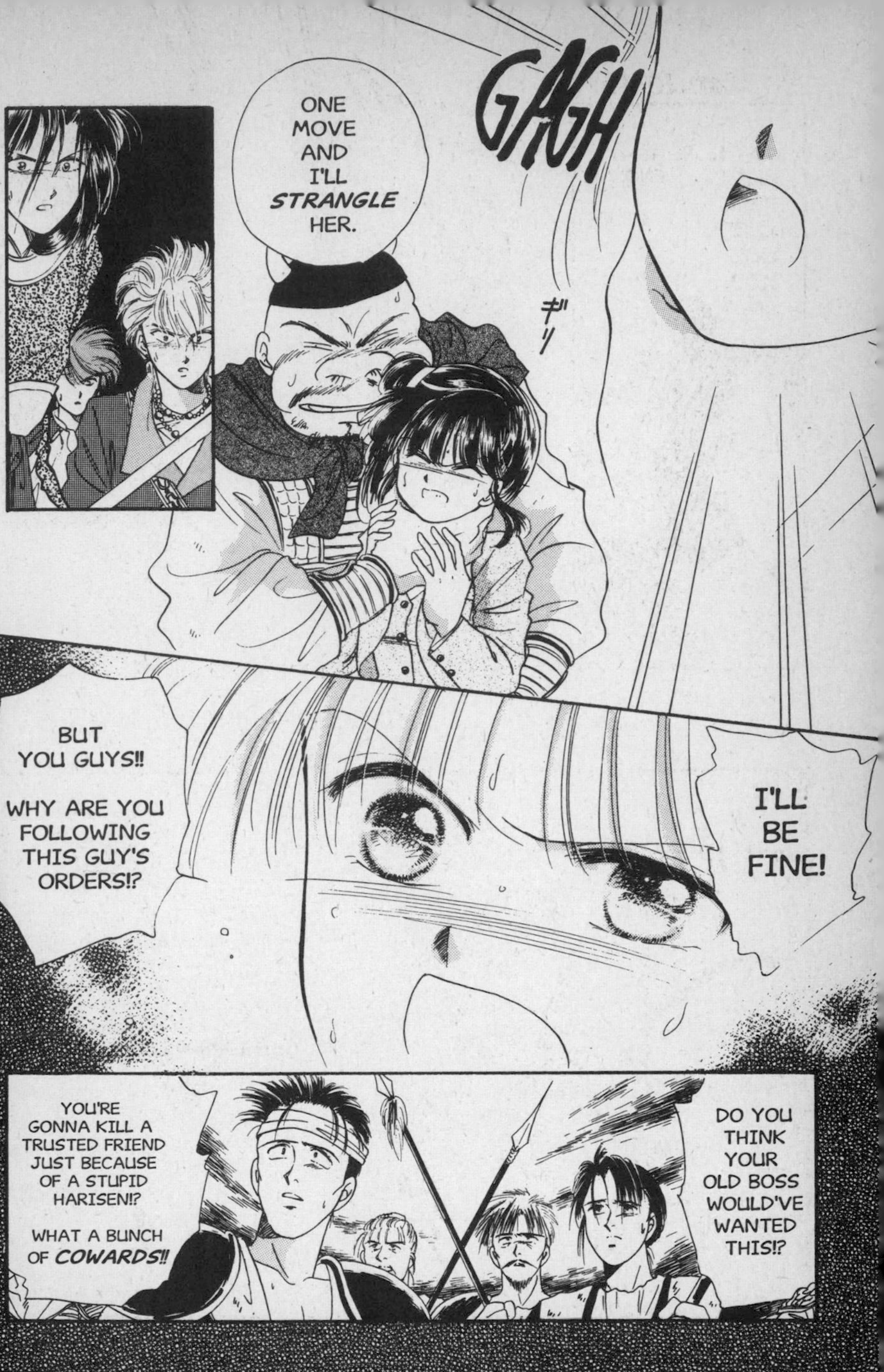
GAGH
ギリ
ONE MOVE AND I'LL *STRANGLE* HER.
I'LL BE FINE!
BUT YOU GUYS!!
WHY ARE YOU FOLLOWING THIS GUY'S ORDERS!?
DO YOU THINK YOUR OLD BOSS WOULD'VE WANTED THIS!?
YOU'RE GONNA KILL A TRUSTED FRIEND JUST BECAUSE OF A STUPID HARISEN!?
WHAT A BUNCH OF *COWARDS!!*

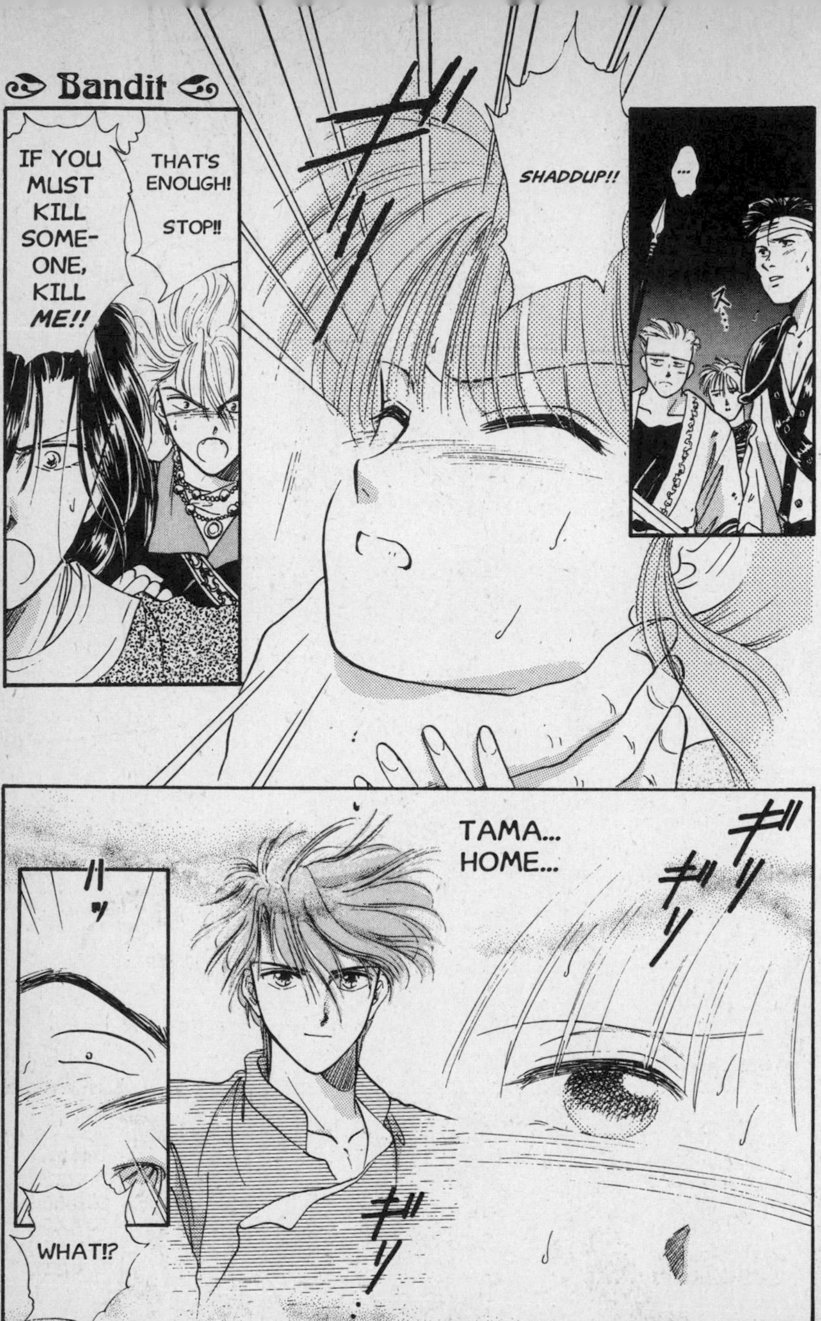
...
SHADDUP!!
THAT'S ENOUGH!
STOP!!
IF YOU MUST KILL SOME-ONE, KILL ME!!
TAMA... HOME...
WHAT!?

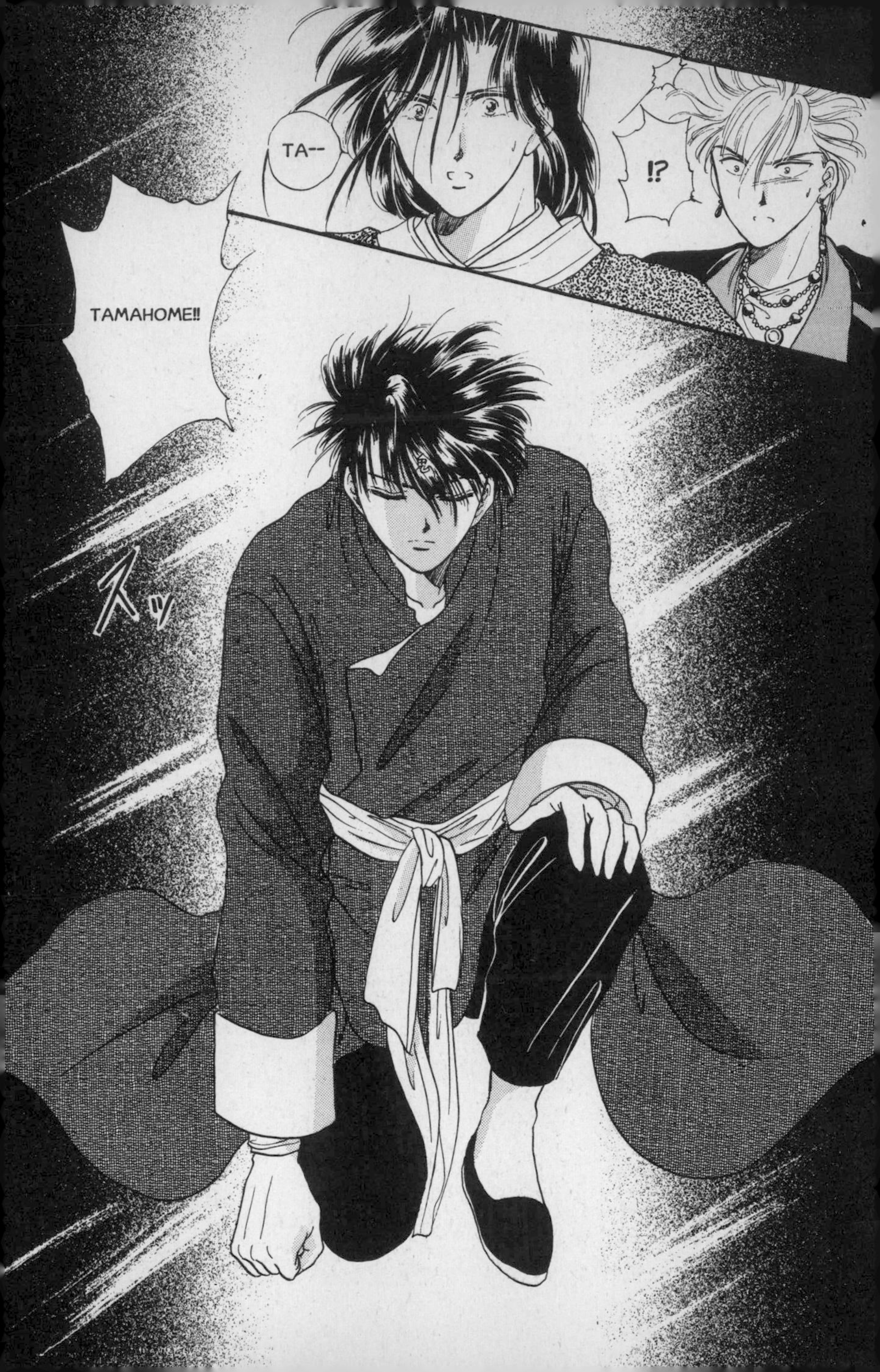
!?
TA--
TAMAHOME!!
スッ

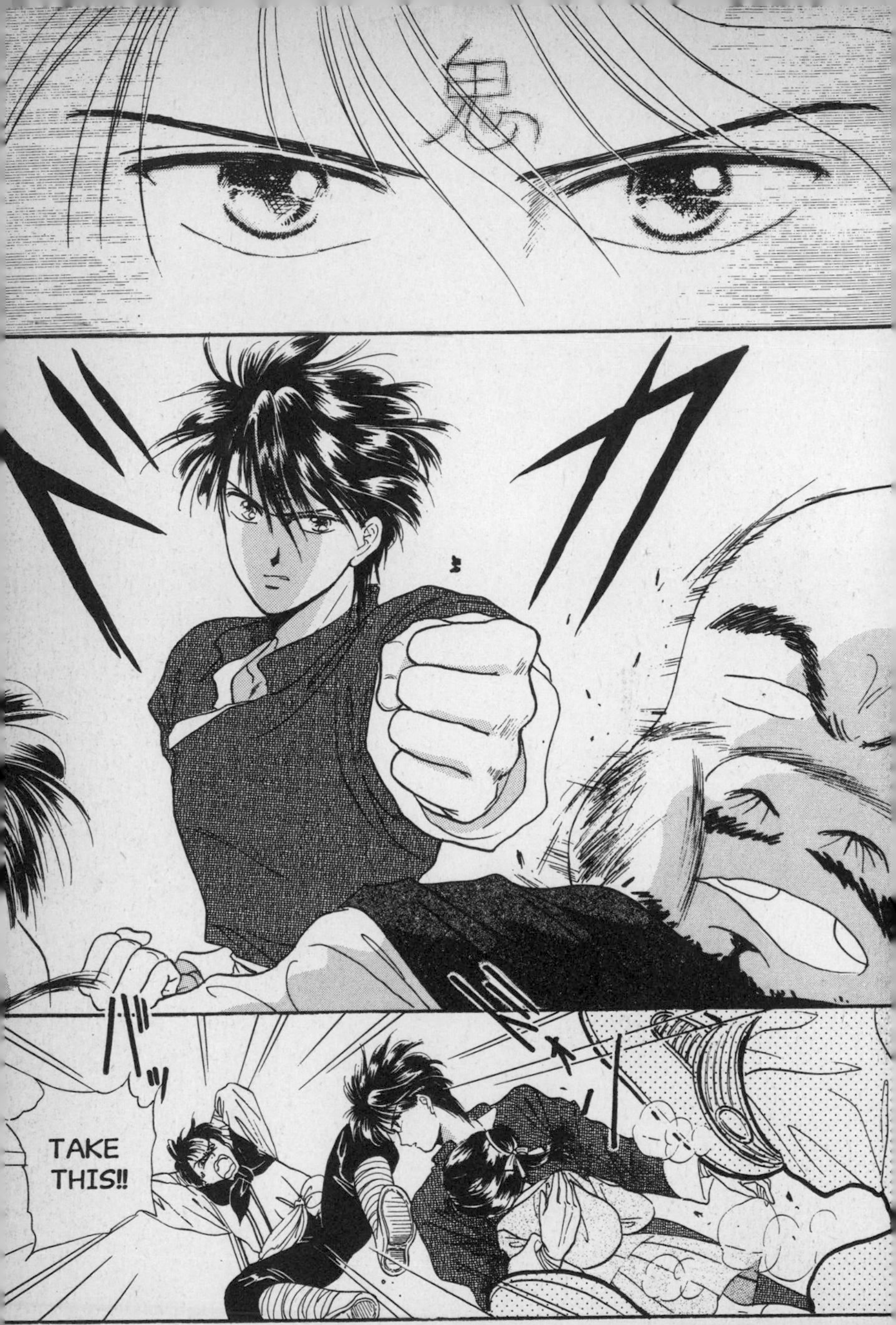
鬼
ドカ
TAKE THIS!!

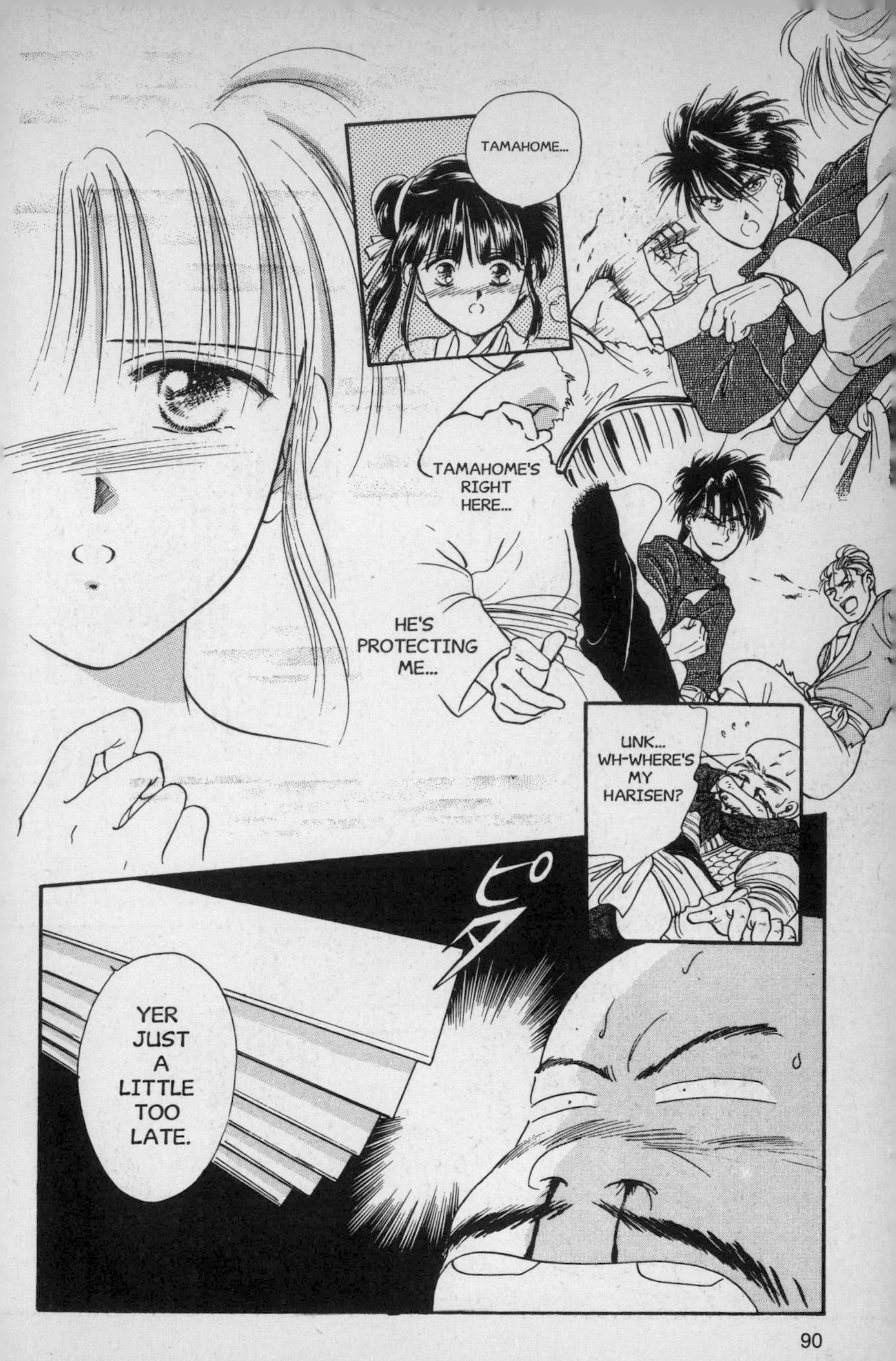
TAMAHOME...
TAMAHOME'S RIGHT HERE...
HE'S PROTECTING ME...
UNK... WH-WHERE'S MY HARISEN?
YER JUST A LITTLE TOO LATE.

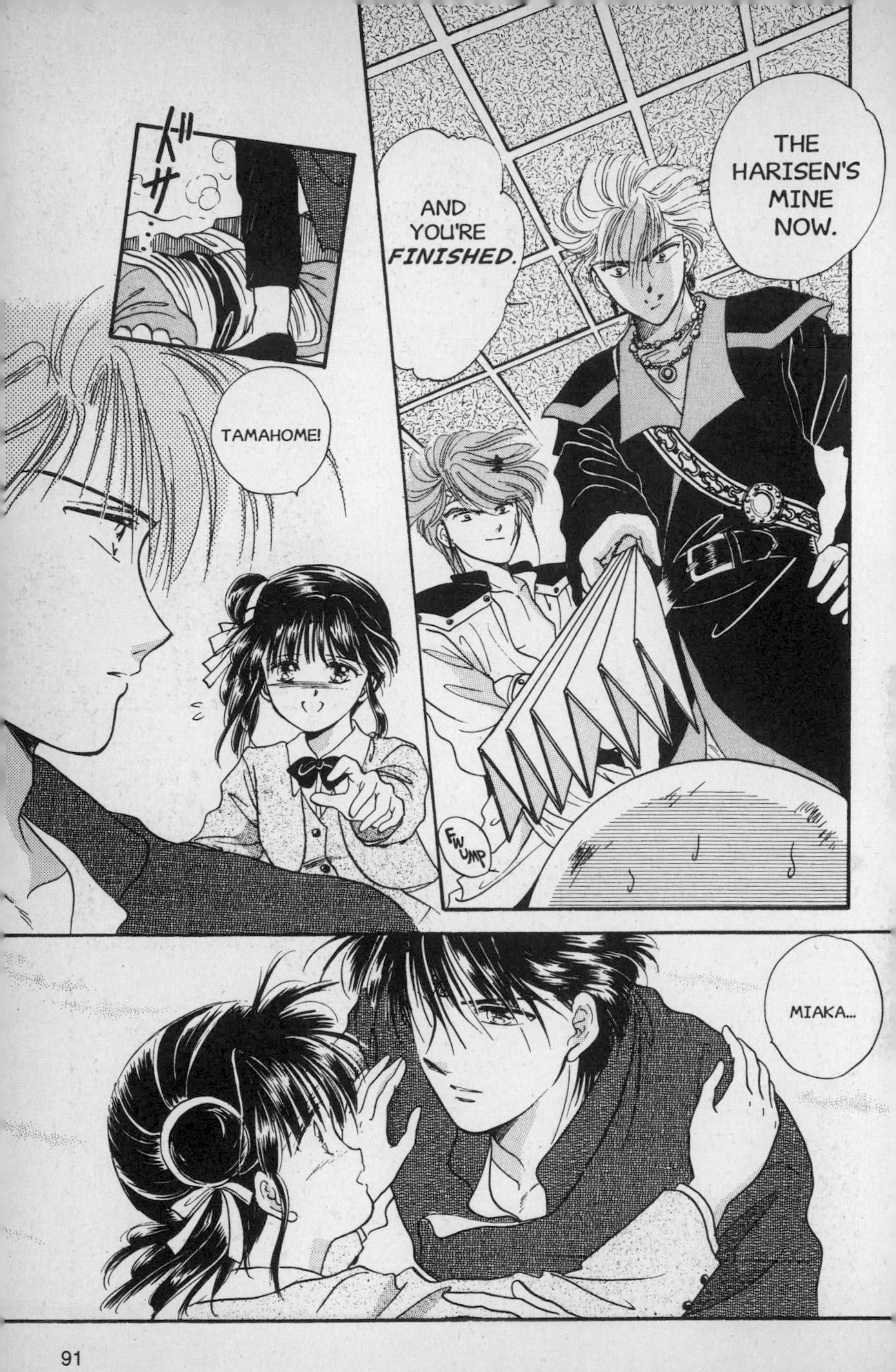
THE HARISEN'S MINE NOW.
AND YOU'RE *FINISHED*.
FWUMP
TAMAHOME!
MIAKA...

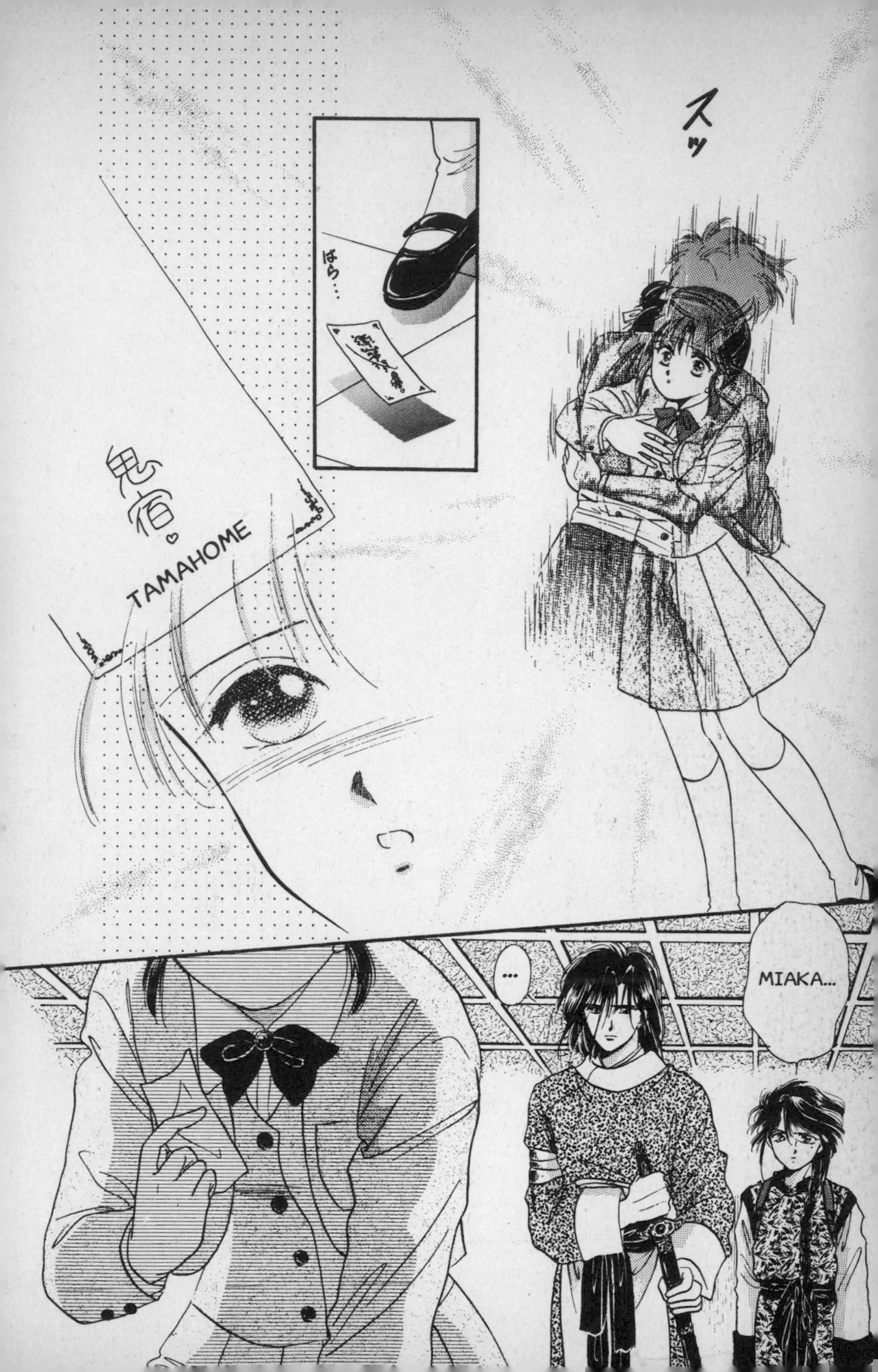
スッ
ぱら…
鬼宿♡
TAMAHOME
MIAKA...
...

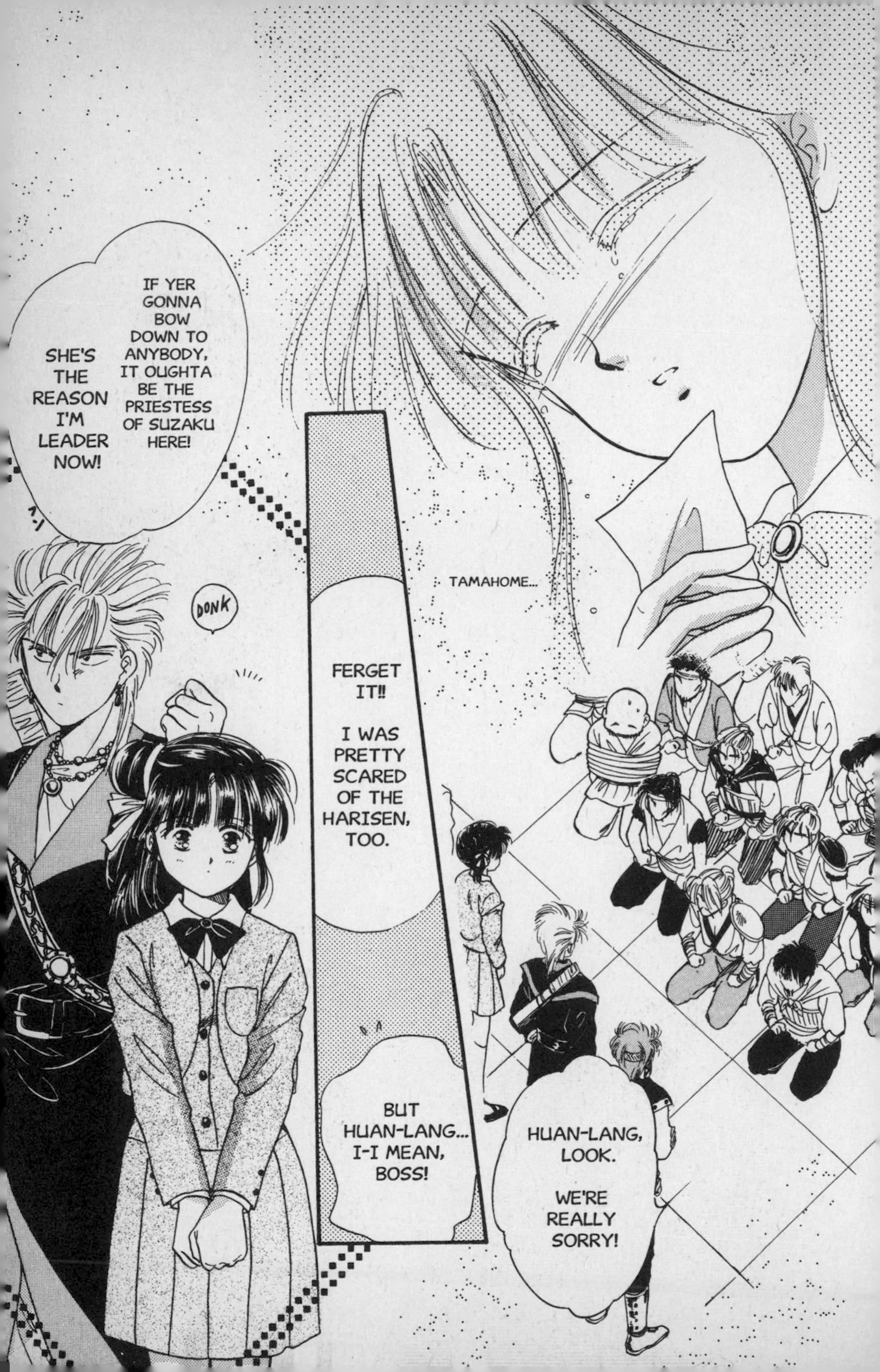
TAMAHOME...
HUAN-LANG, LOOK. WE'RE REALLY SORRY!
FERGET IT!! I WAS PRETTY SCARED OF THE HARISEN, TOO.
BUT HUAN-LANG... I-I MEAN, BOSS!
IF YER GONNA BOW DOWN TO ANYBODY, IT OUGHTA BE THE PRIESTESS OF SUZAKU HERE!
SHE'S THE REASON I'M LEADER NOW!
DONK

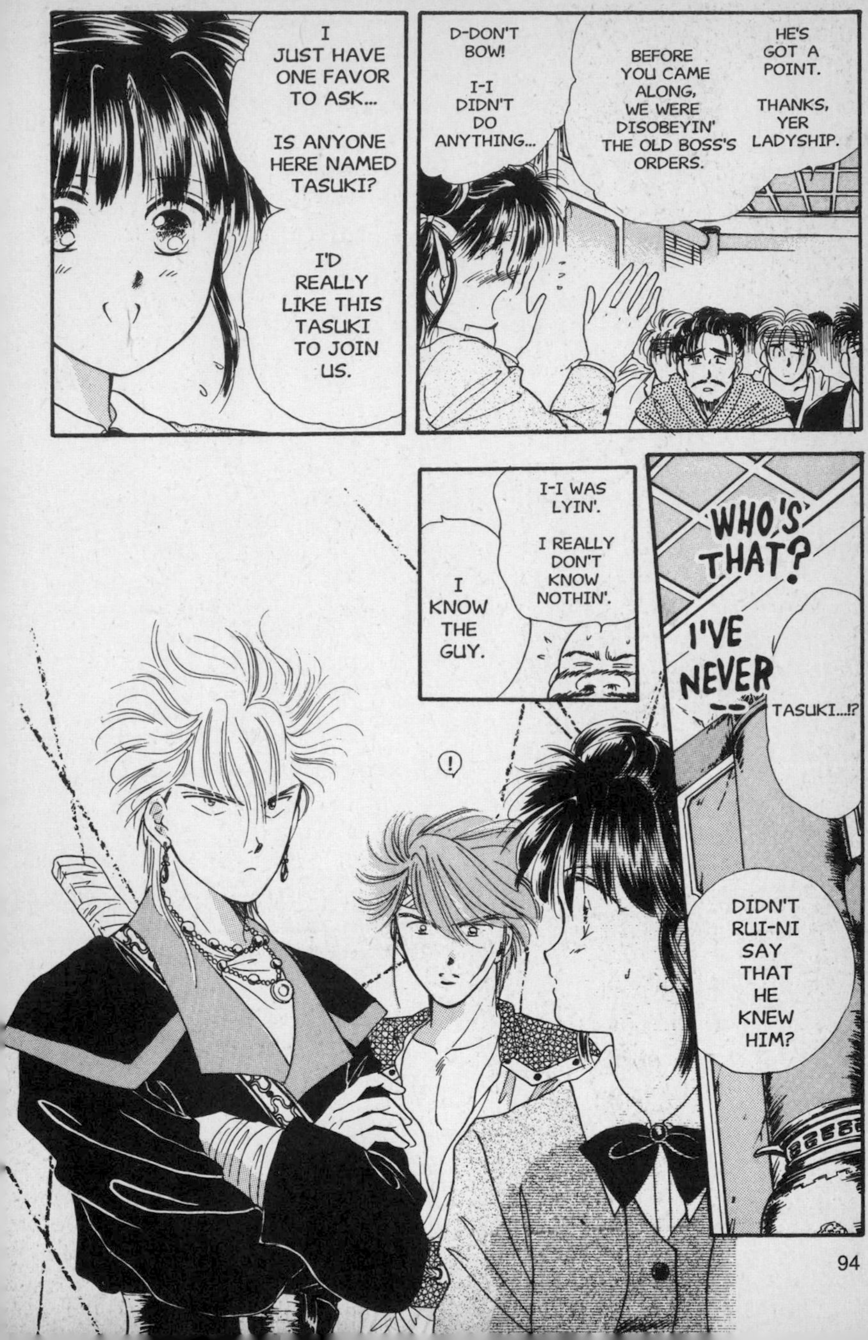
HE'S GOT A POINT. THANKS, YER LADYSHIP.
BEFORE YOU CAME ALONG, WE WERE DISOBEYIN' THE OLD BOSS'S ORDERS.
D-DON'T BOW! I-I DIDN'T DO ANYTHING...
I JUST HAVE ONE FAVOR TO ASK... IS ANYONE HERE NAMED TASUKI?
I'D REALLY LIKE THIS TASUKI TO JOIN US.
WHO'S THAT?
I'VE NEVER--
TASUKI...!?
DIDN'T RUI-NI SAY THAT HE KNEW HIM?
I-I WAS LYIN'. I REALLY DON'T KNOW NOTHIN'.
I KNOW THE GUY.
!

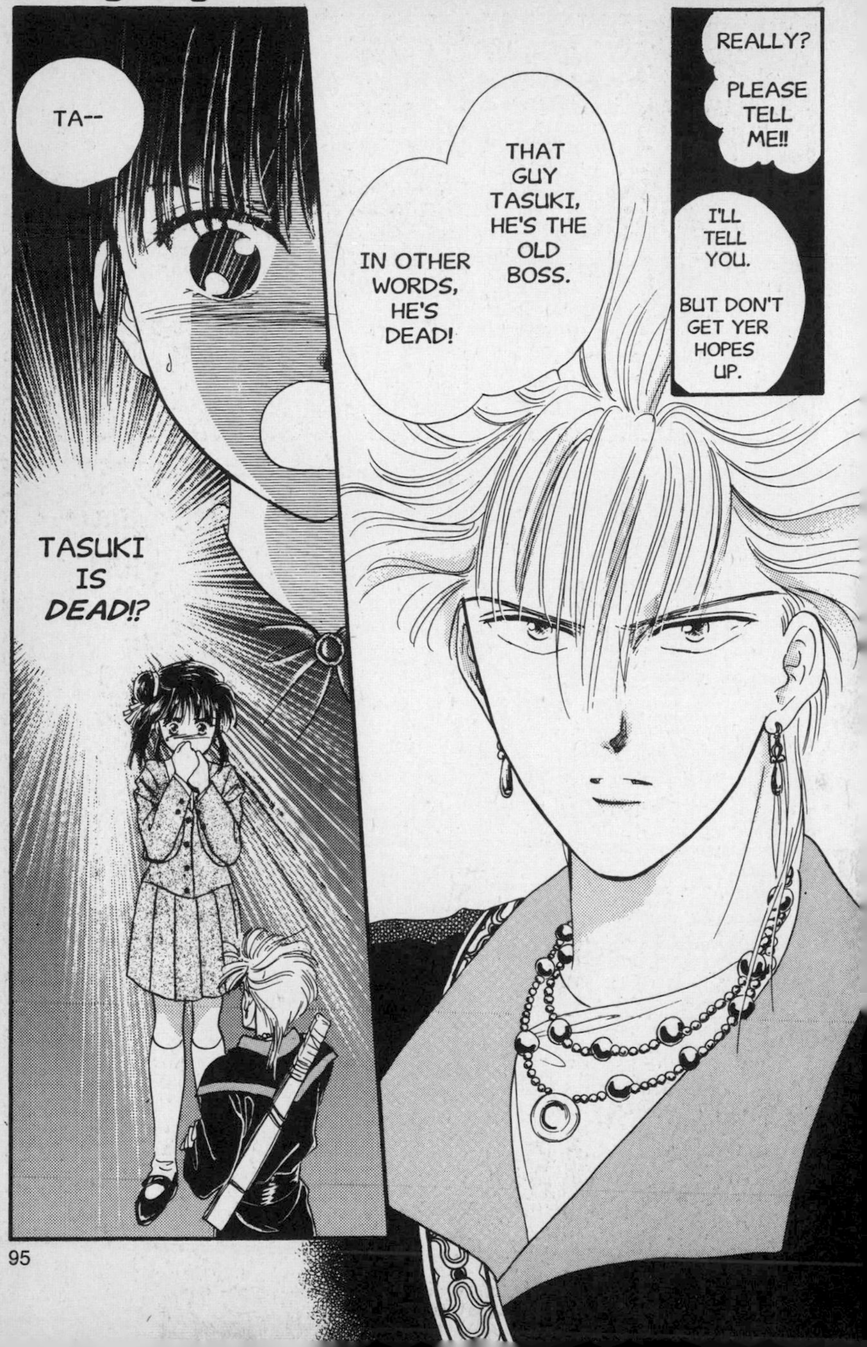
REALLY?
PLEASE TELL ME!!
I'LL TELL YOU.
BUT DON'T GET YER HOPES UP.
THAT GUY TASUKI, HE'S THE OLD BOSS.
IN OTHER WORDS, HE'S DEAD!
TA--
TASUKI IS *DEAD!?*

EASILY

YOU TOO CAN DO IT!! CHICHIRI FASHION!!

(MAYBE THIS IS JUST COSPLAY...)

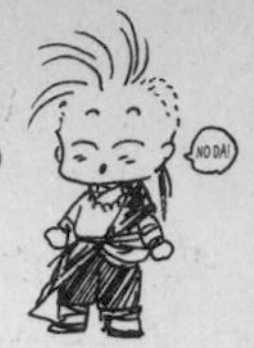
NO DA!

① First, prepare white T or V neck shirt, a large handkerchief, white boots, black string and belt, black sweat pants.

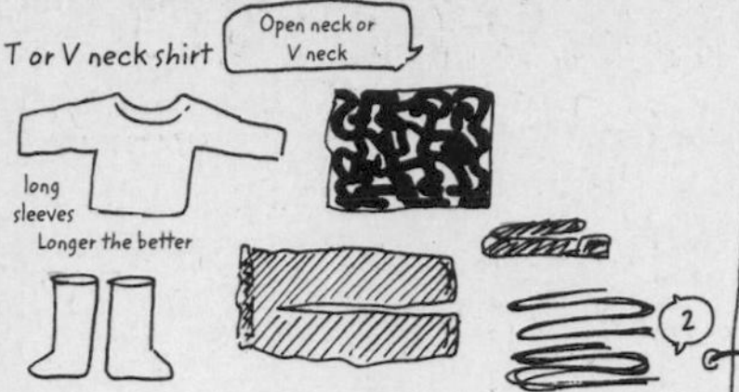
T or V neck shirt
Open neck or V neck
long sleeves
Longer the better
2

② Wear pants and then white shirt over pants.

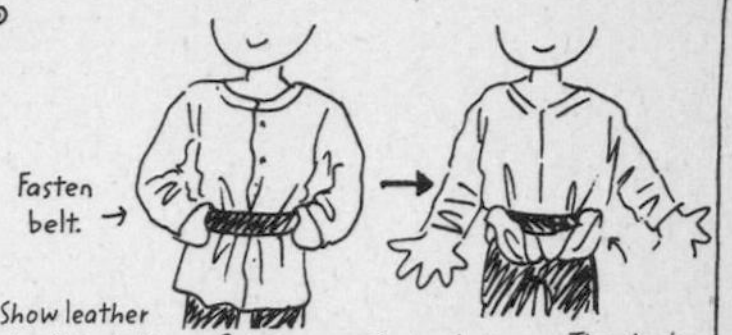
Fasten belt.

Show leather side of the belt. (from right to left)

Bring up sleeves slightly to leave some slack in them.

Tuck only the tips of the shirt in.

Then tuck in shirt through belt.

③ Wear boots and wrap black string around them. Shoes are critical.

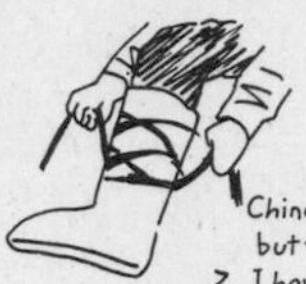

If you have Chinese shoes you're fine, but for those who don't, I have a secret solution I'm revealing!!

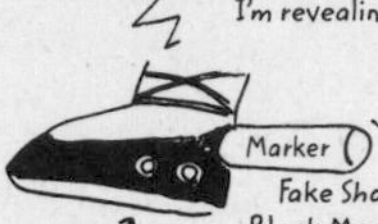
Marker

Fake Shoes Using Black Magic Marker

Make sure there are two open holes for air passage.

④ Now all you have to do is wear the furoshiki cloth like a surplice over your shoulder and your outfit's complete!

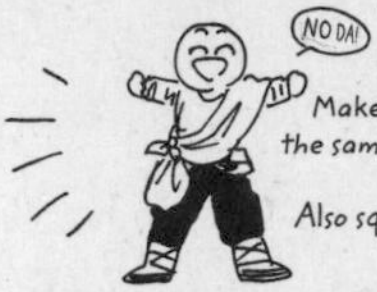
NO DA!

Make sure you speak with the same idiosyncrasies as him.

Also squint your eyes to make them thinner.

We have an advanced section below for those of you not quite satisfied.

ADVANCED SECTION

① I'm sure most of you have noticed that Chichiri's key possession is the ROSARY! You might not find such big rosaries.

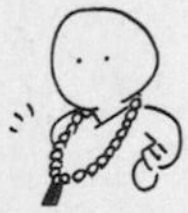

You might have to go to a temple or occult group to find one.

② Not enough? Of course not. The second key props are...
THE STAFF AND BAMBOO HAT!!

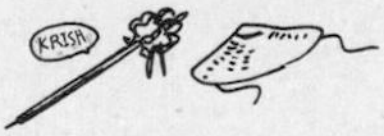
KRISH

Wait for that night when a traveling priest knocks on your door to ask for a night's lodging.

③ If you've gone this far, nothing can stop you! There is one last detail to be Chichiri and that's...THE MOHAWK!!

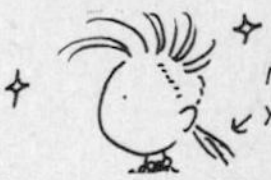

Note: Make sure you keep your hair here.

Bring a portrait of Chichiri to the beauty parlor and they'll be glad to cut your hair accordingly, I'm sure.

※ For those who have dared to go this far, with regard to being alienated from your neighbors or family, or ending up committing family suicide, I assume no responsibility. It might be best at least for the sake of world peace if you train yourself to disappear into your bamboo hat and leave this world for good.

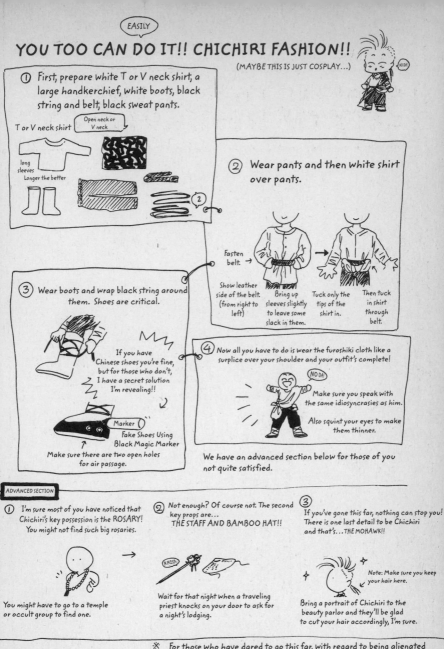

CHAPTER TWENTY-TWO
CITY OF RESURRECTION

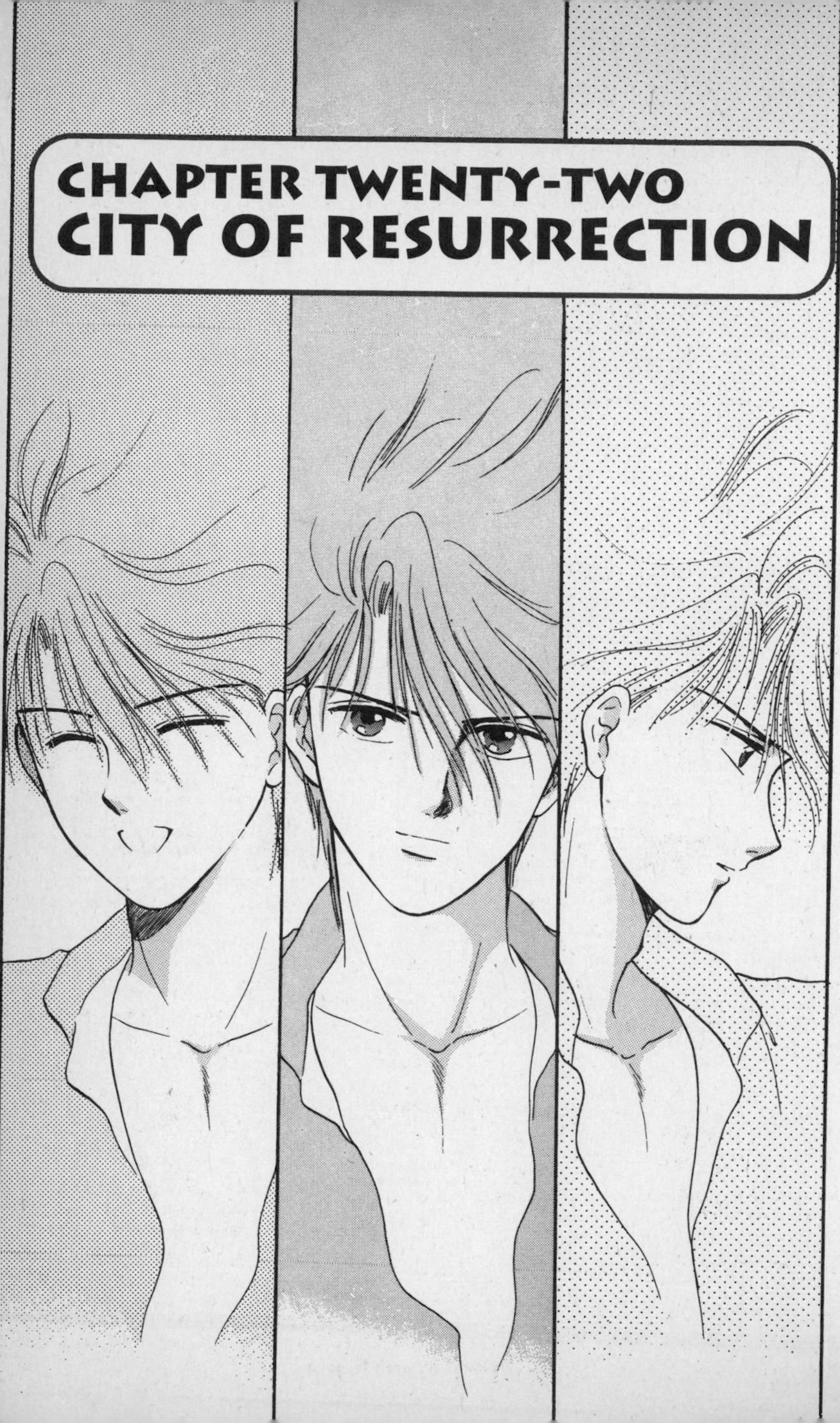

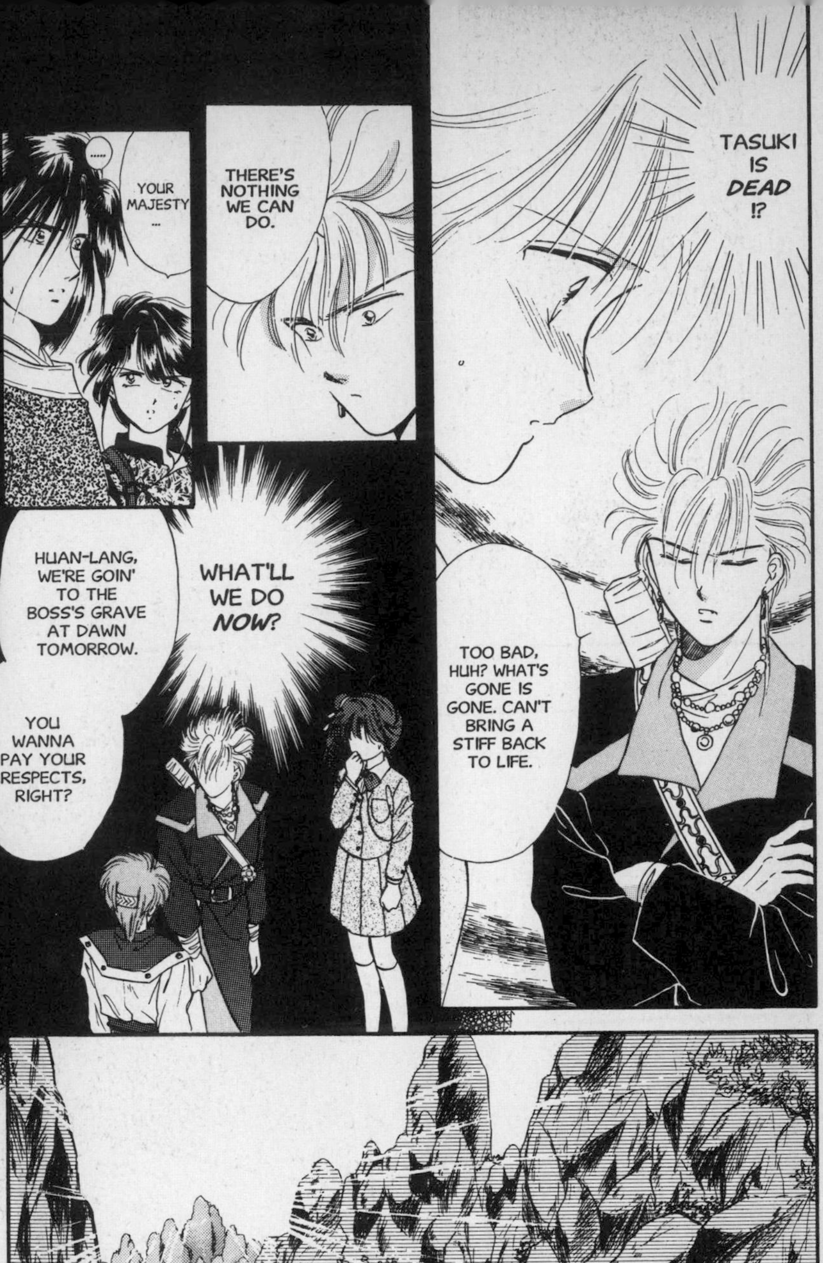
TASUKI IS *DEAD* !?
TOO BAD, HUH? WHAT'S GONE IS GONE. CAN'T BRING A STIFF BACK TO LIFE.
THERE'S NOTHING WE CAN DO.
......
YOUR MAJESTY ...
WHAT'LL WE DO *NOW?*
HUAN-LANG, WE'RE GOIN' TO THE BOSS'S GRAVE AT DAWN TOMORROW.
YOU WANNA PAY YOUR RESPECTS, RIGHT?

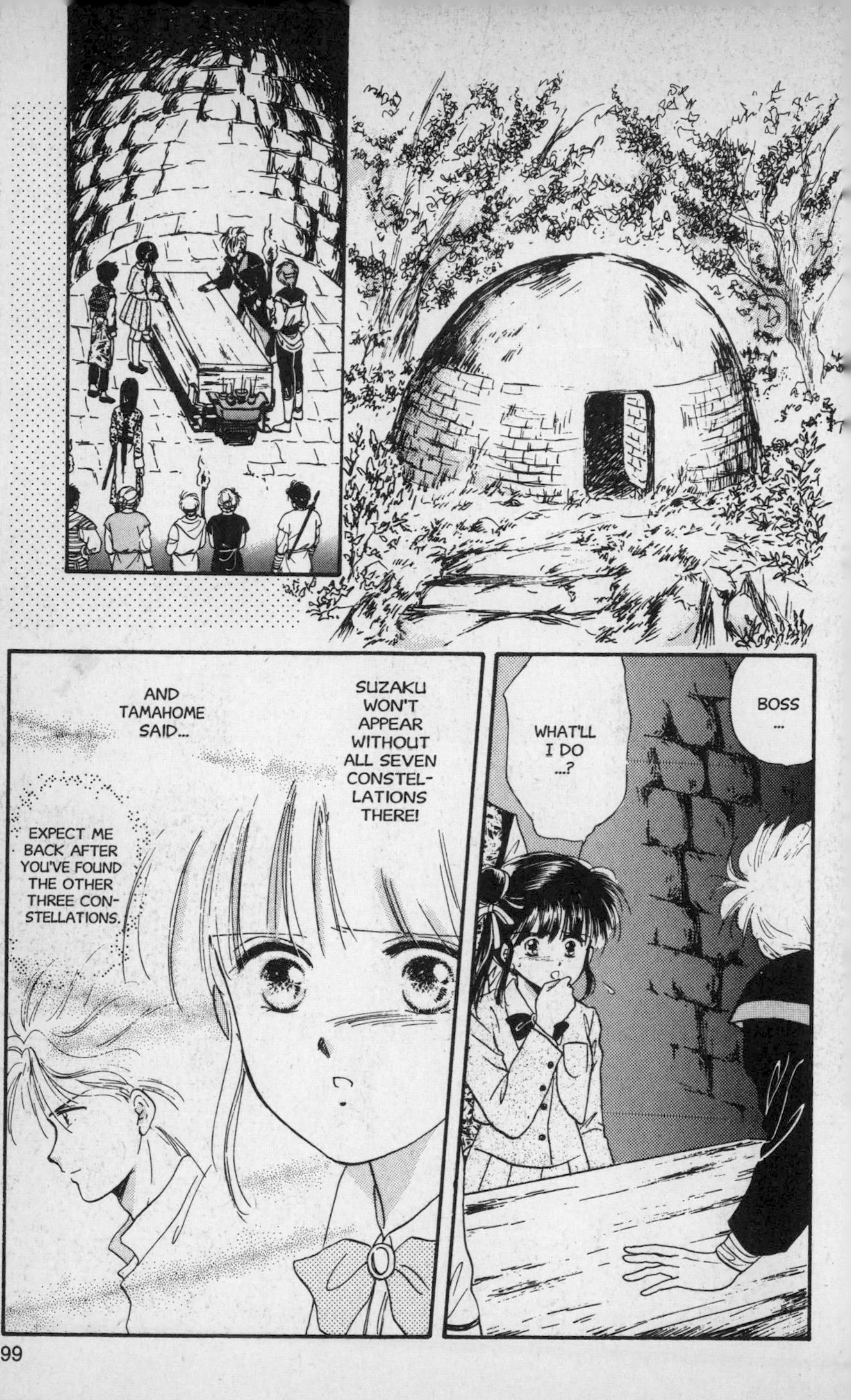
BOSS ...
WHAT'LL I DO ...?
SUZAKU WON'T APPEAR WITHOUT ALL SEVEN CONSTEL-LATIONS THERE!
AND TAMAHOME SAID...
EXPECT ME BACK AFTER YOU'VE FOUND THE OTHER THREE CON-STELLATIONS.

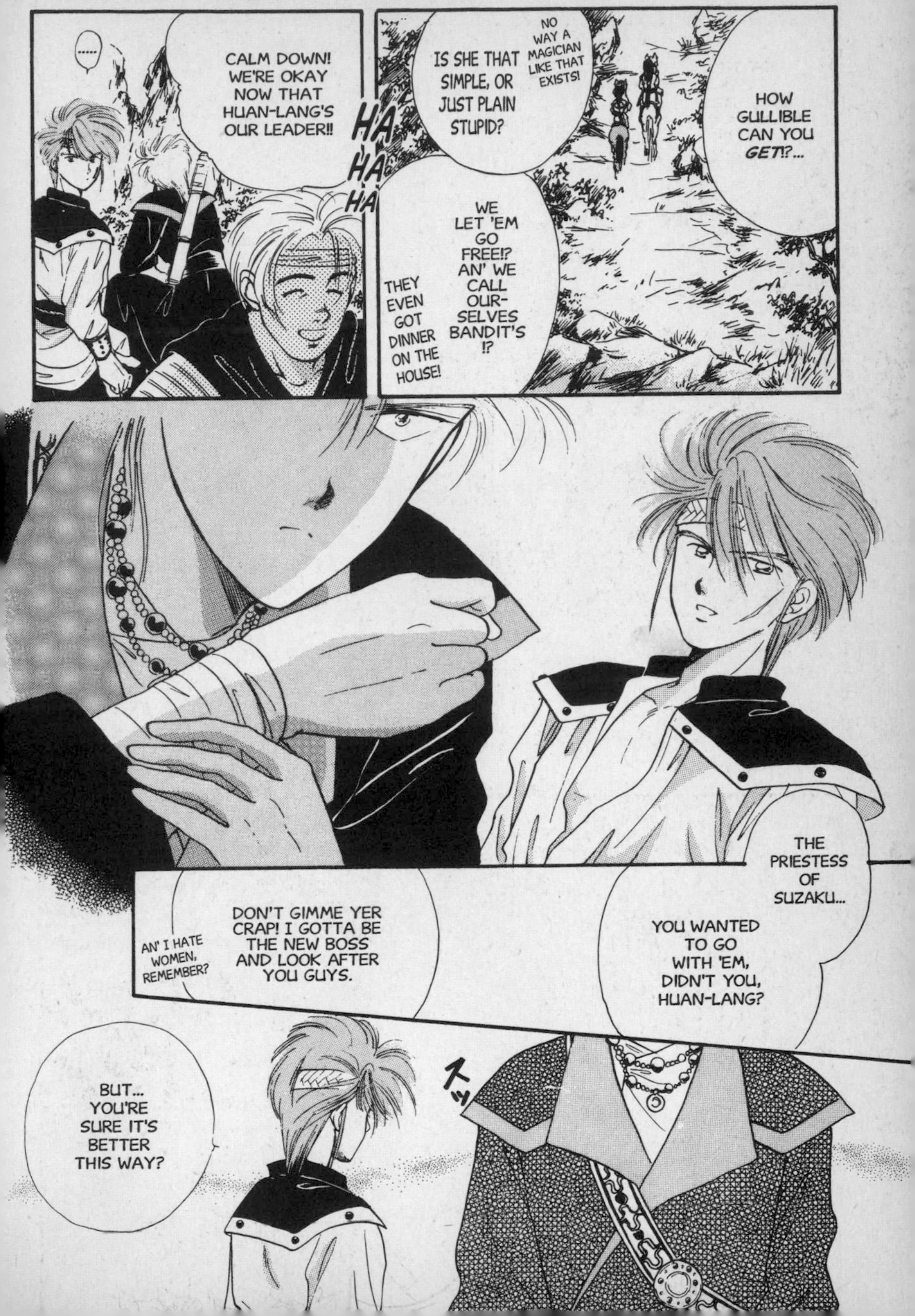
HOW GULLIBLE CAN YOU GET!?...
NO WAY A MAGICIAN LIKE THAT EXISTS!
IS SHE THAT SIMPLE, OR JUST PLAIN STUPID?
WE LET 'EM GO FREE!? AN' WE CALL OURSELVES BANDIT'S !?
THEY EVEN GOT DINNER ON THE HOUSE!
HA HA HA
CALM DOWN! WE'RE OKAY NOW THAT HUAN-LANG'S OUR LEADER!!
......
THE PRIESTESS OF SUZAKU...
YOU WANTED TO GO WITH 'EM, DIDN'T YOU, HUAN-LANG?
DON'T GIMME YER CRAP! I GOTTA BE THE NEW BOSS AND LOOK AFTER YOU GUYS.
AN' I HATE WOMEN, REMEMBER?
スッ
BUT... YOU'RE SURE IT'S BETTER THIS WAY?

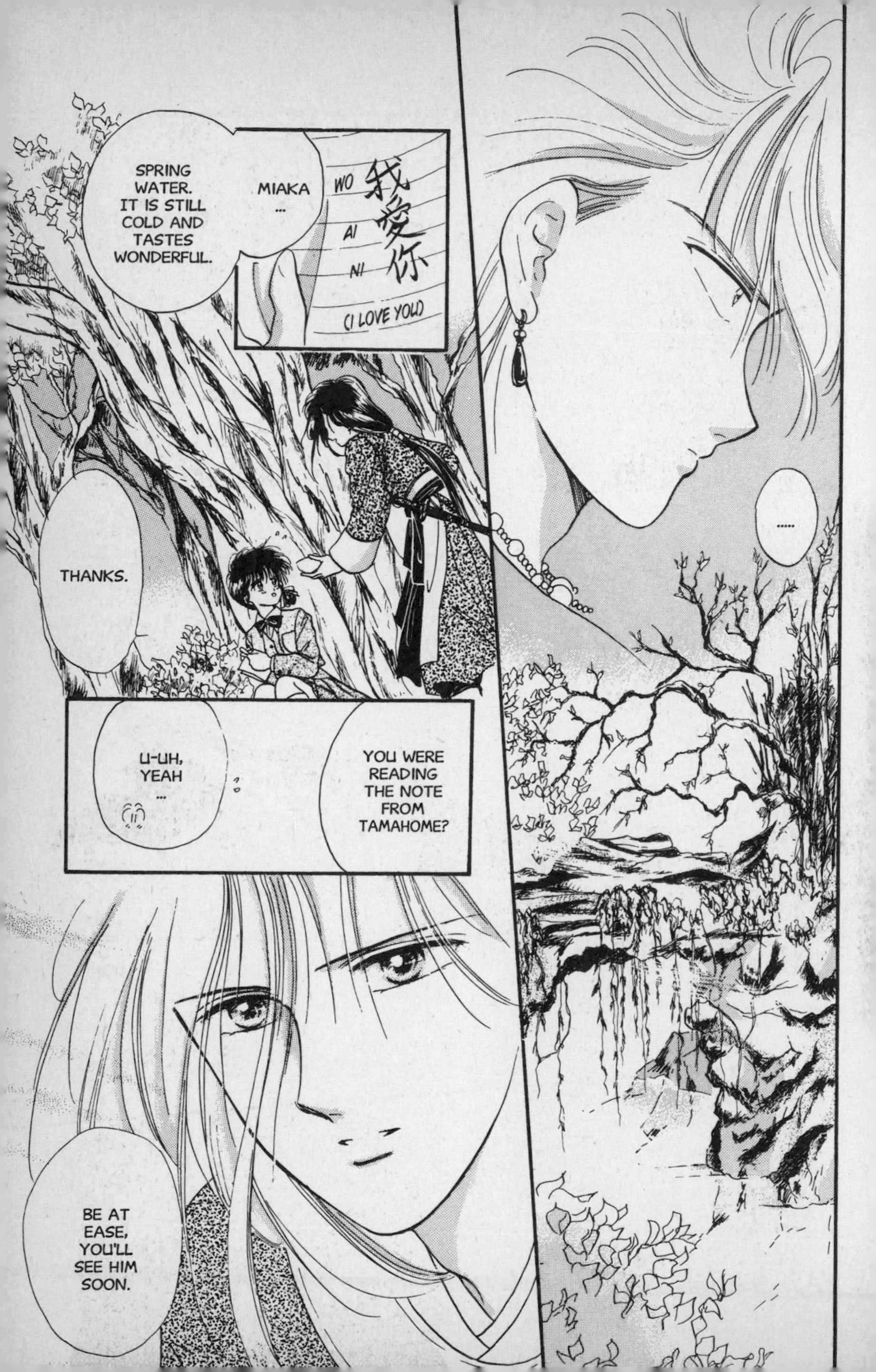
......
我愛你
WO AI NI
(I LOVE YOU)
MIAKA ...
SPRING WATER. IT IS STILL COLD AND TASTES WONDERFUL.
THANKS.
YOU WERE READING THE NOTE FROM TAMAHOME?
U-UH, YEAH ...
BE AT EASE, YOU'LL SEE HIM SOON.

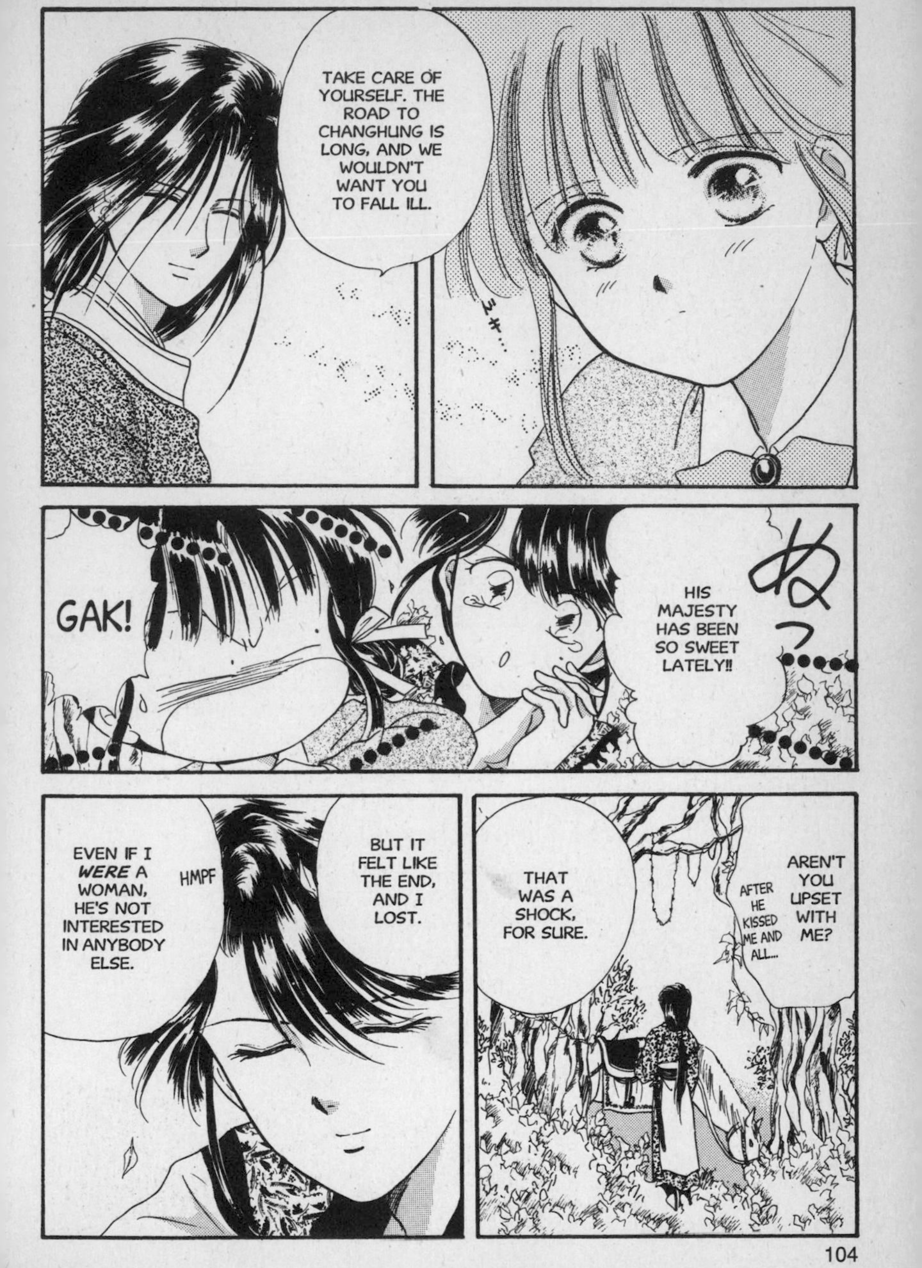
TAKE CARE OF YOURSELF. THE ROAD TO CHANGHUNG IS LONG, AND WE WOULDN'T WANT YOU TO FALL ILL.
ぬっ
HIS MAJESTY HAS BEEN SO SWEET LATELY!!
GAK!
AREN'T YOU UPSET WITH ME?
AFTER HE KISSED ME AND ALL...
THAT WAS A SHOCK, FOR SURE.
BUT IT FELT LIKE THE END, AND I LOST.
HMPF
EVEN IF I *WERE* A WOMAN, HE'S NOT INTERESTED IN ANYBODY ELSE.

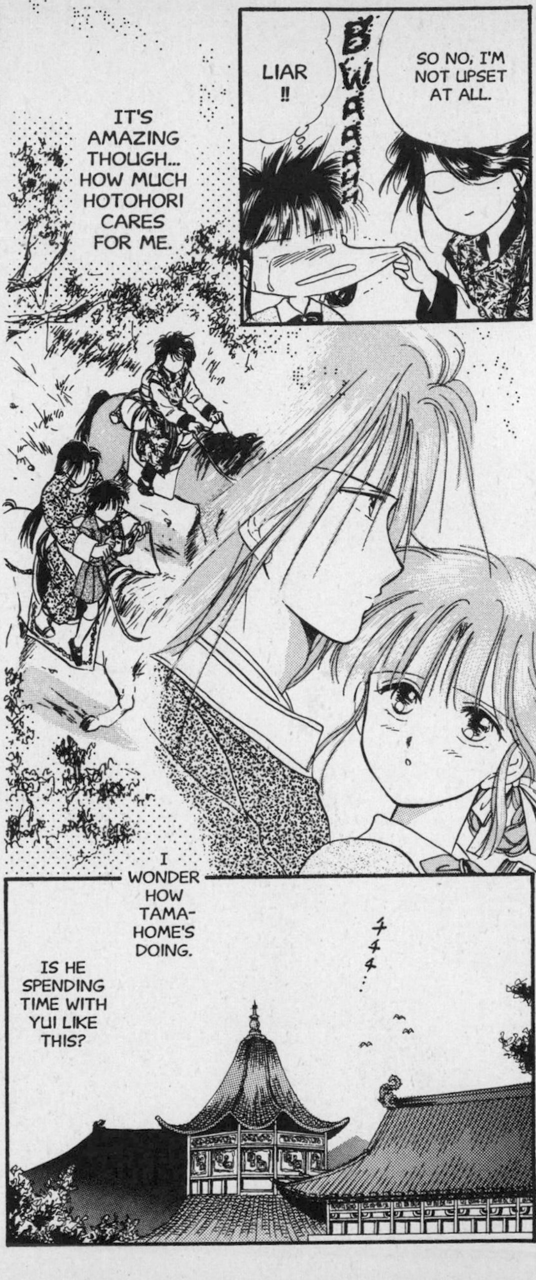
SO NO, I'M NOT UPSET AT ALL.
LIAR !!
BWAAAAH
IT'S AMAZING THOUGH... HOW MUCH HOTOHORI CARES FOR ME.
I WONDER HOW TAMA-HOME'S DOING.
IS HE SPENDING TIME WITH YUI LIKE THIS?

Bandit

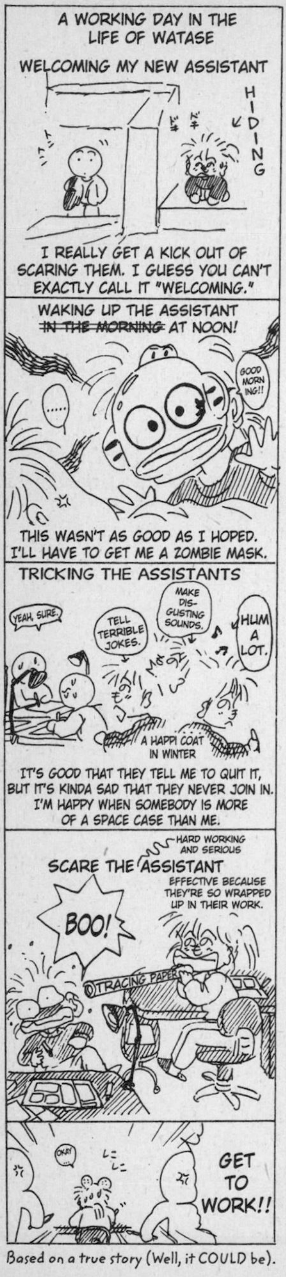
A WORKING DAY IN THE LIFE OF WATASE
WELCOMING MY NEW ASSISTANT
HIDING
I REALLY GET A KICK OUT OF SCARING THEM. I GUESS YOU CAN'T EXACTLY CALL IT "WELCOMING."
WAKING UP THE ASSISTANT ~~IN THE MORNING~~ AT NOON!
GOOD MORNING!!
......
THIS WASN'T AS GOOD AS I HOPED. I'LL HAVE TO GET ME A ZOMBIE MASK.
TRICKING THE ASSISTANTS
YEAH, SURE.
TELL TERRIBLE JOKES.
MAKE DISGUSTING SOUNDS.
HUM A LOT.
A HAPPI COAT IN WINTER
IT'S GOOD THAT THEY TELL ME TO QUIT IT, BUT IT'S KINDA SAD THAT THEY NEVER JOIN IN. I'M HAPPY WHEN SOMEBODY IS MORE OF A SPACE CASE THAN ME.
SCARE THE ASSISTANT
HARD WORKING AND SERIOUS
EFFECTIVE BECAUSE THEY'RE SO WRAPPED UP IN THEIR WORK.
BOO!
TRACING PAPER
OKAY...
GET TO WORK!!

Based on a true story (Well, it COULD be).

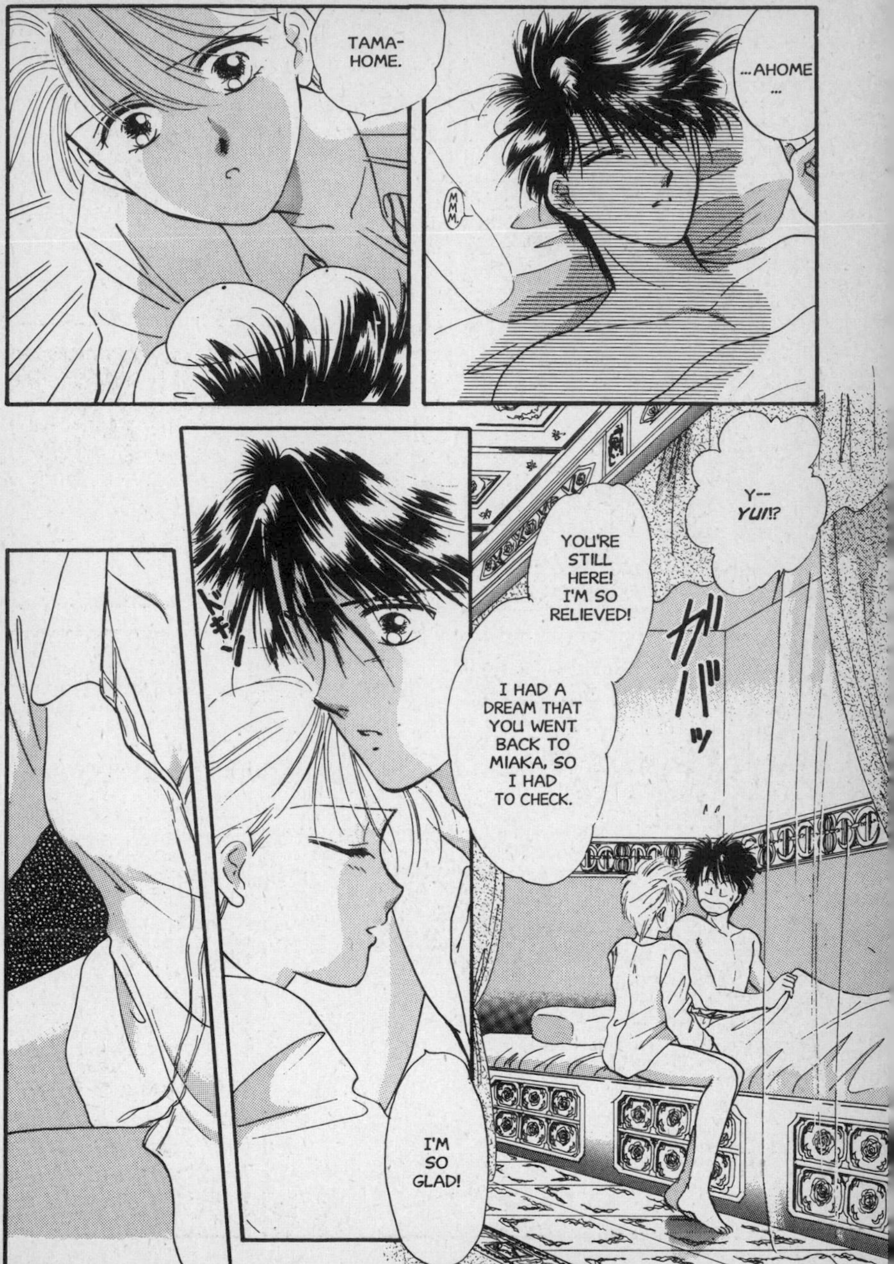
...AHOME ...
MMM
TAMA-HOME.
Y-- YUI!?
ガバッ
YOU'RE STILL HERE! I'M SO RELIEVED!
I HAD A DREAM THAT YOU WENT BACK TO MIAKA, SO I HAD TO CHECK.
I'M SO GLAD!

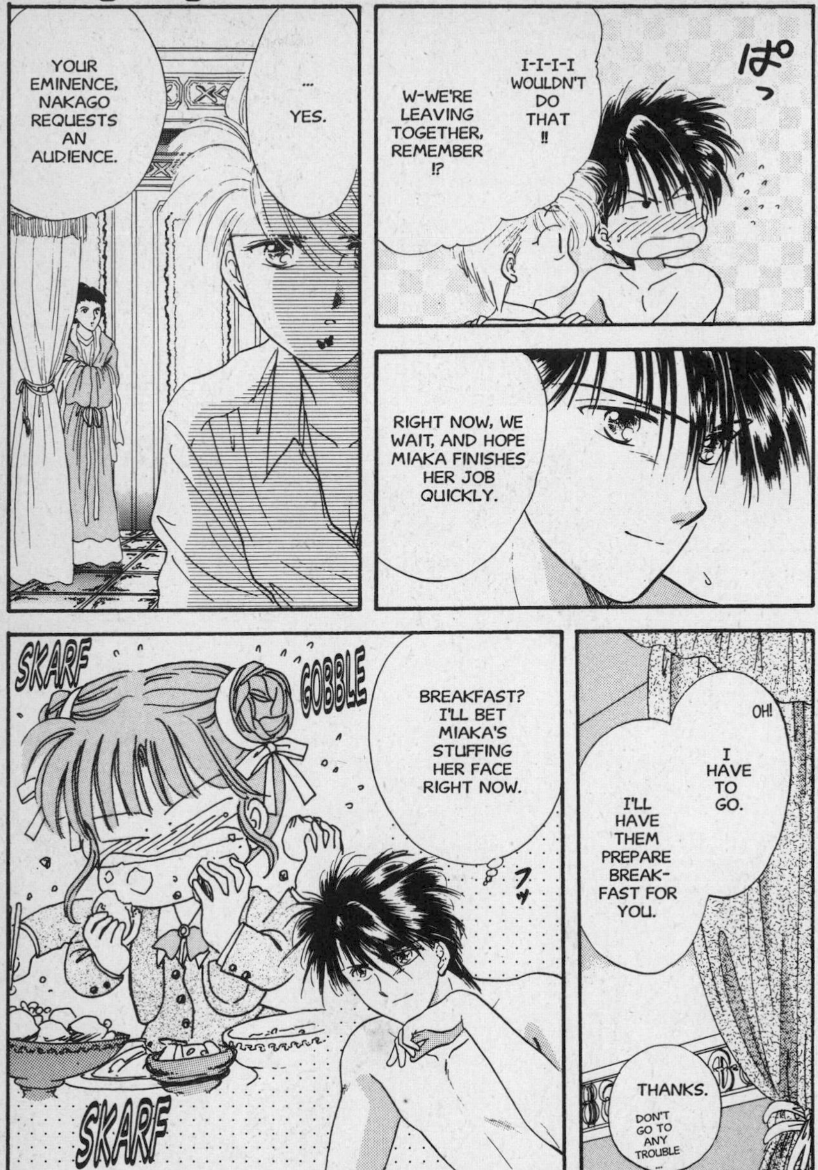
ぱっ
I-I-I-I WOULDN'T DO THAT!!
W-WE'RE LEAVING TOGETHER, REMEMBER!?
RIGHT NOW, WE WAIT, AND HOPE MIAKA FINISHES HER JOB QUICKLY.
... YES.
YOUR EMINENCE, NAKAGO REQUESTS AN AUDIENCE.
OH!
I HAVE TO GO.
I'LL HAVE THEM PREPARE BREAKFAST FOR YOU.
THANKS.
DON'T GO TO ANY TROUBLE ...
BREAKFAST? I'LL BET MIAKA'S STUFFING HER FACE RIGHT NOW.
フッ
GOBBLE
SKARF
SKARF

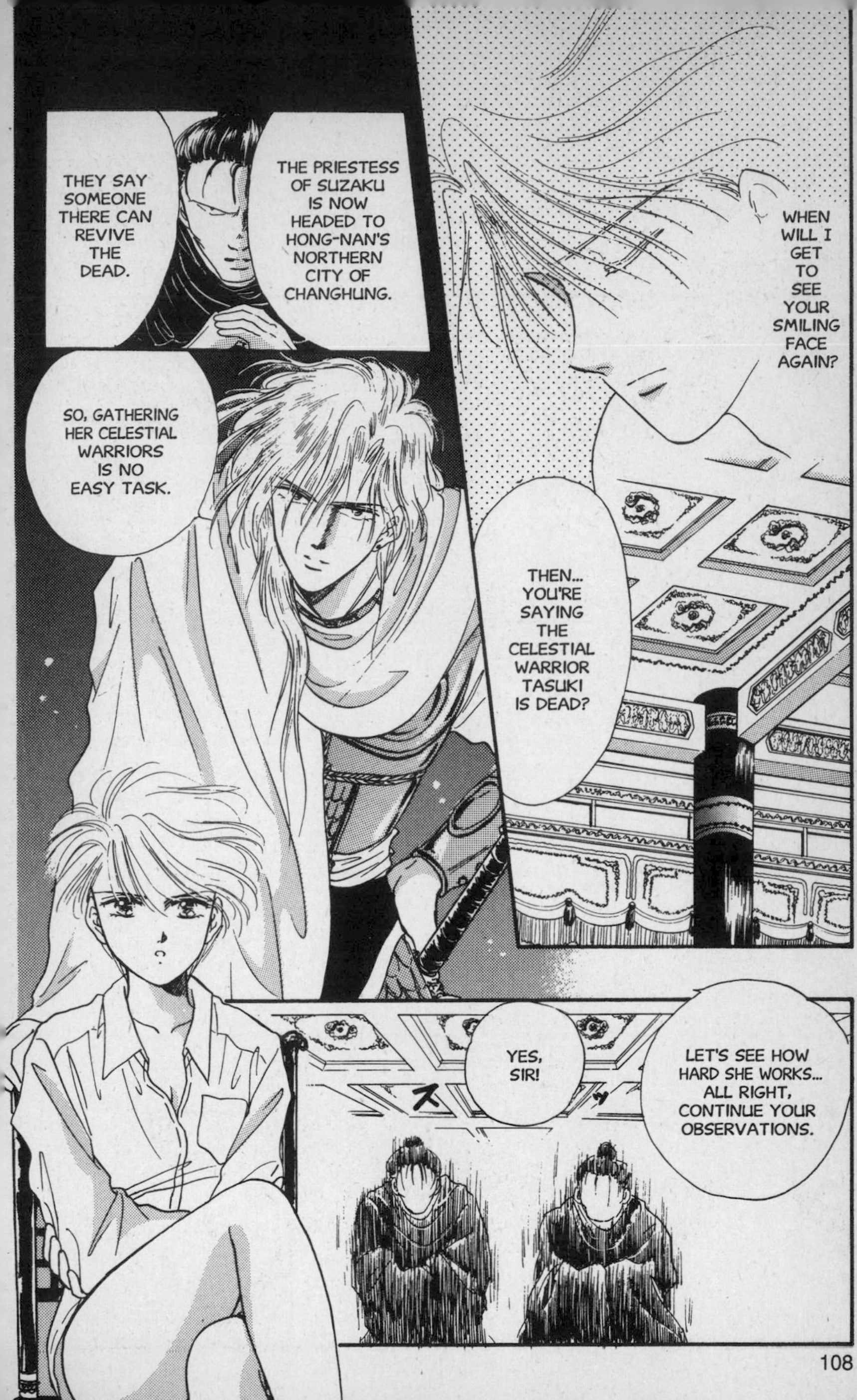
WHEN WILL I GET TO SEE YOUR SMILING FACE AGAIN?
THEN... YOU'RE SAYING THE CELESTIAL WARRIOR TASUKI IS DEAD?
THE PRIESTESS OF SUZAKU IS NOW HEADED TO HONG-NAN'S NORTHERN CITY OF CHANGHUNG.
THEY SAY SOMEONE THERE CAN REVIVE THE DEAD.
SO, GATHERING HER CELESTIAL WARRIORS IS NO EASY TASK.
LET'S SEE HOW HARD SHE WORKS... ALL RIGHT, CONTINUE YOUR OBSERVATIONS.
ッ
ス
YES, SIR!

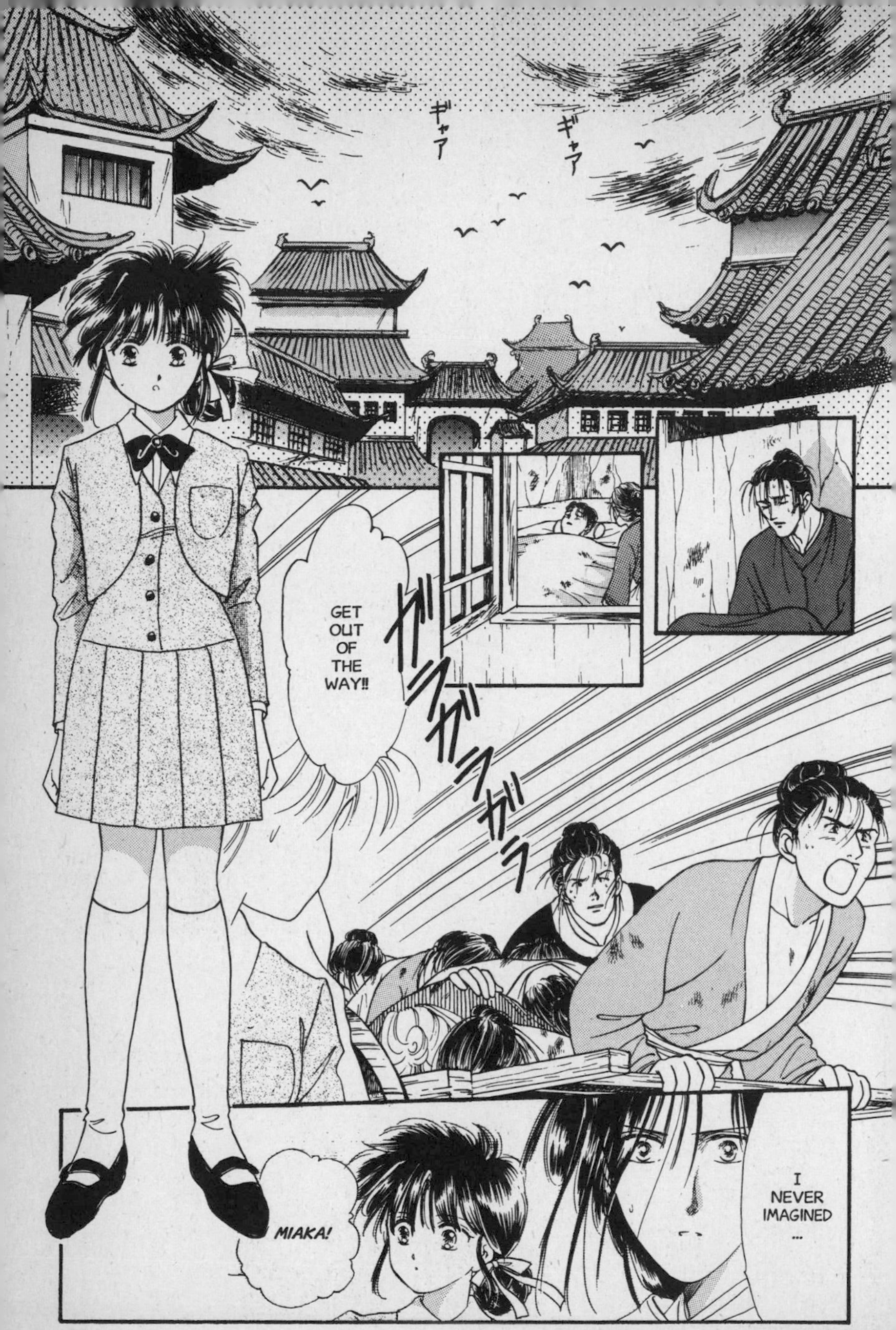

ギャア
ギャア
ガラガラガラ
GET OUT OF THE WAY!!
I NEVER IMAGINED ...
MIAKA!

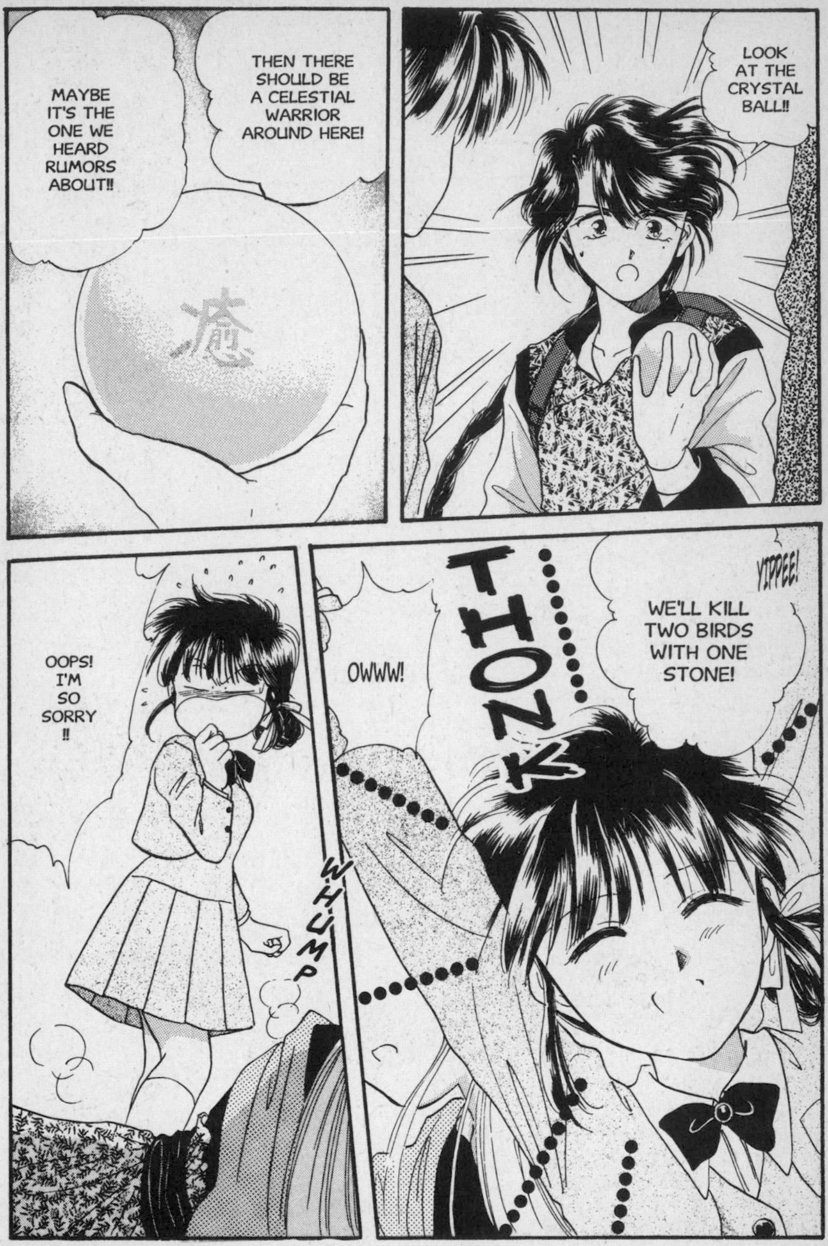
LOOK AT THE CRYSTAL BALL!!
THEN THERE SHOULD BE A CELESTIAL WARRIOR AROUND HERE!
MAYBE IT'S THE ONE WE HEARD RUMORS ABOUT!!
YIPPEE!
WE'LL KILL TWO BIRDS WITH ONE STONE!
THONK
OWWW!
WHUMP
OOPS! I'M SO SORRY !!

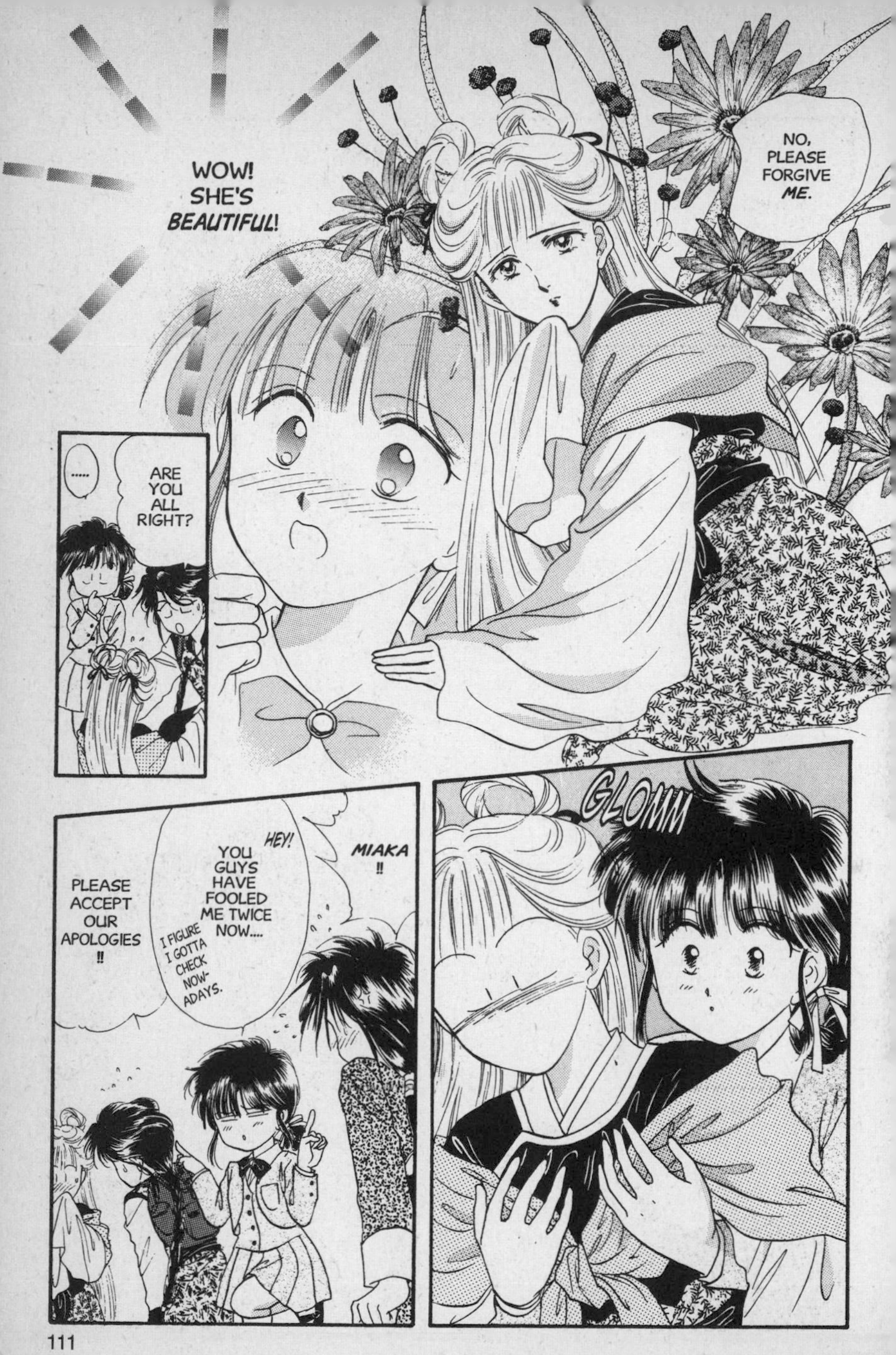
NO, PLEASE FORGIVE *ME*.
WOW! SHE'S *BEAUTIFUL*!
ARE YOU ALL RIGHT?
......
GLOMM
MIAKA !!
HEY! YOU GUYS HAVE FOOLED ME TWICE NOW....
I FIGURE I GOTTA CHECK NOW-ADAYS.
PLEASE ACCEPT OUR APOLOGIES !!

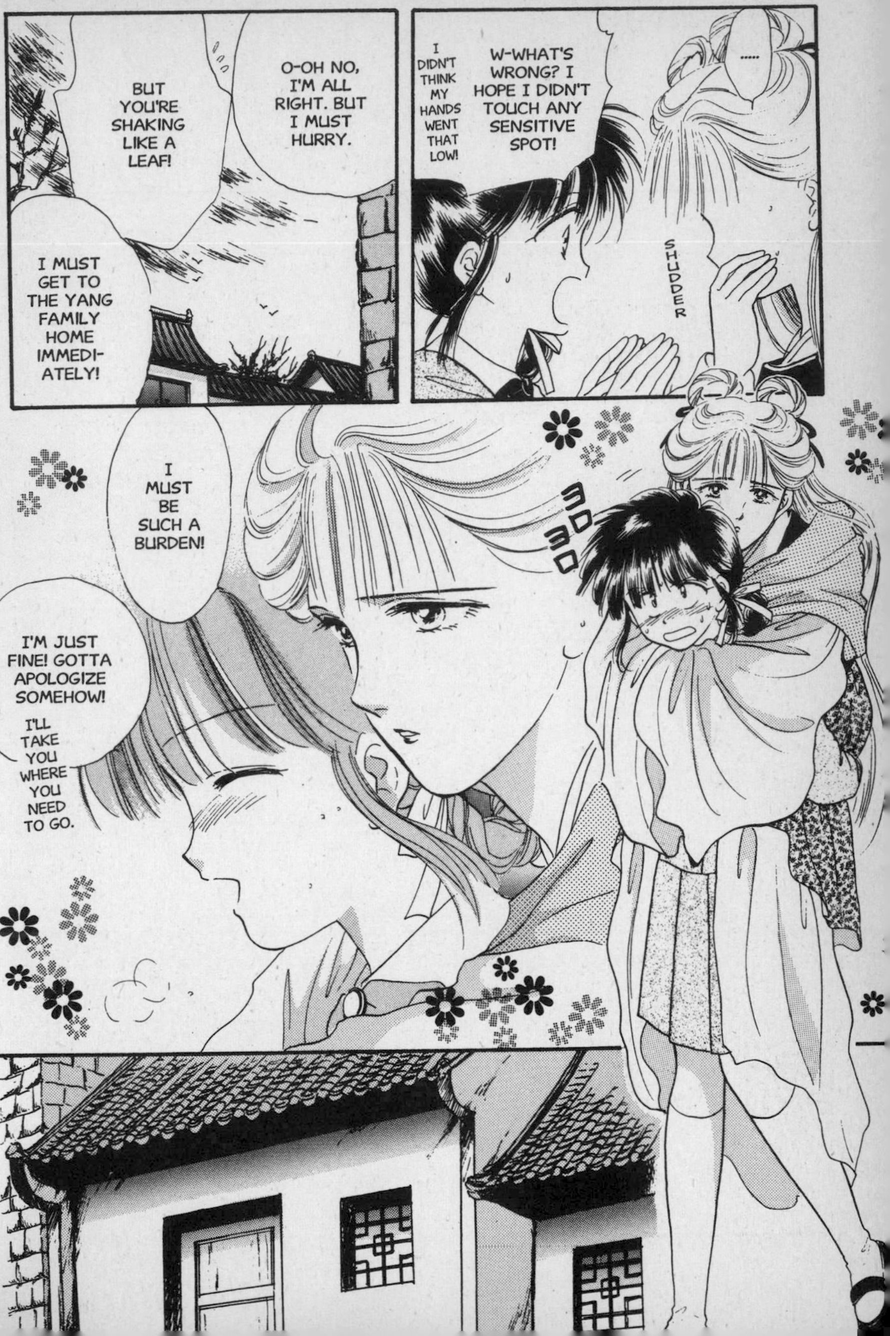
......
W-WHAT'S WRONG? I HOPE I DIDN'T TOUCH ANY SENSITIVE SPOT!
I DIDN'T THINK MY HANDS WENT THAT LOW!
SHUDDER
O-OH NO, I'M ALL RIGHT. BUT I MUST HURRY.
BUT YOU'RE SHAKING LIKE A LEAF!
I MUST GET TO THE YANG FAMILY HOME IMMEDIATELY!
ヨロヨロ
I MUST BE SUCH A BURDEN!
I'M JUST FINE! GOTTA APOLOGIZE SOMEHOW!
I'LL TAKE YOU WHERE YOU NEED TO GO.

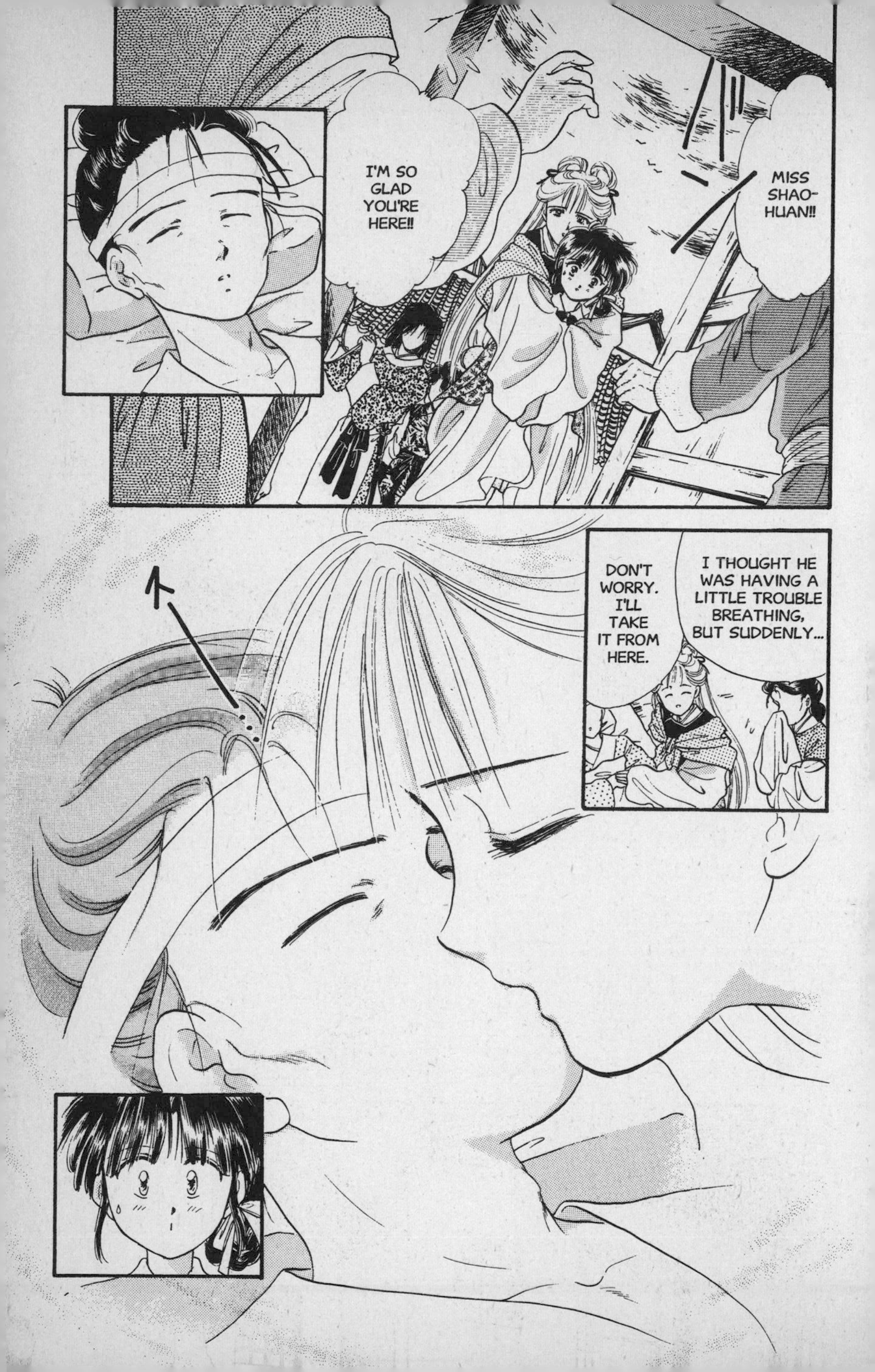
MISS SHAO-HUAN!!
I'M SO GLAD YOU'RE HERE!!
I THOUGHT HE WAS HAVING A LITTLE TROUBLE BREATHING, BUT SUDDENLY...
DON'T WORRY. I'LL TAKE IT FROM HERE.

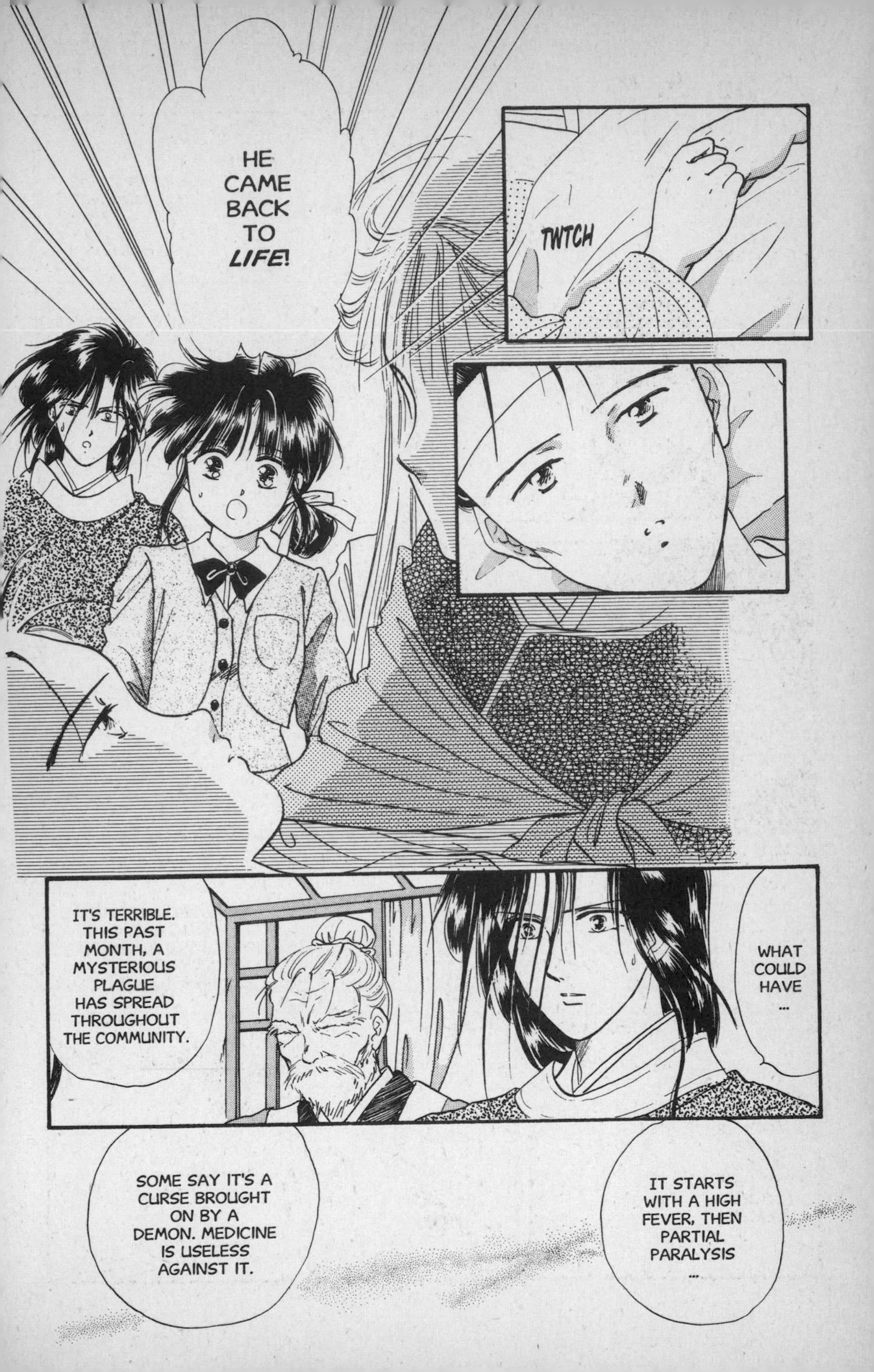
TWTCH
HE CAME BACK TO LIFE!
WHAT COULD HAVE ...
IT'S TERRIBLE. THIS PAST MONTH, A MYSTERIOUS PLAGUE HAS SPREAD THROUGHOUT THE COMMUNITY.
IT STARTS WITH A HIGH FEVER, THEN PARTIAL PARALYSIS ...
SOME SAY IT'S A CURSE BROUGHT ON BY A DEMON. MEDICINE IS USELESS AGAINST IT.

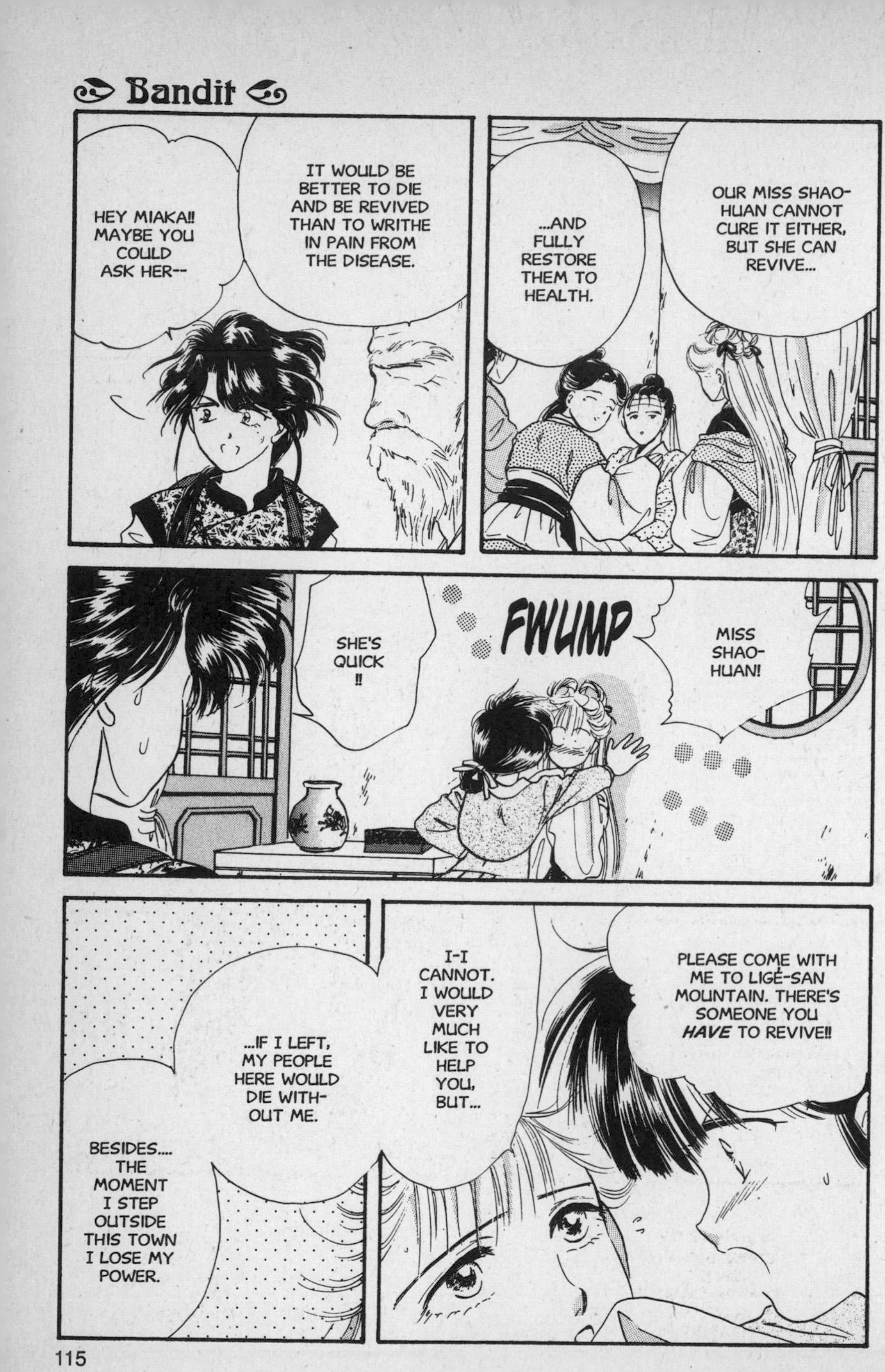
OUR MISS SHAO-HUAN CANNOT CURE IT EITHER, BUT SHE CAN REVIVE...
...AND FULLY RESTORE THEM TO HEALTH.
IT WOULD BE BETTER TO DIE AND BE REVIVED THAN TO WRITHE IN PAIN FROM THE DISEASE.
HEY MIAKA!! MAYBE YOU COULD ASK HER--
MISS SHAO-HUAN!
FWUMP
SHE'S QUICK !!
PLEASE COME WITH ME TO LIGÉ-SAN MOUNTAIN. THERE'S SOMEONE YOU ***HAVE*** TO REVIVE!!
I-I CANNOT. I WOULD VERY MUCH LIKE TO HELP YOU, BUT...
...IF I LEFT, MY PEOPLE HERE WOULD DIE WITH-OUT ME.
BESIDES.... THE MOMENT I STEP OUTSIDE THIS TOWN I LOSE MY POWER.

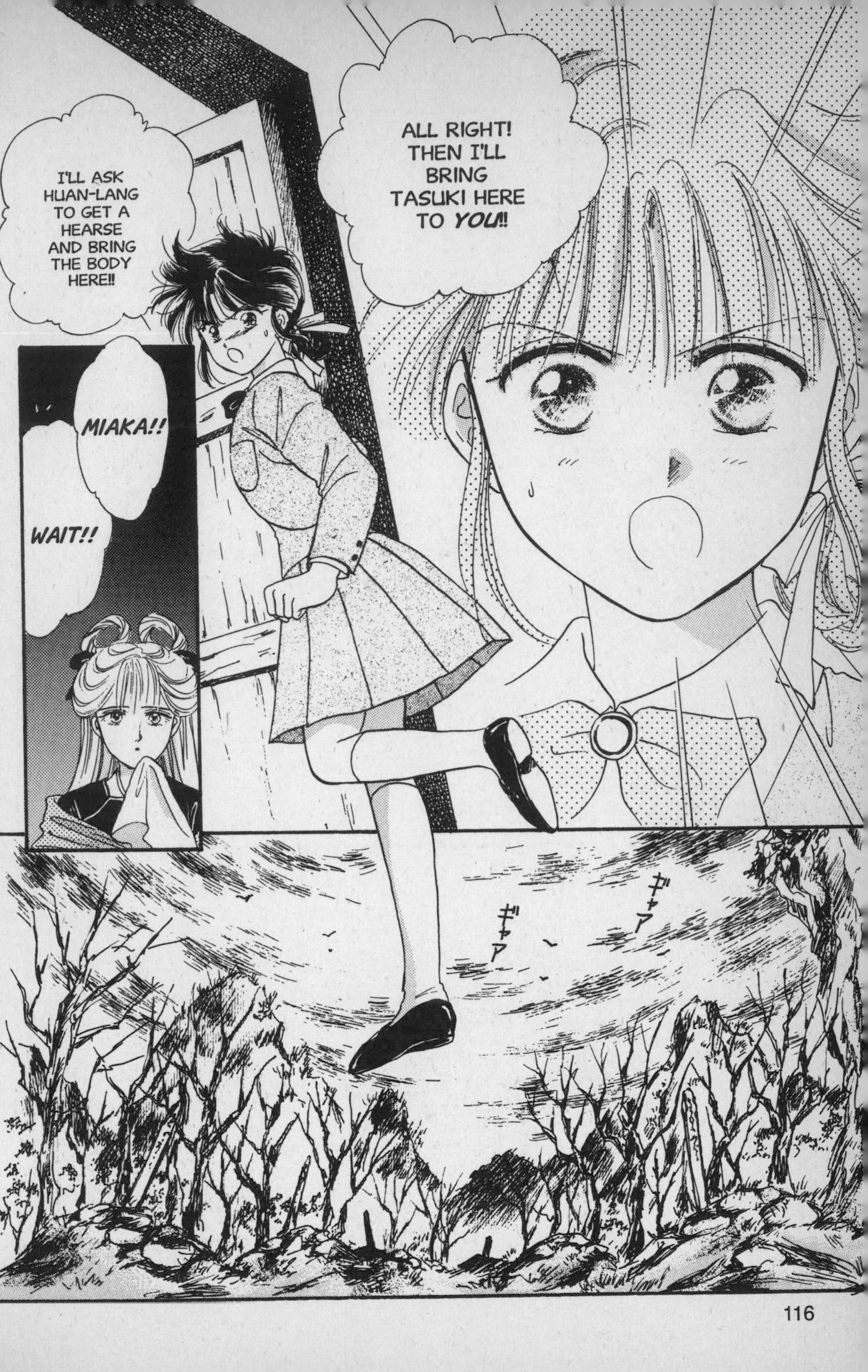
ALL RIGHT! THEN I'LL BRING TASUKI HERE TO *YOU*!!
I'LL ASK HUAN-LANG TO GET A HEARSE AND BRING THE BODY HERE!!
MIAKA!!
WAIT!!
ギャア
ギャア

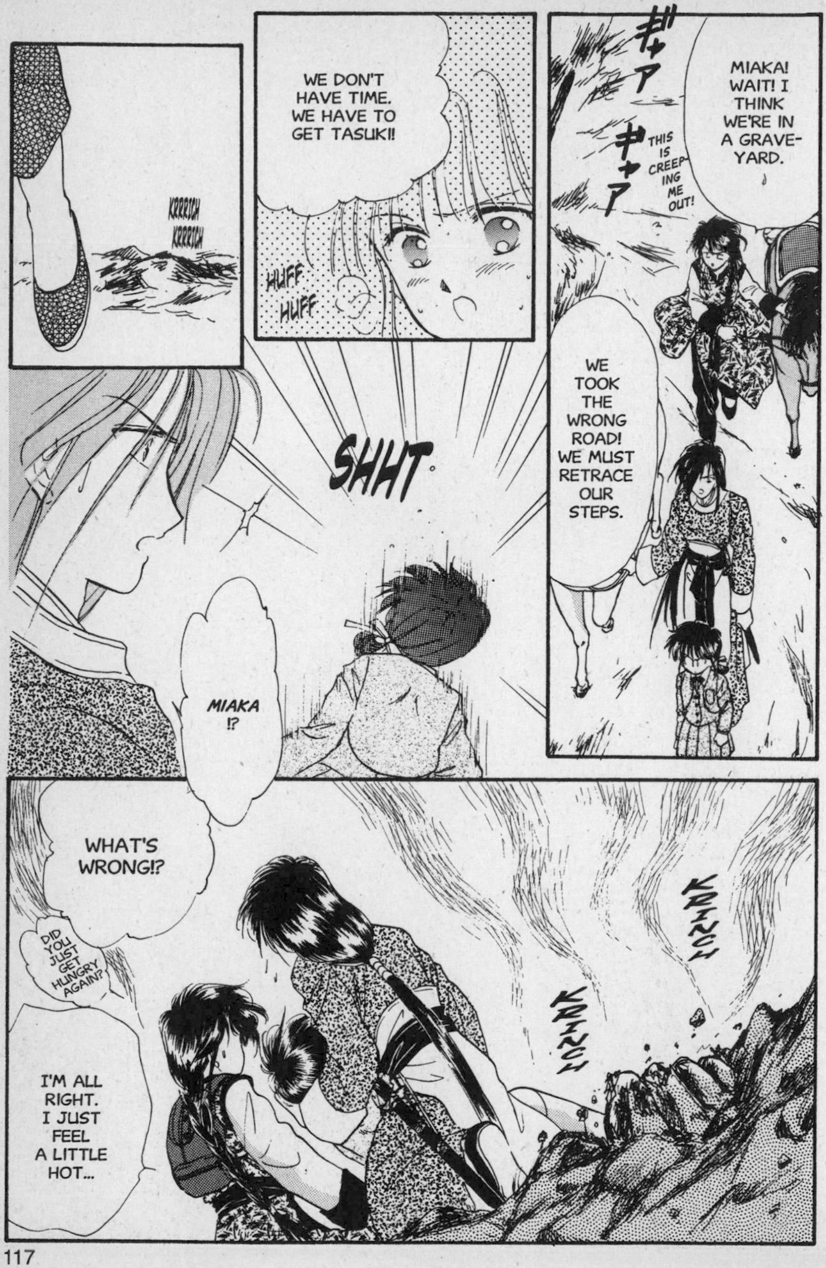
MIAKA! WAIT! I THINK WE'RE IN A GRAVEYARD.
ギャア ギャア
THIS IS CREEPING ME OUT!
WE TOOK THE WRONG ROAD! WE MUST RETRACE OUR STEPS.
WE DON'T HAVE TIME. WE HAVE TO GET TASUKI!!
HUFF HUFF
KRRRICH KRRRICH
SHHT
MIAKA!?
WHAT'S WRONG!?
DID YOU JUST GET HUNGRY AGAIN?
I'M ALL RIGHT. I JUST FEEL A LITTLE HOT...
KRINCH
KRINCH

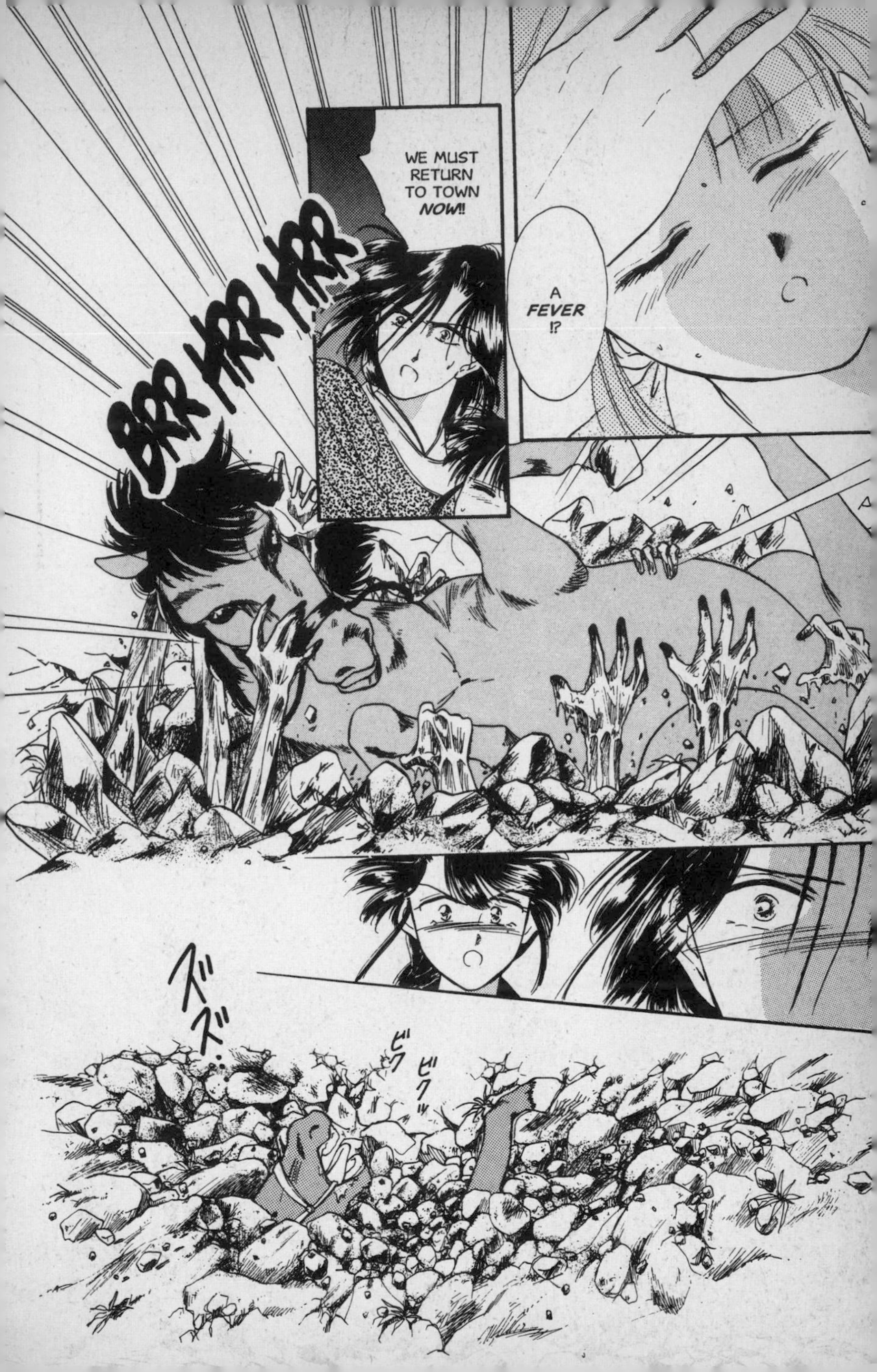
A FEVER !?
WE MUST RETURN TO TOWN NOW!!
BRR HRR HRR
ズズ
ビク ビクッ

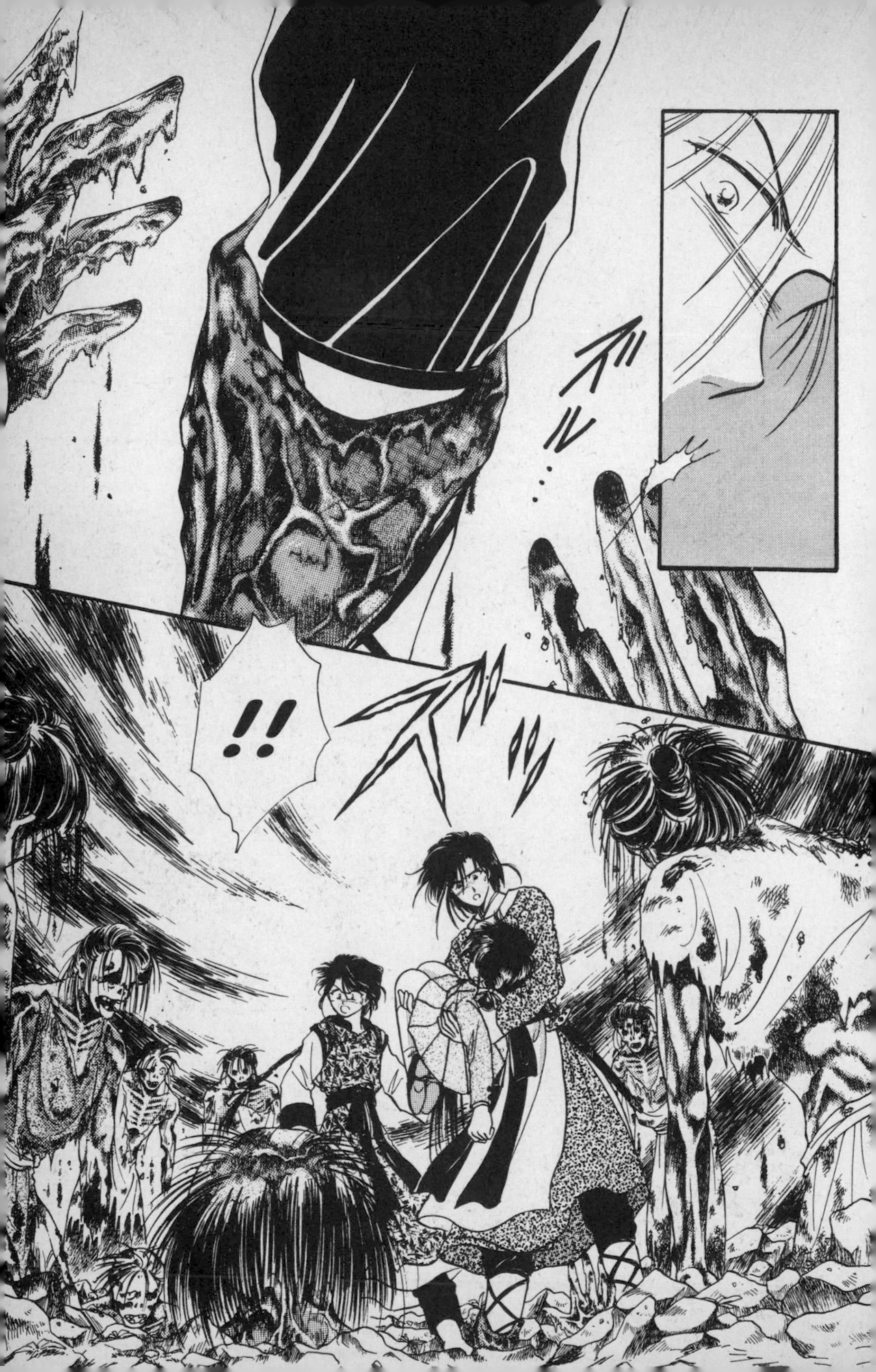
ズル…
!!
ズル

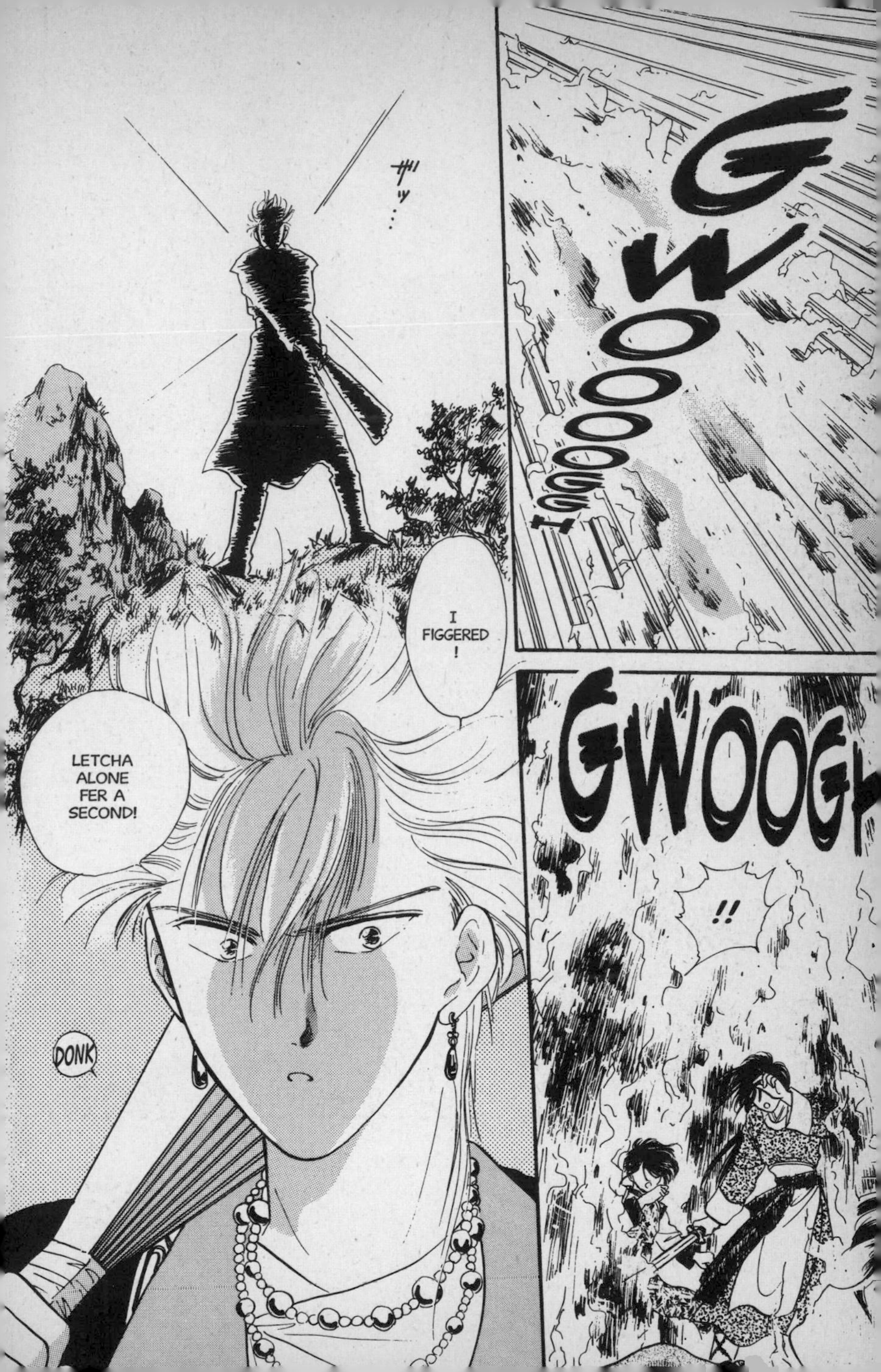
GWOOOOGG!
GWOOGH
!!
I FIGGERED!
LETCHA ALONE FER A SECOND!
DONK

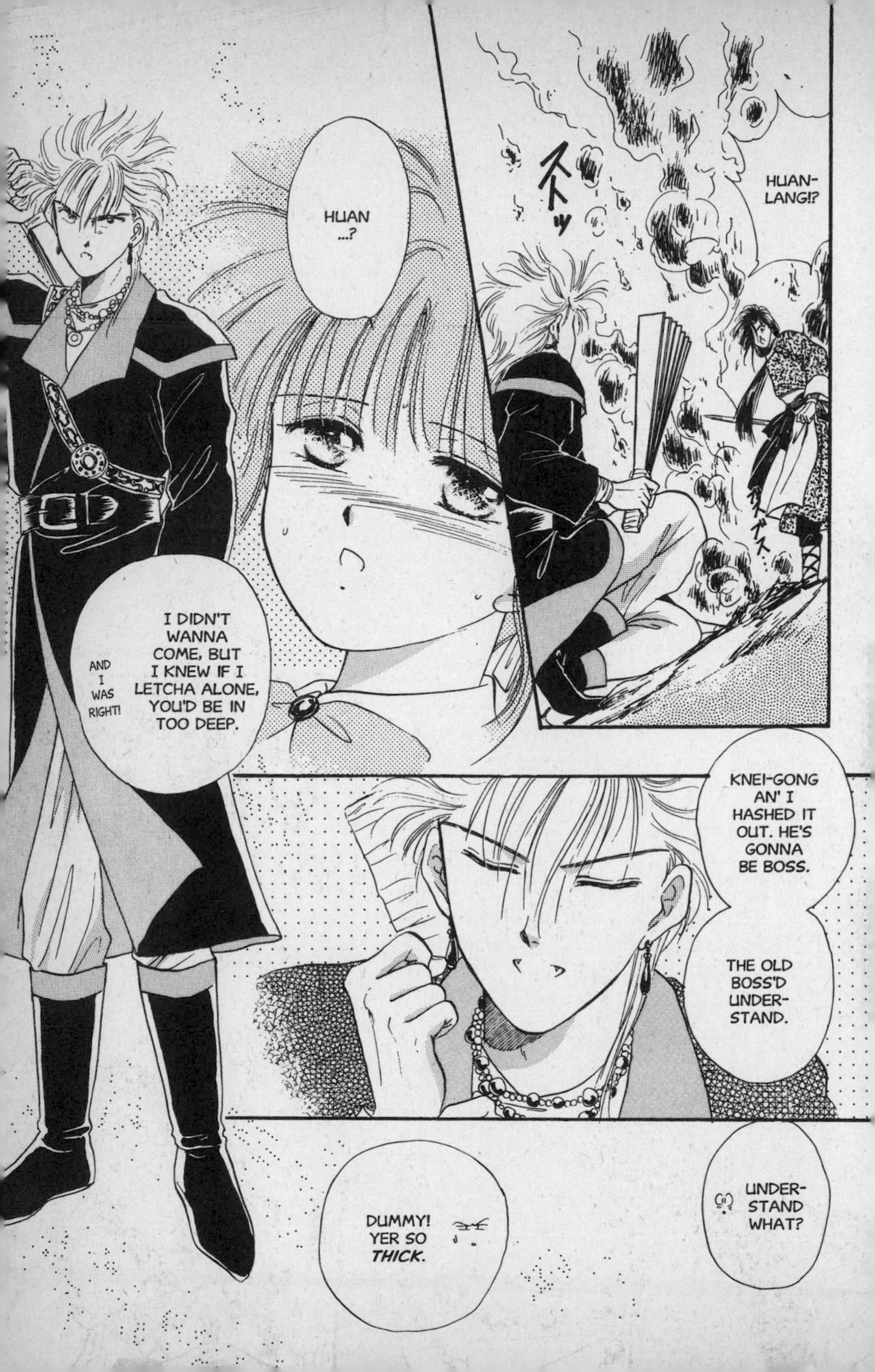

HUAN-LANG!?
ストッ
HUAN ...?
I DIDN'T WANNA COME, BUT I KNEW IF I LETCHA ALONE, YOU'D BE IN TOO DEEP.
AND I WAS RIGHT!
KNEI-GONG AN' I HASHED IT OUT. HE'S GONNA BE BOSS.
THE OLD BOSS'D UNDER-STAND.
UNDER-STAND WHAT?
DUMMY! YER SO *THICK*.

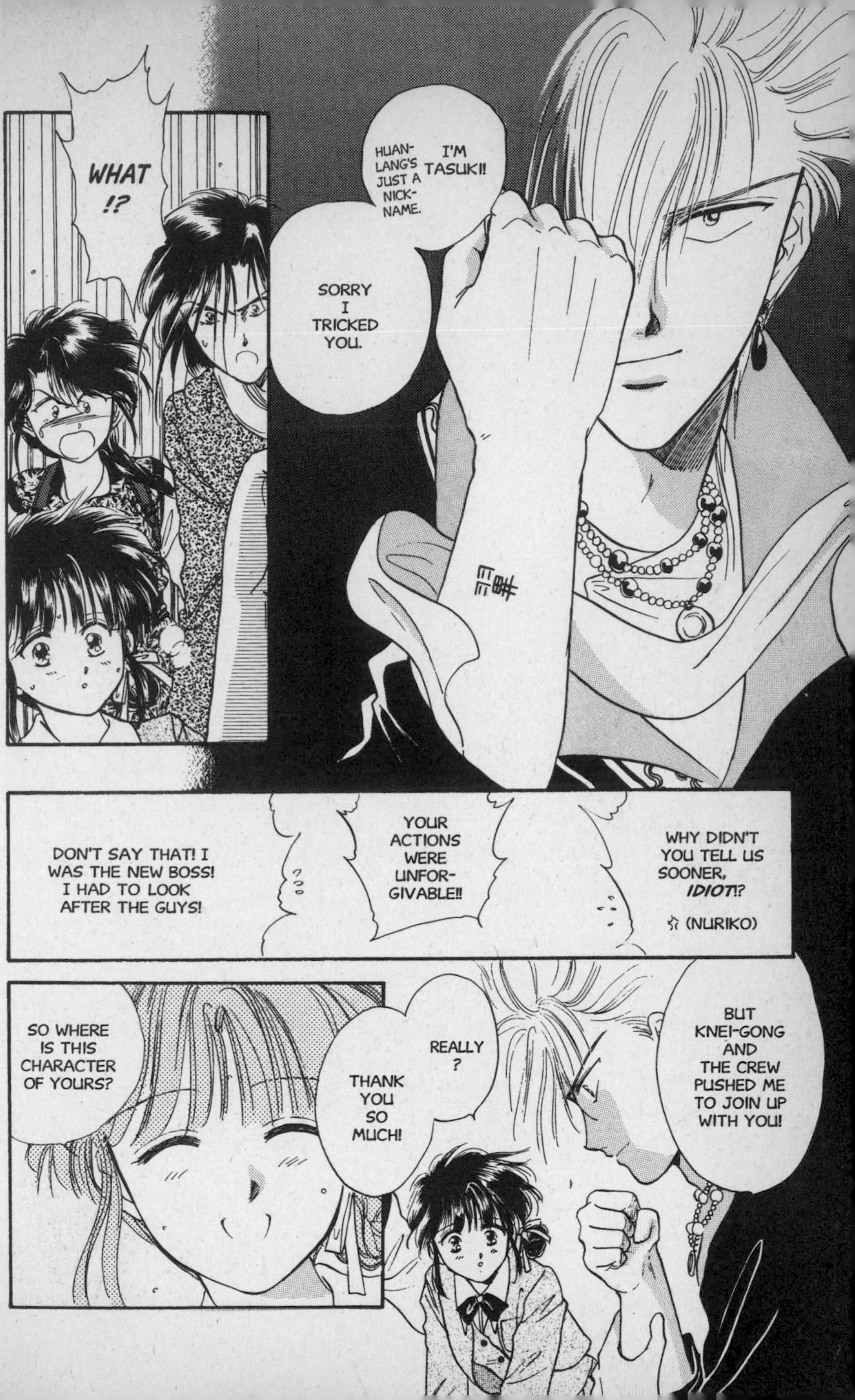
I'M TASUKI!!
HUAN-LANG'S JUST A NICK-NAME.
SORRY I TRICKED YOU.
WHAT!?
WHY DIDN'T YOU TELL US SOONER, *IDIOT*!?
☆ (NURIKO)
YOUR ACTIONS WERE UNFORGIVABLE!!
DON'T SAY THAT! I WAS THE NEW BOSS! I HAD TO LOOK AFTER THE GUYS!
BUT KNEI-GONG AND THE CREW PUSHED ME TO JOIN UP WITH YOU!
REALLY?
THANK YOU SO MUCH!
SO WHERE IS THIS CHARACTER OF YOURS?

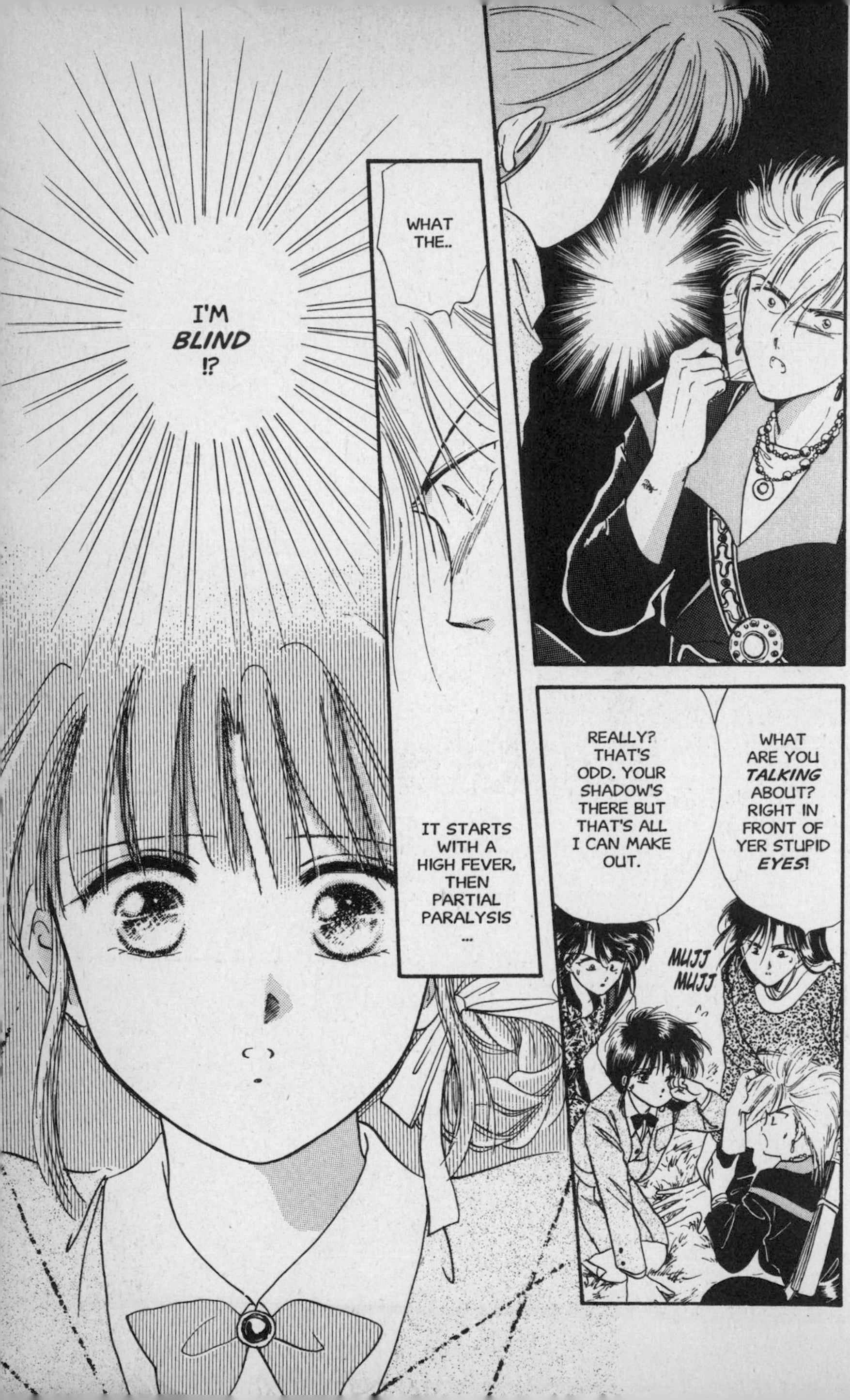
WHAT ARE YOU *TALKING* ABOUT? RIGHT IN FRONT OF YER STUPID *EYES*!
REALLY? THAT'S ODD. YOUR SHADOW'S THERE BUT THAT'S ALL I CAN MAKE OUT.
MUJJ MUJJ
WHAT THE..
IT STARTS WITH A HIGH FEVER, THEN PARTIAL PARALYSIS ...
I'M *BLIND* !?

TASUKI

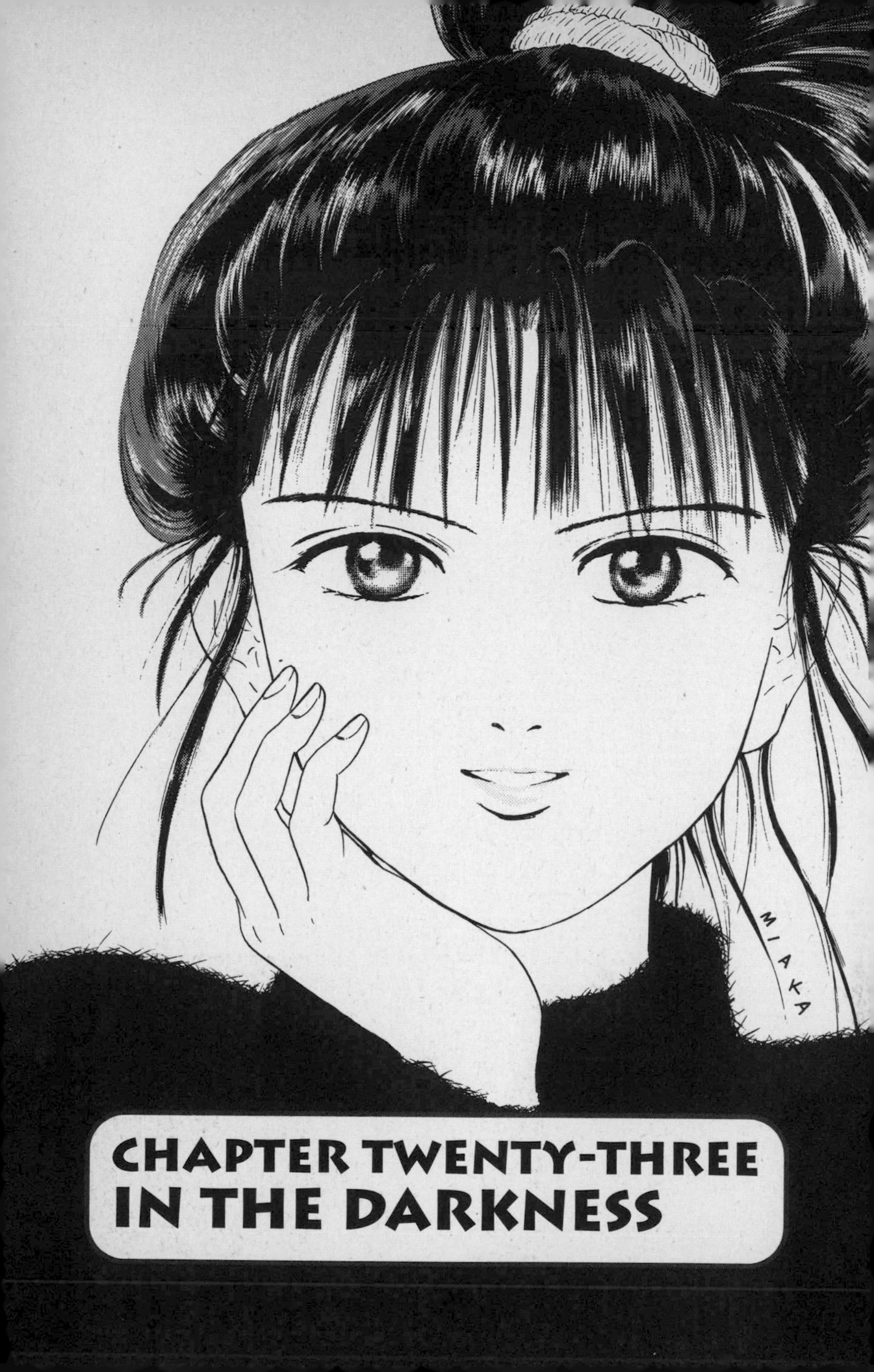
MIAKA

CHAPTER TWENTY-THREE
IN THE DARKNESS

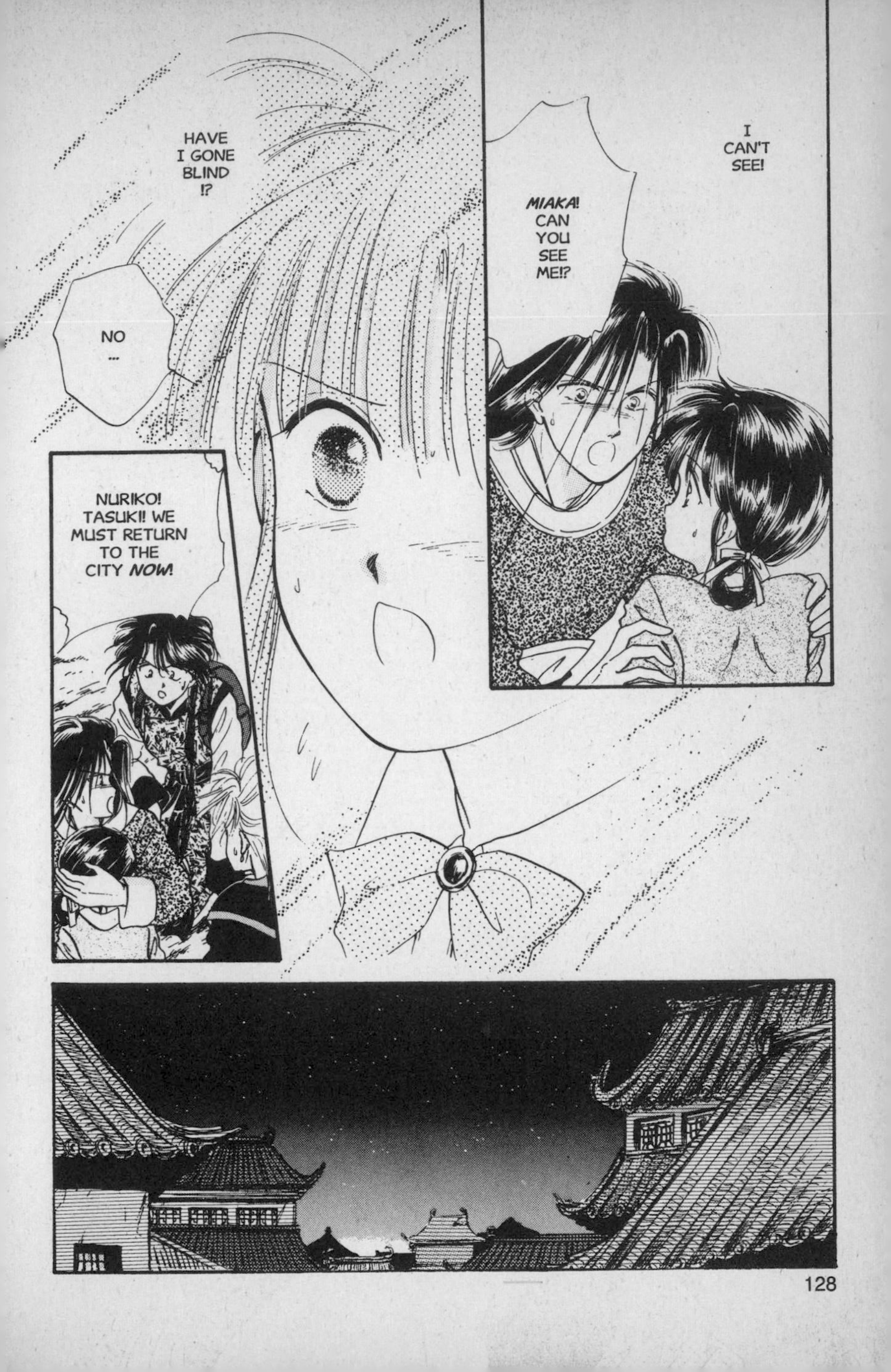
I CAN'T SEE!
MIAKA! CAN YOU SEE ME!?
HAVE I GONE BLIND !?
NO ...
NURIKO! TASUKI! WE MUST RETURN TO THE CITY *NOW*!

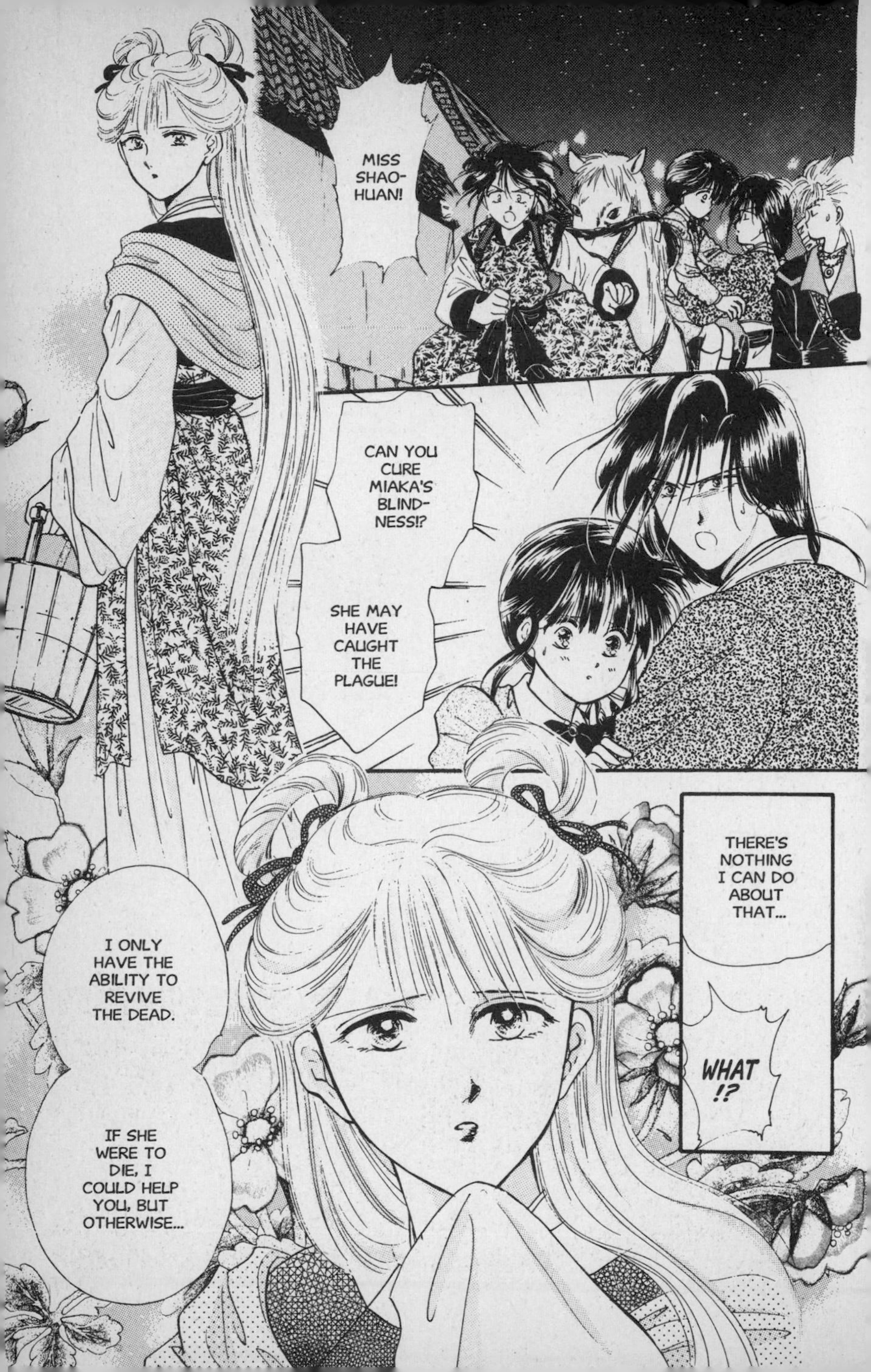
MISS SHAO-HUAN!
CAN YOU CURE MIAKA'S BLINDNESS!?
SHE MAY HAVE CAUGHT THE PLAGUE!
THERE'S NOTHING I CAN DO ABOUT THAT...
WHAT!?
I ONLY HAVE THE ABILITY TO REVIVE THE DEAD.
IF SHE WERE TO DIE, I COULD HELP YOU, BUT OTHERWISE...

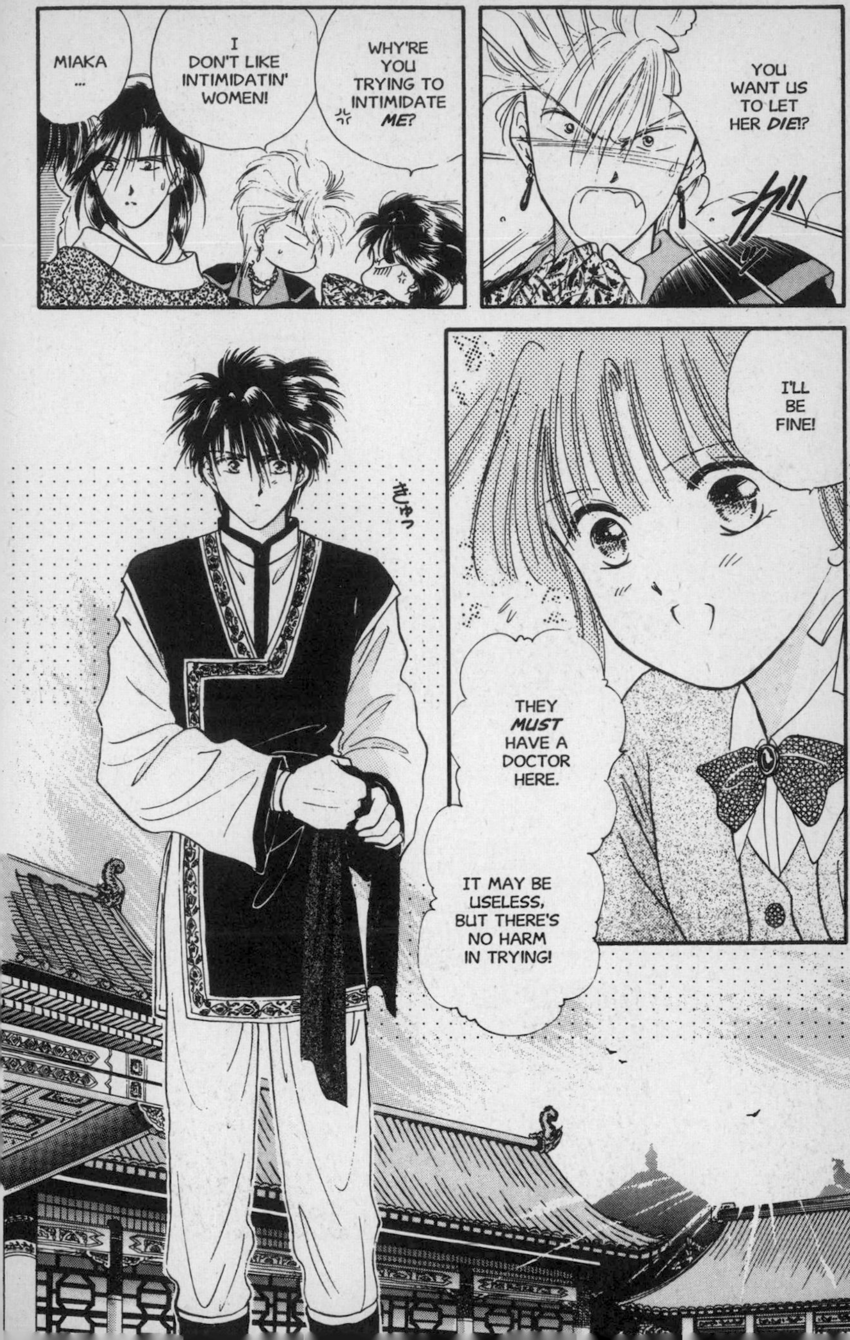
YOU WANT US TO LET HER *DIE*!?
ガッ
WHY'RE YOU TRYING TO INTIMIDATE *ME*?
I DON'T LIKE INTIMIDATIN' WOMEN!
MIAKA ...
I'LL BE FINE!
THEY *MUST* HAVE A DOCTOR HERE.
IT MAY BE USELESS, BUT THERE'S NO HARM IN TRYING!
きゅっ

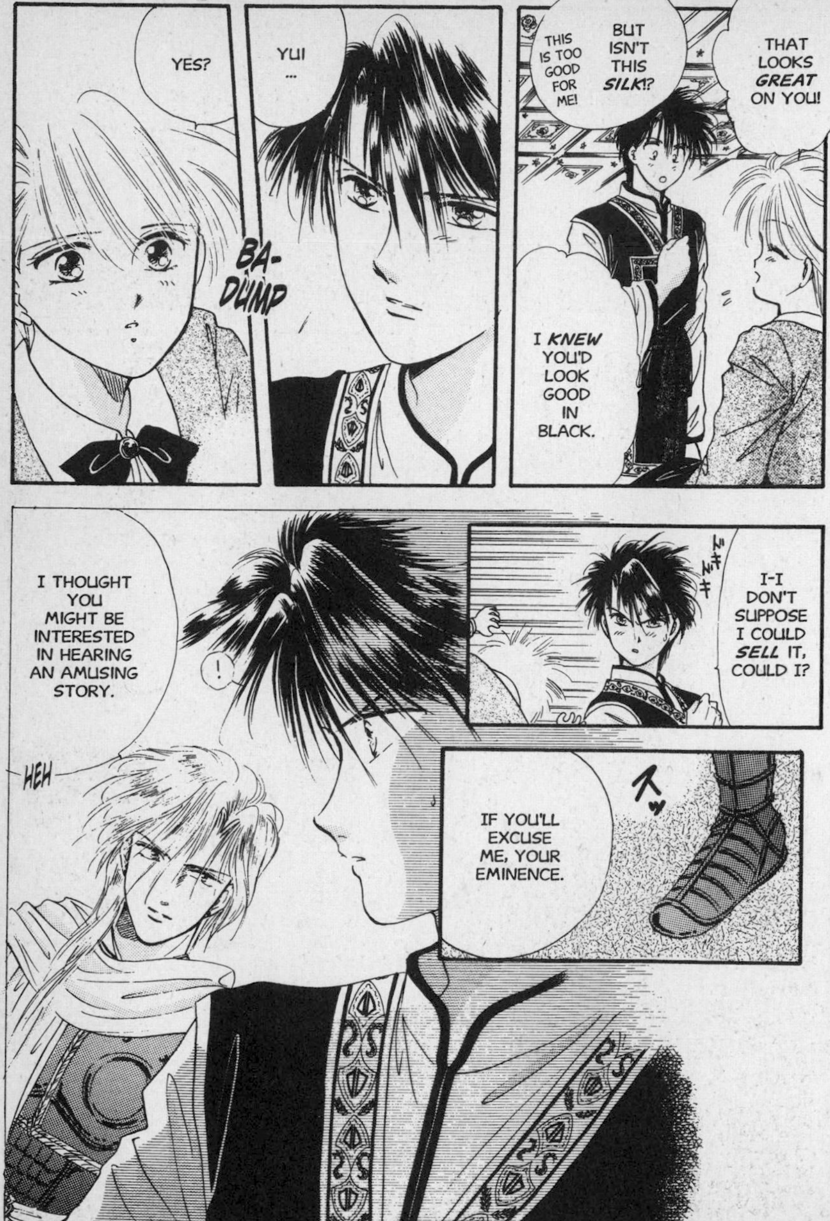
THAT LOOKS GREAT ON YOU!
BUT ISN'T THIS SILK!?
THIS IS TOO GOOD FOR ME!
I KNEW YOU'D LOOK GOOD IN BLACK.
YUI ...
BA-DUMP
YES?
I-I DON'T SUPPOSE I COULD SELL IT, COULD I?
スッ
IF YOU'LL EXCUSE ME, YOUR EMINENCE.
I THOUGHT YOU MIGHT BE INTERESTED IN HEARING AN AMUSING STORY.
!
HEH

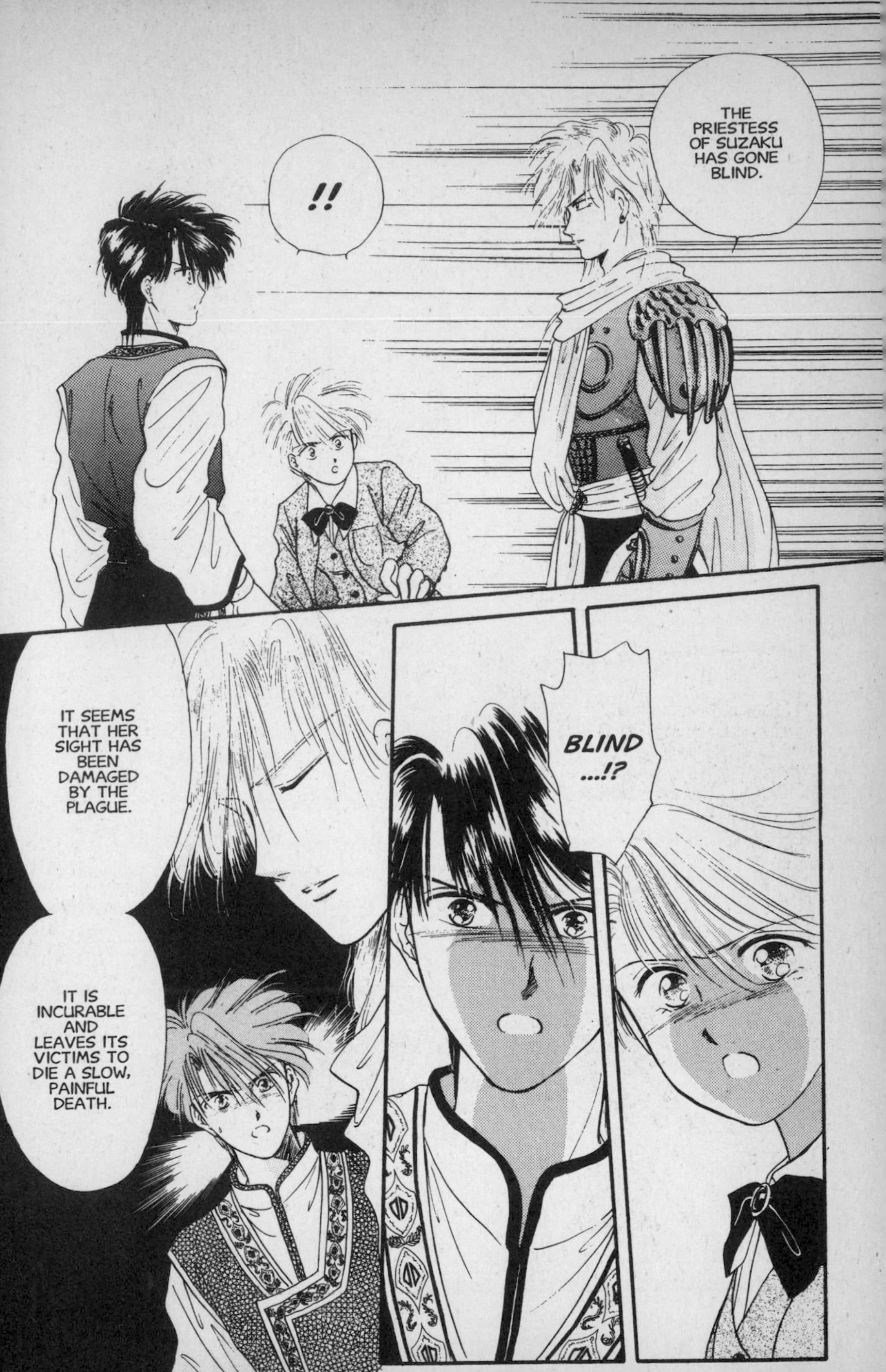
THE PRIESTESS OF SUZAKU HAS GONE BLIND.
!!
BLIND ...!?
IT SEEMS THAT HER SIGHT HAS BEEN DAMAGED BY THE PLAGUE.
IT IS INCURABLE AND LEAVES ITS VICTIMS TO DIE A SLOW, PAINFUL DEATH.

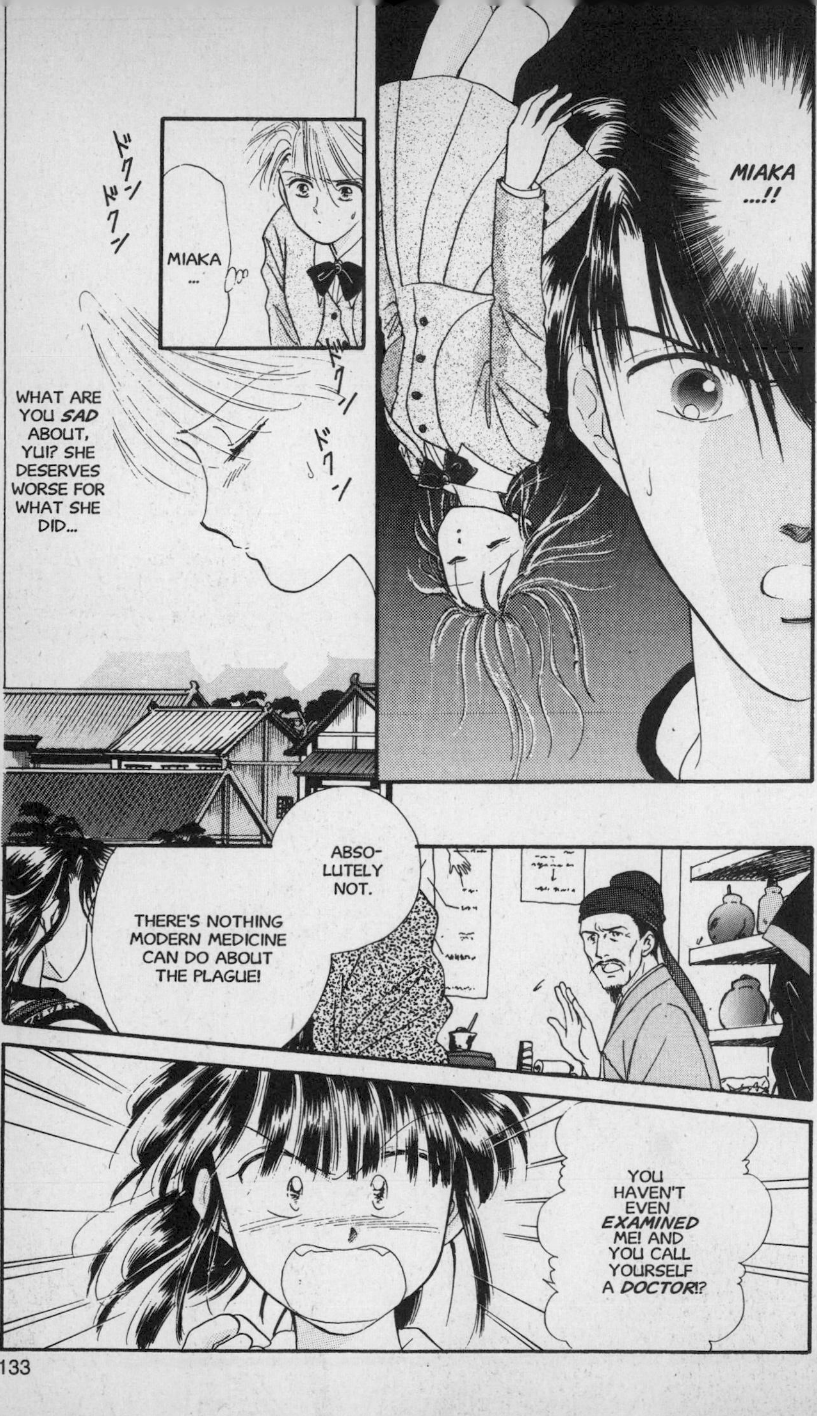
MIAKA ...!!
ドクン ドクン
MIAKA ...
ドクン ドクン
WHAT ARE YOU *SAD* ABOUT, YUI? SHE DESERVES WORSE FOR WHAT SHE DID...
ABSO-LUTELY NOT.
THERE'S NOTHING MODERN MEDICINE CAN DO ABOUT THE PLAGUE!
YOU HAVEN'T EVEN *EXAMINED* ME! AND YOU CALL YOURSELF A *DOCTOR*!?

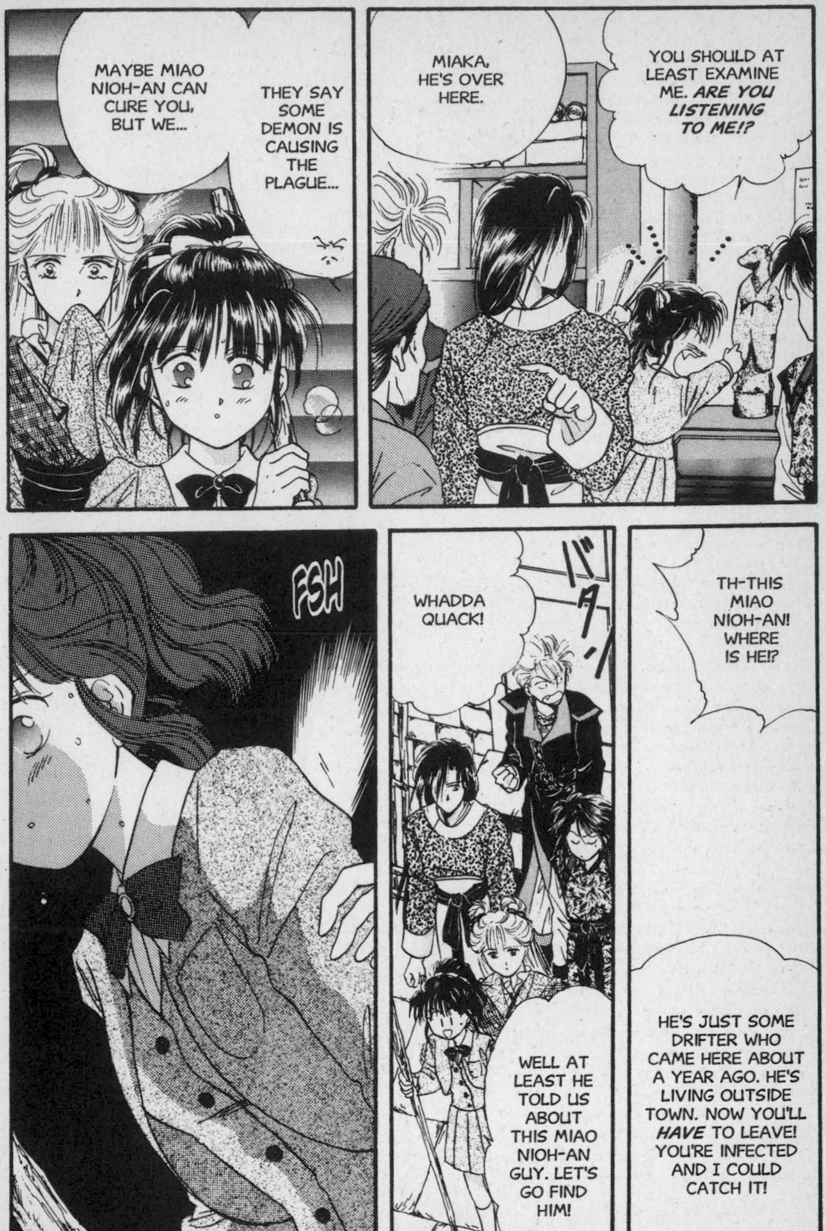
YOU SHOULD AT LEAST EXAMINE ME. ***ARE YOU LISTENING TO ME!?***
MIAKA, HE'S OVER HERE.
THEY SAY SOME DEMON IS CAUSING THE PLAGUE...
MAYBE MIAO NIOH-AN CAN CURE YOU, BUT WE...
TH-THIS MIAO NIOH-AN! WHERE IS HE!?
HE'S JUST SOME DRIFTER WHO CAME HERE ABOUT A YEAR AGO. HE'S LIVING OUTSIDE TOWN. NOW YOU'LL ***HAVE*** TO LEAVE! YOU'RE INFECTED AND I COULD CATCH IT!
バタン
WHADDA QUACK!
WELL AT LEAST HE TOLD US ABOUT THIS MIAO NIOH-AN GUY. LET'S GO FIND HIM!
FSH

Bandit

So... Twin Peaks is about to begin! Today is Saturday. Shogakukan's editorial offices should be closed. So why do I get a calls from my editor!? Comic editors work on the weekend. Let's applaud all their hard work. Now then, lately I haven't found any interesting TV shows so I've been watching Sekai Fushigi Hakken ("Strange Discoveries!") and The Wonder Zone, as well as Terebi Tokusōbu ("Special Investigation TV"). Beat Takeshi is the best! Bokutachi no Drama Series ("Our Drama Series") and Hōkago ("After School") are just remakes of the masterpiece Tenkōsei ("Transfer Student") so I haven't been watching them, but I have been watching Sono Toki, Heart wa Nusumareta ("That Was When My Heart Was Stolen"). I guess none of this will matter by the time this is printed, but a character in that series really reminds me of Yui. My assistant agrees! She wears a brown school uniform; she has her hair cut short; and she even slashed her wrists. But Yui is purer. There aren't that many girls who are that jaded at the age of 15 or 16. Well, maybe there are. It's supposed to be a high-school romantic comedy, but there's also this stuff about who slept with whom--it's a bit much. The youth of today! Don't they have anything more interesting to think about? Huh? Not very convincing coming from me? Well, I guess I depict my share of kissing scenes, corny men's dialogue and racy scenes... hold on I just realized I've dug myself into a hole. I tell you though, art work can be really hard.

Now then, how else do I spend my day? I read the Asahi News. I'm so sophisticated! Actually, I mostly read the funnies, but I really do read the articles. The mother in Tonari no Yamada-kun ("My Neighbors, the Yamadas") reminds me a lot of my mom. They both speak in a Kansai dialect, although my mom's thinner. Their conversations are just like the ones I have with my mom. My mom plays passive, while I'm always the aggressor. Why is it always that way? That's just the how folks in the Kansai area are, I guess. Daily conversations are a comedy routine. That's why I like Tasuki so much!

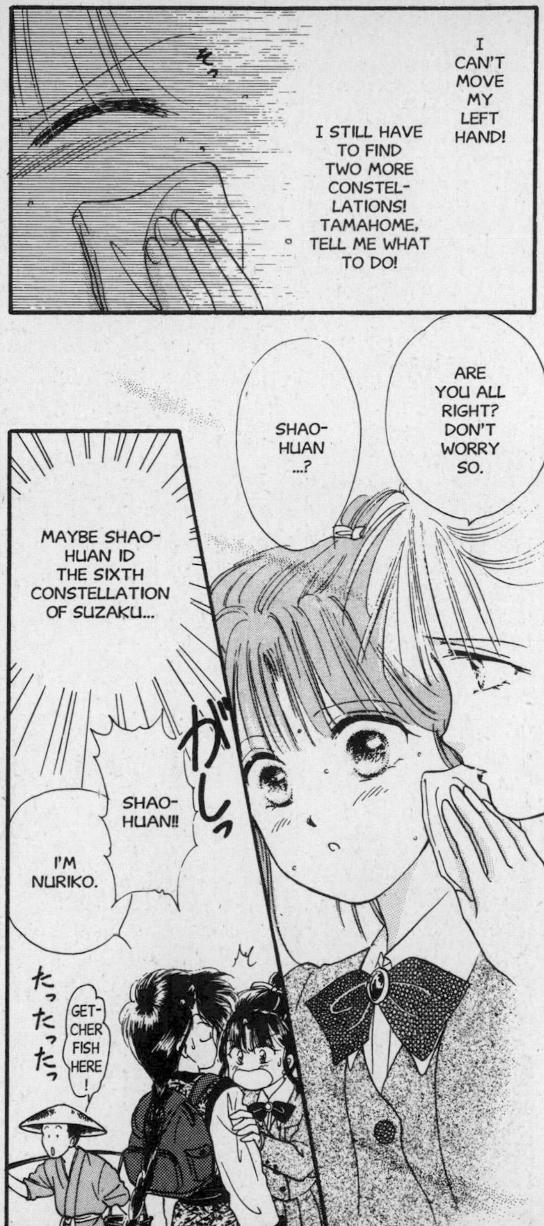
I CAN'T MOVE MY LEFT HAND!
I STILL HAVE TO FIND TWO MORE CONSTEL-LATIONS! TAMAHOME, TELL ME WHAT TO DO!
ARE YOU ALL RIGHT? DON'T WORRY SO.
SHAO-HUAN ...?
MAYBE SHAO-HUAN ID THE SIXTH CONSTELLATION OF SUZAKU...
がしっ
SHAO-HUAN!!
I'M NURIKO.
たったった
GET-CHER FISH HERE!

Isn't Miaka supposed to be sick!?

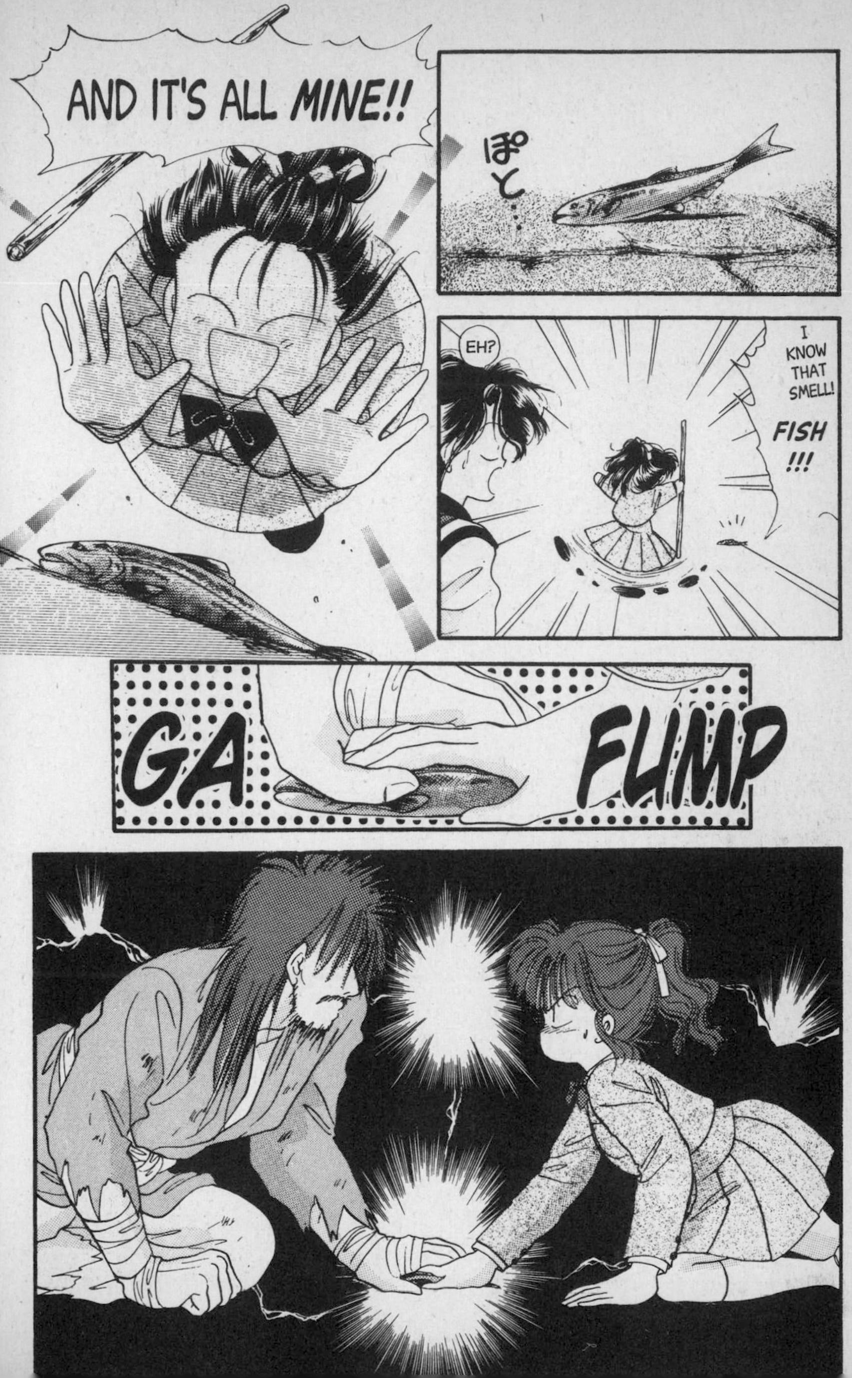
ぽと…
I KNOW THAT SMELL!
FISH !!!
EH?
AND IT'S ALL MINE!!
GA FUMP

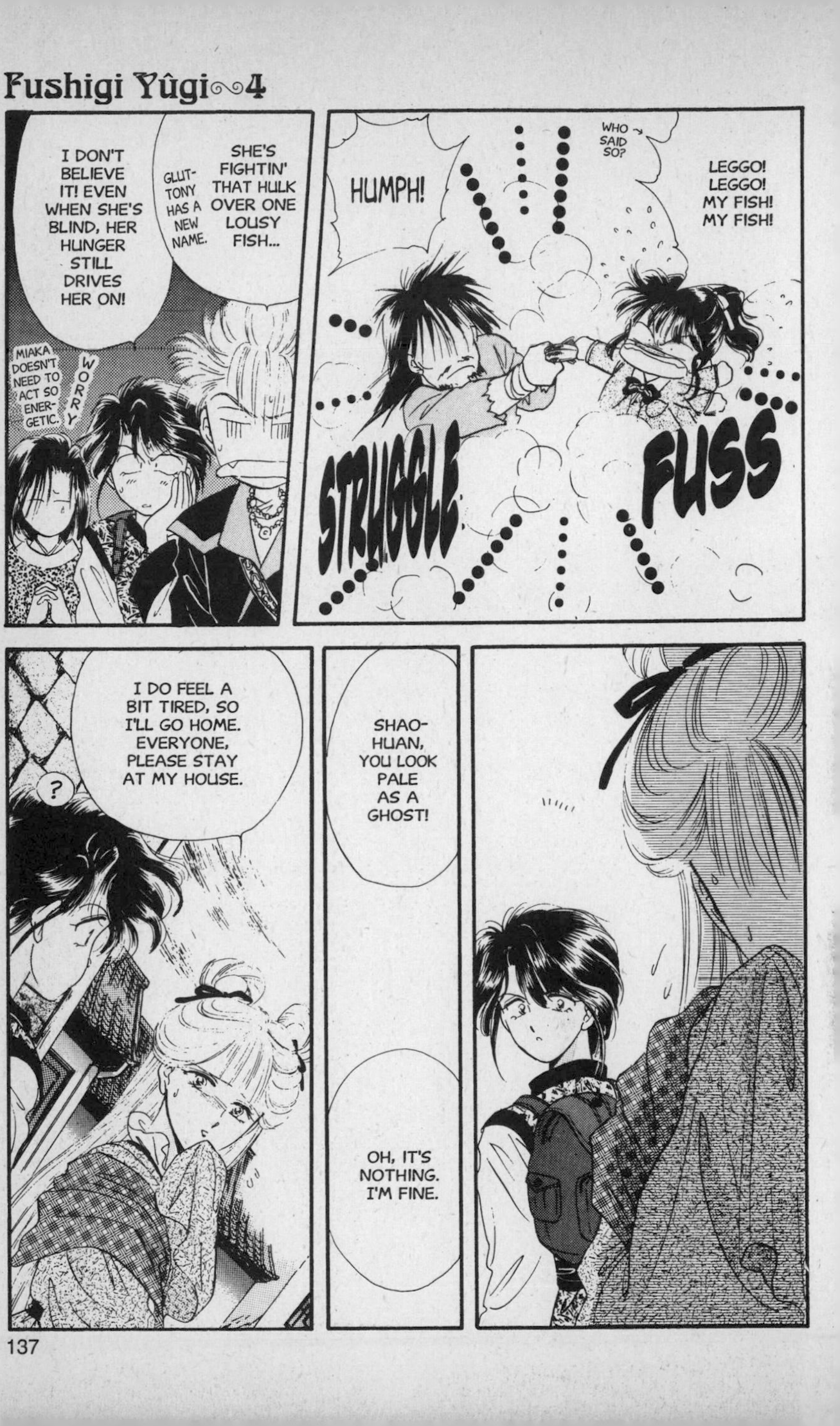
LEGGO! LEGGO! MY FISH! MY FISH!
WHO SAID SO?
HUMPH!
FUSS
STRUGGLE
SHE'S FIGHTIN' THAT HULK OVER ONE LOUSY FISH...
GLUT-TONY HAS A NEW NAME.
I DON'T BELIEVE IT! EVEN WHEN SHE'S BLIND, HER HUNGER STILL DRIVES HER ON!
WORRY
MIAKA DOESN'T NEED TO ACT SO ENER-GETIC.
SHAO-HUAN, YOU LOOK PALE AS A GHOST!
OH, IT'S NOTHING. I'M FINE.
I DO FEEL A BIT TIRED, SO I'LL GO HOME. EVERYONE, PLEASE STAY AT MY HOUSE.
?

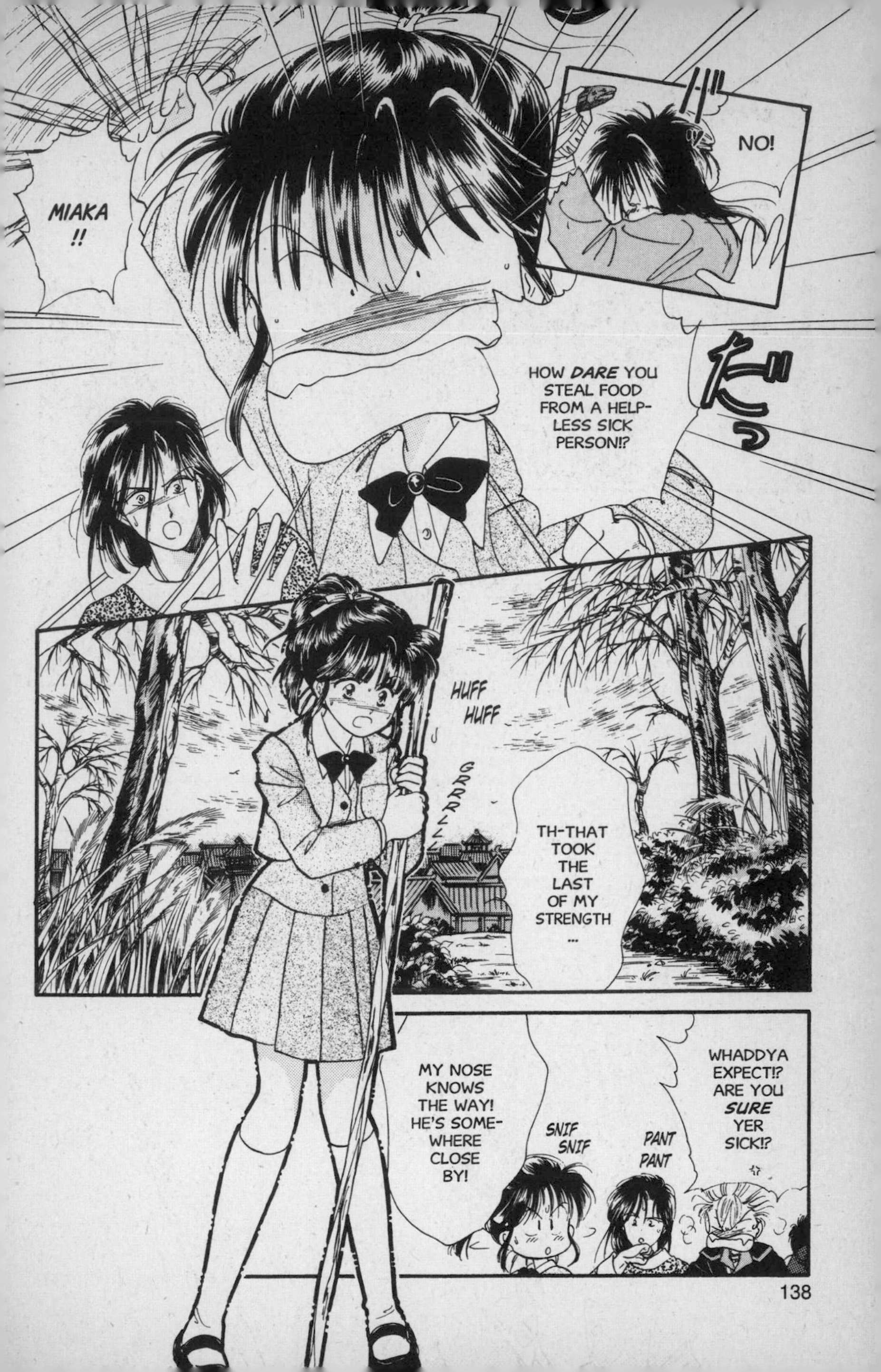
NO!
だっ
HOW *DARE* YOU STEAL FOOD FROM A HELP-LESS SICK PERSON!?
MIAKA !!
TH-THAT TOOK THE LAST OF MY STRENGTH ...
HUFF HUFF
GRRRR...
WHADDYA EXPECT!? ARE YOU *SURE* YER SICK!?
PANT PANT
SNIF SNIF
MY NOSE KNOWS THE WAY! HE'S SOME-WHERE CLOSE BY!

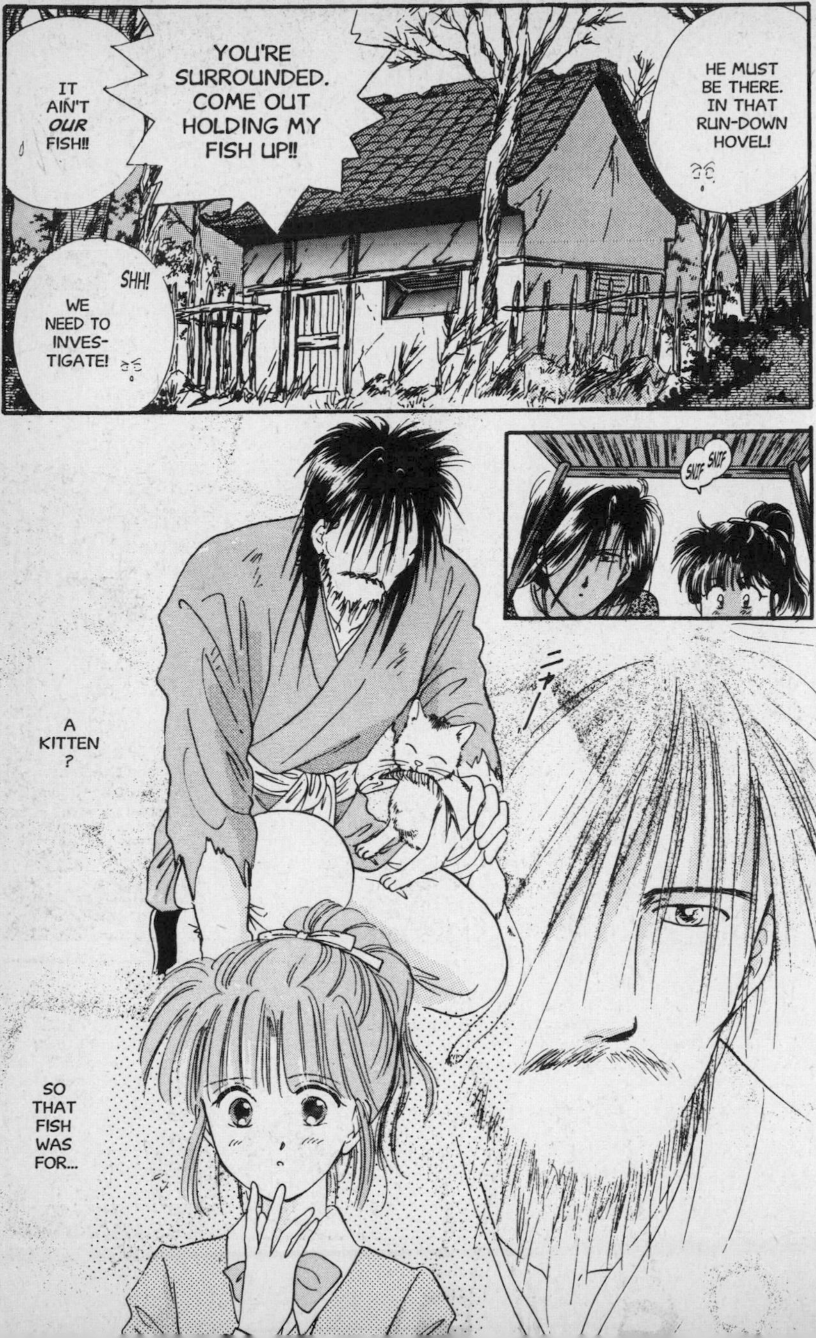
HE MUST BE THERE. IN THAT RUN-DOWN HOVEL!
YOU'RE SURROUNDED. COME OUT HOLDING MY FISH UP!!
IT AIN'T *OUR* FISH!!
SHH!
WE NEED TO INVES-TIGATE!
SNIF SNIF
ニャー
A KITTEN ?
SO THAT FISH WAS FOR...

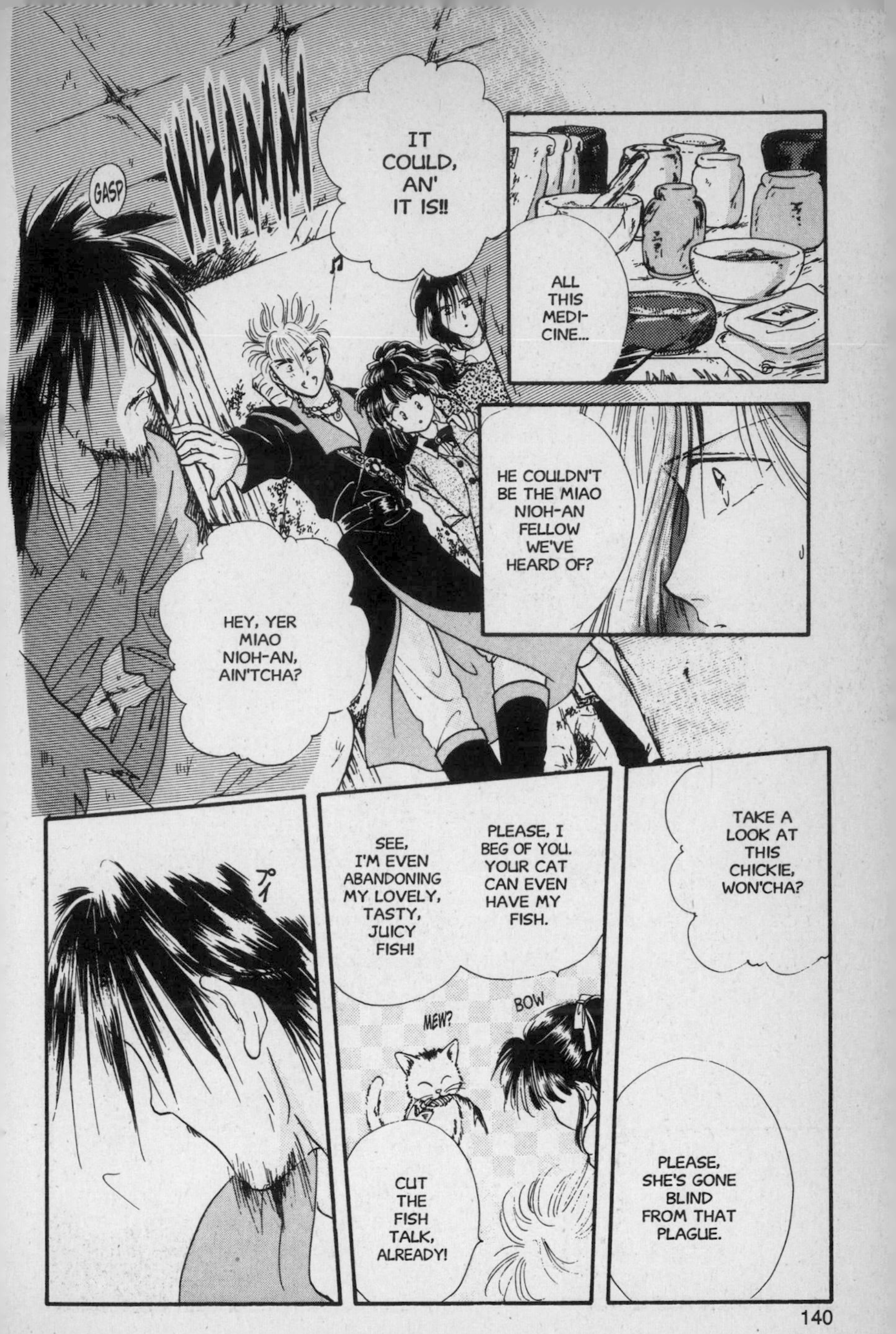
ALL THIS MEDICINE...
HE COULDN'T BE THE MIAO NIOH-AN FELLOW WE'VE HEARD OF?
IT COULD, AN' IT IS!!
WHAMM
GASP
HEY, YER MIAO NIOH-AN, AIN'TCHA?
TAKE A LOOK AT THIS CHICKIE, WON'CHA?
PLEASE, SHE'S GONE BLIND FROM THAT PLAGUE.
PLEASE, I BEG OF YOU. YOUR CAT CAN EVEN HAVE MY FISH.
SEE, I'M EVEN ABANDONING MY LOVELY, TASTY, JUICY FISH!
BOW
MEW?
CUT THE FISH TALK, ALREADY!
プイ

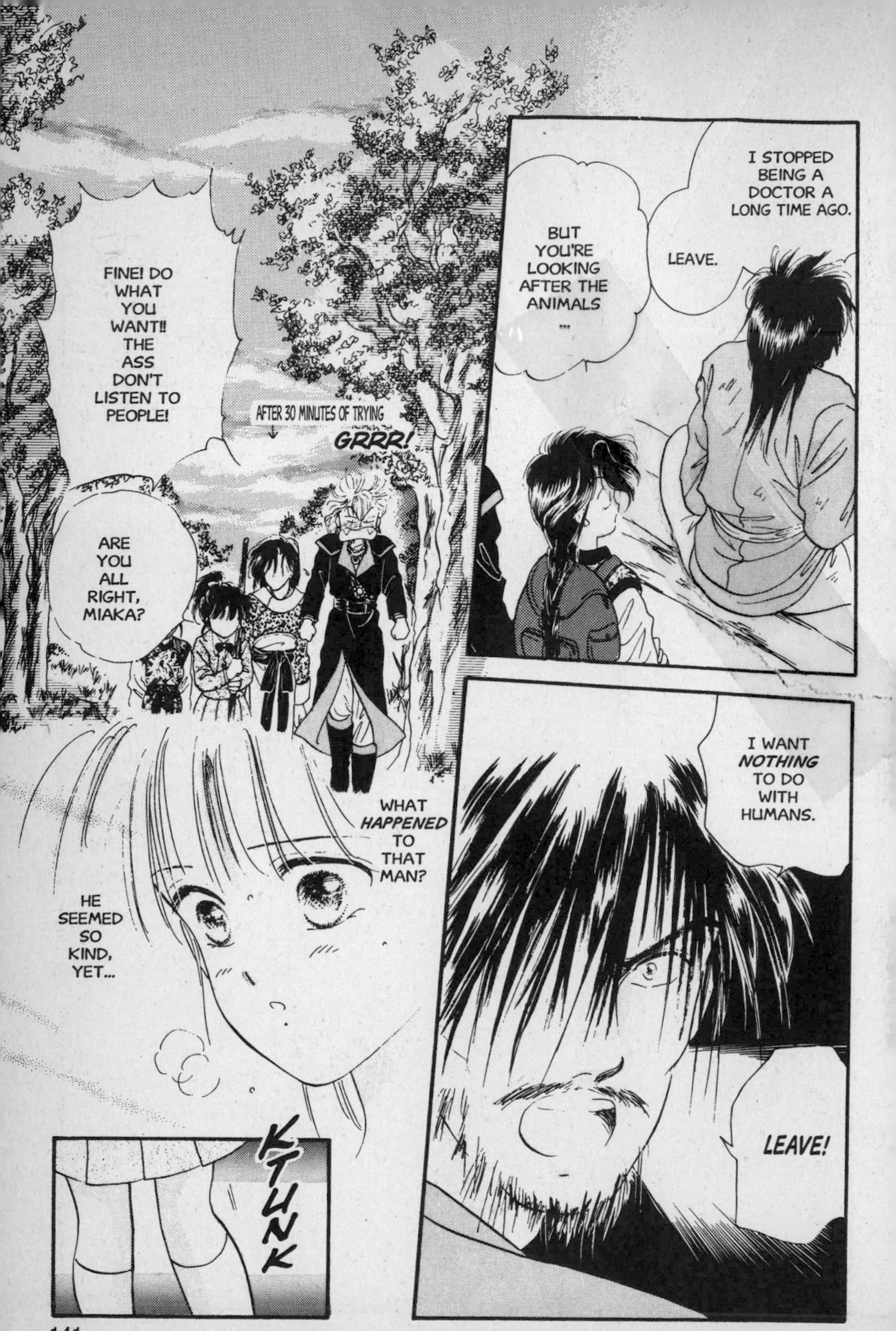
I STOPPED BEING A DOCTOR A LONG TIME AGO.
LEAVE.
BUT YOU'RE LOOKING AFTER THE ANIMALS ...
I WANT *NOTHING* TO DO WITH HUMANS.
LEAVE!
FINE! DO WHAT YOU WANT!! THE ASS DON'T LISTEN TO PEOPLE!
AFTER 30 MINUTES OF TRYING
GRRR!
ARE YOU ALL RIGHT, MIAKA?
WHAT *HAPPENED* TO THAT MAN?
HE SEEMED SO KIND, YET...
KTUNK

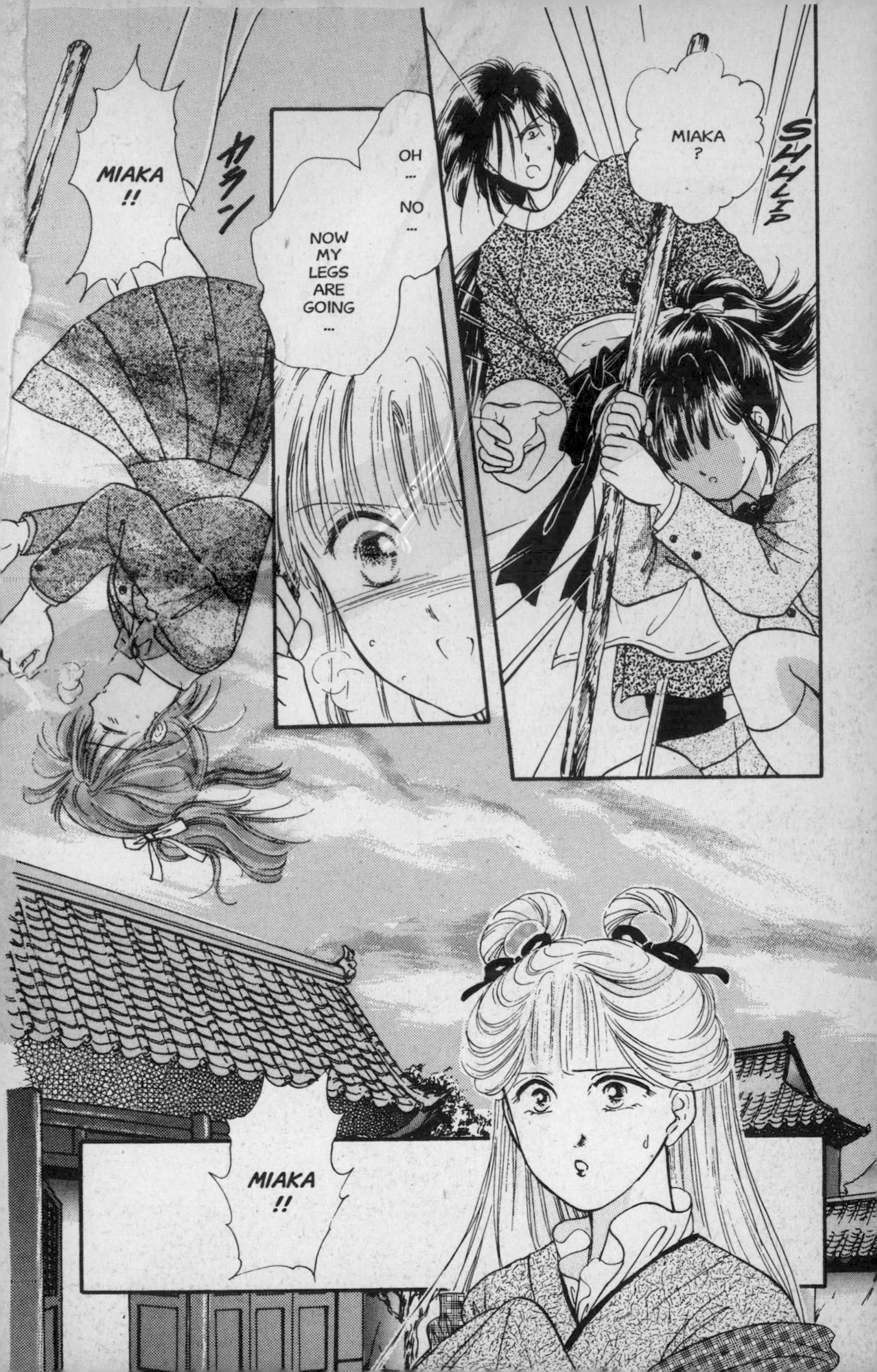
SHHLIP
MIAKA ?
OH ... NO ... NOW MY LEGS ARE GOING ...
カラン
MIAKA !!
MIAKA !!

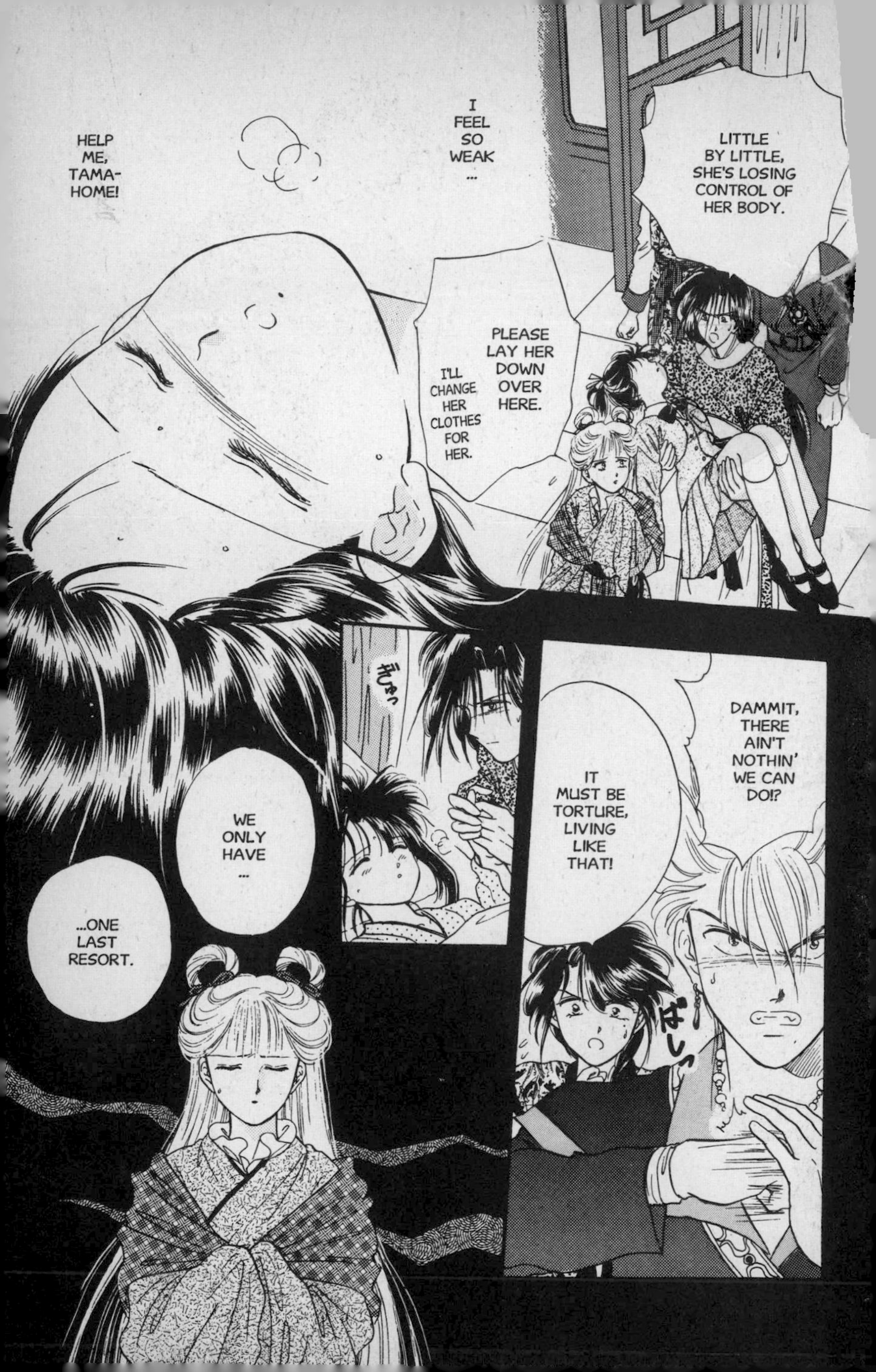
LITTLE BY LITTLE, SHE'S LOSING CONTROL OF HER BODY.
PLEASE LAY HER DOWN OVER HERE.
I'LL CHANGE HER CLOTHES FOR HER.
I FEEL SO WEAK ...
HELP ME, TAMA-HOME!
DAMMIT, THERE AIN'T NOTHIN' WE CAN DO!?
IT MUST BE TORTURE, LIVING LIKE THAT!
ぱしっ
ぎゅっ
WE ONLY HAVE ...
...ONE LAST RESORT.

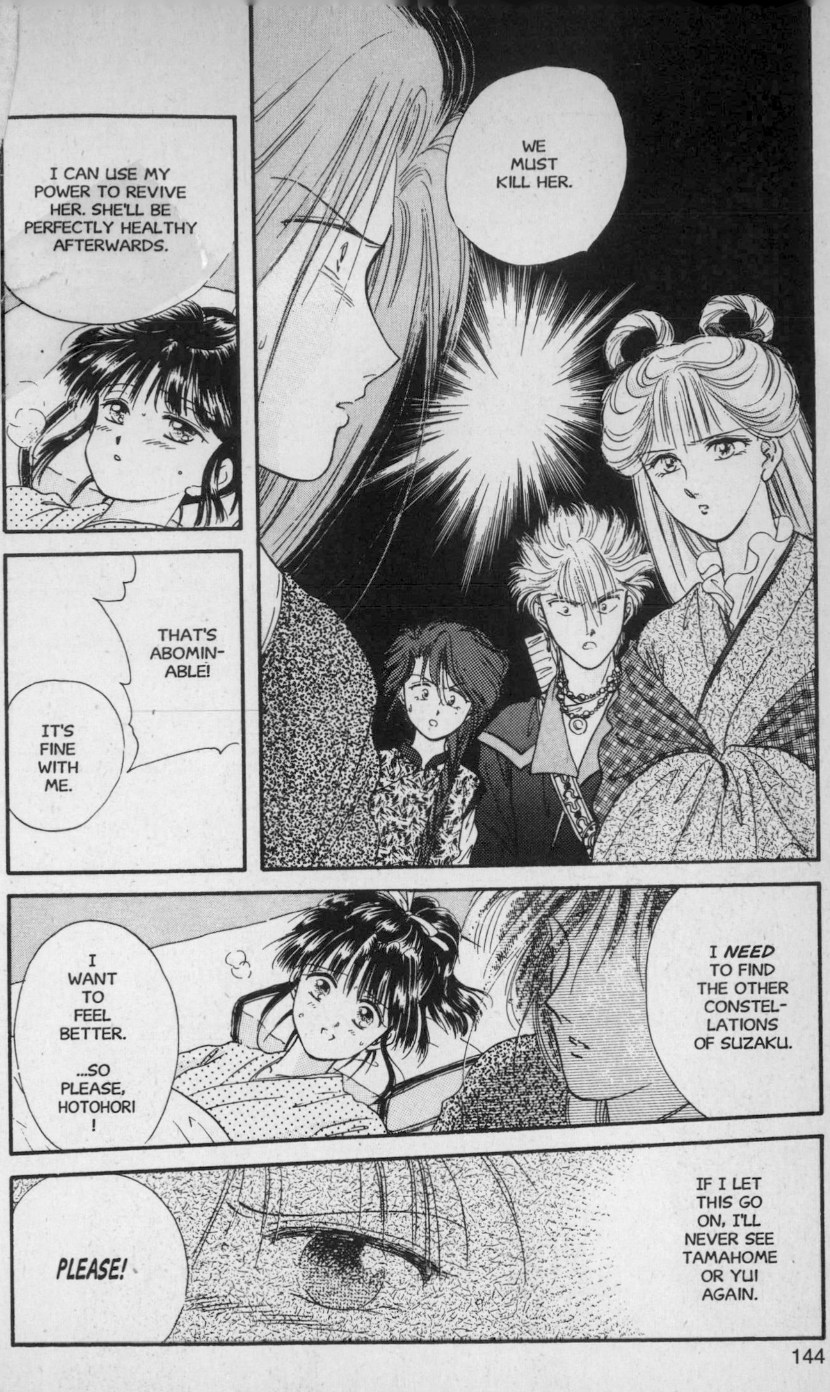
WE MUST KILL HER.
I CAN USE MY POWER TO REVIVE HER. SHE'LL BE PERFECTLY HEALTHY AFTERWARDS.
THAT'S ABOMINABLE!
IT'S FINE WITH ME.
I *NEED* TO FIND THE OTHER CONSTEL-LATIONS OF SUZAKU.
I WANT TO FEEL BETTER.
...SO PLEASE, HOTOHORI!
IF I LET THIS GO ON, I'LL NEVER SEE TAMAHOME OR YUI AGAIN.
PLEASE!

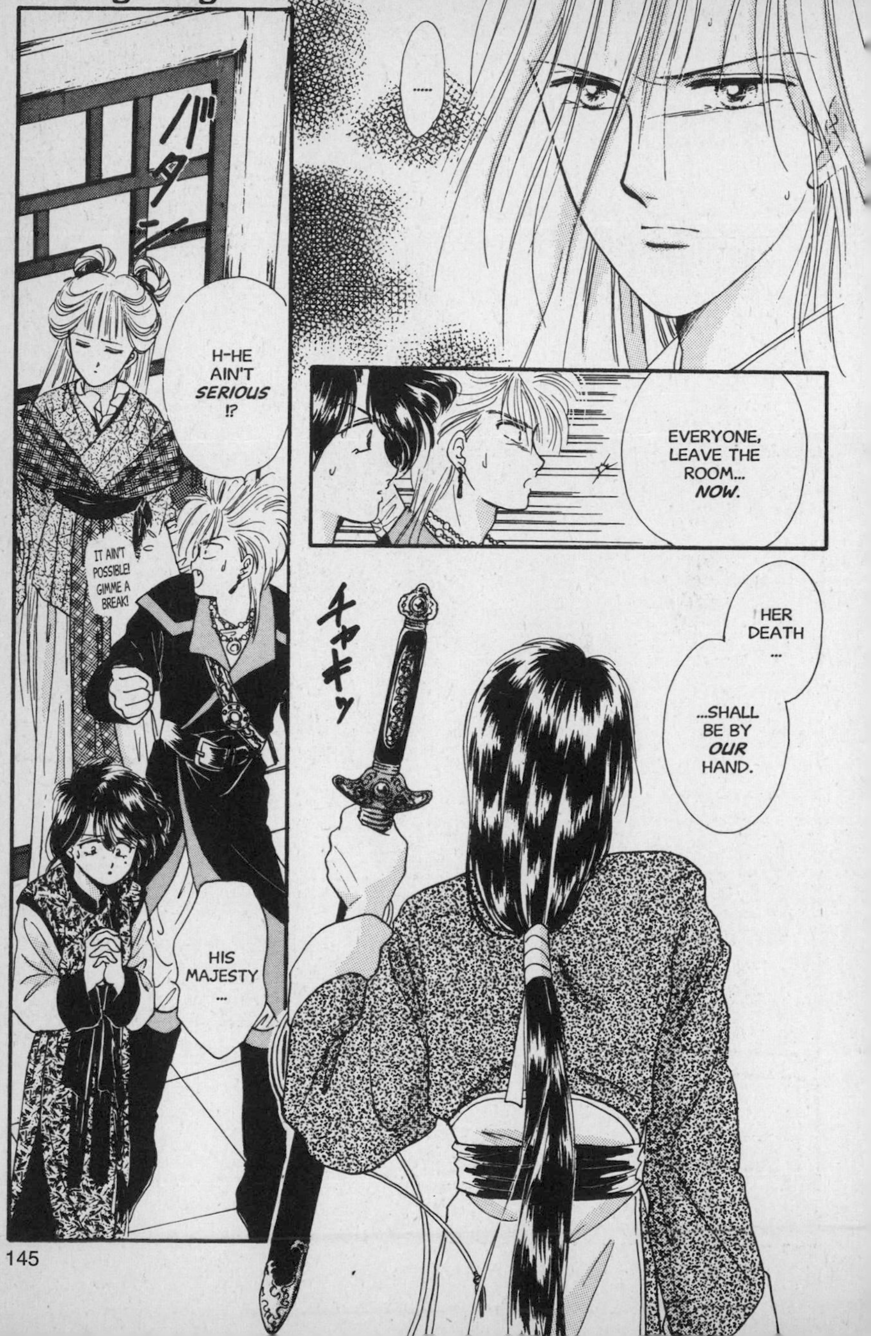
......
EVERYONE, LEAVE THE ROOM... *NOW.*
チャキッ
HER DEATH...
...SHALL BE BY *OUR* HAND.
バタン
H-HE AIN'T *SERIOUS* !?
IT AIN'T POSSIBLE! GIMME A BREAK!
HIS MAJESTY...

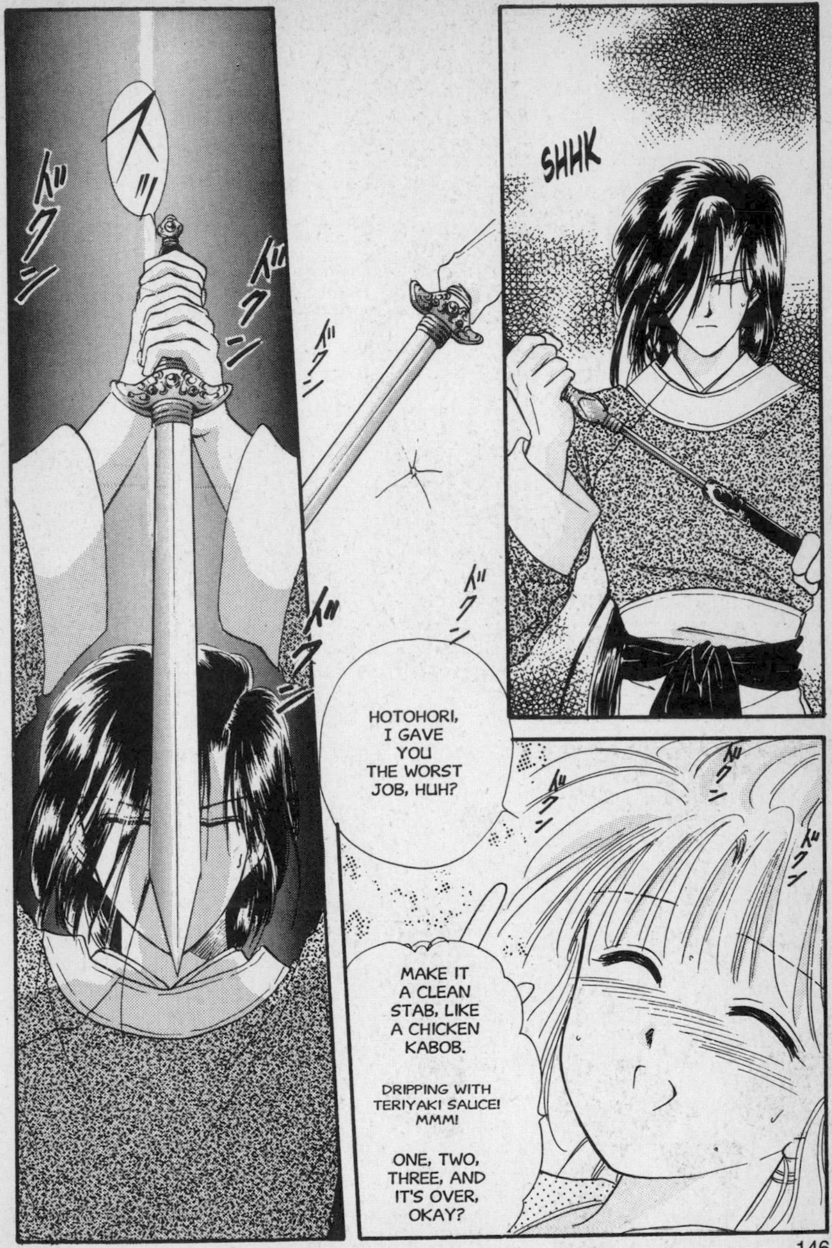
SHHK
ドクン
HOTOHORI, I GAVE YOU THE WORST JOB, HUH?
ドクン
ドクン
ドクン
MAKE IT A CLEAN STAB, LIKE A CHICKEN KABOB.
DRIPPING WITH TERIYAKI SAUCE! MMM!
ONE, TWO, THREE, AND IT'S OVER, OKAY?
ドクン
ドクン
ズ
ドクン
ドクン
ドクン

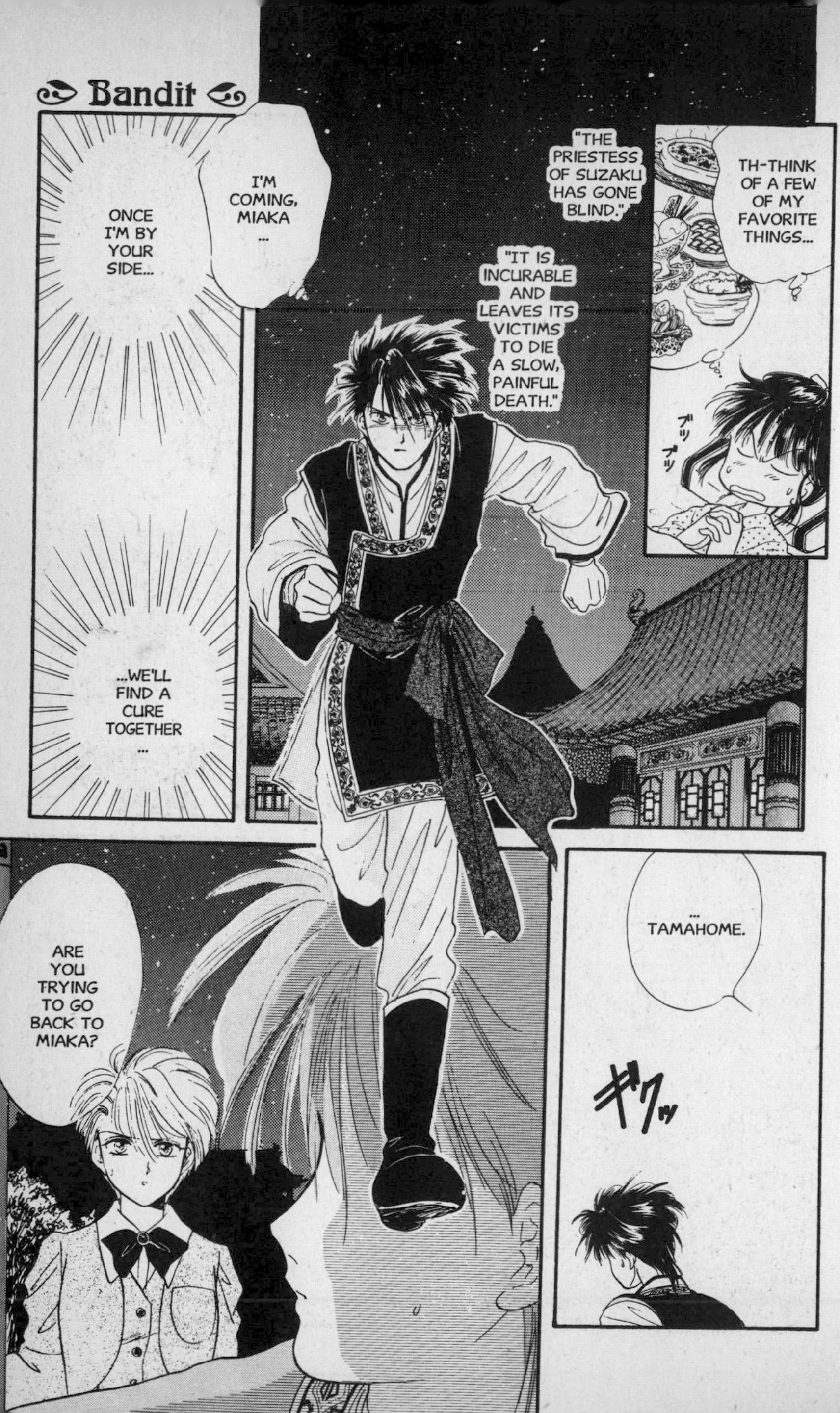
TH-THINK OF A FEW OF MY FAVORITE THINGS...
ブツ ブツ
"THE PRIESTESS OF SUZAKU HAS GONE BLIND."
"IT IS INCURABLE AND LEAVES ITS VICTIMS TO DIE A SLOW, PAINFUL DEATH."
I'M COMING, MIAKA ...
ONCE I'M BY YOUR SIDE...
...WE'LL FIND A CURE TOGETHER ...
... TAMAHOME.
ギクッ
ARE YOU TRYING TO GO BACK TO MIAKA?

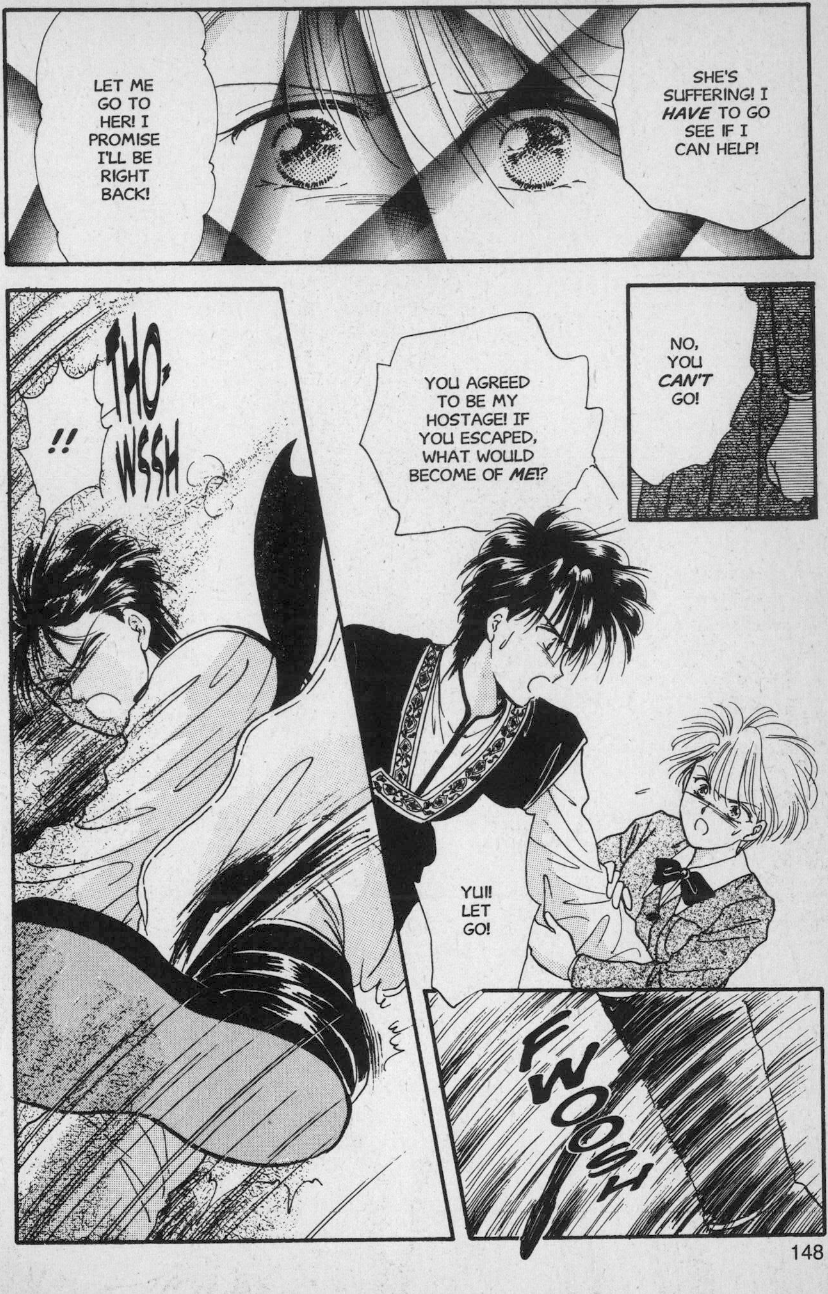
SHE'S SUFFERING! I *HAVE* TO GO SEE IF I CAN HELP!
LET ME GO TO HER! I PROMISE I'LL BE RIGHT BACK!
NO, YOU *CAN'T* GO!
YOU AGREED TO BE MY HOSTAGE! IF YOU ESCAPED, WHAT WOULD BECOME OF *ME*!?
YUI! LET GO!
FWOOSH
THO-WSSH
!!

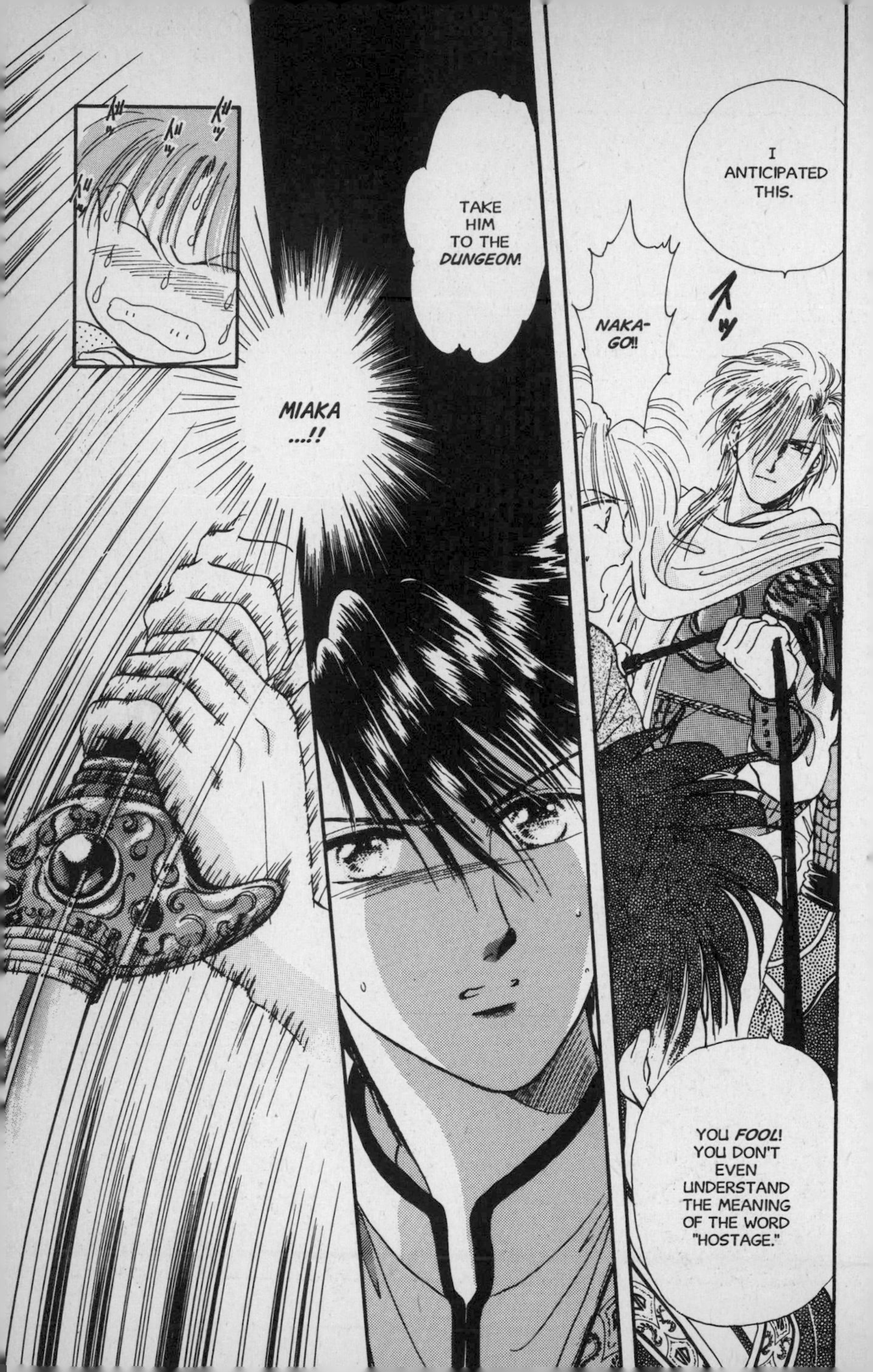
I ANTICIPATED THIS.
NAKA-GO!!
YOU *FOOL*! YOU DON'T EVEN UNDERSTAND THE MEANING OF THE WORD "HOSTAGE."
TAKE HIM TO THE *DUNGEON*!
MIAKA ...!!

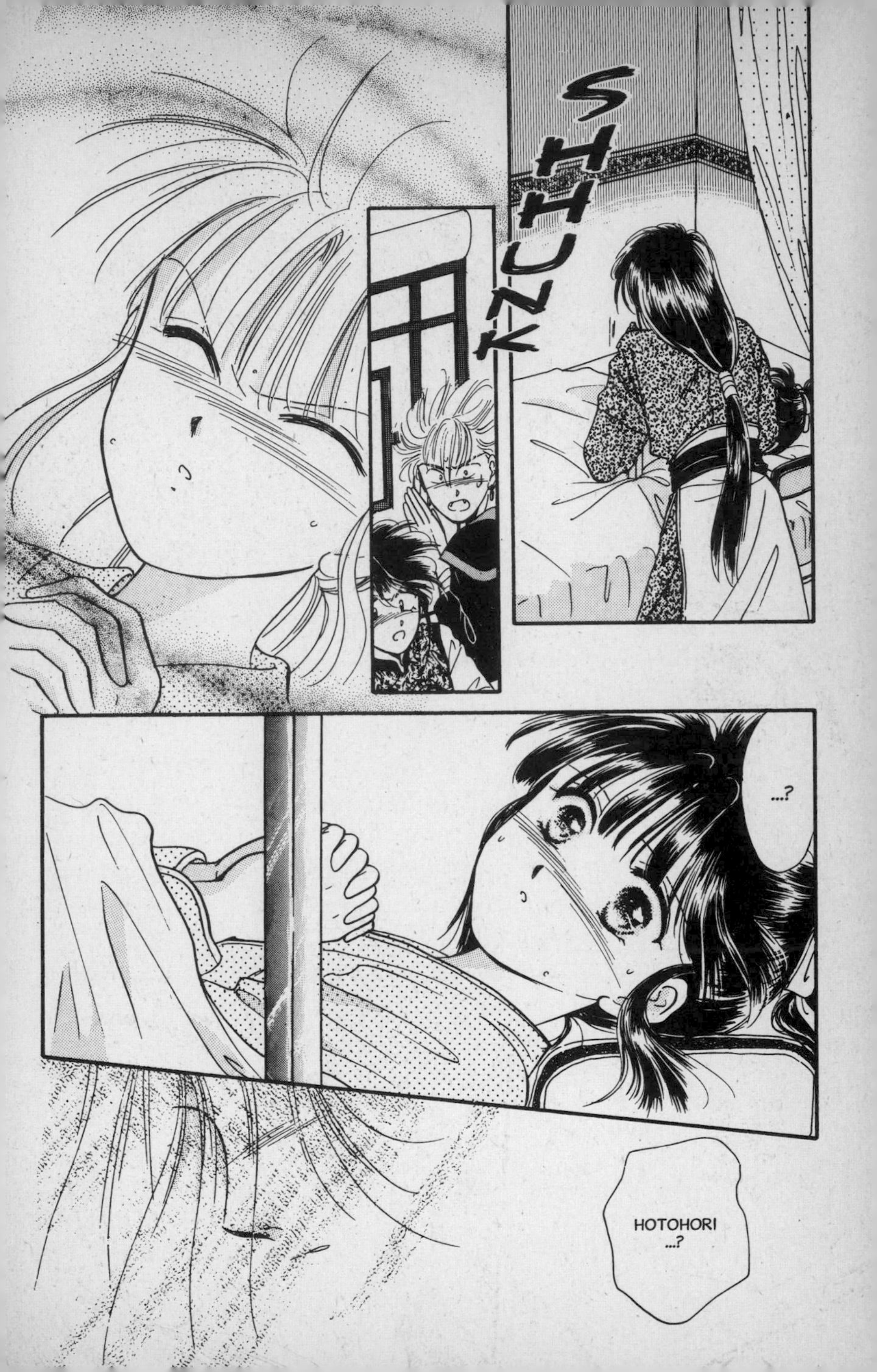
SHHUNK
...?
HOTOHORI ...?

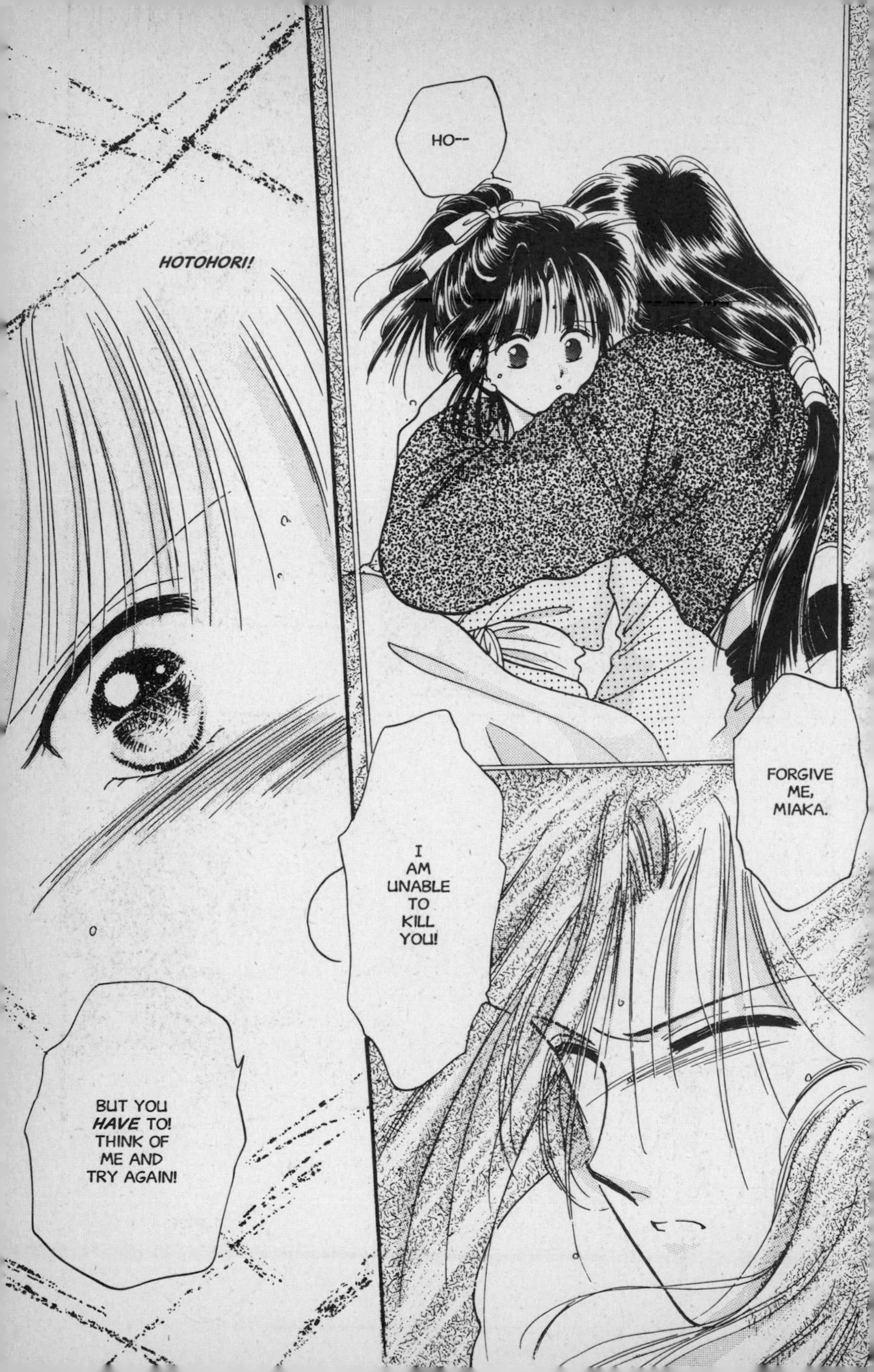
HO--
FORGIVE ME, MIAKA.
I AM UNABLE TO KILL YOU!
HOTOHORI!
BUT YOU *HAVE* TO! THINK OF ME AND TRY AGAIN!

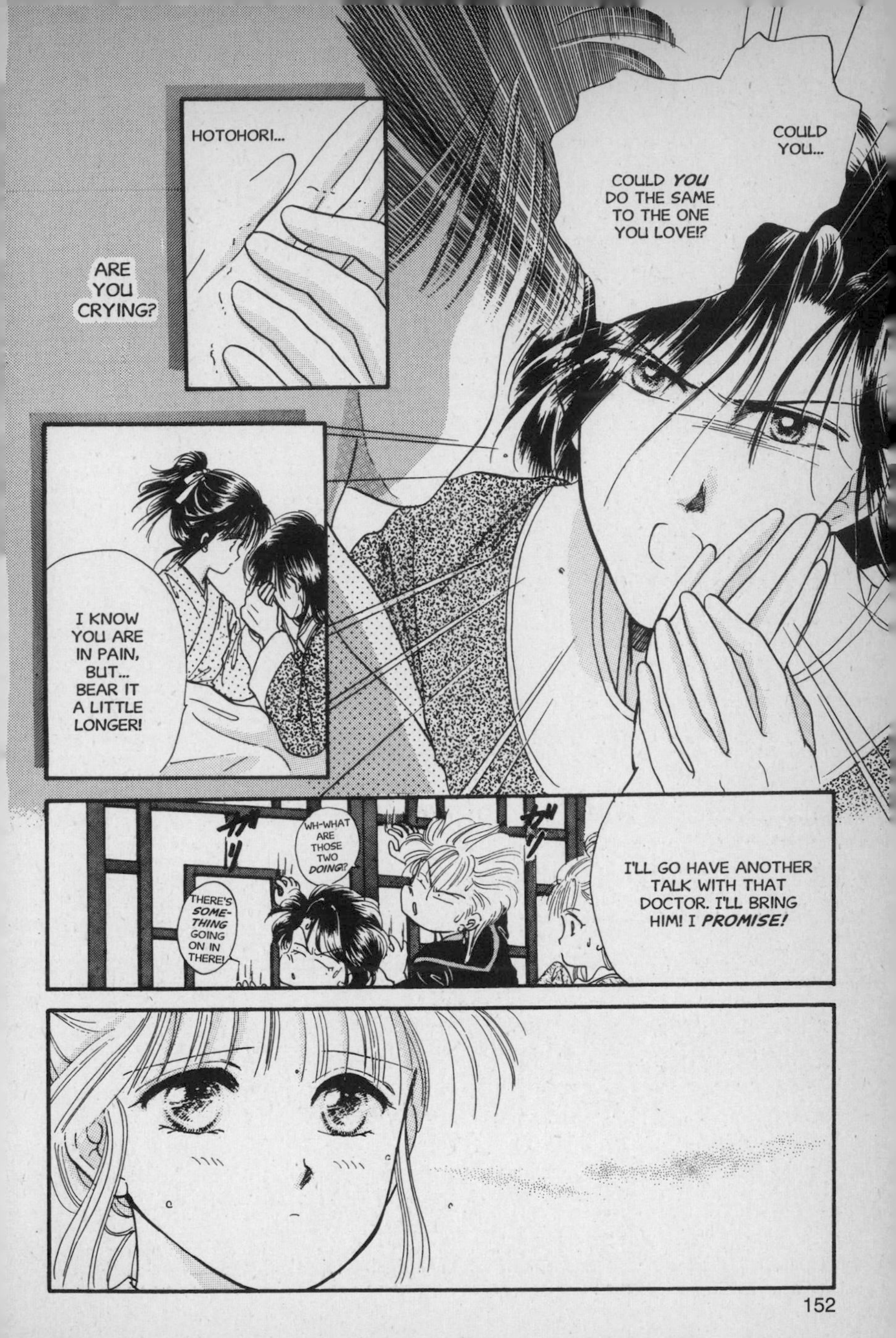
COULD YOU...
COULD YOU DO THE SAME TO THE ONE YOU LOVE!?
HOTOHORI...
ARE YOU CRYING?
I KNOW YOU ARE IN PAIN, BUT... BEAR IT A LITTLE LONGER!
I'LL GO HAVE ANOTHER TALK WITH THAT DOCTOR. I'LL BRING HIM! I PROMISE!
WH-WHAT ARE THOSE TWO DOING?!
THERE'S SOMETHING GOING ON IN THERE!

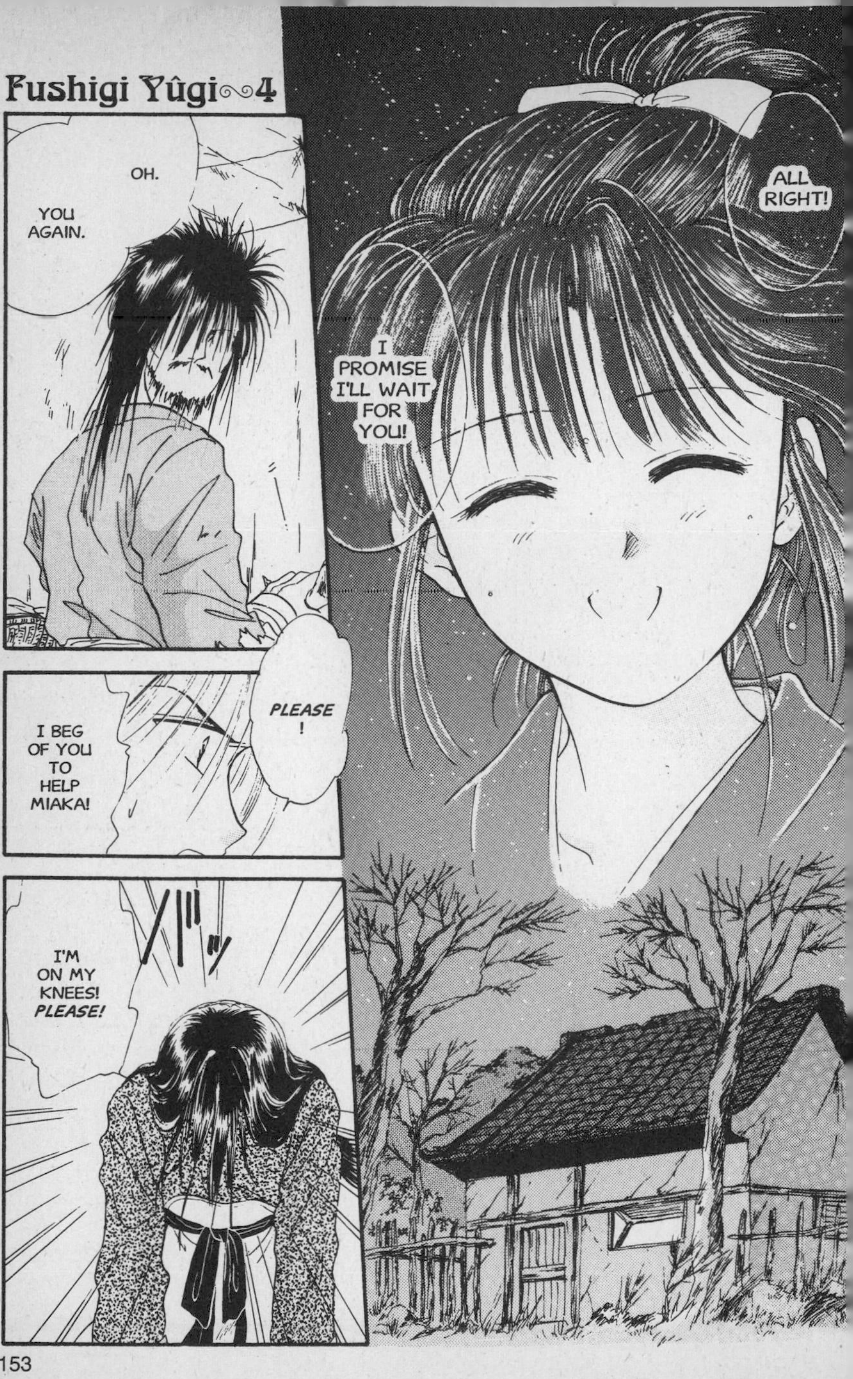
ALL RIGHT!
I PROMISE I'LL WAIT FOR YOU!
OH.
YOU AGAIN.
PLEASE !
I BEG OF YOU TO HELP MIAKA!
I'M ON MY KNEES! *PLEASE!*

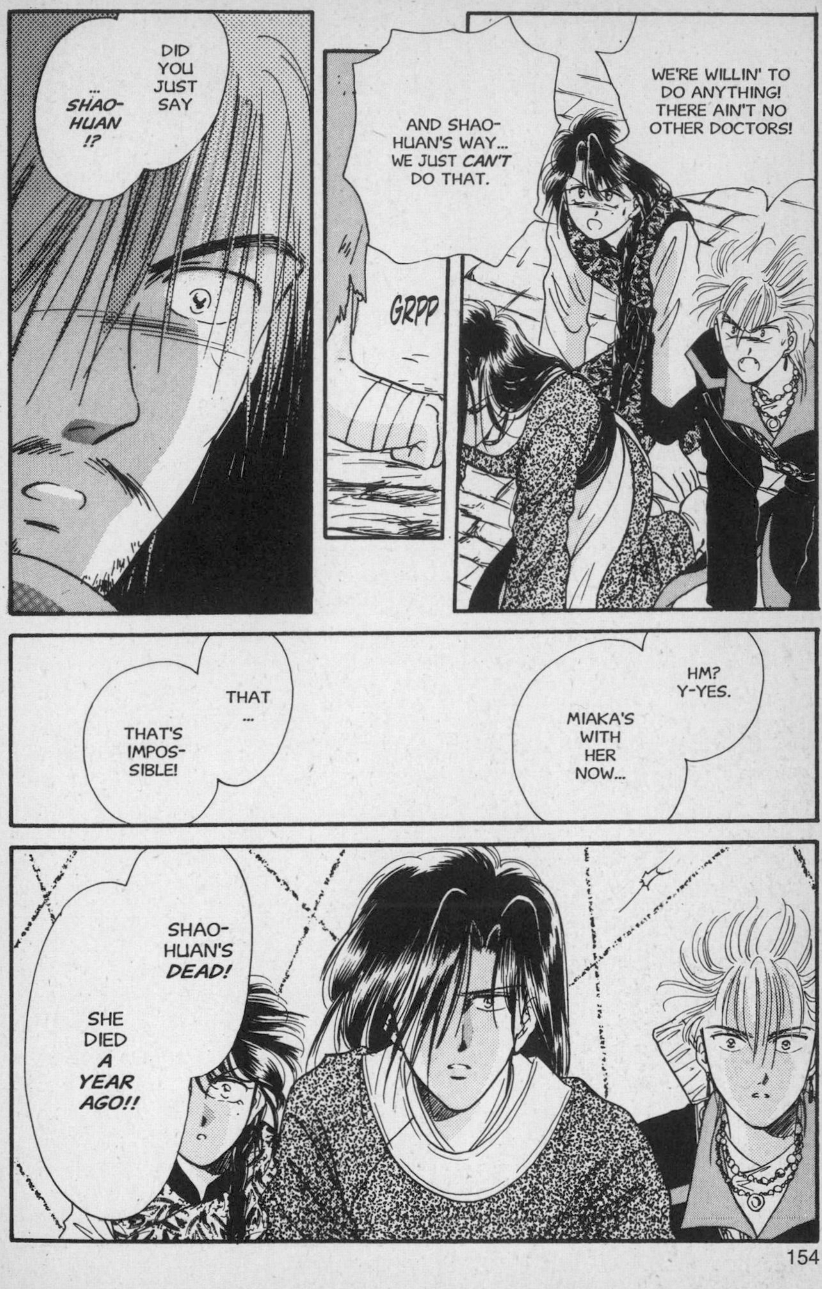
WE'RE WILLIN' TO DO ANYTHING! THERE AIN'T NO OTHER DOCTORS!
AND SHAO-HUAN'S WAY... WE JUST CAN'T DO THAT.
GRPP
DID YOU JUST SAY ...SHAO-HUAN!?
HM? Y-YES.
MIAKA'S WITH HER NOW...
THAT...
THAT'S IMPOSSIBLE!
SHAO-HUAN'S DEAD!
SHE DIED A YEAR AGO!!

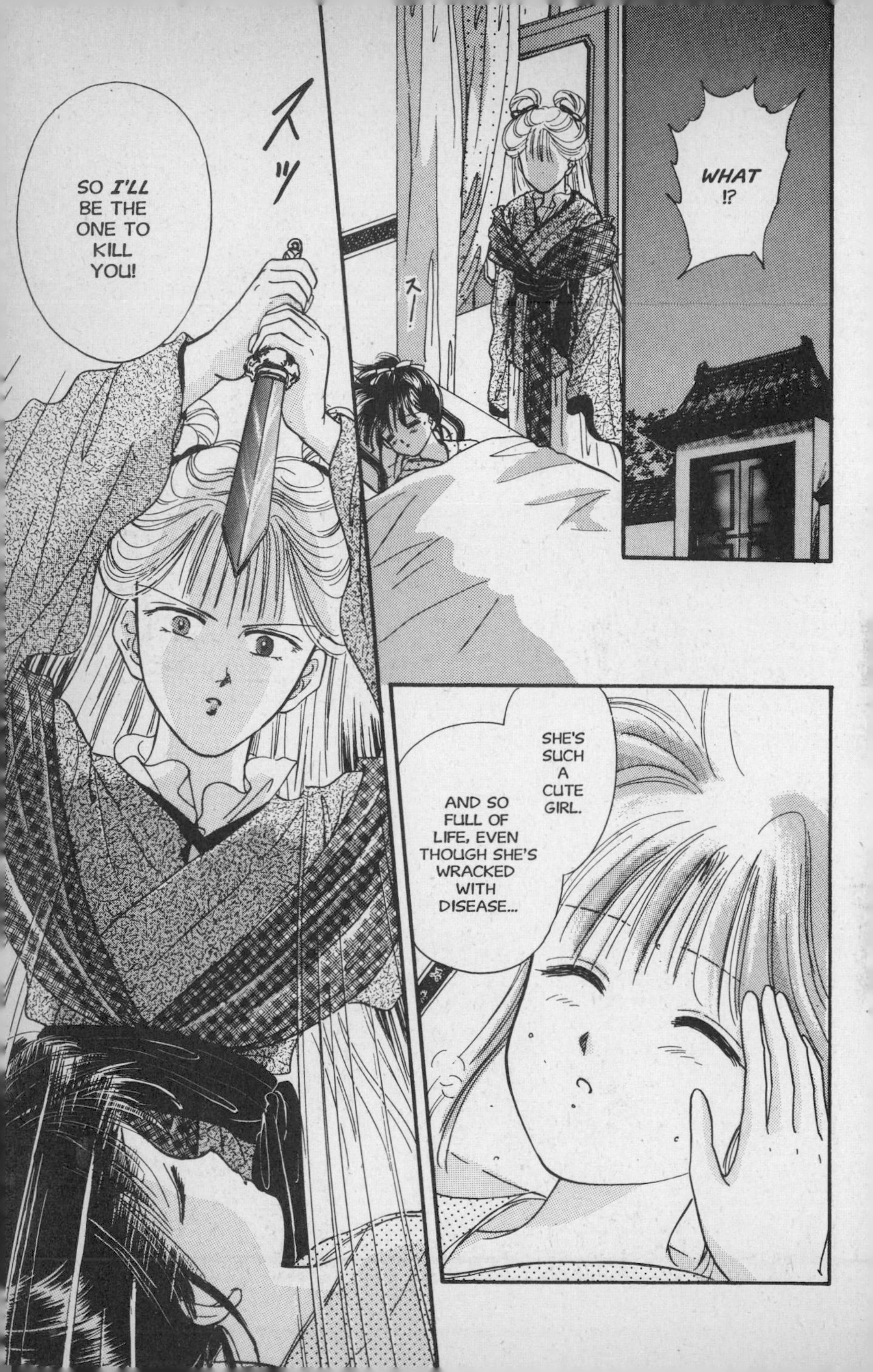
WHAT !?
スー
SHE'S SUCH A CUTE GIRL.
AND SO FULL OF LIFE, EVEN THOUGH SHE'S WRACKED WITH DISEASE...
スッ
SO *I'LL* BE THE ONE TO KILL YOU!

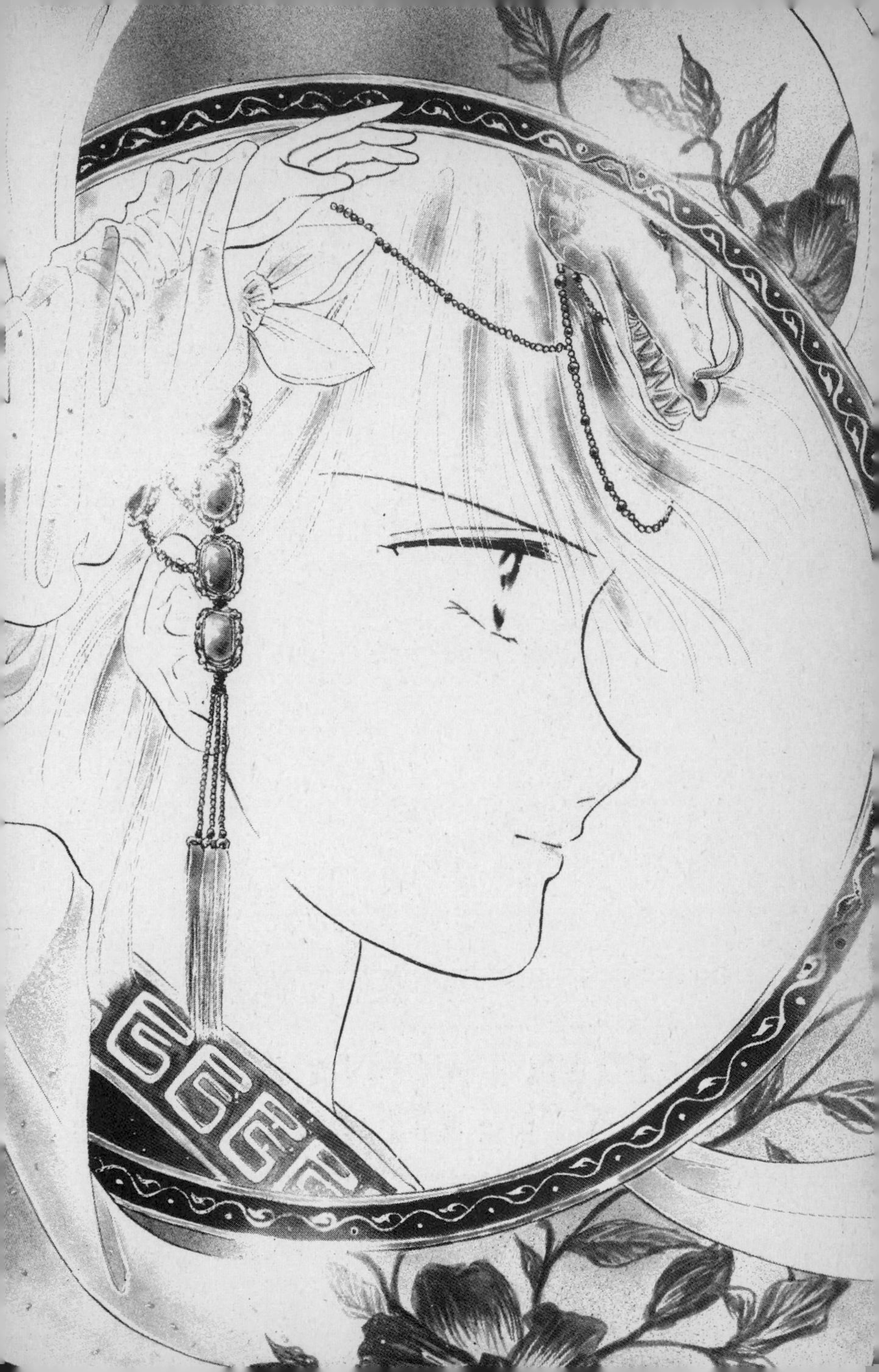

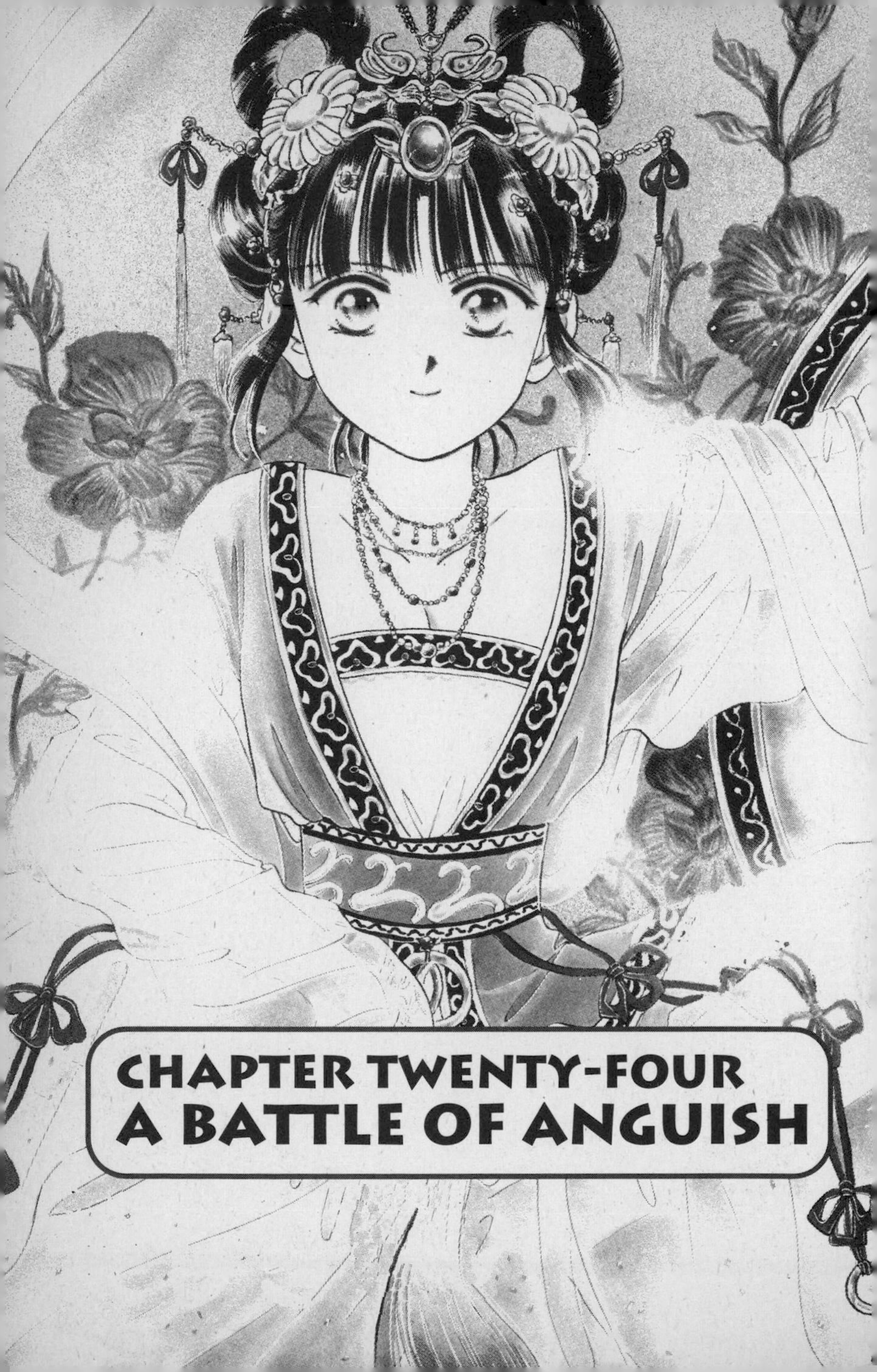
CHAPTER TWENTY-FOUR
A BATTLE OF ANGUISH

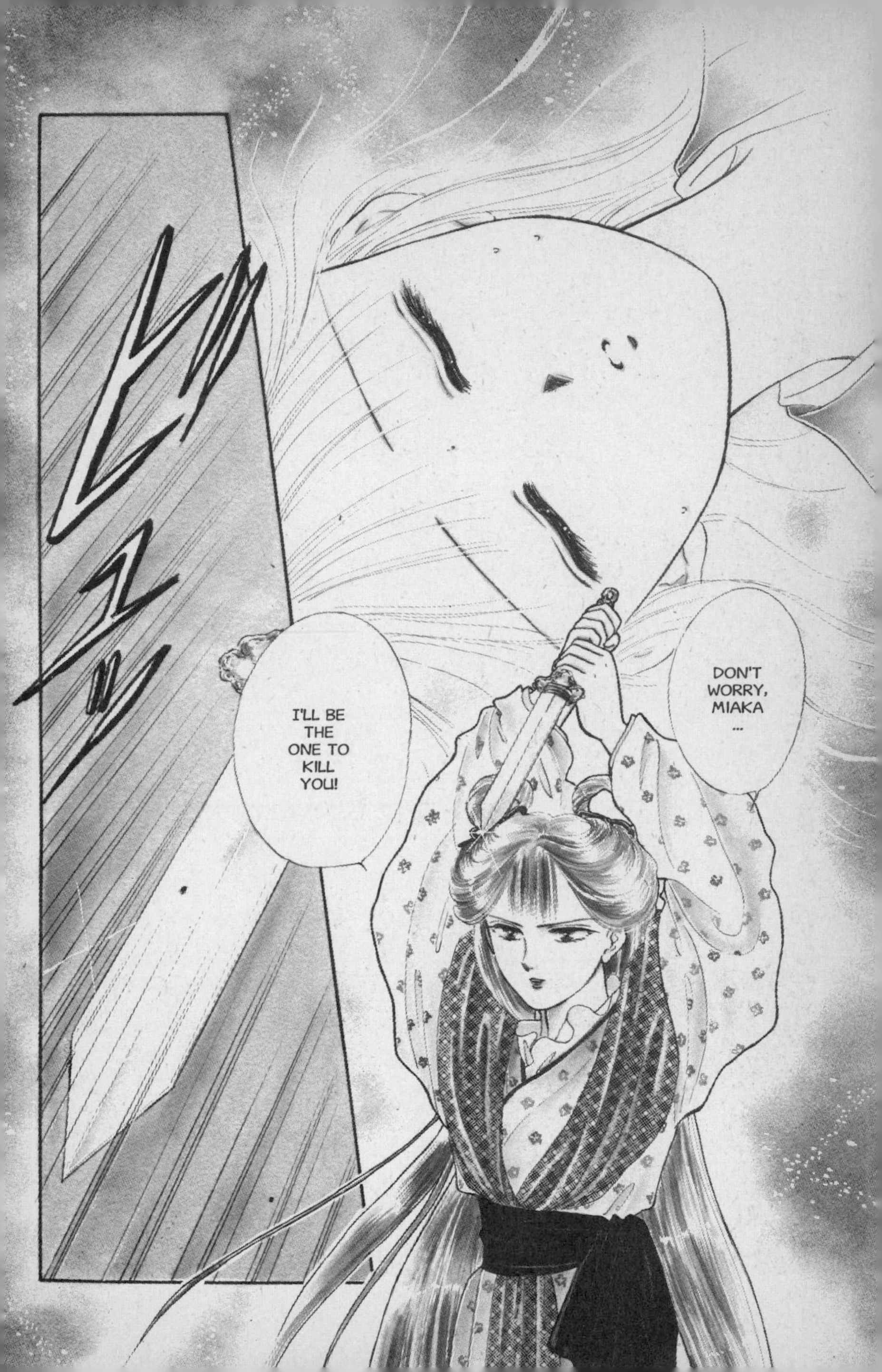
DON'T WORRY, MIAKA ...
I'LL BE THE ONE TO KILL YOU!

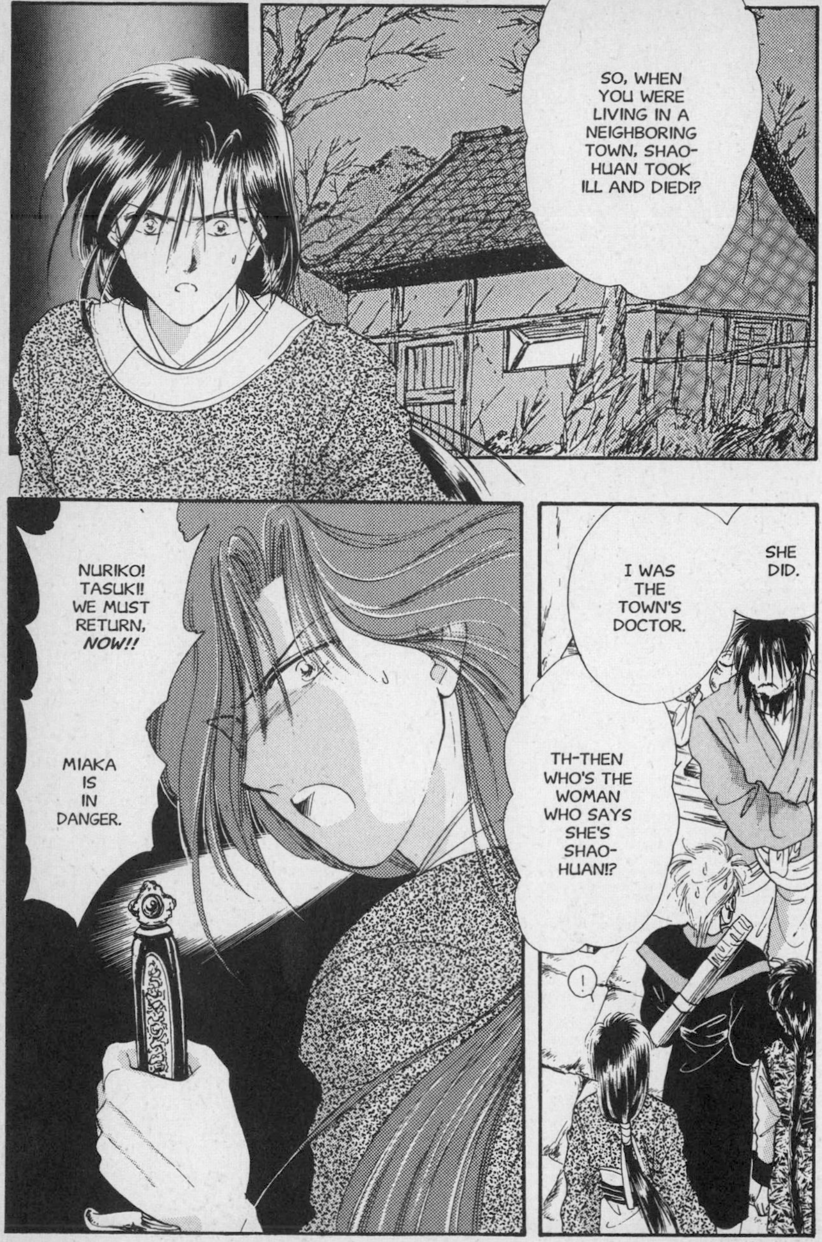

SO, WHEN YOU WERE LIVING IN A NEIGHBORING TOWN, SHAO-HUAN TOOK ILL AND DIED!?
SHE DID.
I WAS THE TOWN'S DOCTOR.
TH-THEN WHO'S THE WOMAN WHO SAYS SHE'S SHAO-HUAN!?
!
NURIKO! TASUKI! WE MUST RETURN, *NOW!!*
MIAKA IS IN DANGER.

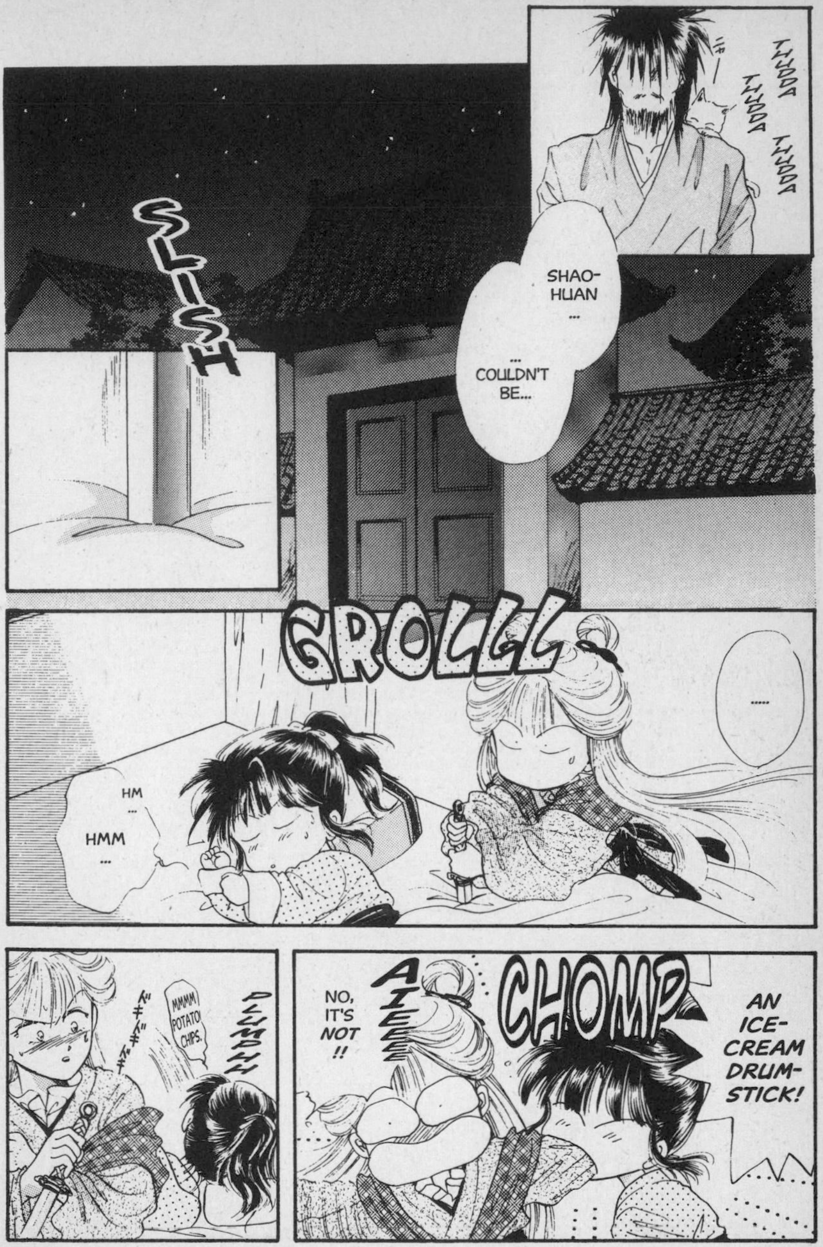

THUDDA THUDDA THUDDA
SHAO-HUAN ...
... COULDN'T BE...
SLISH
.....
GROLLL
HM ... HMM ...
AN ICE-CREAM DRUMSTICK!
CHOMP
AIEEEE
NO, IT'S NOT !!
PLUMPHH
MMMM POTATO CHIPS.

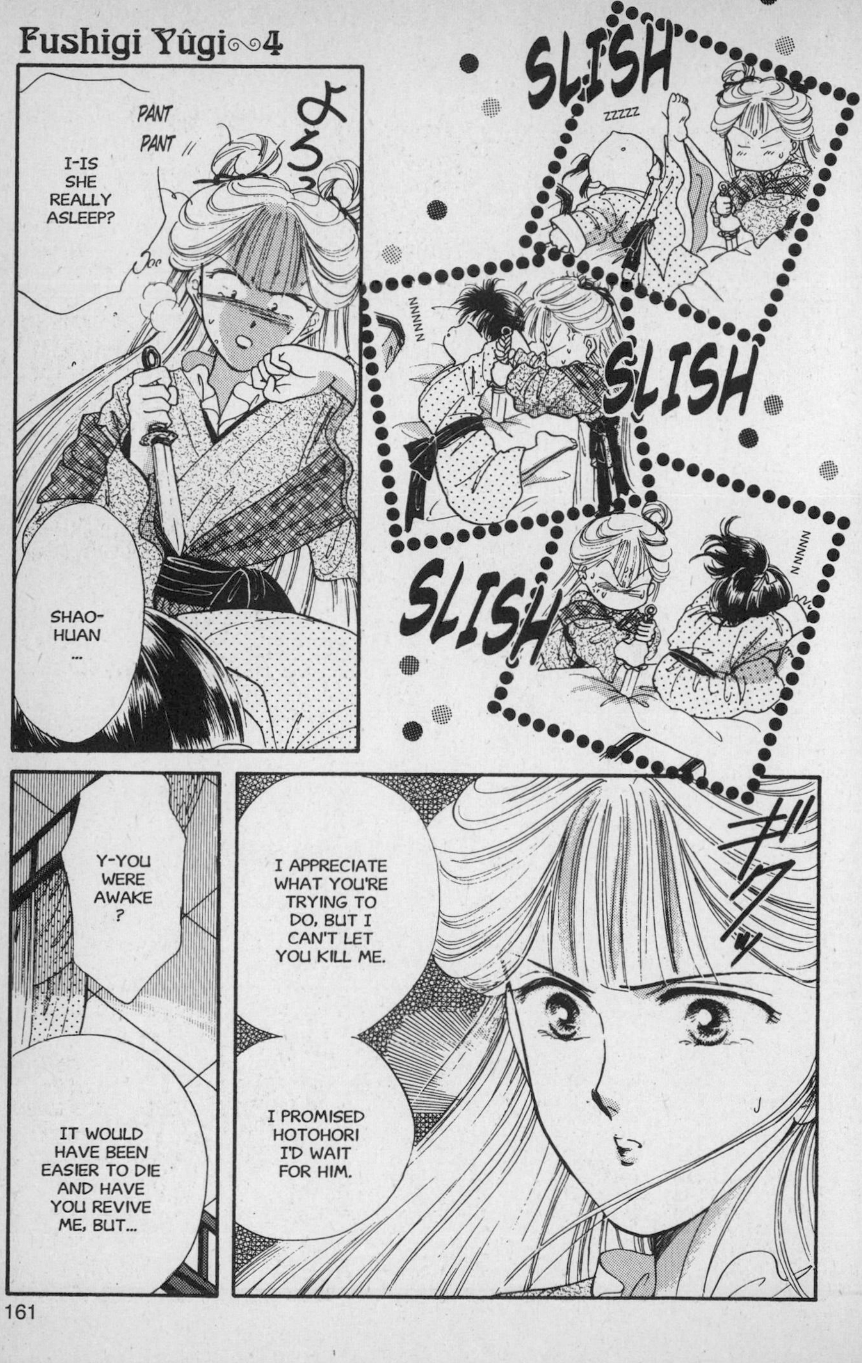
SLISH
ZZZZZ
SLISH
NNNNN
SLISH
NNNNN
よろ
PANT PANT
I-IS SHE REALLY ASLEEP?
SHAO-HUAN ...
I APPRECIATE WHAT YOU'RE TRYING TO DO, BUT I CAN'T LET YOU KILL ME.
I PROMISED HOTOHORI I'D WAIT FOR HIM.
Y-YOU WERE AWAKE ?
IT WOULD HAVE BEEN EASIER TO DIE AND HAVE YOU REVIVE ME, BUT...

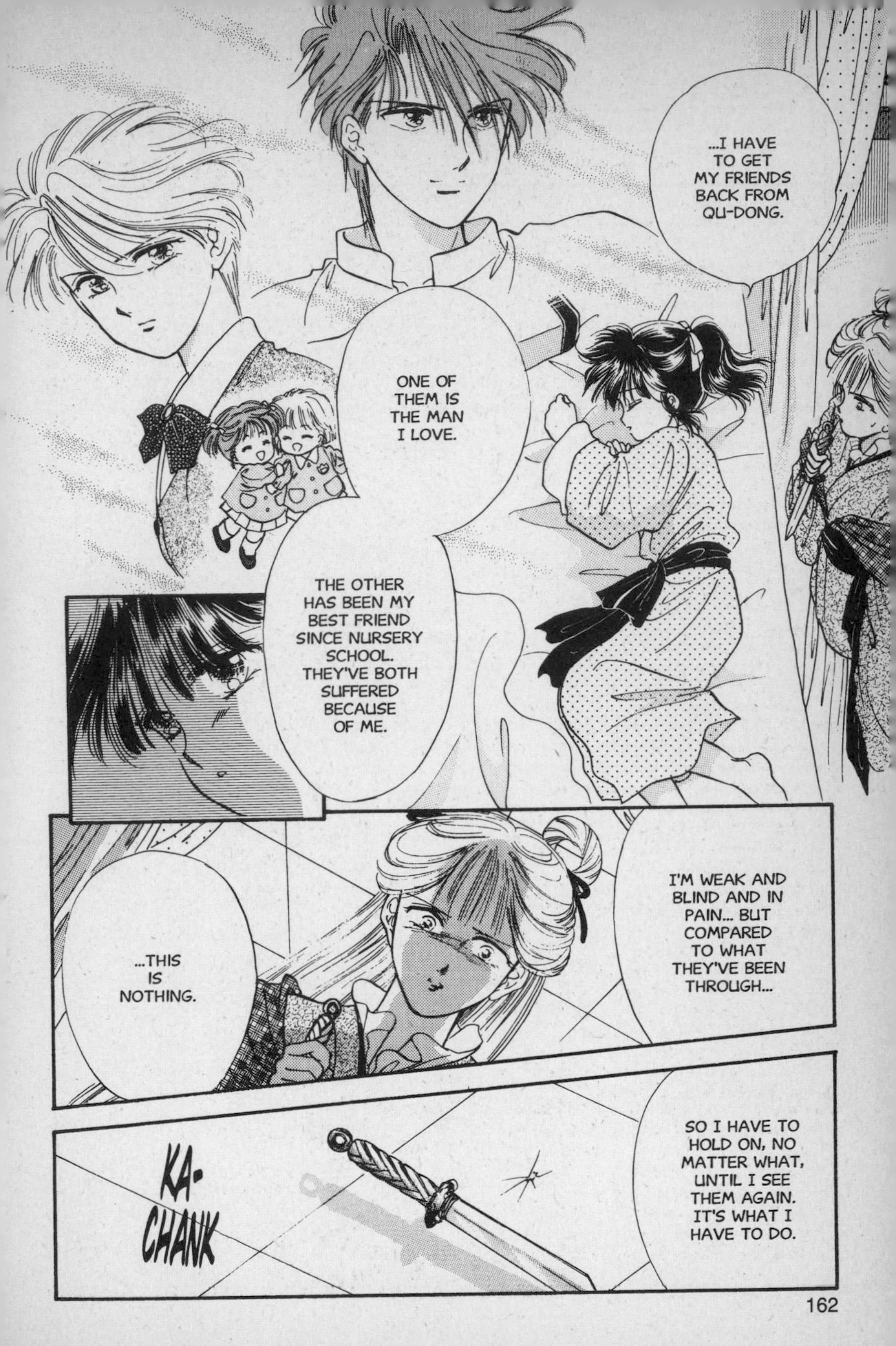
...I HAVE TO GET MY FRIENDS BACK FROM QU-DONG.
ONE OF THEM IS THE MAN I LOVE.
THE OTHER HAS BEEN MY BEST FRIEND SINCE NURSERY SCHOOL. THEY'VE BOTH SUFFERED BECAUSE OF ME.
I'M WEAK AND BLIND AND IN PAIN... BUT COMPARED TO WHAT THEY'VE BEEN THROUGH...
...THIS IS NOTHING.
SO I HAVE TO HOLD ON, NO MATTER WHAT, UNTIL I SEE THEM AGAIN. IT'S WHAT I HAVE TO DO.
KA-CHANK

Bandit

One thing I find interesting in the Asahi News is the letters to the editor. There are so many interesting opinions. There was a really interesting piece on corporal punishment recently. If you push a teacher too far...hey, he's only human. A teacher can't get carried away, but you need to maintain some discipline in the classroom. When I was young, my parents put me in my place all the time. But everybody says I've got a great relationship with my mother. She'd scold me, or she'd praise me whenever the occasion called for it. But slapping your child, like Miaka's mom did, might not be appropriate. In any case, don't just use the paper for the TV listings! You don't learn anything about the world. So let's read a few articles now and again! You hear me, people?

Oh, no! It's 2 AM already. I'm half asleep. ⊖⊖ I'm huuungry! They say that manga reveals the artist's personality. I wonder whether Miaka's appetite says something about me... (The editorial department thinks that my first editor, Ms. Y., is the model.) I washed my face and applied some skin lotion. This is the way I spend my free time. And the lotion's yogurt smell just gets me going!! It's addictive! When I met with my editor at the cafe, I ordered some cocoa, and it looked so delicious, I couldn't contain my smile. I don't hold back at mealtime... Hey! It's healthy! No matter how determined I am to lose weight, when I try to control myself, I wind up eating. We're human, aren't we? We gotta eat! My pen's running out of ink!

The stuffed cabbage I had for dinner was so good! But right now, I have a craving for crab. The next time I visit home, I have a reservation for Chanko Nabe.

I don't know what to do! I have to wrap this up! (And I've written to the point where I have to find a good conclusion to this chat section!) It's no conclusion, but I've filled up enough space.

DUM DA DA DUM DUM--DUM DUM (curtain)

What the heck was this chat section about?

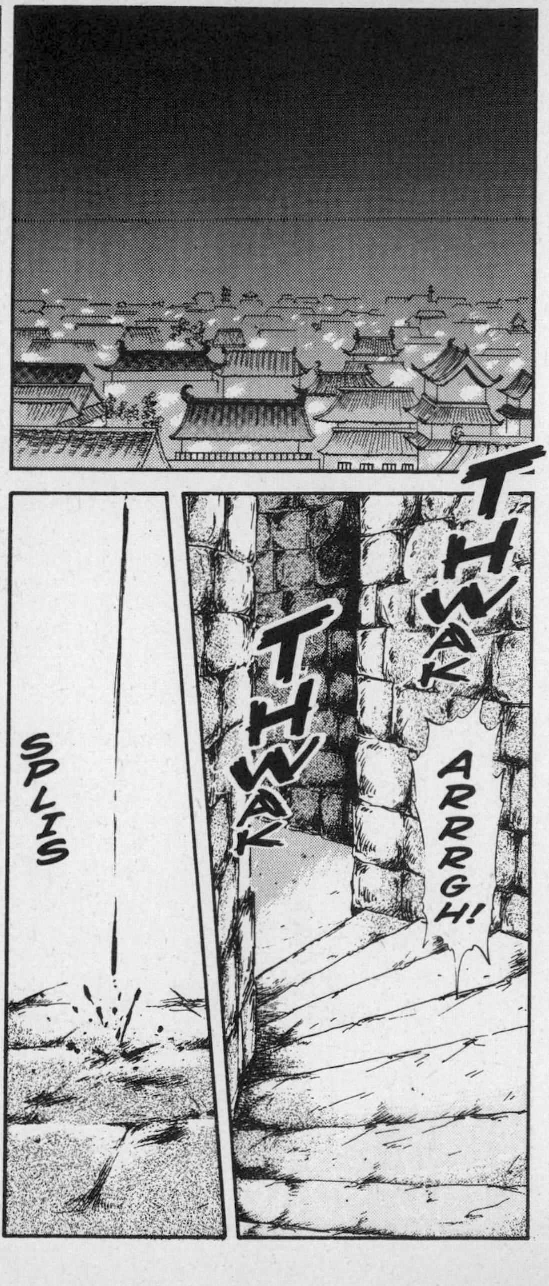
THWAK
THWAK
ARRRGH!
SPLIS

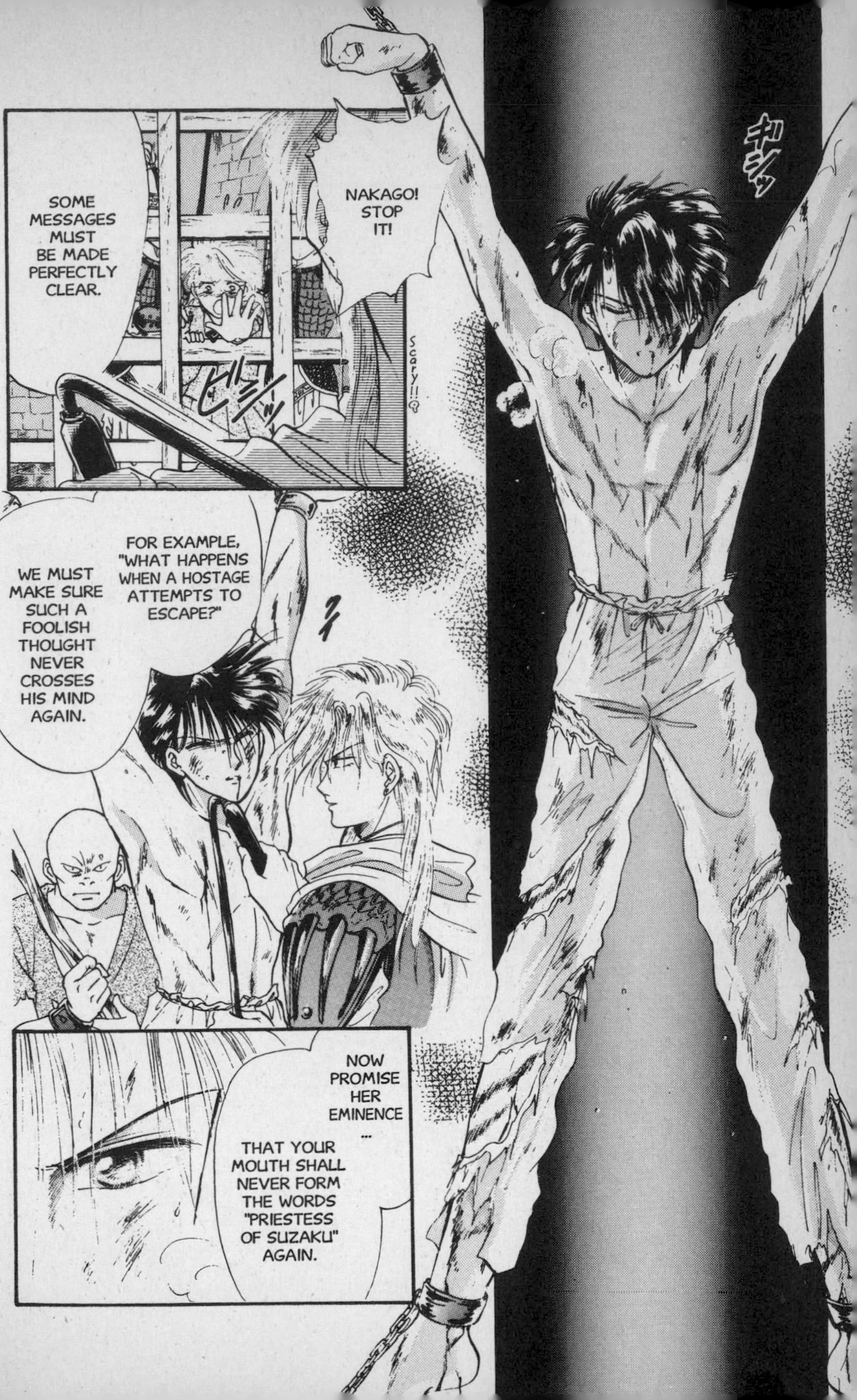
ギシッ
NAKAGO! STOP IT!
SOME MESSAGES MUST BE MADE PERFECTLY CLEAR.
Scary!!
FOR EXAMPLE, "WHAT HAPPENS WHEN A HOSTAGE ATTEMPTS TO ESCAPE?"
WE MUST MAKE SURE SUCH A FOOLISH THOUGHT NEVER CROSSES HIS MIND AGAIN.
NOW PROMISE HER EMINENCE ...
THAT YOUR MOUTH SHALL NEVER FORM THE WORDS "PRIESTESS OF SUZAKU" AGAIN.

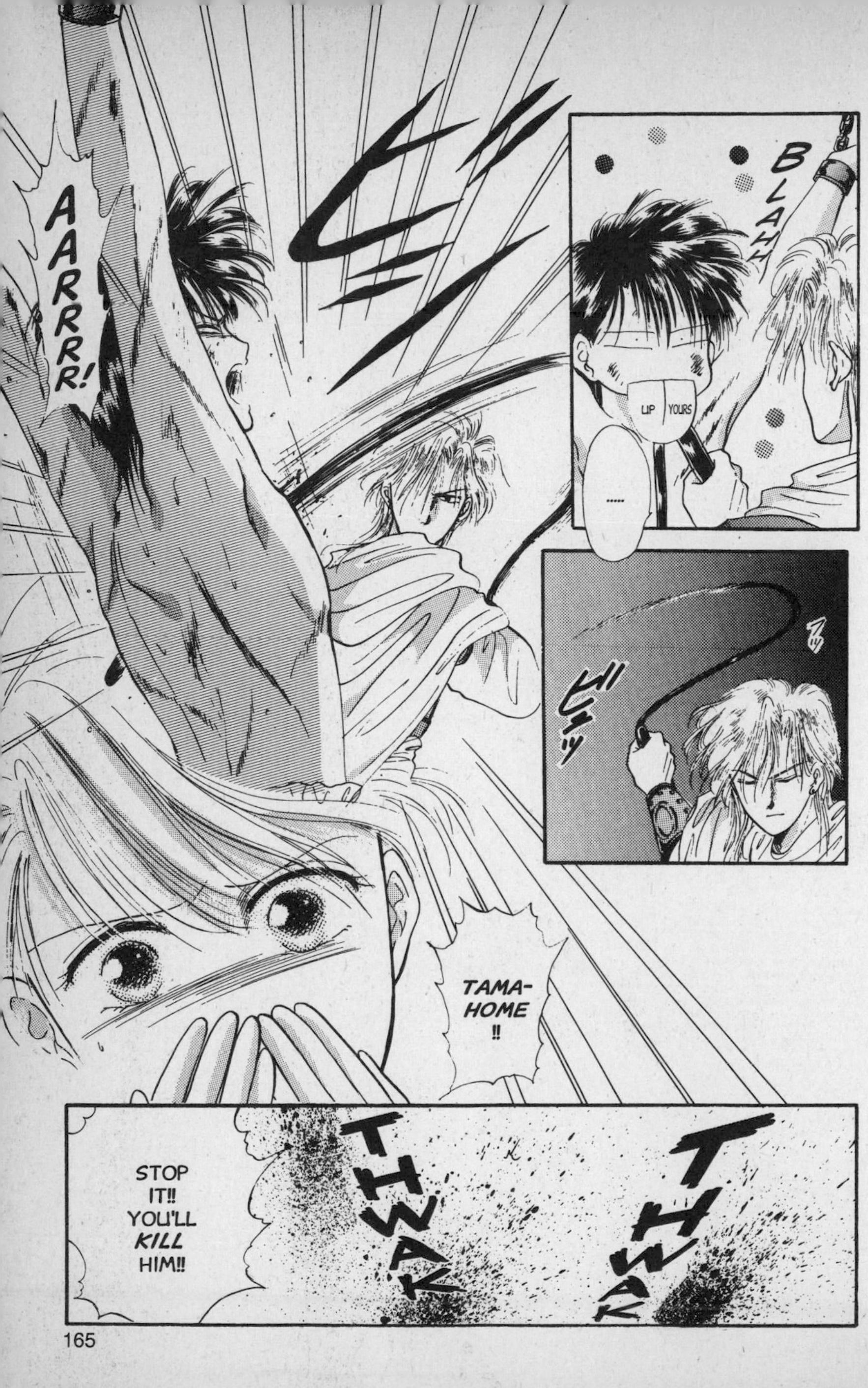
BLAHH
UP YOURS
......
ビシッ
AARRRR!
TAMA-HOME!!
THWAK
THWAK
STOP IT!! YOU'LL *KILL* HIM!!

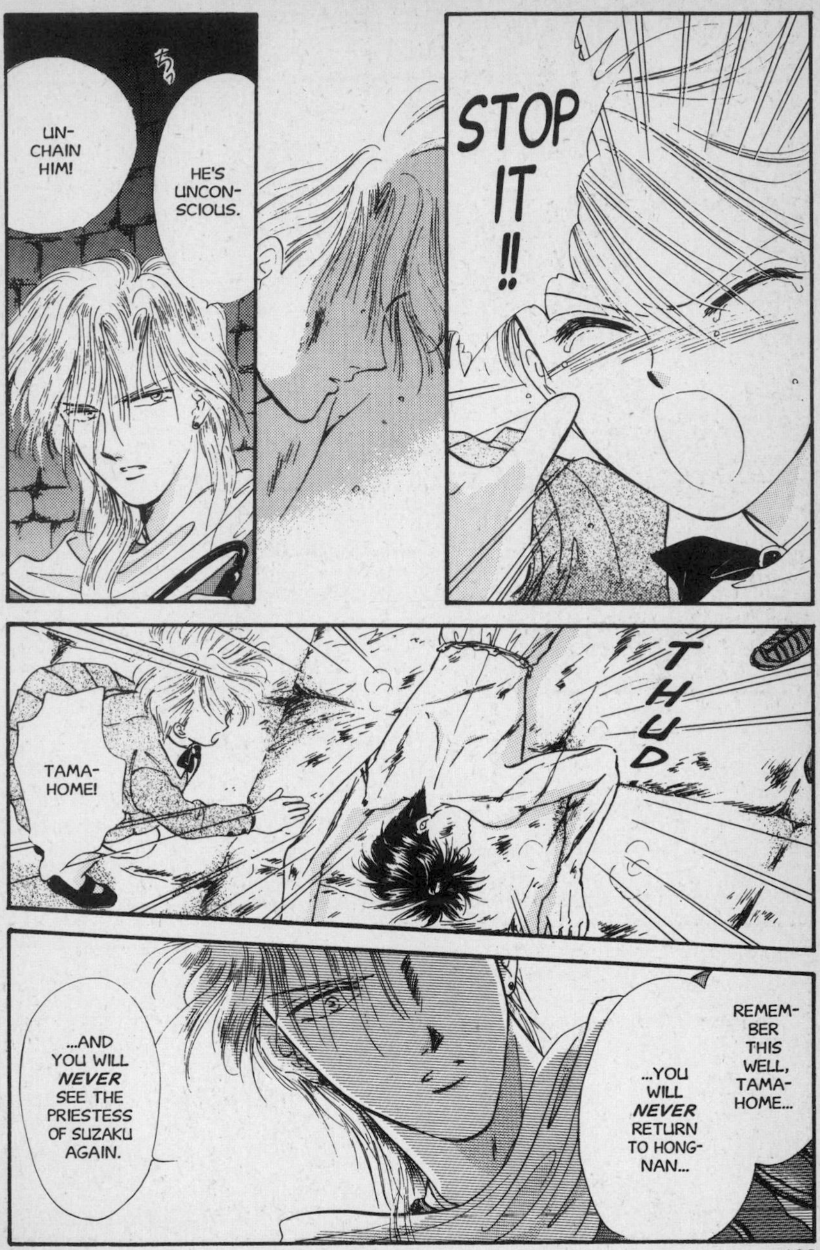
STOP IT!!
HE'S UNCONSCIOUS.
UN-CHAIN HIM!
THUD
TAMA-HOME!
REMEMBER THIS WELL, TAMA-HOME...
...YOU WILL *NEVER* RETURN TO HONG-NAN...
...AND YOU WILL *NEVER* SEE THE PRIESTESS OF SUZAKU AGAIN.

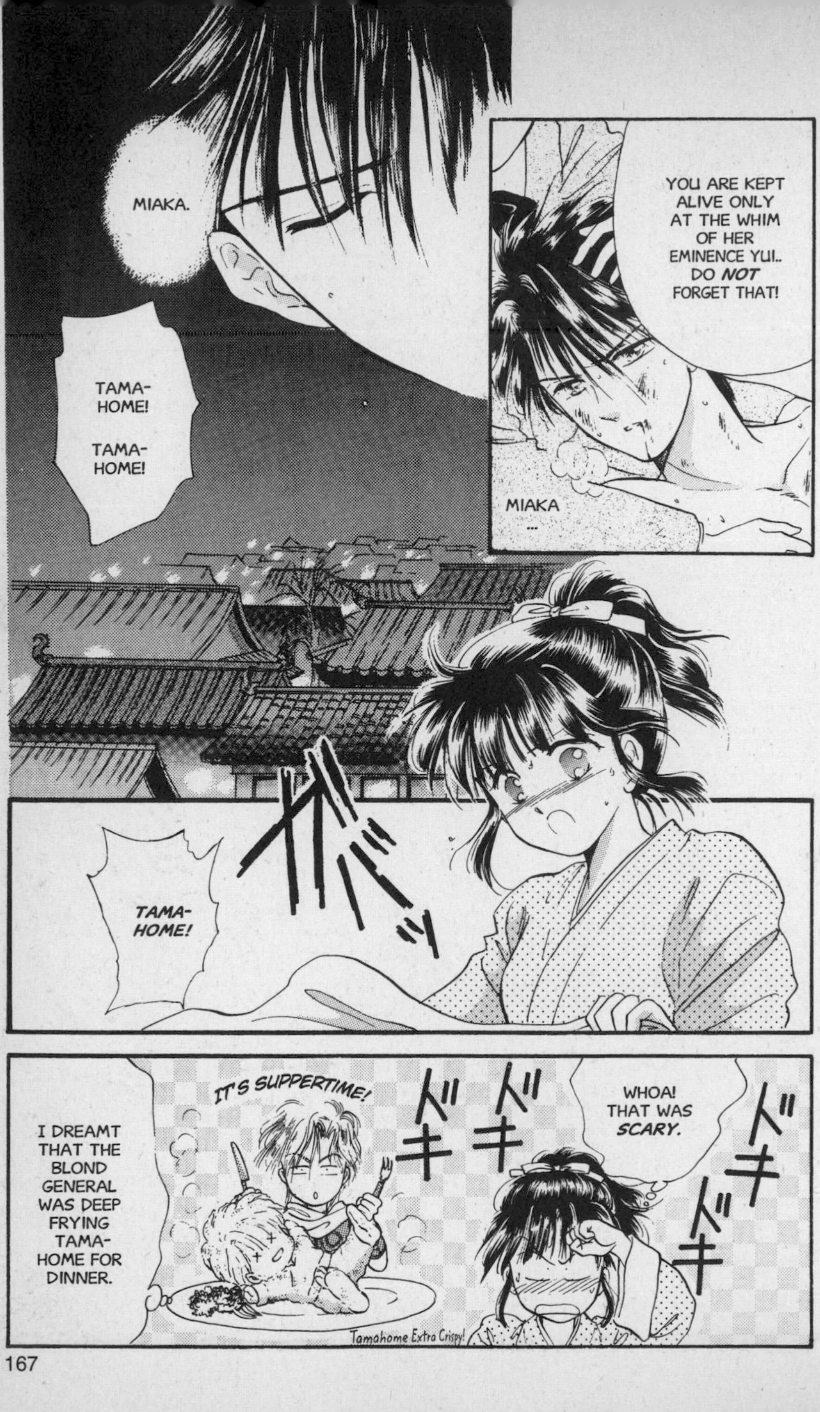
YOU ARE KEPT ALIVE ONLY AT THE WHIM OF HER EMINENCE YUI.. DO *NOT* FORGET THAT!
MIAKA ...
MIAKA.
TAMA-HOME! TAMA-HOME!
TAMA-HOME!
ツ
ドキ
ドキ
WHOA! THAT WAS *SCARY.*
ドキ
ドキ
I DREAMT THAT THE BLOND GENERAL WAS DEEP FRYING TAMA-HOME FOR DINNER.
IT'S SUPPERTIME!
Tamahome Extra Crispy!

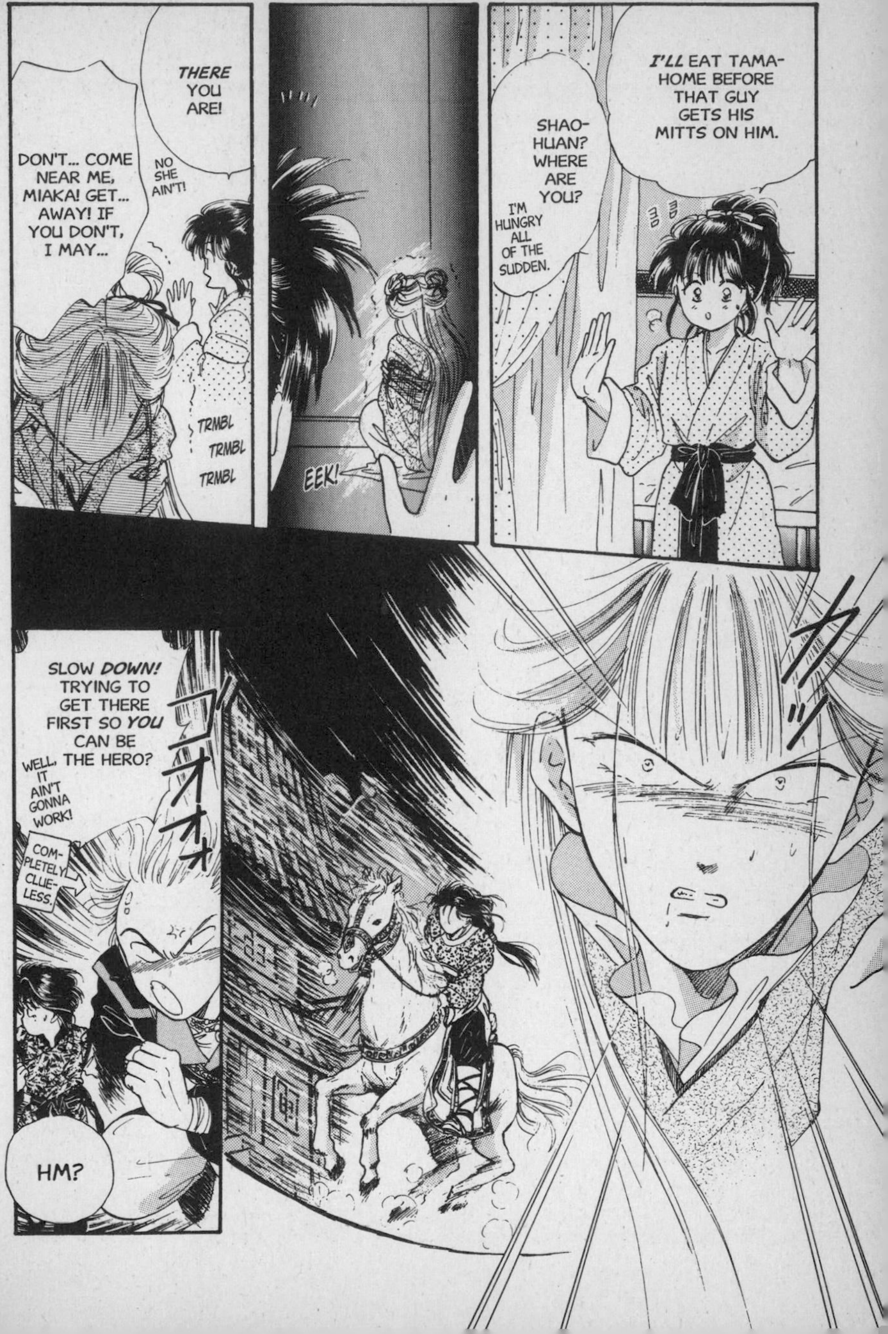
I'LL EAT TAMA-HOME BEFORE THAT GUY GETS HIS MITTS ON HIM.
SHAO-HUAN? WHERE ARE YOU?
I'M HUNGRY ALL OF THE SUDDEN.
EEK!
THERE YOU ARE!
NO SHE AIN'T!
DON'T... COME NEAR ME, MIAKA! GET... AWAY! IF YOU DON'T, I MAY...
TRMBL TRMBL TRMBL
SLOW DOWN! TRYING TO GET THERE FIRST SO YOU CAN BE THE HERO?
WELL, IT AIN'T GONNA WORK!
COMPLETELY CLUELESS.
HM?

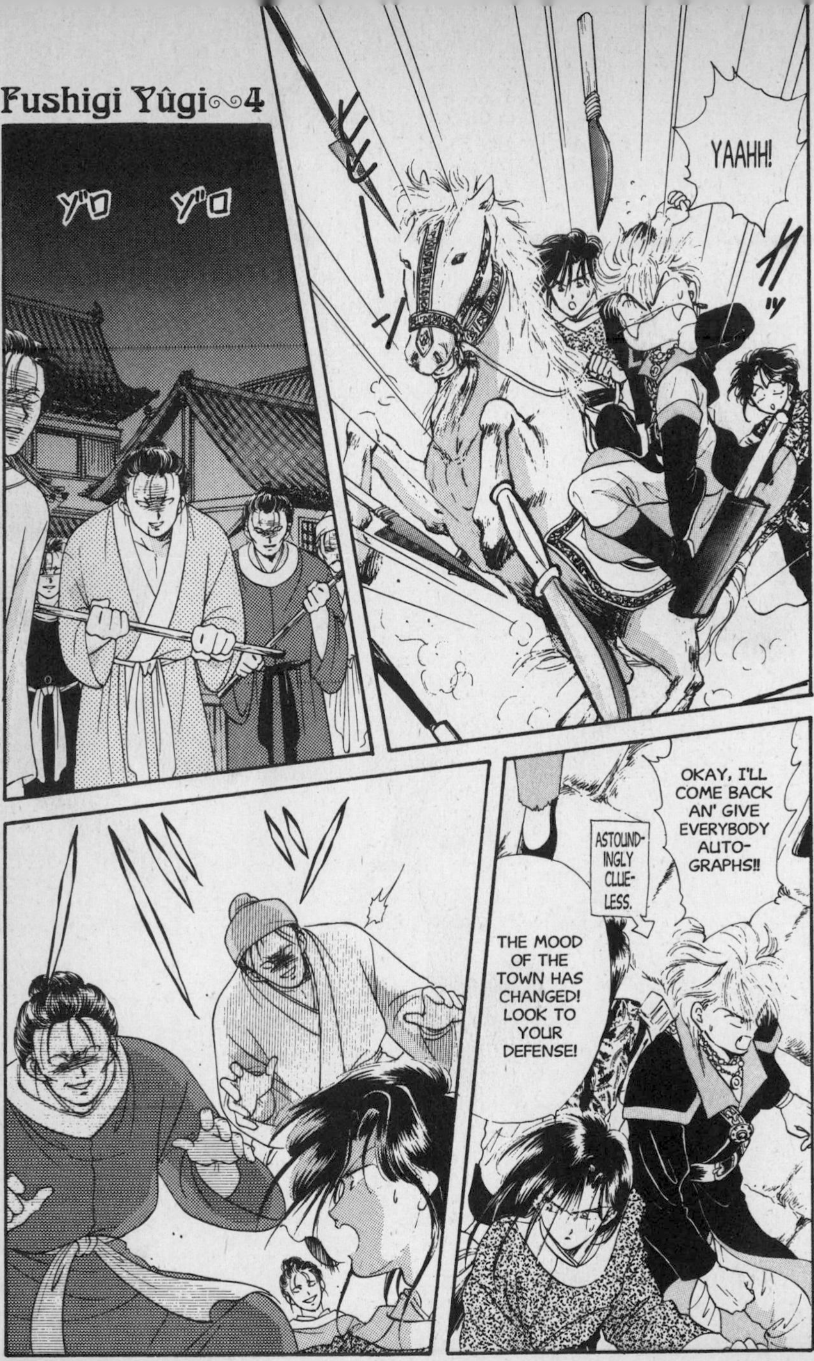
YAAHH!
ッ
ゾロ ゾロ
OKAY, I'LL COME BACK AN' GIVE EVERYBODY AUTO-GRAPHS!!
ASTOUND-INGLY CLUE-LESS.
THE MOOD OF THE TOWN HAS CHANGED! LOOK TO YOUR DEFENSE!

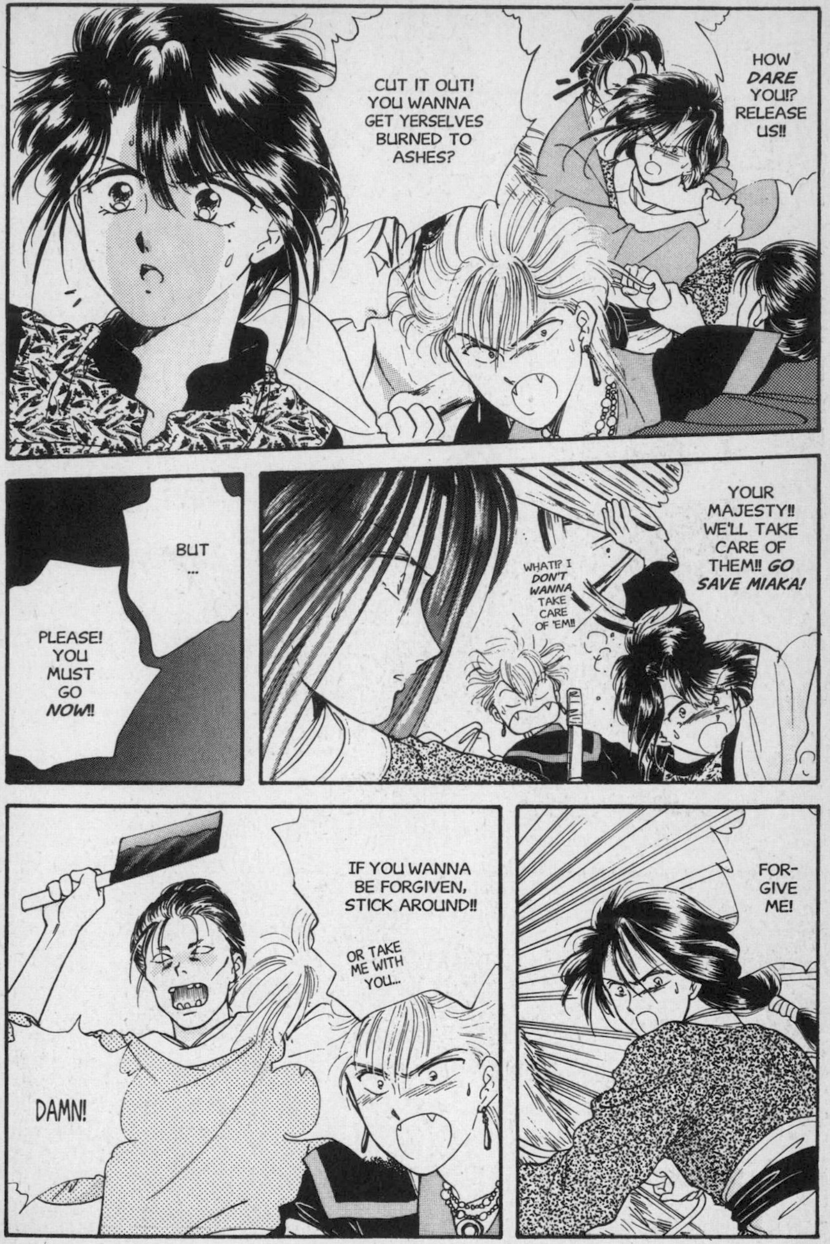
HOW DARE YOU!? RELEASE US!!
CUT IT OUT! YOU WANNA GET YERSELVES BURNED TO ASHES?
YOUR MAJESTY!! WE'LL TAKE CARE OF THEM!! GO SAVE MIAKA!
WHAT!? I DON'T WANNA TAKE CARE OF 'EM!!
BUT ...
PLEASE! YOU MUST GO NOW!!
FOR-GIVE ME!
IF YOU WANNA BE FORGIVEN, STICK AROUND!!
OR TAKE ME WITH YOU...
DAMN!

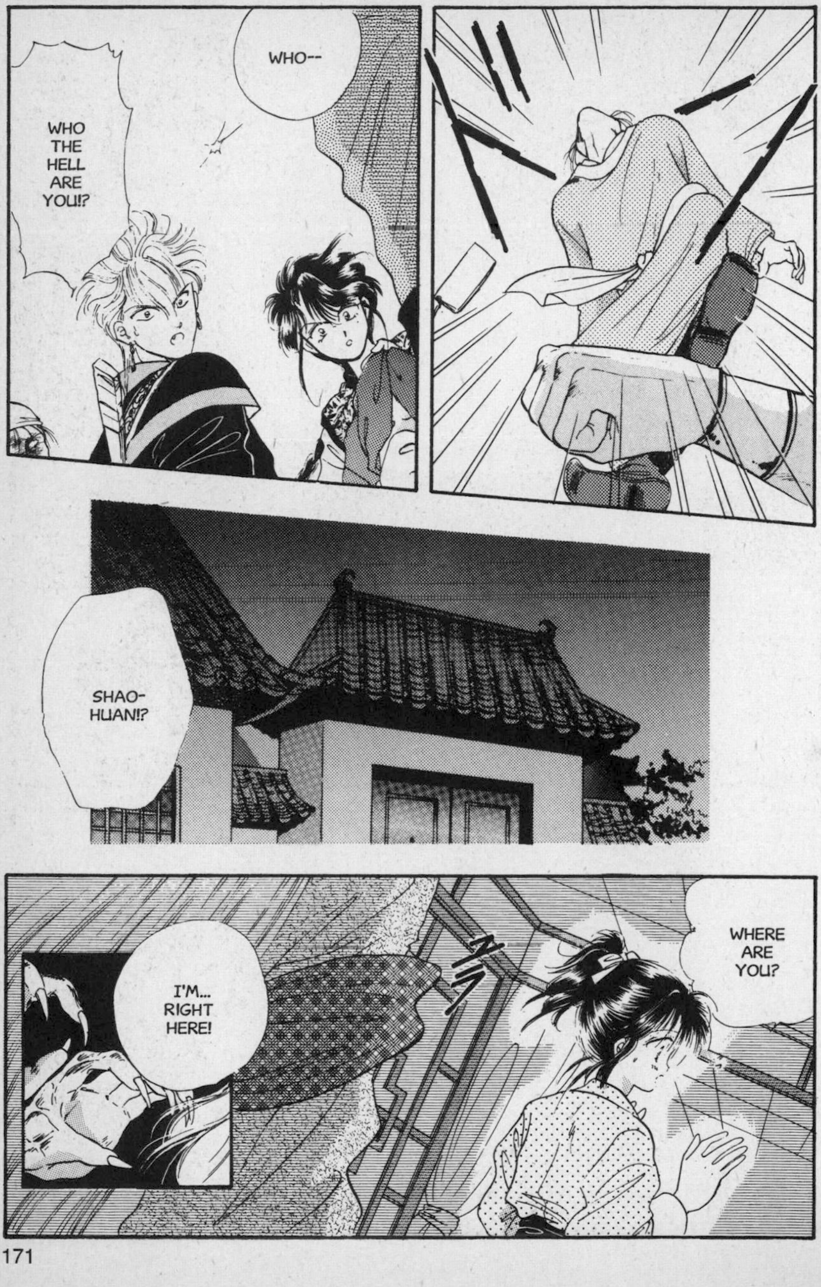
WHO--
WHO THE HELL ARE YOU!?
SHAO-HUAN!?
WHERE ARE YOU?
I'M... RIGHT HERE!

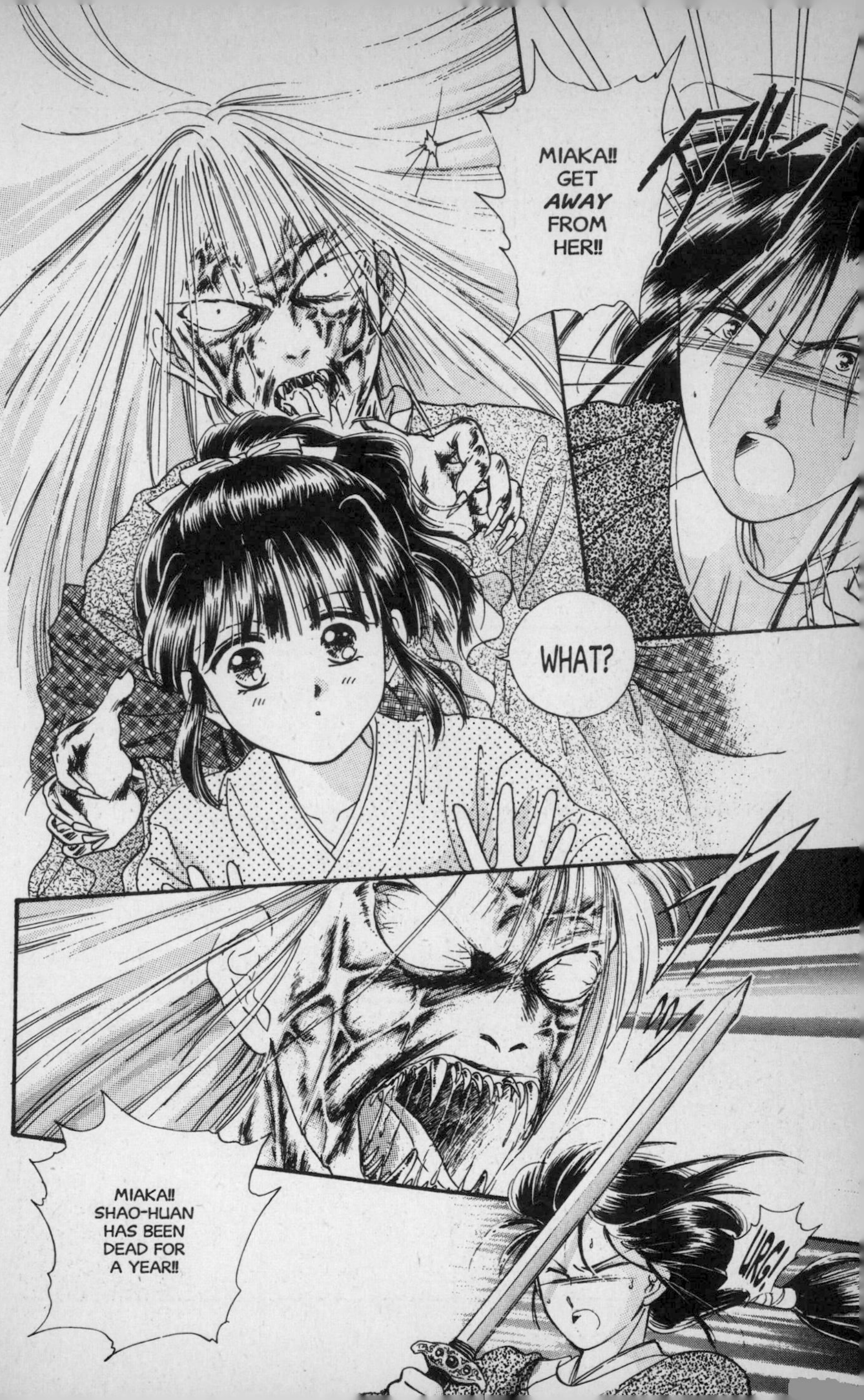
MIAKA!! GET AWAY FROM HER!!
WHAT?
URG!
MIAKA!! SHAO-HUAN HAS BEEN DEAD FOR A YEAR!!

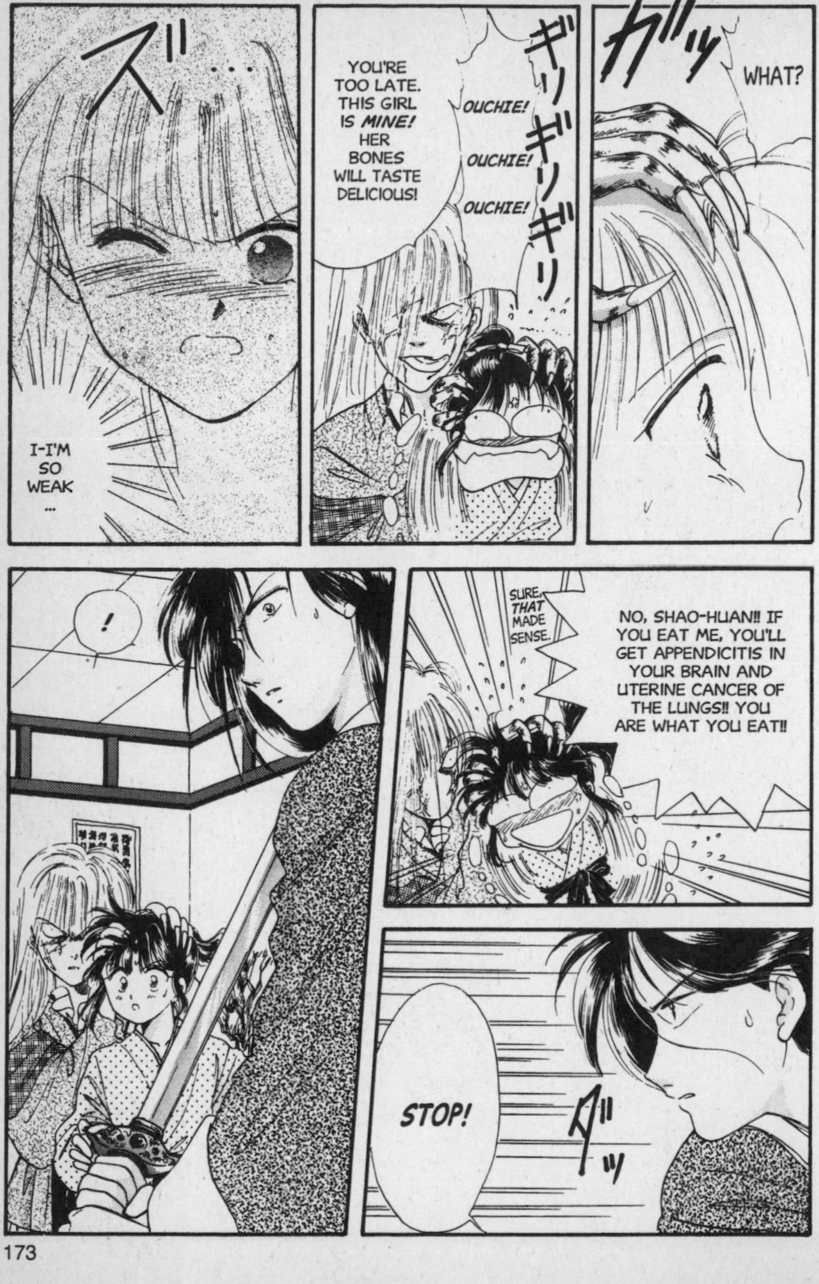
ガッ
WHAT?
ギリギリ
OUCHIE!
OUCHIE!
OUCHIE!
YOU'RE TOO LATE. THIS GIRL IS *MINE!* HER BONES WILL TASTE DELICIOUS!
ズ…
I-I'M SO WEAK ...
NO, SHAO-HUAN!! IF YOU EAT ME, YOU'LL GET APPENDICITIS IN YOUR BRAIN AND UTERINE CANCER OF THE LUNGS!! YOU ARE WHAT YOU EAT!!
SURE, *THAT* MADE SENSE.
ダッ
STOP!
!

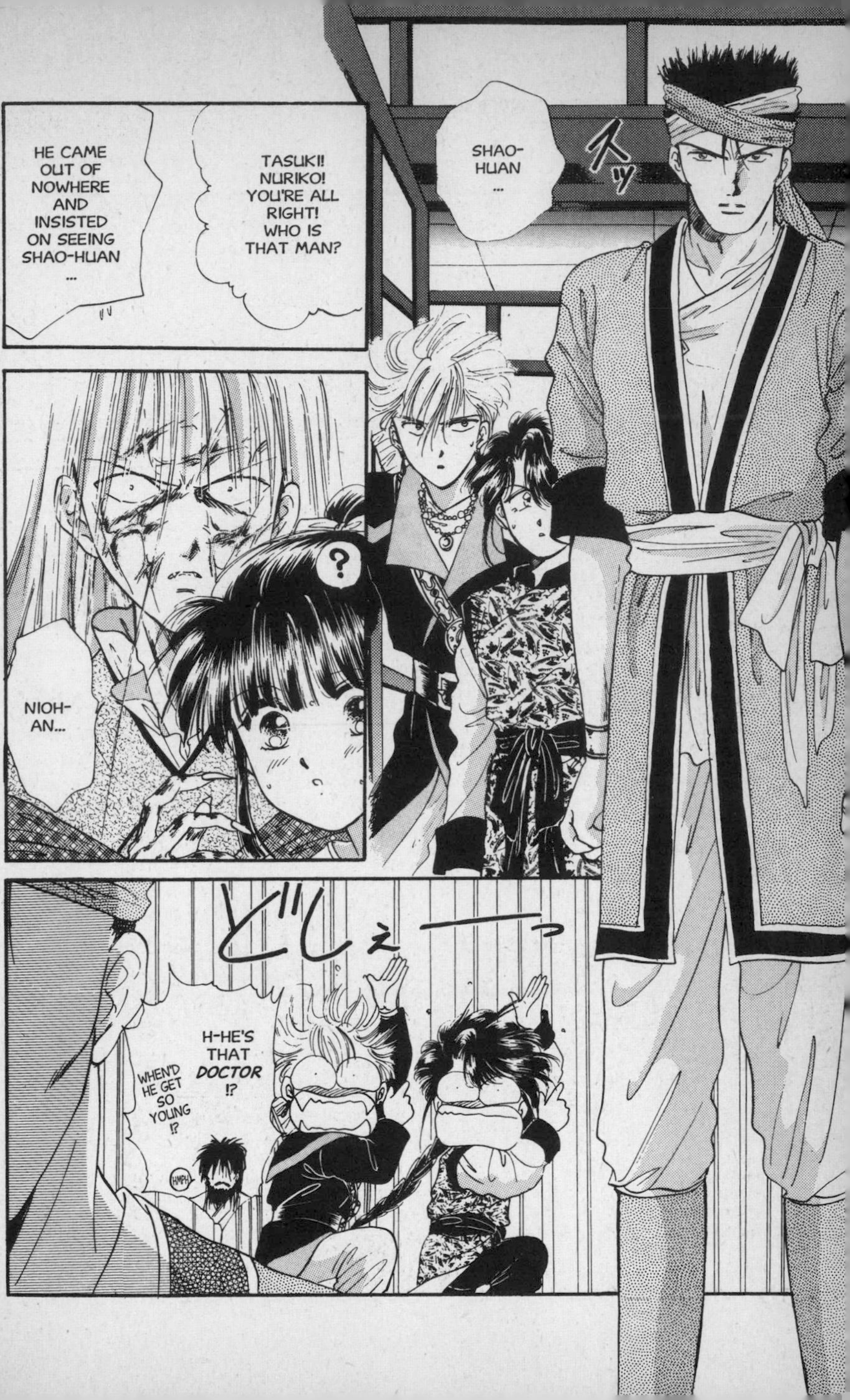
スッ
SHAO-HUAN ...
TASUKI! NURIKO! YOU'RE ALL RIGHT! WHO IS THAT MAN?
HE CAME OUT OF NOWHERE AND INSISTED ON SEEING SHAO-HUAN ...
NIOH-AN...
どしぇーーっ
H-HE'S THAT *DOCTOR* !?
WHEN'D HE GET SO YOUNG !?
HMPH

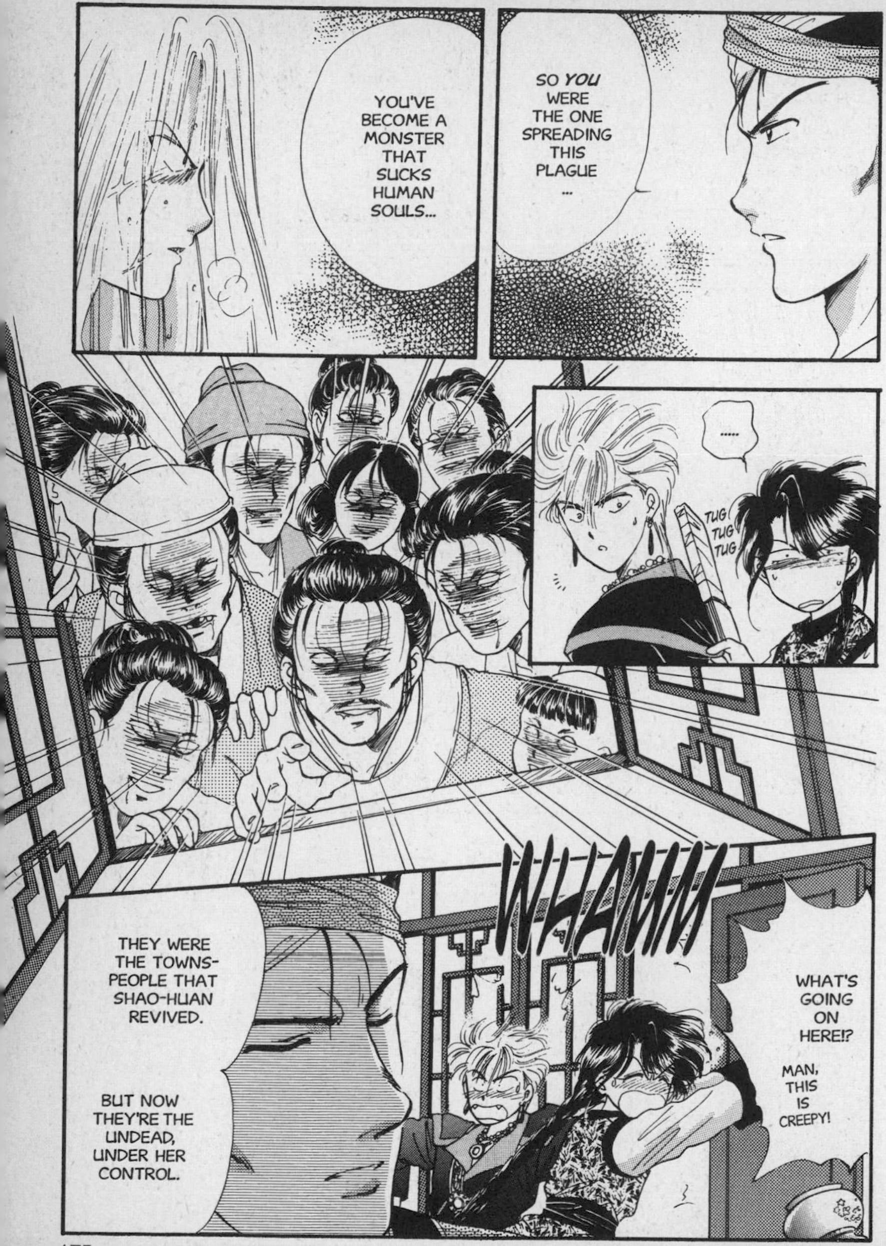
SO *YOU* WERE THE ONE SPREADING THIS PLAGUE ...
YOU'VE BECOME A MONSTER THAT SUCKS HUMAN SOULS...
.....
TUG TUG TUG
WHAMM
WHAT'S GOING ON HERE!?
MAN, THIS IS CREEPY!
THEY WERE THE TOWNS-PEOPLE THAT SHAO-HUAN REVIVED.
BUT NOW THEY'RE THE UNDEAD, UNDER HER CONTROL.

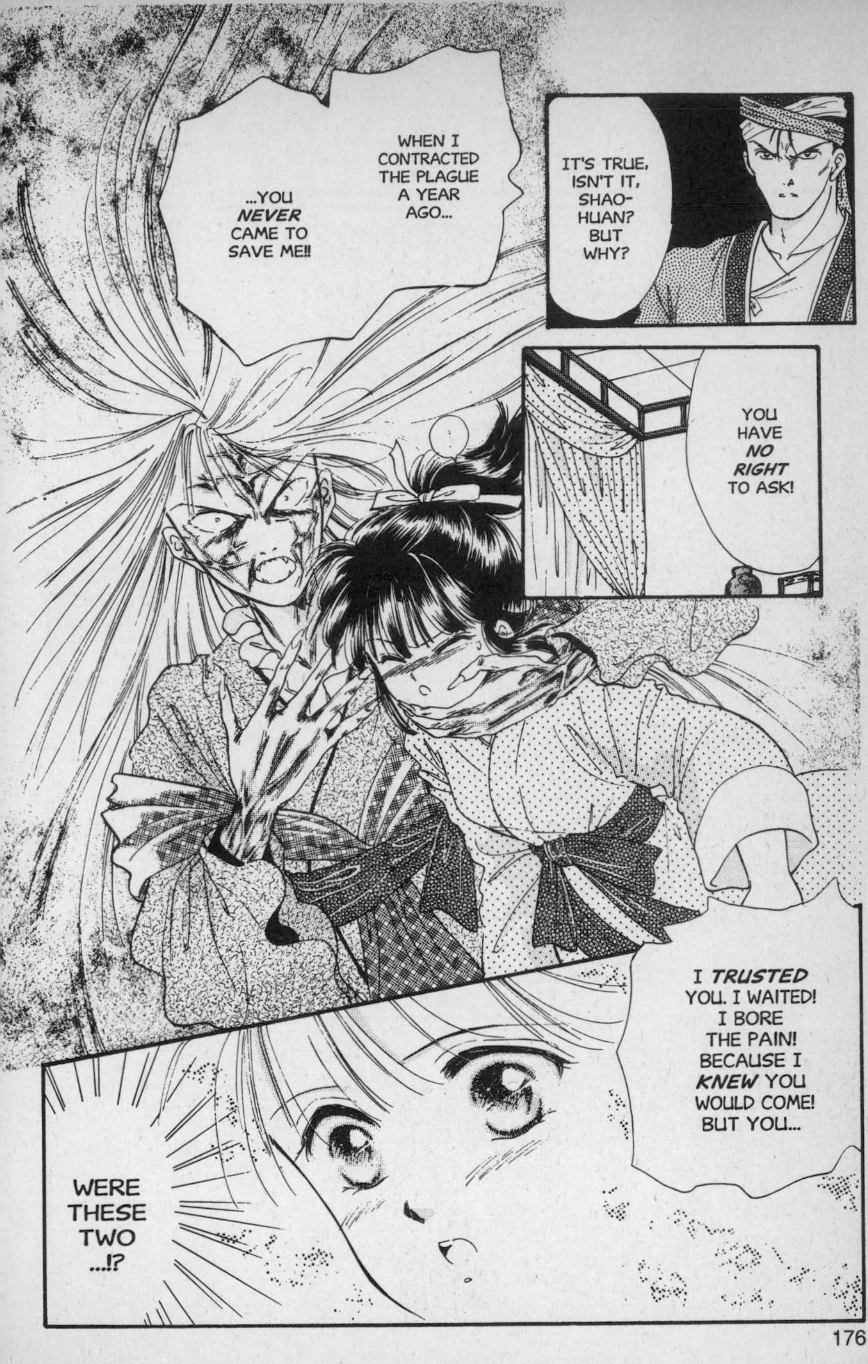
IT'S TRUE, ISN'T IT, SHAO-HUAN? BUT WHY?
YOU HAVE *NO RIGHT* TO ASK!
WHEN I CONTRACTED THE PLAGUE A YEAR AGO...
...YOU *NEVER* CAME TO SAVE ME!!
I *TRUSTED* YOU. I WAITED! I BORE THE PAIN! BECAUSE I *KNEW* YOU WOULD COME! BUT YOU...
WERE THESE TWO ...!?

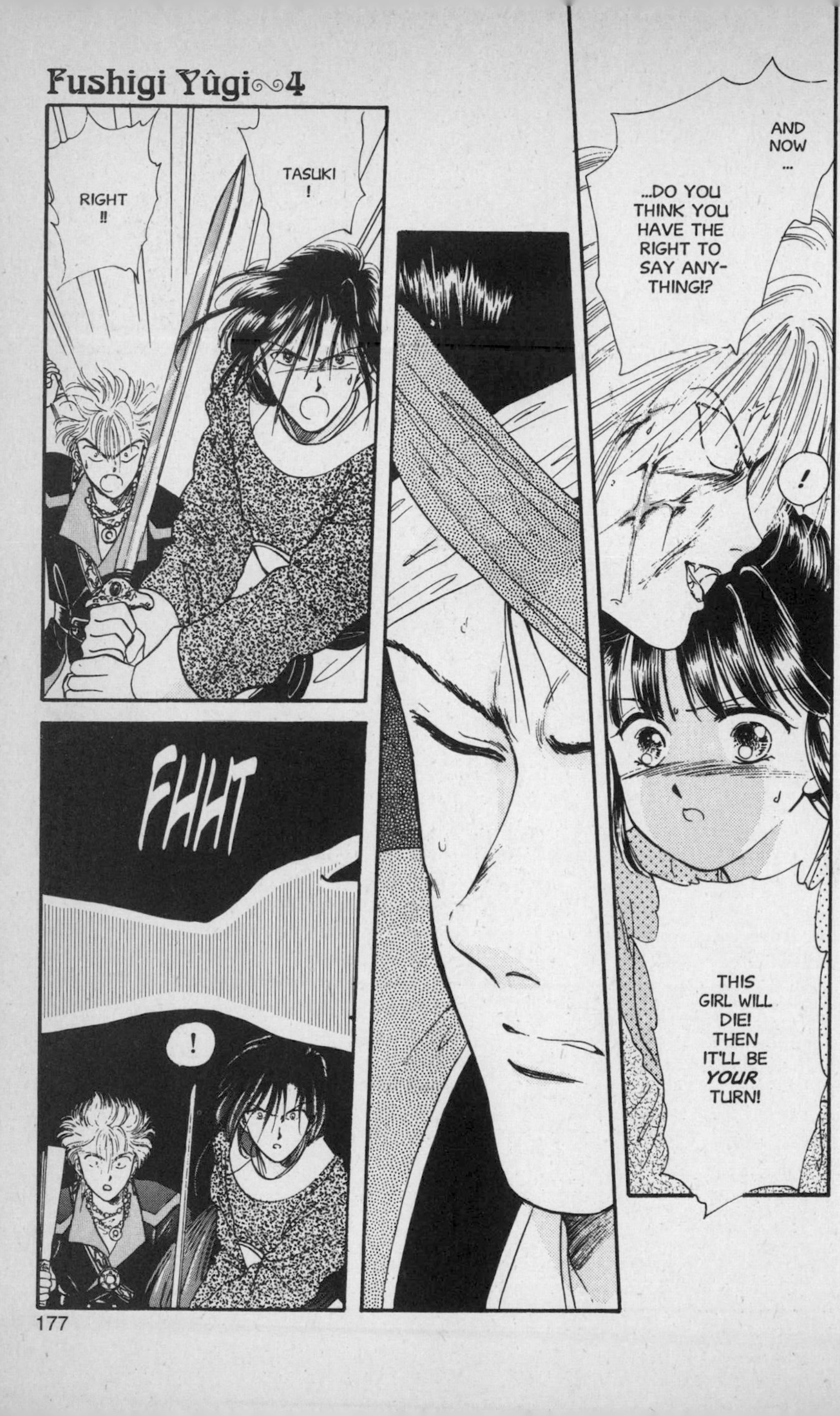
AND NOW ...
...DO YOU THINK YOU HAVE THE RIGHT TO SAY ANY-THING!?
!
THIS GIRL WILL DIE! THEN IT'LL BE ***YOUR*** TURN!
TASUKI !
RIGHT !!
FHHT
!

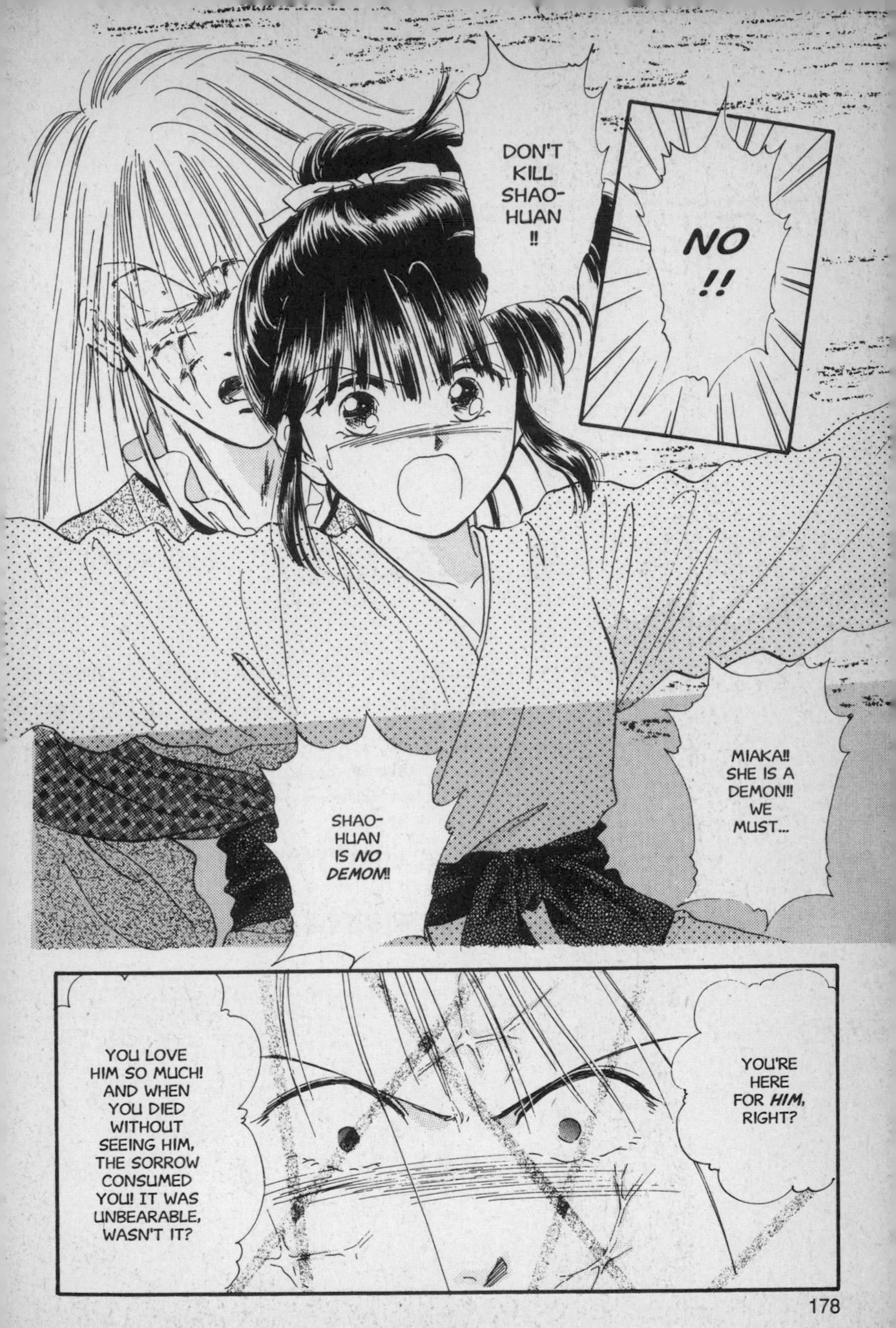
NO !!
DON'T KILL SHAO-HUAN !!
MIAKA!! SHE IS A DEMON!! WE MUST...
SHAO-HUAN IS *NO DEMON*!
YOU'RE HERE FOR *HIM*, RIGHT?
YOU LOVE HIM SO MUCH! AND WHEN YOU DIED WITHOUT SEEING HIM, THE SORROW CONSUMED YOU! IT WAS UNBEARABLE, WASN'T IT?

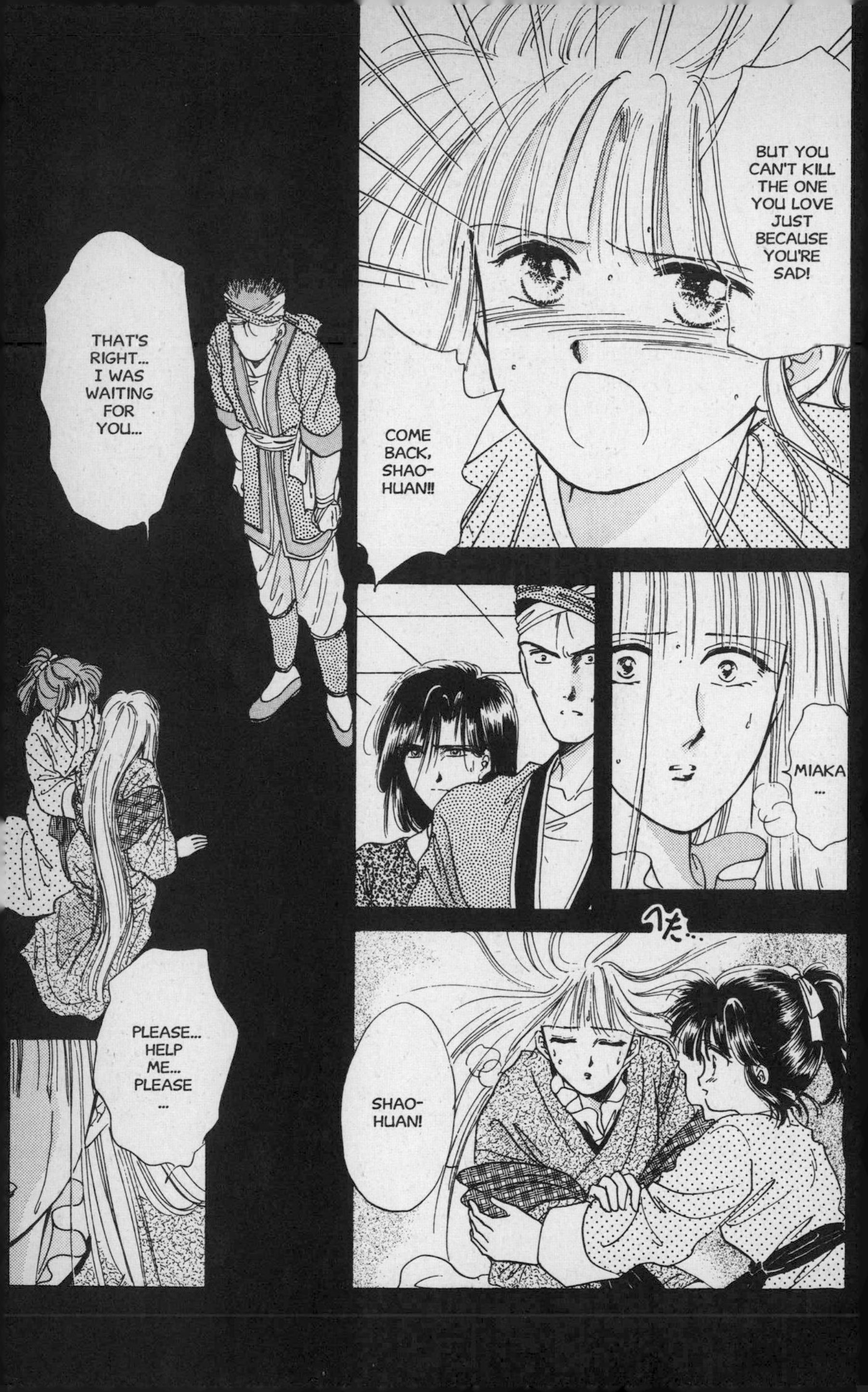
BUT YOU CAN'T KILL THE ONE YOU LOVE JUST BECAUSE YOU'RE SAD!
COME BACK, SHAO-HUAN!!
MIAKA ...
へた...
SHAO-HUAN!
THAT'S RIGHT... I WAS WAITING FOR YOU...
PLEASE... HELP ME... PLEASE ...

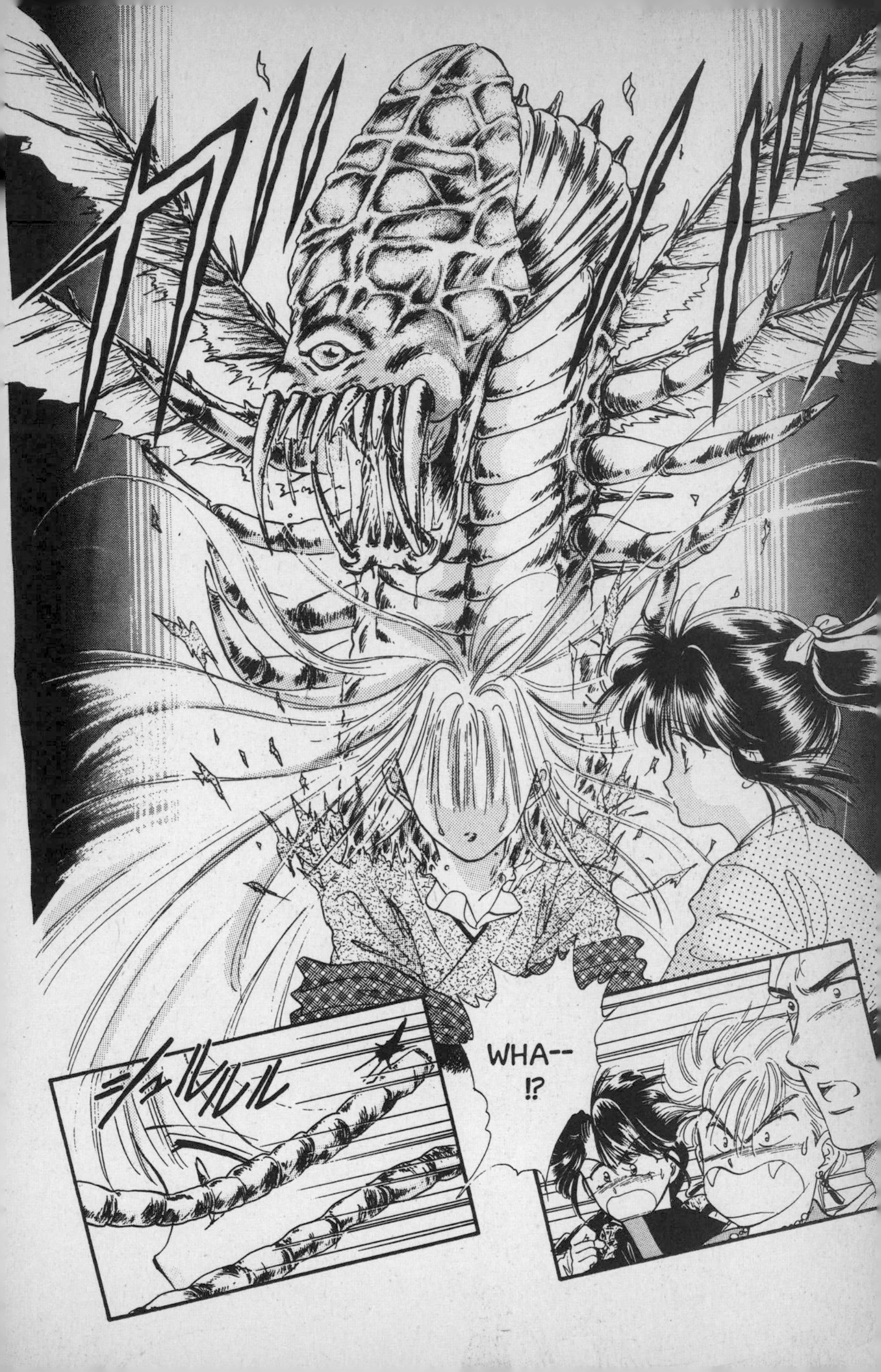
WHA-- !?
シュルルルル

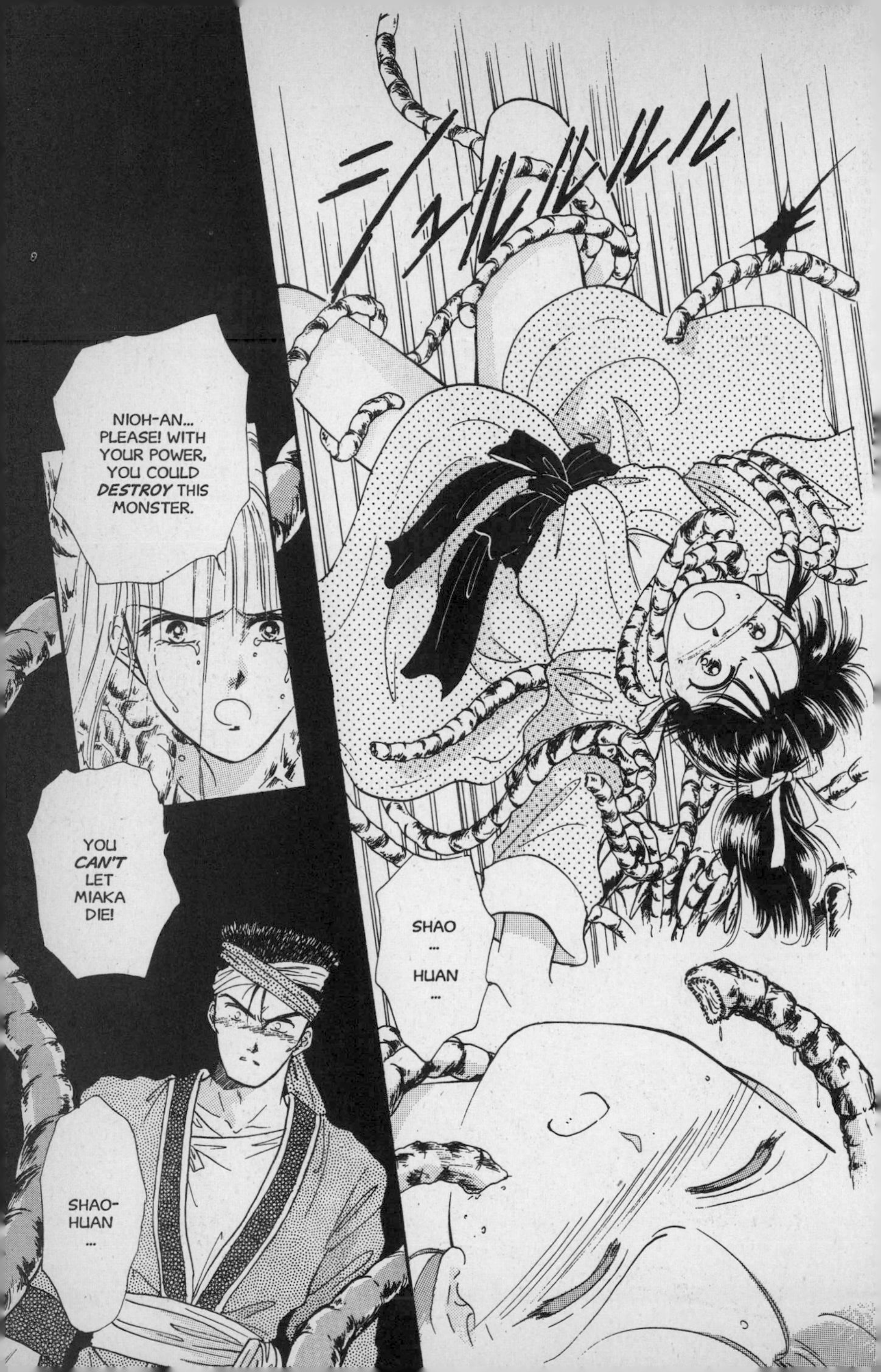
SHAO ... HUAN ...
NIOH-AN... PLEASE! WITH YOUR POWER, YOU COULD *DESTROY* THIS MONSTER.
YOU *CAN'T* LET MIAKA DIE!
SHAO-HUAN ...

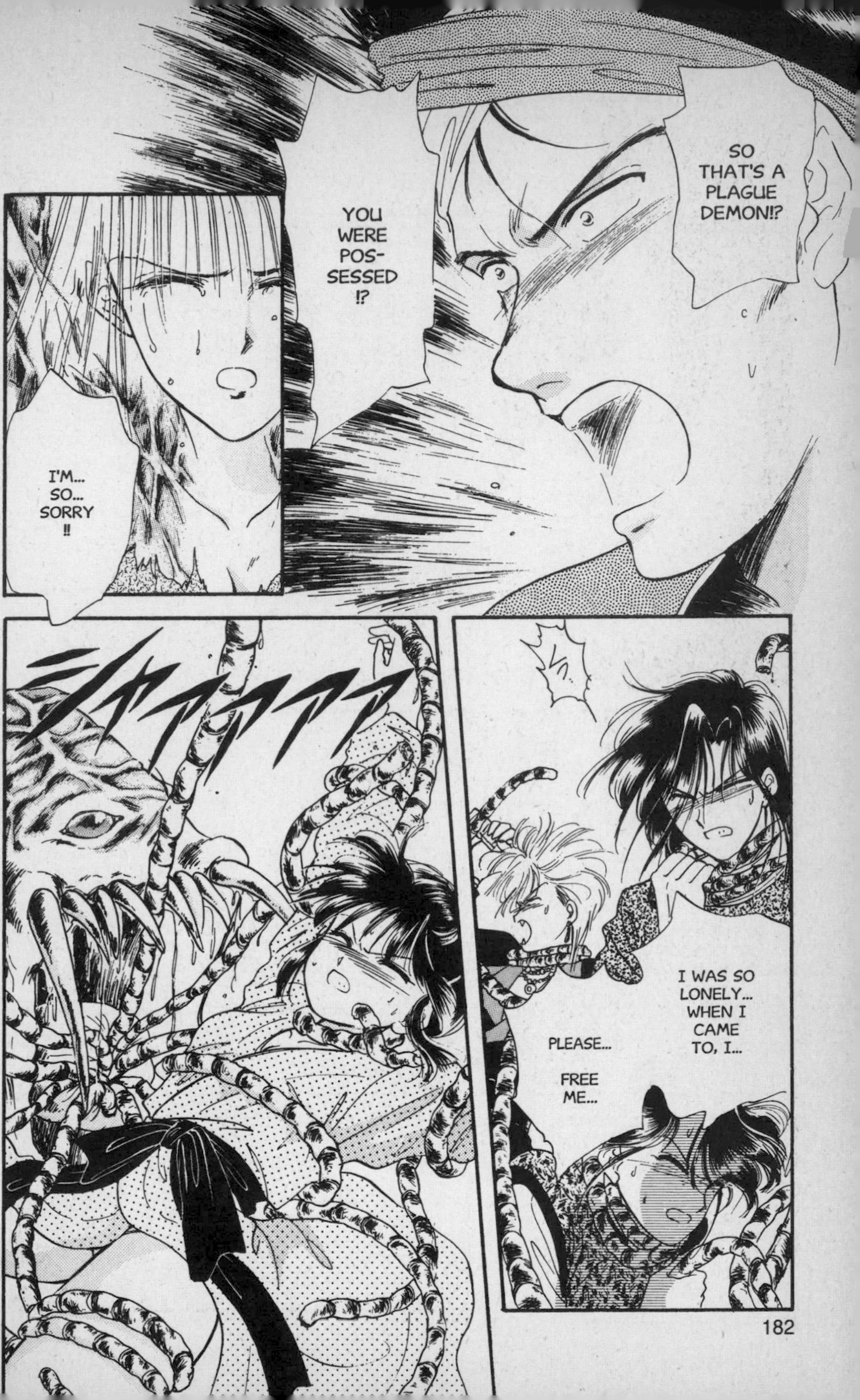
SO THAT'S A PLAGUE DEMON!?
YOU WERE POS-SESSED !?
I'M... SO... SORRY !!
I WAS SO LONELY... WHEN I CAME TO, I...
PLEASE...
FREE ME...
シャアアアアア

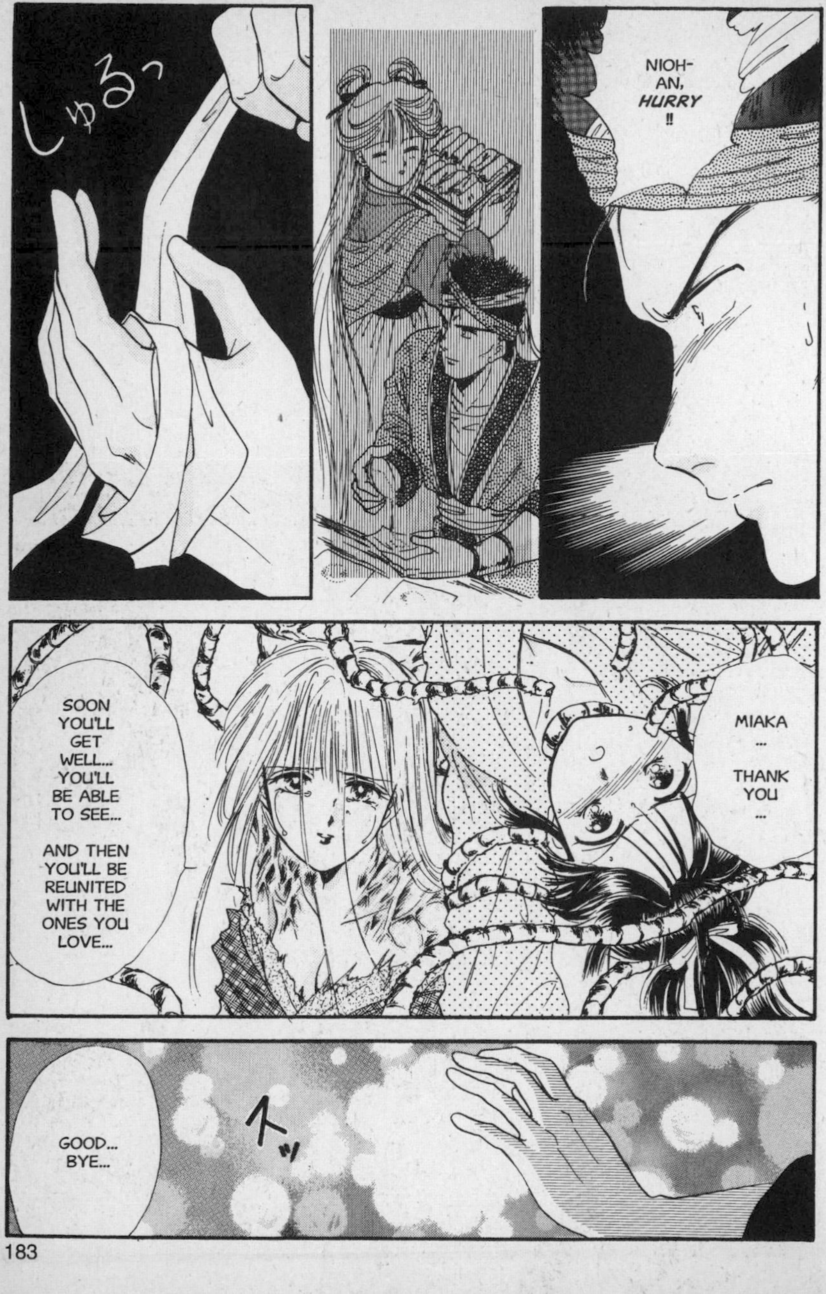
NIOH-AN, HURRY!!
しゅるっ
MIAKA ... THANK YOU ...
SOON YOU'LL GET WELL... YOU'LL BE ABLE TO SEE...
AND THEN YOU'LL BE REUNITED WITH THE ONES YOU LOVE...
スッ
GOOD... BYE...

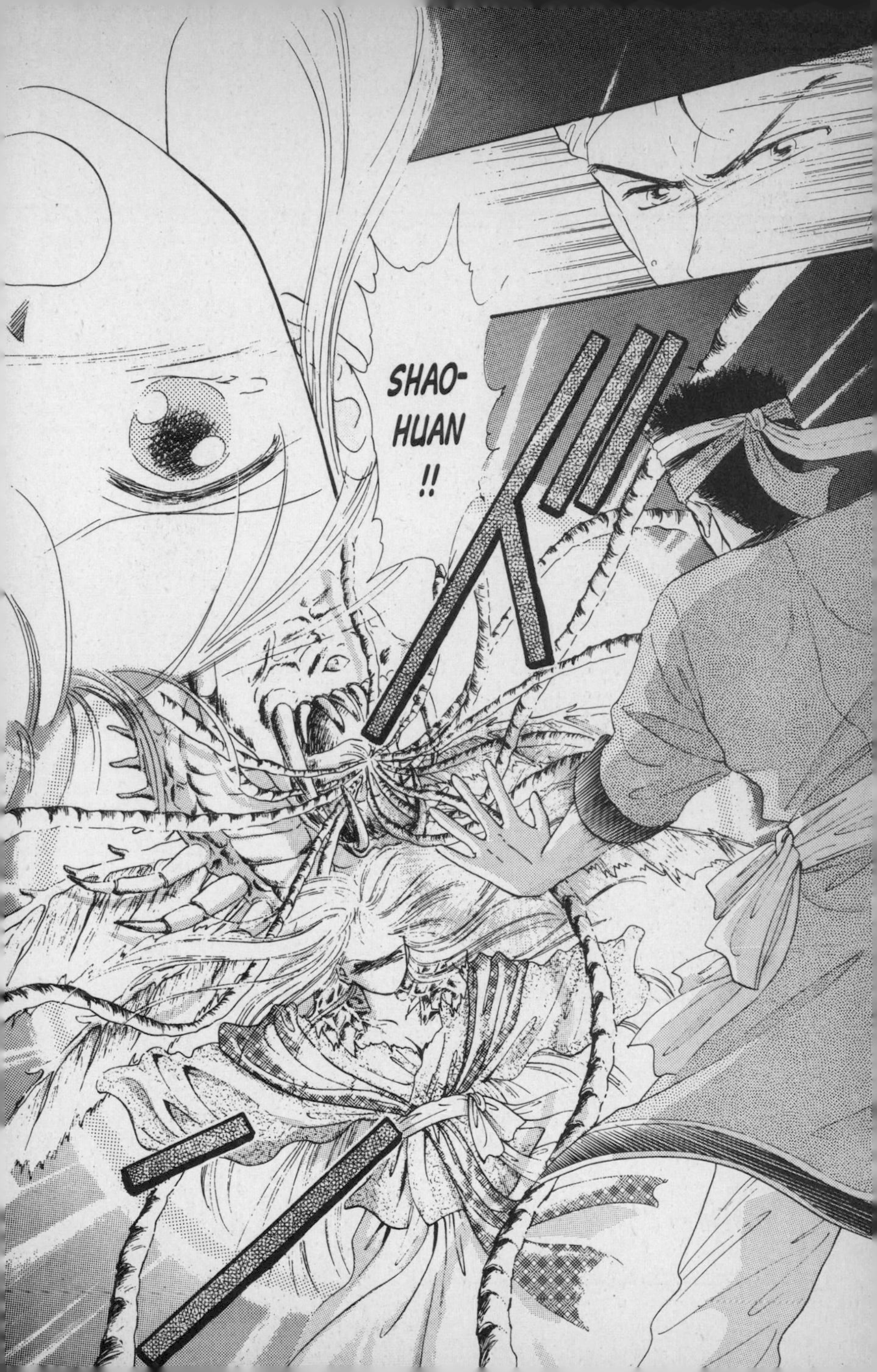
SHAO-HUAN !!

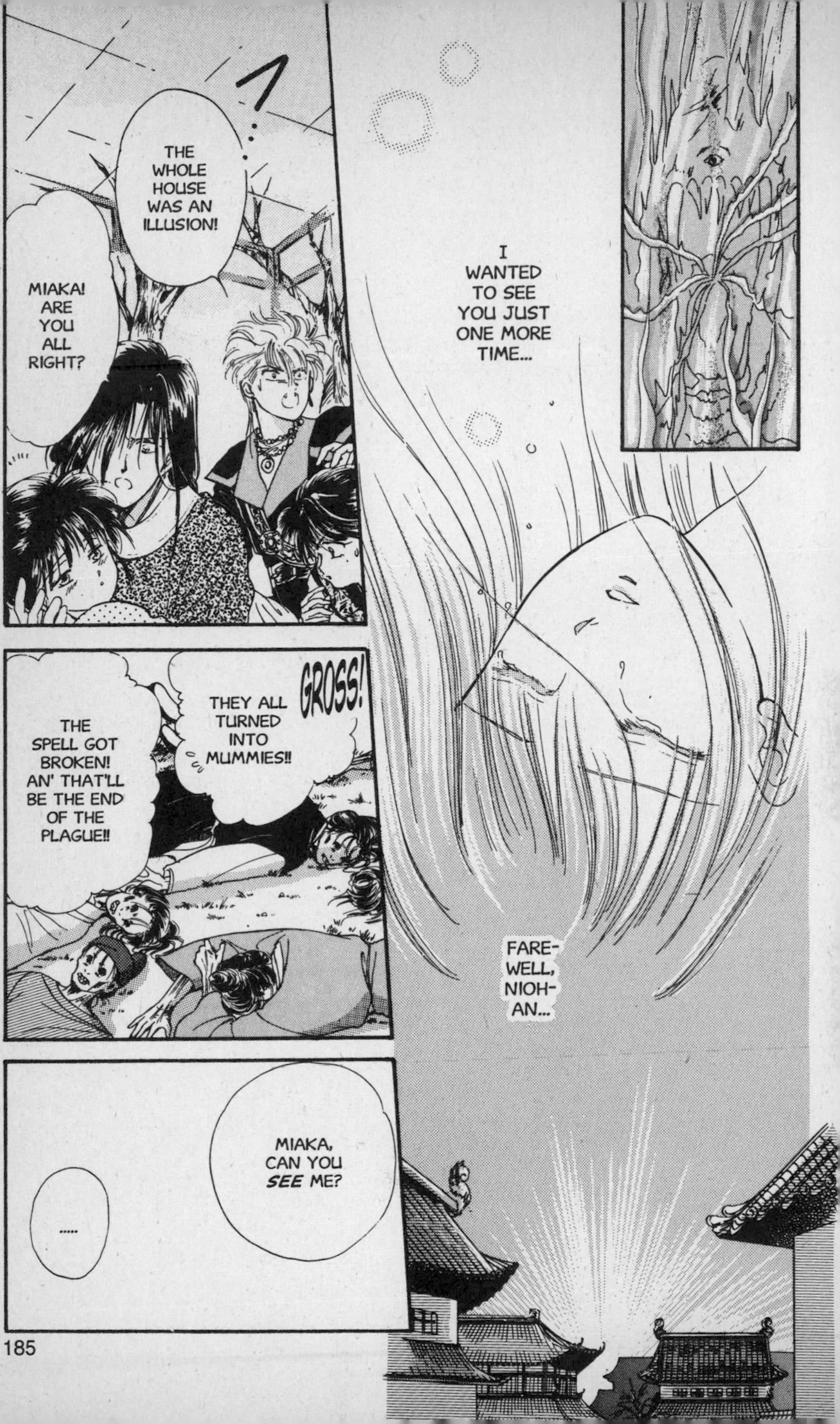
I WANTED TO SEE YOU JUST ONE MORE TIME...
FARE-WELL, NIOH-AN...
THE WHOLE HOUSE WAS AN ILLUSION!
MIAKA! ARE YOU ALL RIGHT?
GROSS!
THEY ALL TURNED INTO MUMMIES!!
THE SPELL GOT BROKEN! AN' THAT'LL BE THE END OF THE PLAGUE!!
MIAKA, CAN YOU *SEE* ME?
.....

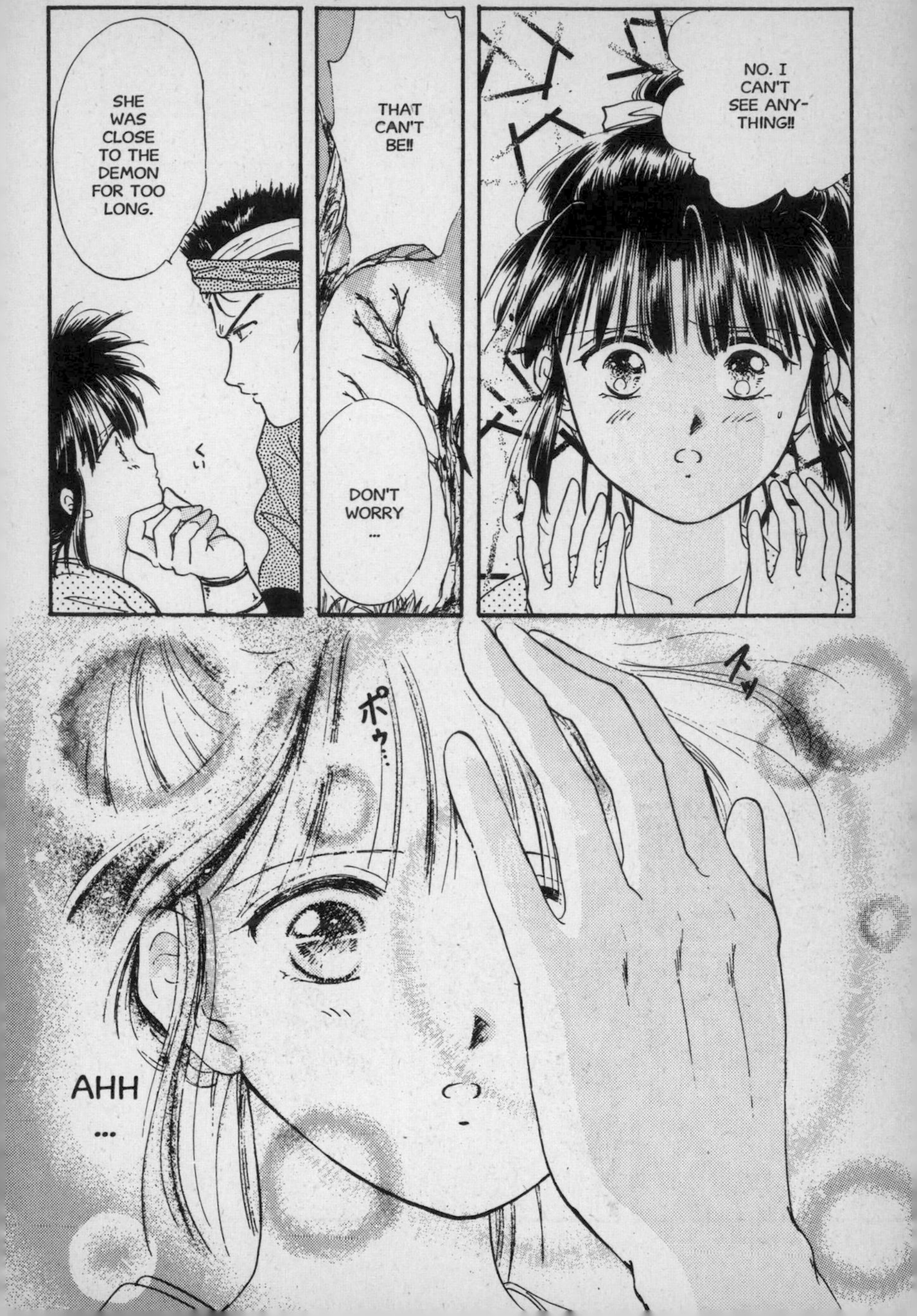
NO. I CAN'T SEE ANYTHING!!
THAT CAN'T BE!!
DON'T WORRY ...
SHE WAS CLOSE TO THE DEMON FOR TOO LONG.
くい
ポゥ…
AHH ...

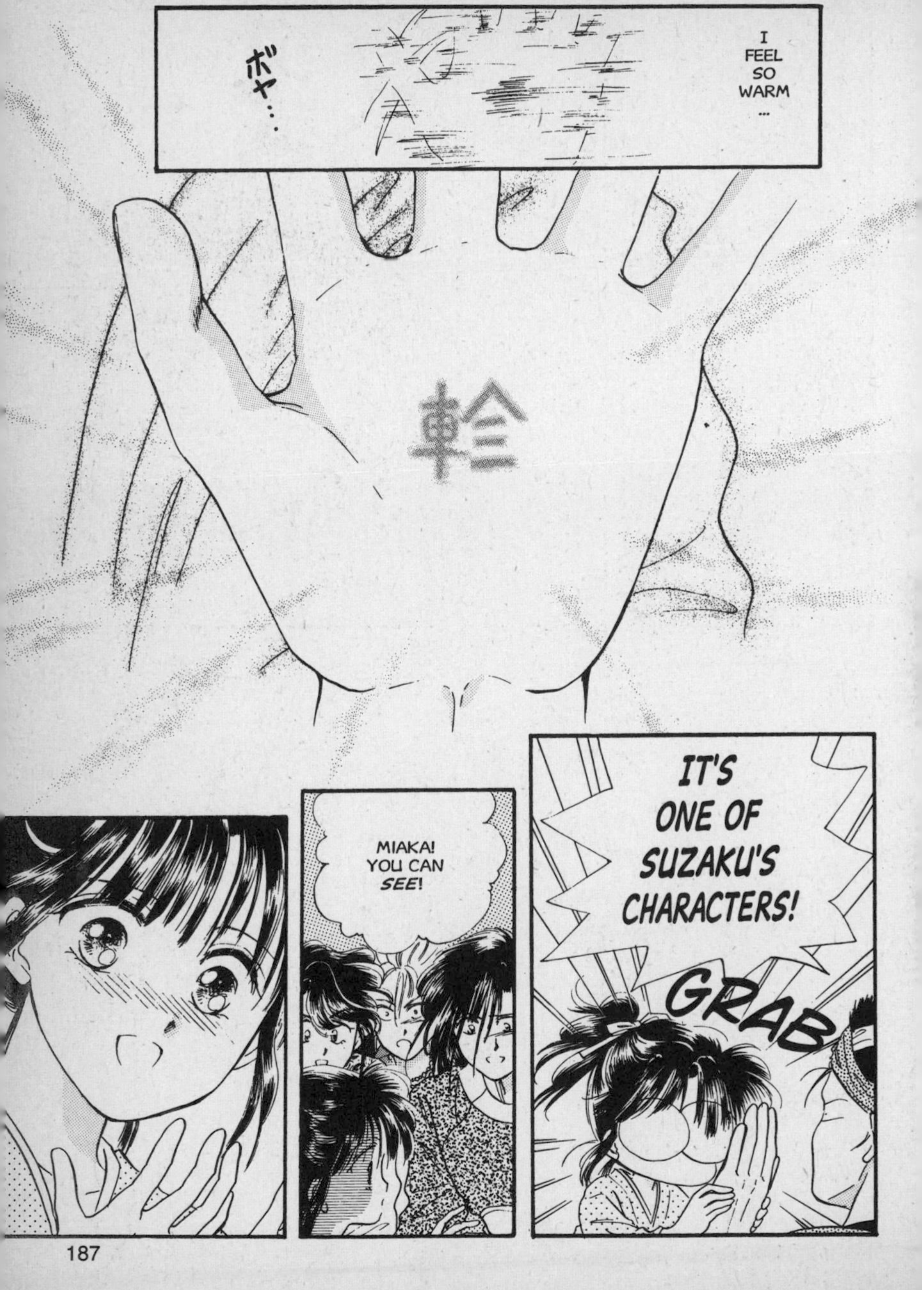
ボヤ…
I FEEL SO WARM ...
IT'S ONE OF SUZAKU'S CHARACTERS!
GRAB
MIAKA! YOU CAN *SEE*!

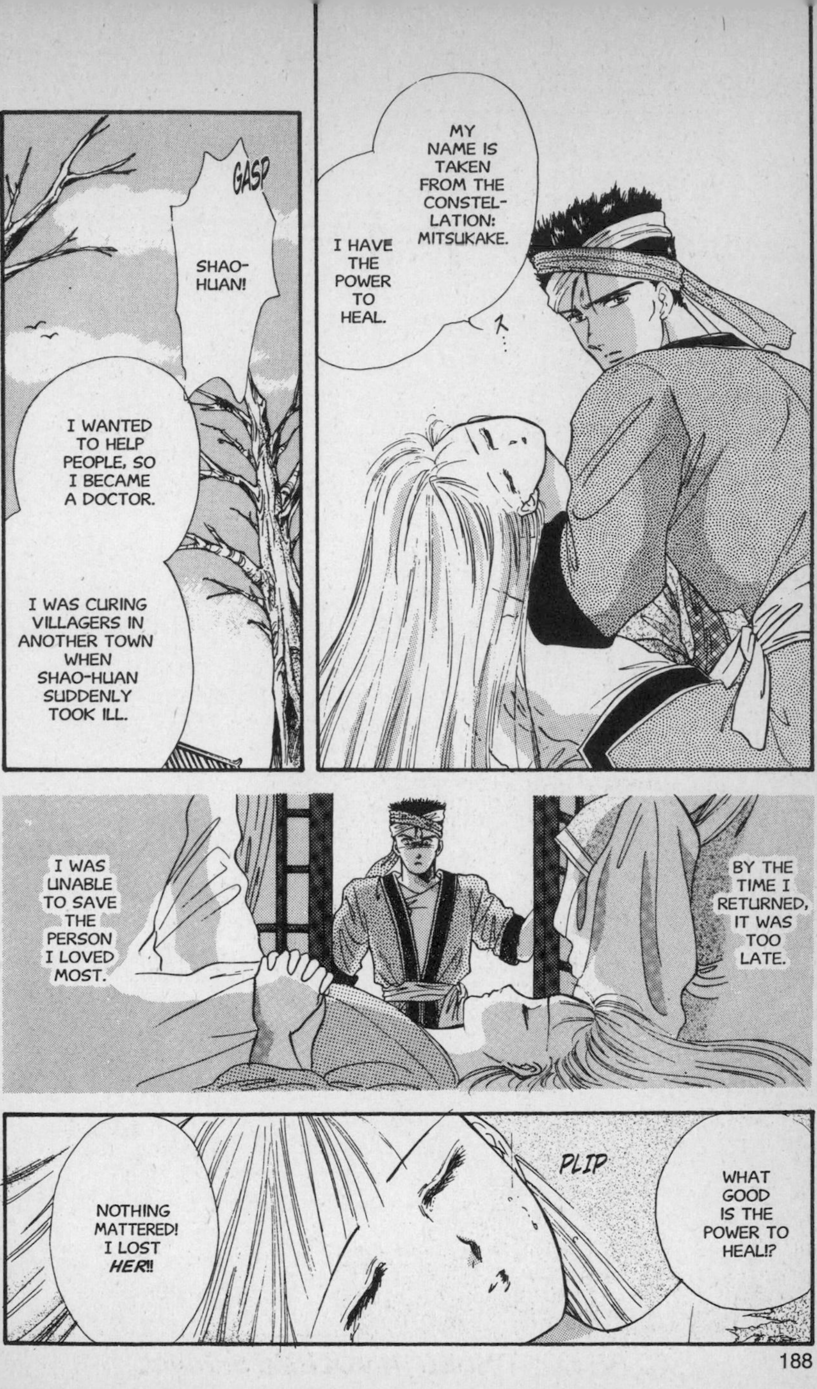
MY NAME IS TAKEN FROM THE CONSTEL-LATION: MITSUKAKE.
I HAVE THE POWER TO HEAL.
GASP
SHAO-HUAN!
I WANTED TO HELP PEOPLE, SO I BECAME A DOCTOR.
I WAS CURING VILLAGERS IN ANOTHER TOWN WHEN SHAO-HUAN SUDDENLY TOOK ILL.
BY THE TIME I RETURNED, IT WAS TOO LATE.
I WAS UNABLE TO SAVE THE PERSON I LOVED MOST.
WHAT GOOD IS THE POWER TO HEAL!?
PLIP
NOTHING MATTERED! I LOST *HER*!!

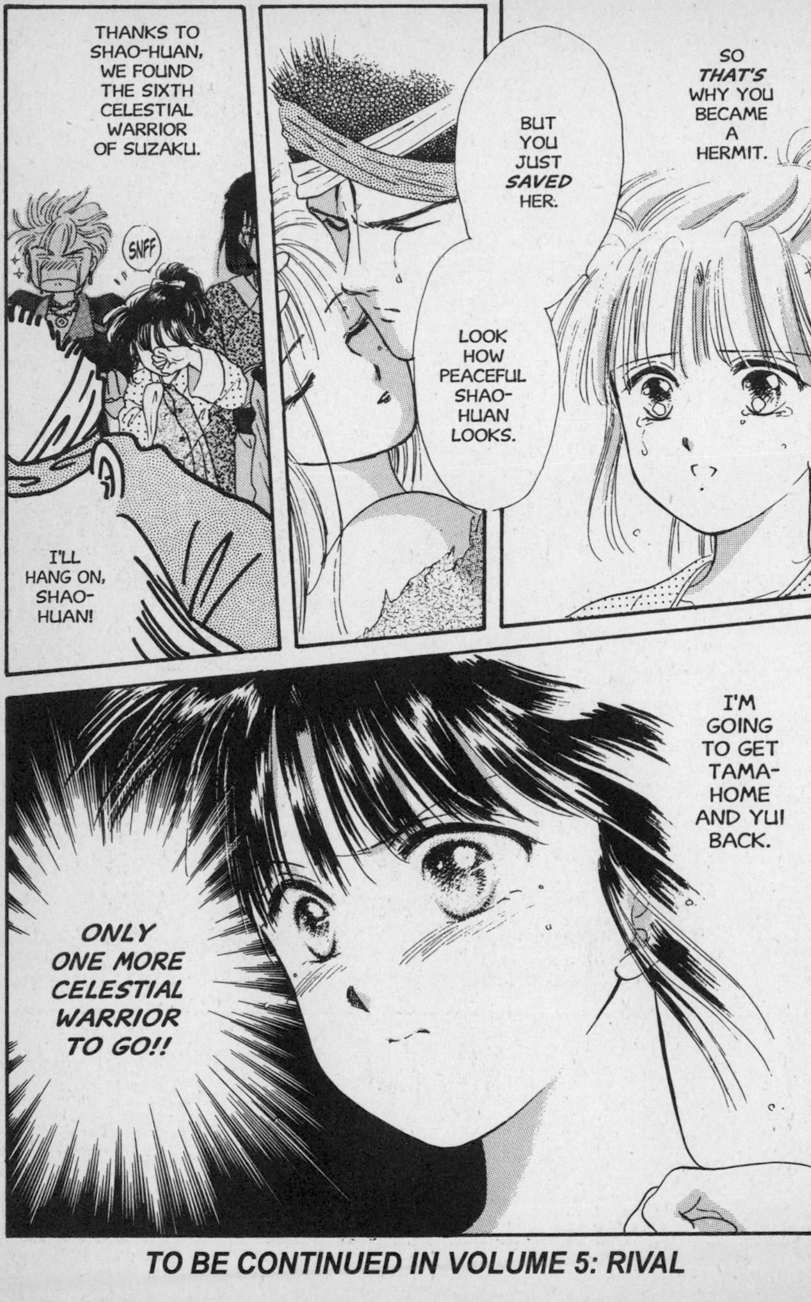
SO *THAT'S* WHY YOU BECAME A HERMIT.
BUT YOU JUST *SAVED* HER.
LOOK HOW PEACEFUL SHAO-HUAN LOOKS.
THANKS TO SHAO-HUAN, WE FOUND THE SIXTH CELESTIAL WARRIOR OF SUZAKU.
SNFF
I'LL HANG ON, SHAO-HUAN!
I'M GOING TO GET TAMA-HOME AND YUI BACK.
ONLY ONE MORE CELESTIAL WARRIOR TO GO!!

TO BE CONTINUED IN VOLUME 5: RIVAL

ABOUT THE AUTHOR

Yû Watase was born on March 5 in a town near Osaka, Japan, and she was raised there before moving to Tokyo to follow her dream of creating manga. In the decade since her debut short story, *PAJAMA DE OJAMA* ("An Intrusion in Pajamas"), she has produced more than 50 compiled volumes of short stories and continuing series. Her latest series, *ZETTAI KARESHI* ("He'll Be My Boyfriend"), is currently running in the anthology magazine *SHÔJO COMIC*. Watase's long-running horror/romance story *CERES: CELESTIAL LEGEND* and her most recent completed series, *ALICE 19TH*, are now available in North America published by VIZ. She loves science fiction, fantasy and comedy.

The Fushigi Yûgi Guide to Sound Effects

Most of the sound effects in FUSHIGI YÛGI are the way Yû Watase created them, in their original Japanese.

We created this glossary for a page-by-page, panel-by-panel explanation of the action and background noises. By using this guide, you may even learn some Japanese.

The glossary lists page and panel number. For example, page 1, panel 3, would be listed as 1.3.

26.1	FX: Zulu (zlup)
27.1	FX: Ka ka (caw caw)
27.5	FX: Kasa (rustle)
32.1	FX: Ba (wrench)
32.3	FX: Za (zoosh)
33.3	FX: Dosa (whud)
33.4	FX: Za (zash)

CHAPTER TWENTY:
WOLF OF THE FORTRESS

36.2	FX: Ha (gasp)
36.3	FX: Gaba (umph)
37.2	FX: Zuki (zing)
37.4	FX: Ha (gasp)
40.2	FX: Hyoi (lift)
41.1	FX: Zulu zulu zulu (drag)
41.1	FX: Gashi (grasp)
42.1	FX: Pafu pafu (poof poof)
42.2	FX: Kulu (turn)
43.3	FX: Kotsu kotsu (klink klink)
43.4	FX: Gui (yank)
47.3	FX: Gacha (gachak)
47.5	FX: Pon (pat)
48.5	FX: Zozooo (shudder)
	FX: Peko (bow)
49.1	FX: Ki (glare)
50.2	FX: Chila (glance)

CHAPTER NINETEEN:
WO AI NI

6.2	FX: Ha (gasp)
6.3	FX: Ha (gasp)
7.2	FX: Bishi (zap)
7.3	FX: Shu (fwish)
7.5	FX: Gyu (grasp)
9.1	FX: Gyu (clench)
10.4	FX: Su (tiptoe)
11.1	FX: Kui (tug)
13.1	FX: Suu (zzz)
13.3	FX: Su (swff)
13.4	FX: Suto (shff)
13.5	FX: Su (swff)
14.2	FX: Chichichi (chirp chirp)
16.4	FX: Bata bata (flap flap)
18.2	FX: Kapo kapo (klop klop)
18.4	FX: Pou (glow)
19.4	FX: Gatan (gatunk)
22.1	FX: Jala (jingle)
24.1	FX: Zulu (slip)
24.3	FX: Bishi (vwap)
24.5	FX: Baki (crack)
25.1	FX: Doka (thwack)
25.2	FX: Ba (vwah)

78.4   FX: Ban ban (slap slap)

79.1   FX: O-oooh (y-yeah)

80.4   FX: Za (zoosh)

81.1   FX: Za (zoosh)
81.5   FX: Koso (slink)

82.3   FX: Sa (swish)
82.4   FX: Pon (ponf)

84.1   FX: Boo (bwooof)

85.2   FX: Da (dash)
85.3   FX: Gashi (grip)

86.1   FX: Gili (squeeze)

87.1   FX: Su (slump)
87.2   FX: Gili (clench)
87.4   FX: Gili gili gili (squeeze)
87.5   FX: Ha (gasp)

88.2   FX: Su (swff)

89.2   FX: Doka (bam)
89.3   FX: Doon (thud)
89.3   FX: Ba (bwah)

90.4   FX: Pita (stop)

92.1   FX: Su (fwoosh)
92.2   FX: Hala (fwah)

51.2   FX: Gaba (grab)
51.2   FX: Aaa? (huh?)
51.3   FX: Shu (swish)
51.4   FX: Pashi (fwap)

53.2   FX: Ha (gasp)

54.2   FX: Su (slide)
54.4   FX: Pala pala (crumble)

55.1   FX: Dokooo (kaboom)
55.3   FX: Ta (dash)

57.2   FX: Pita (point)
57.3   FX: Za (zash)
57.3   FX: Ha (gasp)
57.5   FX: Su (swff)

58.3   FX: Su (swff)

59.1   FX: Fu (fwoosh)
59.3   FX: Ha (gasp)
59.4   FX: Ta (tump)

61.4   FX: Su (swoosh)
63.1   FX: Ba (bwah)

63.2   FX: Gau (roar)
63.3   FX: Fu (fwoosh)

CHAPTER TWENTY-ONE:
ILLUSION'S EMBRACE

67.3   FX: Gaa (graaah)
67.4   FX: Zan (zwoosh)

68.2   FX: Gau galulu (rrrooooar grrrr)
68.3   FX: Za (zwoosh)
68.4   FX: Goo (gwoooh)

69.2   FX: Koso (sneak)
69.3   FX: Gusha (crush)

70.2   FX: Dosa (whump)
70.3   FX: Basa (thud)
70.4   FX: Gui (tug)

71.5   FX: Kulu (turn)

EDITOR'S RECOMMENDATIONS

Did you like *FUSHIGI YÛGI?* Here's what VIZ recommends you try next:

CERES: CELESTIAL LEGEND

From the acclaimed author of *FUSHIGI YÛGI* comes this darkly romantic story of love, betrayal and revenge. On her sixteenth birthday, Aya's world is turned upside-down after her family tries to kill her to protect a terrifying secret. Her struggle to survive pits her against nearly everyone she loves, including her beloved twin brother Aki.

REVOLUTIONARY GIRL UTENA

As a little girl, Utena was once saved by a beautiful prince and she's dreamed of finding him ever since. Now all grown up, she's vowed to follow him, even if it means becoming a prince just like him! Drawn to the elite Ohtori Private Academy, Utena is forced to duel for the hand of the mysterious Rose Bride in her search for the true identify of her elusive savior.

SAIKANO

Soon after they start dating, Shuji discovers that his girl-friend Chise has a horrible secret—she's been engineered by the military to transform into a devastating weapon! Chise's deadly power grows, threatening to tear the young couple apart, along with Chise herself, who's caught between her role as a fighting machine and her life as an ordinary teenager.

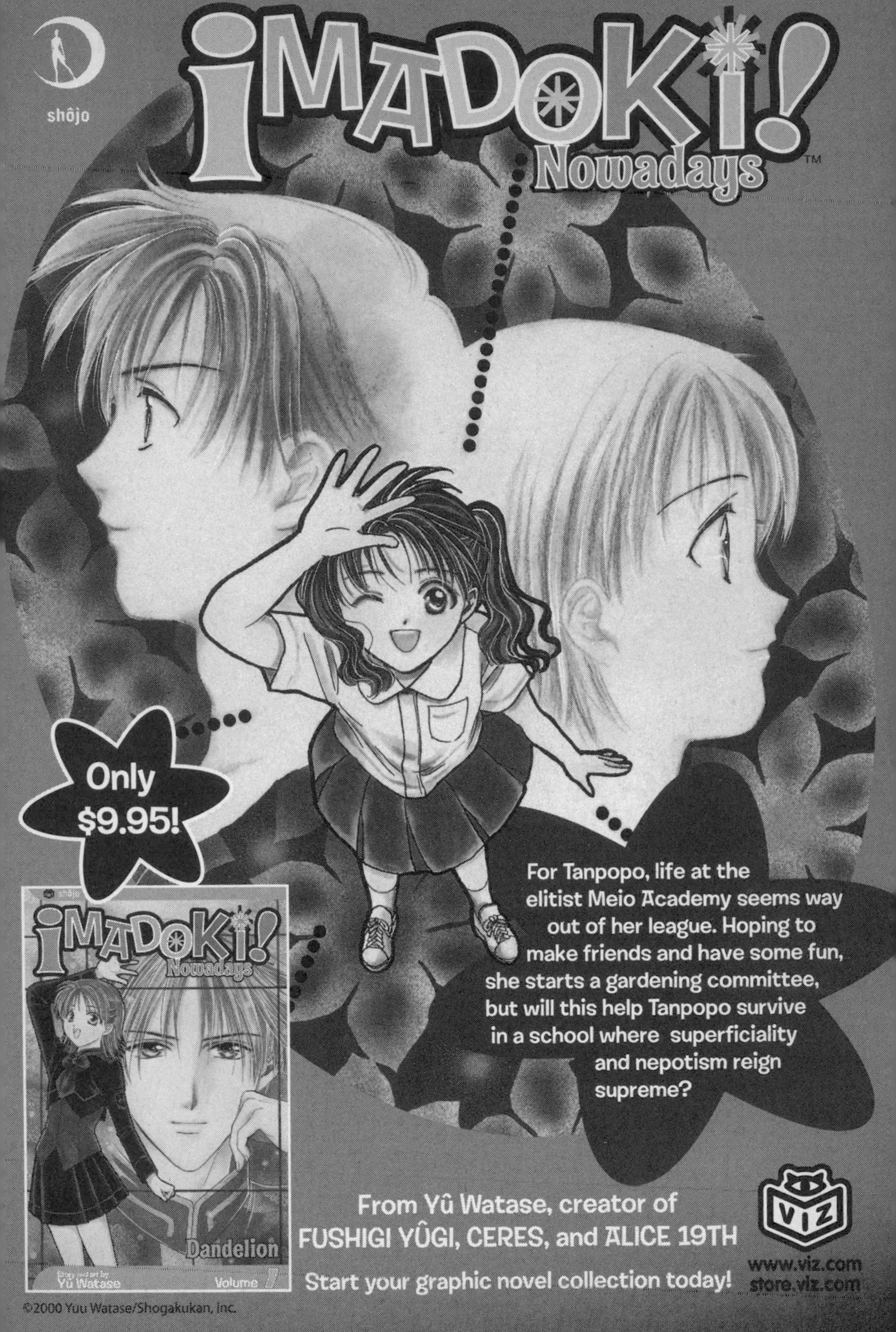
shôjo
IMADOKI!
Nowadays™
Only $9.95!
For Tanpopo, life at the elitist Meio Academy seems way out of her league. Hoping to make friends and have some fun, she starts a gardening committee, but will this help Tanpopo survive in a school where superficiality and nepotism reign supreme?
IMADOKI! Nowadays
Dandelion
Yû Watase
Volume 1
From Yû Watase, creator of
FUSHIGI YÛGI, CERES, and ALICE 19TH
Start your graphic novel collection today!
VIZ
www.viz.com
store.viz.com